Metropolitan Economic Development

Metropolitan areas are home to a significant proportion of the world's population and its economic output. Taking Mexico as a case study and weaving in comparisons from Latin America and developed countries, this book explores current trends and policy issues around urbanisation, metropolisation, economic development and city-region governance.

Despite their fundamental economic relevance, the analysis and monitoring of metropolitan economies in Mexico and other countries in the Global South under a comparative perspective are relatively scarce. This volume contains empirical analysis based on comparative perspectives with relation to international experiences.

It will be of interest to advanced students, researchers and policymakers in urban policy, urban economics, regional studies, economic geography and Latin American studies.

Alejandra Trejo Nieto is an economist and holds a PhD in Development Studies from the University of East Anglia in the UK. She is currently a professor at the Centre for Demographic, Urban and Environmental Studies, El Colegio de Mexico.

Regions and Cities

Series Editor in Chief
Joan Fitzgerald, *Northeastern University, USA*

Editors
Ron Martin, *University of Cambridge, UK*
Maryann Feldman, *University of North Carolina, USA*
Gernot Grabher, *HafenCity University Hamburg, Germany*
Kieran P. Donaghy, *Cornell University, USA*

In today's globalised, knowledge-driven and networked world, regions and cities have assumed heightened significance as the interconnected nodes of economic, social and cultural production, and as sites of new modes of economic and territorial governance and policy experimentation. This book series brings together incisive and critically engaged international and interdisciplinary research on this resurgence of regions and cities, and should be of interest to geographers, economists, sociologists, political scientists and cultural scholars, as well as to policy-makers involved in regional and urban development.

For more information on the Regional Studies Association visit www.regionalstudies.org

There is a **30% discount** available to RSA members on books in the *Regions and Cities* series, and other subject related Taylor and Francis books and e-books including Routledge titles. To order just e-mail Emilia Falcone, Emilia.Falcone@tandf.co.uk, or phone on +44 (0)20 3377 3369 and declare your RSA membership. You can also visit the series page at www.routledge.com/Regions-and-Cities/book-series/RSA and use the discount code: **RSA0901**

The Theory, Practice and Potential of Regional Development
The Case of Canada
Edited by Kelly Vodden, David J.A. Douglas, Sean Markey, Sarah Minnes and Bill Reimer

Social and Economic Development in Central and Eastern Europe
Stability and Change after 1990
Edited by Grzegorz Gorzelak

Metropolitan Economic Development
The Political Economy of Urbanisation in Mexico
Alejandra Trejo Nieto

For more information about this series, please visit: www.routledge.com/Regions-and-Cities/book-series/RSA

Metropolitan Economic Development

The Political Economy of Urbanisation in Mexico

Alejandra Trejo Nieto

LONDON AND NEW YORK

First published 2020
by Routledge
2 Park Square, Milton Park, Abingdon, Oxon OX14 4RN

and by Routledge
605 Third Avenue, New York, NY 10017

First issued in paperback 2021

Routledge is an imprint of the Taylor & Francis Group, an informa business

British Library Cataloguing-in-Publication Data
A catalogue record for this book is available from the British Library

Library of Congress Cataloging-in-Publication Data
A catalog record for this book has been requested

ISBN 13: 978-0-367-77756-2 (pbk)
ISBN 13: 978-1-138-31584-6 (hbk)

Typeset in Bembo
by Apex CoVantage, LLC

This book is dedicated with love and affection to my father, in Memorian, to my mother Minerva, my brothers Angel, Adán and Ernesto, and my nephew Memito.

Contents

List of figures   ix
List of tables   xi
Acknowledgements   xiii

Introduction   1

PART I
The rise of a metropolitan world   13

1   The intersection of the urban, the metropolitan and the
    regional: concepts, theories and international experiences   15

2   Urbanisation in Mexico and Latin America: a comparative
    assessment   44

3   The spatial distribution of population: a study of
    metropolitan patterns and dynamics in Mexico   73

PART II
Metropolitan economic development in Mexico:
patterns, trends and drivers   103

4   The economic significance of metropolitan areas: patterns
    of economic performance and disparities   105

5   Public financing in metropolitan areas   135

6   Exploring the driving forces of metropolitan economic
    development   165

PART III
Local experiences: metropolisation, governance and
public policies   185

7   The metropolisation process and spatial structure in
     Mexico City: a giant's tale   187

8   Provision of urban services: how Mexico City performs
     compared to other metropolitan areas in Latin America   213

9   Urban policy agendas, governance and metropolitan
     economic development   243

     Conclusions   265

     Index   282

Figures

1.1	Urbanisation-related concepts	18
1.2	Drivers of urbanisation	21
1.3	Urbanisation levels by region, 1950–2050 (%)	32
1.4	Urbanisation degree by countries' income level, 1950–2050 (%)	33
1.5	Distribution of global urban population by region, 1950–2050 (%)	34
1.6	Distribution of global urban population by countries' income level, 1950–2056 (%)	35
1.7	Top 30 largest cities of the world, 2015	39
1.8	World's largest metropolitan regions by LBA (billions)	40
2.1	Countries by percentage of regional population, 2018	54
2.2	Urbanisation levels in Latin America, 2018	57
2.3	Mexico urbanisation and industrialisation stages, 1900–2010	63
2.4	Peripheral dynamic insufficiency in urban contexts	69
3.1	Estimated number of metropolitan areas with more than 100,000 inhabitants in selected regions, 2000 and 2010	75
3.2	Sources of urban expansion (%)	76
3.3	Factors in the expansion of Mexican cities	81
3.4	Metropolitan areas in Mexico in 1960	83
3.5	The metropolitanisation process: some indicators	84
3.6	Number of metropolitan municipalities in Mexico by category	85
3.7	Metropolitan areas according to population size, 2015	87
3.8	Zipf's law in Mexican metropolitan areas, 1990, 2000, 2010 and 2015	89
3.9	Metropolitan municipalities by migration category, 2000	94
3.10	Metropolitan municipalities by migration category, 2010	95
4.1	Generic and specific economic advantages of metropolitan areas	108
4.2	Compound annual growth rates in the world's largest metropolitan areas, 2014–2016 (%)	109
4.3	Metropolitan share of total gross production, 2013 (%)	116
4.4	Total gross production per capita, 2013	117
4.5	Labour informality rate, fourth quarter 2017 (%)	125
4.6	Poverty rates by metropolitan area by population size, 2010 (%)	126

4.7   Malmquist total factor productivity index by metropolitan
       area, 1998–2013   130
5.1   General guidelines for a model of metropolitan public finances 138
5.2   Municipal public finances, 1978–2000   143
5.3   Total revenue and main items, 1989–2016
       (Mexican pesos, 2010 = 100)   146
5.4   Average annual revenue variation, 1989–2016 (%)   147
5.5   Local government tax revenue as a percentage of GDP, 2015   147
5.6   Property tax as a percentage of local taxation, 2015   148
5.7   Revenue structure in federal OECD countries, 2015 (%)   148
5.8   Revenue composition by item, 1989–2016 (%)   149
5.9   Total expenditure and main items, 1989–2016 (2010 = 100)   151
5.10   Average annual expenditure variation rates, 1989–2016 (%)   152
5.11   Structure of public expenditure in OECD countries, 2015   152
5.12   Spending composition by item, 1989–2016 (2010 = 100)   153
5.13   Average per capita budgets, 1989–2016   156
5.14   Evolution of disparities, 1989–2016   157
5.15   Metropolitan areas by public finance performance, 1989–2016 159
6.1   Theoretical approaches to economic development   167
7.1   The cycle of the urban corporatism and the land market   195
7.2   Mexico City Metropolitan Area's municipalities and
       boroughs by population, 2015   199
7.3   Global Moran's index of labour supply, 2010   201
7.4   Local indicators of spatial association of labour supply, 2010 202
7.5   Global Moran's index of labour demand, 2008   203
7.6   Local indicators of spatial association of labour demand, 2008 204
7.7   Bivariate global Moran's index labour demand and supply   205
7.8   Bivariate LISAs labour demand and supply   206
8.1   Models of metropolitan government   216
8.2   The institutional collective action approach to metropolitan
       governance   219
8.3   Production schemes of public services in MCMA   222
8.4   Coverage of daily water provision   226
8.5   Coverage of transport services   227
8.6   Coverage of waste collection services   228
9.1   Urban economic development framework, Habitat III Policy
       Papers   246

Tables

1.1	Varying definitions of urban centres	17
1.2	World urban indicators, 1950–2050	30
1.3	Number of cities, urban population and urbanisation by city size, 1950–2030	37
1.4	The 30 largest urban agglomerations by population size, 1950, 2015 and 2035	38
2.1	Larger Mexican cities and demographic change during the Porfiriato era	48
2.2	Latin America: urban indicators, 1950–2050	51
2.3	Urban indicators by subregion, 1950–2050	55
2.4	Number of cities, urban population and urbanisation by city size in Latin America, 1950–2030	60
3.1	Total urban extension and average built-up area of selected cities by region, 2015	75
3.2	Population distribution in Mexico, 2015	87
3.3	Metropolitan areas by population growth rate	91
3.4	Distribution of metropolitan municipalities according to migration category	94
3.5	Mexico's population, distribution and growth in 1990, 2000, 2010 and 2015	97
4.1	Largest metropolitan economies by region (light-based activity)	111
4.2	Main metropolitan economies in Latin America, 2007	112
4.3	Largest metropolitan economies in Mexico (share in metropolitan gross production) and geographic concentration indices, 1998, 2003, 2008 and 2013	115
4.4	Per capita production in metropolitan areas, 1998, 2003, 2008 and 2013	117
4.5	Specialisation in metropolitan areas and economic function, 2013	118
4.6	Metropolitan areas by average annual growth rates, 2010–2015 (%)	122
4.7	Highest and lowest average years of schooling by metropolitan area, 1990, 2000, 2010 and 2015	124
4.8	Efficient metropolitan areas and mean efficiency, 1998, 2003, 2008 and 2013	128

4.9   Summary of total factor productivity changes, 1998–2013   129
5.1   Indicators of public finances of metropolitan performance   157
5.2   Criteria for the categorisation of metropolitan areas   158
5.3   Classification of metropolitan areas based on performance
      indicators, 1989–2016   158
6.1   Keynesian theories of development   168
6.2   Transition theories of development   169
6.3   Seven categories of global cities, 2015   171
6.4   Independent variables used to study metropolitan economic
      development   178
6.5   Estimation of the model for productivity   180
6.6   Estimation of the model for GDP pc   181
7.1   The stages of metropolisation of Mexico City   193
8.1   Governance of urban services in MCMA   224
8.2   Governance experiences in Monterrey and Guadalajara
      metropolitan areas   229
8.3   Stakeholders in the levels of governance in provision of
      services in Lima   232
8.4   Governance of urban services in Lima   233
8.5   Stakeholders in the levels of governance in provision of
      services in Bogota   235
8.6   Governance of urban services in Bogota   237
9.1   NUPs in three federal OECD countries   250
9.2   Priorities and challenges in NUPs by region   251
9.3   Latin American NUPs with an extensive level of attention to
      economic development   252
9.4   Components of local economic development policy   254

Acknowledgements

I start by thanking my family for their love. I am eternally grateful to my parents who taught me discipline, respect, humbleness, and all that has helped me achieve my goals. Thank you to my friends and colleagues who were supportive and encouraging during the writing process of this book, especially to Faby. Thank you, Roberto, for the time, company, support and caring during those few months.

None of this would have been possible without the interest of my publisher. Special thanks to Natalie Tomlinson and Lisa Lavelle for their guidance, patience and assistance. The writing process started when I was a Fulbright-Garcia Robles visiting scholar at the Center for U.S.–Mexican Studies, University of California in San Diego. Special gratitude to Melissa Flocca, the associate director of the centre, for supporting my application and research project. I also thank my fellow fellows, especially Yesica Mayet for sharing her office, laughs, chocolate biscuits and burritos, as well as for her support and help during my recovery from my fall while running in the Rose Canyon hills.

I spent two months writing some chapters at the Regional Management Centre for Productivity and Innovation of Boyaca (CREPIB) in Tunja, Colombia. Thanks to Mariana Palacios, the director, and Jose Niño for receiving me as a visiting researcher, and for the pleasant days in Tibasosa and Bogota with their lovely families. They made me feel at home.

The last and busiest stage of the writing process was spent in Brussels while on a three-month visiting fellowship at the Brussels Centre for Urban Studies, Vrije Universiteit. Thank you to colleagues who attended the Cosmopolis lunch seminar where I presented the book project and to Sylvie Gadeyne from the Interface Demography group for inviting me to give a lecture in the lecture series 'European Social and Population Issues'. Special thanks to Patrick Deboosere and David Bassens for supporting my application for this fellowship and for their help.

Last but not least, thank you to my research assistants Adrian Trejo, Carmen Morales and Fernanda Muñoz. And thank you, Sally Sutton, for proofreading my chapters and for your support. Thanks to all.

Alejandra Trejo Nieto
Brussels, April 12, 2019

Introduction

Urbanisation, metropolitan areas and enduring economic underdevelopment

The year 2007 marked a turning point in world history when the share of the world's population living in urban areas exceeded that of the rural population. At that point, from the demographic point of view, we were in the course of the urban millennium (UN, 2014). In the twenty-first century increasing percentages of population are living in urban centres, with some 70 per cent of the world's inhabitants forecasted to live in cities by 2050. Also by 2050, cities in the developing world will absorb more than 2 billion new urban residents, representing 95 per cent of global urban growth (UN, 2018). Despite the recent preoccupation with the exceedingly rapid urban growth occurring in Asia and Africa, where most of the urban population will concentrate in the future, and the problems associated with this (Cohen, 2006), these regions have not yet completed their urban transition (UN, 2018). In contrast, Latin America already has some of the most urbanised countries in the world, and merits special attention to capture the essence of accelerated urbanisation, urban growth and the expansion of twenty-first-century cities worldwide. Moreover, this highly urbanised region has been regarded as one that contains a larger urban population than can be supported by its level of economic development, exemplifying that urbanisation and development are not always inextricably linked (Jedwab & Vollrath, 2015).

In the twentieth century the Latin American region saw a dramatic shift to high urbanisation, particularly in the 1960s, when the urban population grew at annual rates of more than 5 per cent. Demographic urbanisation had already intensified at the beginning of the twentieth century with foreign immigration in the Southern Cone and southern Brazil, followed by accelerated urbanisation pushed by intense rural–urban migration in Mexico and Andean countries from the 1930s onwards (Almandoz, 2008). In 1950, 40 per cent of the region's population lived in cities, but by 1990 this was up to 70 per cent, and today about 80 per cent of the region's population are urban dwellers. UN-Habitat predicts that by 2050 Latin America's cities will include 90 per cent of the region's population (UN, 2018).

In addition to its fast urban growth and urban transition, Latin America's historic and contemporary urbanisation is characterised by urban primacy, with the demographic, social, economic and political dominance of one city, which in most cases is the political capital, monopolising the wealth, income, and economic and administrative functions within its urban system. In countries such as Argentina this primacy is marked, with its primate city four times the size of the next-largest city (Chant & McIlwaine, 2009).

Megacities have been another central component of the region's urbanisation. The number of Latin American cities of more than a million inhabitants increased more than sixfold between 1950 and 1990. High demographic, economic and political concentration in large cities is explained by a longer tradition in the region of centralisation and concentration in one or a small number of cities (Angotti, 1996). Recent trends include the emergence of urban sprawl and metropolisation which has become a key characteristic of Latin American urban context.

Metropolitan areas in Latin America have particular spatial and socioeconomic structural characteristics as a result of their historical roots and structural backgrounds. With metropolitan expansion, urban structures have changed significantly over the decades, with the displacement of population, industries and services from the central city to the periphery, and in some cases the creation of new centres (Rojas, Cuadrado Roura & Fernandez Guell, 2005). The large majority of the people at the margins of a metropolitan area lack access to basic services and infrastructure. The issue of urban peripheries inhabited by the so-called *sectores populares* (low-income population) has been of the utmost concern, with poor urban dwellers frequently driving irregular urban expansion (Ziccardi, 2016). Duality is another predominant feature of Latin America's cities and metropolises. Overall, there is a dichotomy in cities' productive apparatus between innovative high-technology companies integrated with international markets and unproductive and rather undynamic enterprises. There is also high informality, dual labour markets, strong segregation and spatial fragmentation. Moreover, numerous cities and metropolises are being undermined by violence and crime, as well as social and political unrest.

The urban growth rate in Latin America is now falling, but urban footprint is growing faster than population, and medium-sized cities are growing steadily and experiencing metropolitan expansion (Vargas et al., 2017). These trends are accompanied by relatively new migration patterns which add complexity to national urban systems and put increasing pressure on national and local governments.

Now, at the beginning of the twenty-first century, Argentina, Chile, Uruguay, Brazil and Mexico are some of the most urbanised countries in the world, and the region has four of the fifteen largest metropolitan areas: Mexico City, Sao Paulo, Buenos Aires and Rio de Janeiro. Yet these metropolitan areas are not as successful as big metropolises in developed countries. On the contrary, Latin America's metropolitan areas exhibit several of the worst symptoms of the region's underdevelopment.

As mentioned before, the region exemplifies the severe problems faced by countries with a highly urbanised society and fragile economic evolution, and this weak relationship between urbanisation and productive activity has been blamed for Latin America's failed urban transition. The terms 'over-urbanisation' and 'urban explosion' have denoted the broken link between the region's urbanisation and its economic growth and development. Over-urbanisation, in particular, has described the apparent imbalance between urbanisation and industrial development, a situation that is portrayed as abnormal in comparison to the US and Western Europe (Almandoz, 2008).

The relatively poor performance of urbanisation poses enormous challenges for wealth creation and economic, social and sustainable development at all levels of government and society. With few exceptions, the region lacks an urban planning model that can deliver economic growth and a good quality of life to urban populations. Intermediate cities, which are currently growing faster than metropolitan areas, have an important opportunity to develop a more ordered, inclusive and ecological urban model which can increase their economic performance by attracting investment and generating jobs, with positive effects on the economy and society.

Even though globalisation and productive technological restructuring have contributed to defining territorial structures and metropolitan performance, local and idiosyncratic factors contribute to the distinctive patterns of Latin American megacities and shape their future. The problems of Latin American and Caribbean cities are not due exclusively to the size of their population or the pace of their growth. A complex political, social and economic context has been conducive to recent urban patterns, and therefore the increasingly large populations of megacities and metropolitan areas are not the only reason for looking at them carefully.

In recent years some scholars have pointed out the urgent need of a renewed research agenda and new approaches to Latin American urban studies. Rodgers, Beall and Kanbur (2011) highlight how surprisingly few comprehensive overviews of key urbanisation issues had emerged from scholarly research on the region's particular pattern of urban development, and none very recently, because of the significant and varied urban processes still occurring there. The overwhelming majority of research conducted on Latin American cities, they argue, tends to be quite specialised and does not really attempt to deal with the new urban dynamics and patterns. According to these authors, urban research in the 1950s and 1960s focused on general demographic dynamics to describe the accelerated urban transition occurring in different countries in the region; research in the 1970s focused on various aspects of urban life, employment and labour markets; in the 1980s urban politics were the predominant theme; and in the 1990s the main concerns were the social dynamics of city life, inequality, segregation, urban violence and insecurity. They also conclude that research needs to address the strongly growing and significant aspect of Latin American urban development: *metropolitan areas*.

Klaufus and Jaffe (2015) claim that case studies and research developed specifically for Latin American countries and cities could contribute to understanding urban dynamics elsewhere, with cities in the region representing global signposts in urban development. Moreover, they see an opportunity for pragmatic frameworks with a more encompassing and comparative scope that can identify parallels and variations in ways that avoid rigid typology and lead to a more nuanced field of national and international comparative urban studies that includes attention to the specificities of history, territory and politics. They want to see the expansion and renewal of Latin American urban studies via the development of new approaches and empirical insights.

A country case study: Mexico's metropolitan development

Mexico is a middle-income Latin American nation, the tenth most populated country in the world and the fifteenth largest economy. Despite its current fragile socioeconomic and political situation, it is an important international player with a large number of free trade agreements, continuing its track record of three decades as an attractive destination for foreign direct investment. It is a very complex country which now, at the end of the second decade of the twenty-first century, is at what has been considered a historical turning point with a new left-wing president. Medium-term economic stagnation, socioeconomic inequalities, spatial disparities, some political discontent, weak governance and crime-related violence are just some of the tribulations that Mexican society has faced over recent years. Intertwined economic, democratic and urban transitions have been shaping this critical moment and its complexity, with changing trade and industrialisation regimes, high urbanisation and increasing urban expansion and shifting political scenarios the major forces at work in the configuration of Mexico's society today. Even though macro-conditions and external forces such as international migration, the rearrangement of international trade and investment agreements, the reorganisation of the international division of labour and the adjustment of global value chains together capture the national reality well, contributing to shaping the country's situation, urbanisation is a powerful force that helps to provide an understanding of the country's more critical problems from a more local standpoint. As in other nations, Mexico's urban experience has come with an uncommon power, and addressing its challenges must therefore be an ever-more-urgent priority.

With an urban population of 104 million people in 2018, Mexico is 80 per cent urbanised, and is expected to be 88 per cent urbanised by 2050 (UN, 2018). Its urbanisation process echoes the distinct and dramatic urban patterns and trends in the Latin American region in general: accelerated urban growth, super-rapid urban transition, high urbanisation and elevated urban primacy and concentration. National government policy, political interests and institutions played determining roles in its accelerated urbanisation in the mid-twentieth century, with industrialisation policies in particular operating as channels directing resources and investment towards cities and the manufacturing sector from the 1940s to the 1970s, following the so-called 'urban bias' (Trejo, 2017).

This century the country is continuing into the metropolitan age. The physical and functional expansion of its cities is the most outstanding characteristic of its recent urbanisation. While the metropolitan phenomenon originated in the 1940s, for decades urban sprawl had relatively little influence on urban population growth (Trejo, 2013). In the last three decades Mexico's metropolitan areas have added great complexity to its urban realities. In 2015 a total of 75 million inhabitants – 63 per cent of the country's total population and 76 per cent of its urban population – lived in the 74 metropolitan areas (SEDATU, CONAPO & INEGI, 2018).

Thus, metropolitan areas are nowadays the dominant scenario of development processes in the country as they are increasingly concentrating population and facing economic and societal problems. Metropolitan areas are of great concern because they pose serious challenges in terms of mobility, housing, infrastructure and public services, public finances, equity, inclusiveness, employment and the economy, not to mention environmental and climate change problems. The primary obstacles to confronting metropolitan problems have been the formal and informal institutional, political, and policy structures that govern these territories (Sellers & Hoffmann-Martinot, 2008). It has been argued that disordered metropolitan expansion is a reflection of persistent government failure to plan, invest in and proactively manage urban development in the context of extremely rapid urbanisation and formal decentralisation.

As with other countries in the Global South and Latin America, Mexico is characterised by a highly centralised urban system and includes one of the biggest metropolitan areas in the world, Mexico City. The country's capital, Mexico City, is an emblematic metropolitan area of our time and one of the largest in the world, with approximately 21 million inhabitants. In the coming years it will remain among the 10 largest urban agglomerations worldwide. Mexico City Metropolitan Area shares common urban problems with most of the world's big metropolises, yet the national and local contexts influence dramatically the results of metropolitan areas in Mexico when they confront the most critical development issues. A particularly problematic metropolitan governance exacerbates burdens for population, economic activities and governments.

Mexico provides an example of what happens in the urban and economic development of a country when the growth, complexity and expansion of urban areas outpaces the development of governance and institutional structures to manage them. Among the manifold challenges in metropolitan areas, I underline the enormous significance of the economic and financial challenge for metropolitan development. Metropolitan areas face a problematic context in attempting to find adequate and affordable development strategies. Several fragmentations exist, and policy and institutional reforms, as well as a sustainable urban model, need to be implemented. However, a one-size-fits-all approach will not work given the heterogeneity in the country and its urban system.

A pragmatic analytical approach to studying urbanisation, metropolitan areas and development

While much has been written about the general process of urbanisation in the world and in Latin America, perhaps most books on metropolitan development focus mainly on the US and Europe or specific metropolitan areas. Others deal exclusively with government and governance issues or address metropolitan public finances, some offering predominantly theoretical and conceptual discussions. New research and debate, however, must seek to address emerging trends and patterns and illuminate both the historical failures and the potential of urbanisation in different parts of the world. Even though an extensive body of research and literature on cities and urban development issues exists for Mexico because of its advanced stage of urbanisation, few studies have addressed the economic performance of cities or metropolitan areas. In this book I discuss two critical issues of twenty-first-century urbanisation – metropolitan expansion and economic development – contributing to the international debate on and analysis of metropolitan areas and providing new insights into the economic functioning of metropolitan areas and the limitations of the urbanisation models in the countries of the Global South. The book can be situated in the intellectual traditions of international and Latin American urban studies and fills a number of gaps in the current body of empirical work on metropolitan areas and urban development in less-developed countries, and in particular those in our understanding about the dynamics of their urbanisation, economic development and governance. It discusses these three analytical pillars in an attempt to reveal the interplay between politics, society and economics.

Despite those grand narratives of macro-urban development that are applied to the developed world and which automatically link urbanisation to more advanced stages of economic development, we need to identify the key national and local political economic processes that shape urbanisation and the economy in less-developed countries. Another gap, highlighted by Klaufus and Jaffe (2015), must be closed: the need for Latin American urban studies that attend closely to political economic aspects of urban development, addressing the politics at stake more explicitly.

In the analysis of urbanisation and economic development, urban, social, political, economic and geographical theories of urbanisation, as well as development theories, need to be incorporated. Of course, metropolitan development has had its own theoretical developments, with metropolitan areas in their own right posing a significant challenge to academics and researchers seeking to quantify and better understand urban processes and dynamics. Certainly, the intellectual and academic tradition regarding metropolitan areas has predominantly referred to ongoing trends in developed countries, focusing heavily on the issue of adequate and efficient government arrangements and governance structures. In the last decade the general interest has returned to governance issues – why and how the emerging new metropolitan reality is planned, governed and defined. Yet this debate is not separated from general discussion of the urban question.

The debate on metropolitan and urban theory is timely, hot and unsettled. In this respect I consider that there is no unifying and comprehensive theory that explains how urbanisation, cities and metropolitan areas develop in different national or local contexts, why they choose different pathways, and why there are similarities or differences in their processes and challenges. Theories usually navigate between the appeals of specificity and generality. In the absence of a comprehensive theory that can be applied to diverse contexts, analysis tends to draw on either pragmatic frameworks towards a more encompassing and comparative scope to identify the parallels and variations or only report case studies of cities or surveys of general trends. The analysis of urbanisation in this book is based on an eclectic framework which is not necessarily a critique of the urbanisation theory discourses but rather an invitation to develop an understanding of the national, local and idiosyncratic forces that mould urban and economic patterns and dynamics, and at the same time keep an international comparative capacity. I use the idea of the 'urban land nexus' suggested in Scott and Storper (2014) and Storper and Scott (2016) as a helpful tool for leaving room for the idiosyncrasy of particular cases and actors' agency to shape urban realities. Where necessary, the chapters include a specific conceptual or theoretical review relating to the problem or issue at hand.

A number of additional considerations shaped the analytical framework. The book takes a multiscalar approach, presenting international, regional, national and local perspectives of the urbanisation phenomenon in its discussion of mainstream developments in metropolitan areas. I propose to readdress basic but relevant questions about urban, metropolitan and governance issues, including current and historical urbanisation trends and patterns, inter-urban disparities and hierarchies, urban structure mismatches and legal and institutional organisations and structures. Depending on the subject being addressed, in some chapters I take an international comparative approach.

I see some of the key concepts and expressions used in the literature as problematic due to their polysemic nature or incertitude. While economic development has predominantly been associated with economic growth and gains in productivity, over time conceptual developments have incorporated dimensions of development other than income or production such as structural change, sectoral transformation, inclusiveness, sustainability and prosperity. Here I stick mainly to development concepts that refer to growth and efficiency issues. This is more a practical decision based on the availability of data than an intellectual preference. I avoid using the multitude of buzzwords and adjectives that often do not represent or apply to local realities ('global cities', 'creative cities', 'smart cities', and so on). I use the terms 'developing countries', 'the Global South' and 'less-developed countries' interchangeably to refer to nations other than those commonly called 'developed countries', although I consider all of these terms are problematic because although they imply homogeneity there are vast differences among countries.

Most of the chapters in the book are the result of my own individual research agenda on metropolitan areas, economic development and public policy. The exception is Chapter 8 which includes a number of findings of a collective

Brown International Advanced Research Institute (BIARI) seed project on metropolitan governance and the provision of public services in Latin American. The empirical studies are based mainly on quantitative secondary data obtained from open-access international and national sources. Typical data sets are found in national population and housing censuses and economic censuses and United Nations and World Bank country data. Quantitative analysis includes descriptive statistics, specialised indexes, exploratory spatial analysis and econometrics. The research in Chapter 8 employs qualitative data obtained from a mixture of interviews, focus groups and technical visits. Chapter 9 and some sections of other chapters are based on document reviews.

Contents

This introduction situates the work within the intellectual, academic and policy debates on urbanisation, urban economic development and governance. The book consists of nine chapters addressing the patterns and dynamics of urbanisation and urban expansion, the significance of metropolitan areas and the functioning and performance of urban economies. Part I presents a concise review of conceptual and theoretical debates in urban studies and international, regional and national trends and patterns of urban processes. Part II deals with the Mexican urban system, the inter-metropolitan structure and the dynamics of the country case, and Part III deals with local experiences and policy issues. Overall conclusions end the book.

Chapter 1 critically reviews the conceptual frameworks and broad current debates in urban theory, positioning this book among them. The chapter has a twofold objective: (1) it lays out the general principles by which contemporary urbanisation and metropolitan areas can be approached by providing a brief literature review and an account of the scientific debate in urban studies to conceptualise and explain urban and metropolitan patterns and their development; and (2) it delivers an overview of international trends in urbanisation and metropolisation.

Chapter 2 discusses comparative urbanisation and urban development in Latin America. Here I review the precolonial and colonial origins of urbanisation in the region and explain how both historical and contemporary urbanisation in Latin America and Mexico have been characterised by powerful urban primacy, hyper-concentration, and centralisation. The chapter highlights the idea that one of the most significant difference of urban processes in Latin America in relation to advanced economies is the weak link between urbanisation and development, which seems to have broken down in much of the developing world, with Latin America the clearest example. The most significant flaws in the region's urbanisation are identified.

Elucidating the macrodynamics and patterns that characterise Mexico's metropolitan areas, Chapter 3 reviews the origins of the metropolisation process in Mexico and the key features of its metropolitan and urban systems, including their demographics. It also offers a brief account of metropolitan development in Latin America overall, and suggests further investigation of the complex origins of urban sprawl and metropolitan areas in the region. The chapter gives a clear picture of how the Mexican case relates to other countries' experiences regarding the processes and politics driving suburbanisation, urban sprawl and metropolisation. Problematic urban planning, illegality, irregularity, speculative land and housing markets and favourable local and national politics are common elements in the Latin American context that assume specific forms depending on idiosyncratic institutional and legal structures such as land-ownership regimes and regulation to control urban expansion, that is, the urban land nexus. In this respect I underline the convergences and divergences, general categorisations and mainstream developments in relation to the country case.

Analysis, diagnosis and monitoring of metropolitan areas' economic performance is essential to urban planning and the formulation of territorial development strategies. Chapter 4 presents the details of the metropolitan system and hierarchy, examining the dynamics and patterns of economic performance in Mexico's 74 metropolitan areas. The analysis focuses on the spatial patterns of economic performance, the distribution of economic activity, specialisation profiles, poverty levels, informality and inter-metropolitan disparities. I also call attention to the acute problem of the poor availability of data in Mexico for use in the systematic and consistent analysis of metropolitan territories' economic performance and development.

In Chapter 5 I discuss one of the greatest problems at the metropolitan level: public finances. Jurisdictional fragmentation usually disconnects the territorial scope of urban needs from the public resources required to fulfil them. This mismatch occurs in an overall context of constrained public budgets and local authorities being asked to do more with less – a growing and increasingly daunting challenge for metropolitan areas, whose availability, allocation and management of public financial resources determine their potential to achieve their economic and social development objectives. The chapter draws attention to the critical need for a more metropolitan-sensitive approach to public finances. It discusses alternative approaches, explains the frameworks that define local public budgets in Mexico and presents an empirical analysis of metropolitan areas in the country, with a focus on the macroevolution and structure of public budgets, their performance and their inter-metropolitan disparities.

Why do some cities realise their promise as engines of economic growth, development and efficiency, while others fail? Having analysed in Chapter 4 the dynamics and patterns of metropolitan economic development in Mexico according to different performance indicators, the driving forces of urban economic performance and competitiveness must also be identified. Chapter 6 deals with the factors that contribute to boosting economic performance and economic development in metropolitan areas. The effects of a number of variables cited in the theoretical and empirical literature are tested. The data set includes variables for the group of metropolitan areas in two years, 1998 and 2013. An obvious question is whether traditional factors – physical and human capital, economic structure, specialisation – or other factors such as innovation, the creative class, institutions, metropolitan governance and urban structure best explain metropolitan areas' economic performance.

Chapter 7 discusses the urban evolution of Mexico City Metropolitan Area and unfolds the territorial changes that have occurred there over the past century. After recounting the foundation and historical evolution of Mexico City, I discuss the political economy of its territorial transformation and its peripheral urbanisation in the twentieth century. The economy and productive structure of this metropolitan area is depicted to show its relative position and role in the national and global urban systems. An examination of the recent spatial patterns of the labour force and economic activities within the metropolitan area helps to identify the prevailing urban structure which has been blame for much of the social and economic inefficiency in this metropolitan area. The chapter also identifies the governance and political frames in which metropolitan evolution and functioning take place.

Chapter 8 shows how different governance arrangements across Latin American metropolitan areas translate into diverse outcomes when providing urban services such as piped water, waste collection and public transport. These sectors are strategic in urban planning and directly affect the daily lives of the population; they are also typical of the kinds of service that face unique challenges in metropolitan environments. Using a comparative case study analysis of governance, I analyse the provision of those urban services in Mexico City Metropolitan Area, two other metropolitan areas in Mexico (i.e. Guadalajara and Monterrey) and two other metropolises in Latin America (i.e. Lima and Bogota). The analysis focuses on metropolitan governance structures, coordination, financial sustainability and service coverage and quality.

In Chapter 9 I address two central issues in the political economy of metropolitan development: public policies and governance. I review international and national urban development agendas and the policies, strategies and activities that different tiers of government implement to promote economic development in metropolitan areas, with some references to the Mexican experience, particularly regarding urban policy and economic policy. I discuss whether there is room for public policy to shape urban economic development: if the foundation and growth of cities are related to public policy, this raises the question of how much agency political actors have to alter the path of development.

The Conclusion wraps up the findings and discussion against the background of the topics covered in each chapter. Thus, the book is an essential reading for those keen on a comprehensive picture of international, regional, national and local urbanisation and development processes, for empirical research on urbanisation and metropolitan areas in Mexico and Latin America and for an in-depth discussion of urbanisation and metropolitan economic development in Mexico. It also serves as reference for policymakers and others involved in metropolitan policy and governance in both the developed and the developing world.

References

Almandoz, A. (2008). 'Despegues sin madurez: Urbanización, industrialización y desarrollo en la Latinoamérica del siglo XX'. *EURE*, XXXIV(102), 61–76. Available at: www.redalyc.org/articulo.oa?id=19610204.

Angotti, T. (1996). 'Latin American urbanization and planning: Inequality and unsustainability in North and South'. *Latin American Perspectives*, 23(4), 12–34.

Chant, S. & McIlwaine, C. (2009). *Geographies of development in the 21st century: An introduction to the Global South*. Cheltenham: Edward Elgar.

Cohen, B. (2006). 'Urbanization in developing countries: Current trends, future projections, and key challenges for sustainability'. *Technology in Society*, (28), 63–80.

Jedwab, R. & Vollrath, D. (2015). 'Urbanization without growth in historical perspective'. *Explorations in Economic History*, 58(2015), 1–21. Available at: https://doi.org/10.1016/j.eeh.2015.09.002.

Klaufus, C. & Jaffe, R. (2015). 'Latin American and Caribbean urban development'. *European Review of Latin American and Caribbean Studies*, (100), 63–72. Available at: https://doi.org/10.18352/erlacs.10127.

Rodgers, D., Beall, J. & Kanbur, R. (2011). *Latin American urban development into the 21st century: Towards a renewed perspective on the city*. WIDER Working Paper 2011/05, Helsinki: WIDER. Available at: http://hdl.handle.net/10419/54165.

Rojas, E., Cuadrado Roura, J. R. & Fernández Guell, J. M. (2005). *Gobernar las metropolis*. Washington, D.C.: Inter-American Development Bank. Available at: http://site.ebrary.com/id/10201140.

Scott, A. J. & Storper, M. (2014). 'The nature of cities: The scope and limits of urban theory'. *International Journal of Urban and Regional Research*, 39(1), 1–15. Available at: https://doi.org/10.1111/1468-2427.12134.

SEDATU, CONAPO & INEGI. (2018). *Delimitación de las zonas metropolitanas de México 2015*. México, D. F.: Secretaría de Desarrollo Agrario, Territorial y Urbano, Consejo Nacional de Población, Instituto Nacional de Estadística y Geografía. Available at: www.gob.mx/conapo/documentos/delimitacion-de-las-zonas-metropolitanas-de-mexico-2015.

Sellers, J. & Hoffmann-Martinot, V. (2008). Gobernanza metropolitana: United Cities and Local. Washington, D.C.: World Bank, 226–293. Available at: www.cities-localgovernments.org/gold/Upload/gold_report/09_metropolis_es.pdf.

Storper, M. & Scott, A. J. (2016). 'Current debates in urban theory: A critical assessment'. *Urban Studies*, 53(6), 1114–1136. Available at: https://doi.org/10.1177/0042098016634002.

Trejo, A. (2013). 'Las economías de las zonas metropolitanas de México en los albores del siglo XXI'. *Estudios Demográficos y Urbanos*, 28(3), 545–591. Available at: https://doi.org/10.24201/edu.v28i3.1447.

Trejo Nieto, A. (2017). *Localización manufacturera, apertura comercial y disparidades regionales en México*. México, D. F.: El Colegio de México. Available at: www.jstor.org/stable/j.ctv1fxg2x.

UN. (2014). *World urbanization prospects: The 2014 revision, highlights*. New York: United Nations, Department of Economic and Social Affairs and Population Division. Available at: http://esa.un.org/unpd/wup/highlights/wup2014-highlights.pdf.

UN. (2018). *World urbanization prospects: The 2018 revision*. New York: United Nations. Available at: https://population.un.org/wup/Publications/Files/WUP2018-KeyFacts.pdf.

Vargas, J., Brassiolo, P., Sanguinetti, P., Daude, C., Goytia, C., Álvarez, F., Estrada, R. & Fajardo, G. (2017). *RED 2017: Urban growth and access to opportunities: A challenge for Latin America*. Bogota: Banco de Desarrollo de América Latina, CAF. Available at: http://scioteca.caf.com/handle/123456789/1091.

Ziccardi, A. (2016). 'Poverty and urban inequality: The case of Mexico City metropolitan region'. *International Social Science Journal*, 56(217–218), 205–2019.

Part I

The rise of a metropolitan world

1 The intersection of the urban, the metropolitan and the regional

Concepts, theories and international experiences

Introduction

Today, around 55 per cent of the world's population is urban, with some 70 per cent of the world's inhabitants forecasted to live in cities by 2050. Also by 2050, cities in the developing world will absorb more than 2 billion new urban residents, representing 95 per cent of global urban growth (UN, 2014). The current absolute numbers of total urban population are substantial, as the world's population crossed the 7 billion mark in 2011 (Yusuf, 2013). In 1950 there were around 750 million people living in cities, in 2018 there were more than 4 billion, rising to a predicted 6.3 billion by 2050 (UN, 2018). Also, more than ever, cities play an important economic role and are focal points for economic growth, innovation and employment (Fox & Goodfellow, 2016). It has been estimated that today up to 80 per cent of global gross domestic product (GDP) is generated in cities (Dobbs et al., 2011).

Humanity continues on an inexorable urbanisation path that commenced at the end of the eighteenth century in Europe and North America and will likely culminate in Africa at the end of the present century. Whereas in the year 1800 a small percentage of the world population lived in cities, with the Industrial Revolution the city became the main location of the inhabitants of the North. In the countries of the South the city is abruptly becoming the dominant way of life (Sellers & Hoffmann-Martinot, 2008). Cities are outgrowing, and small towns have become cities of several million inhabitants in a few decades.

The pace of recent change at the city level is unprecedented in human history. In both developed and developing countries urbanisation has been tied up with the geographical expansion of cities and urban sprawl. As a result metropolitan areas are emerging as the true functional economies, surpassing the administrative boundaries of the traditional city and exceeding the jurisdictional scope of local authorities, with labour markets that cover several municipalities, sometimes in different states or provinces. Large cities and metropolitan areas are the actual hearts of urban functioning, but tend to be challenged by the 'boundary issue' (Hoornweg & Pope, 2016). This trend explains the increasing percentage of the world's population living in metropolitan areas. It has been estimated that the 300 largest metropolitan areas in the world account for

19 per cent of total population and around one half of production (Bouchet, Lius & Parilla, 2018). Yet cities in the developed world have been surpassed in size and growth by the megacities of the Global South, where cities of unprecedented size are multiplying.

This chapter has a twofold objective. First, it lays out some general principles by which to approach contemporary urbanisation and metropolitan areas. It provides a brief literature review and an account of the scientific debate in urban studies to explain urban and metropolitan patterns and their development. Although the literature includes efforts to incorporate elements particular to less-developed countries and regions, attempts have also been made to provide more universal concepts and explanations of urbanisation and urban patterns. Conceptual categories such as urban growth, urban sprawl, urbanisation and metropolitan areas will be explained. The concept of the metropolitan area, defined in territorial terms and as a complex interrelation of social, economic and institutional factors, occupies central place in this chapter. The overview of relevant explanations of metropolitan areas highlights the interpretation of the metropolitan phenomenon from the economic perspective. The chapter also delivers an overview of international patterns and trends in urbanisation and compares developing and developed countries.

Urbanisation-related concepts

To address the question of what we do and do not know about urbanisation, city growth, metropolitan expansion and economic development, and to consider how we might fill a number of the gaps in the empirical knowledge, a review of the basic conceptual categories is worthwhile. With such categories in mind, it is possible to develop interpretations of metropolitan areas in their connection to broad processes of urbanisation and economic development. As highlighted by McGranahan and Satterthwaite (2014), although there is a consensus that urbanisation is critically important to development, there is also considerable misunderstanding about what it actually involves. Furthermore, the notion of 'urban' remains transitory, changing over time and across political boundaries depending upon the purpose of the definition. A synthetic clarification of concepts is needed.

First, to define urbanisation definitions of the terms 'city' and 'urban centre' are required. Some of the most influential definitions refer to the demographic and physical conditions of the urban environment on the one hand and to the socioeconomic relationships typical of human settlements on the other. Population size, density, heterogeneity, economic functions and the division of labour are factors that have historically defined a city (Fox & Goodfellow, 2016). Whereas there is a general consensus about the essential features of cities, in practice there is no universally established definition. Even though several efforts are underway to produce globally comparable estimates of urban areas based on satellite imagery of land cover and nighttime lights, cities and urban areas are defined and classified very differently across countries, based mainly on administrative criteria or population size (see for instance Florida, Mellander & Gulden, 2009; OECD, 2012; Vargas et al., 2017). The variability shown in Table 1.1 complicates the evaluation and comparison of urban trends across countries in the world.

In addition to the concept of the city, a collection of related notions about urban evolution is present in the literature, including urban growth, urbanisation, urban expansion and sprawl. Among specialists it is generally understood that urbanisation involves a population shift from rural to urban locations. This is a demographic perspective from which urbanisation levels are measured by the urban population share. However, confusion arises when the term 'urbanisation' is used to refer to urban growth or the expansion of urban land cover (McGranahan & Satterthwaite, 2014). 'Urbanisation', 'urban growth' and 'urban expansion' are three distinct terms that describe different phenomena in the urban transition process (Fox & Goodfellow, 2016). Likewise, in some countries, 'urbanisation' has been used to refer to the expansion of built-up areas, to the process of rural–urban migration and to the development of physical infrastructure in cities. A series of misconceptions can emerge when terms describing different but related phenomena are used without caution. Figure 1.1 summarises the fundamental differences between the core concepts of urbanisation, urban growth and urban expansion.

Urbanisation, understood in a static sense, denotes the proportion of the total population living in urban areas, that is, the level or degree of urbanisation. From a dynamic perspective, urbanisation is the speed of change in that level, that is, the urbanisation rate. Thus, urbanisation is simultaneously a process of change and a state of being. Urban growth, on the other hand, represents the increase in the absolute number, rather than the proportion, of urban inhabitants. In contrast, urban expansion is the increase in the physical built-up area of a city or urban area (Fox & Goodfellow, 2016).

Table 1.1 Varying definitions of urban centres

Country	Criteria to define urban centres
Germany	Population density of 150 or more per square kilometre.
Angola	2,000 inhabitants or more.
Australia	Population of at least 1,000 inhabitants.
Botswana	Agglomerations of 5,000 inhabitants or more with 75 per cent of economic activity non-agricultural.
Canada	Areas with 1,000 inhabitants or more and a population density of at least 400 per square kilometre.
Nigeria	Towns with at least 20,000 inhabitants.
Vietnam	Places with a population in excess of 4,000.
Zimbabwe	Urban centres are defined in two ways, as places that are officially designated 'urban'; and places with 2,500 inhabitants or more with at least 50 per cent of employment non-agricultural.

Source: UN (2014).

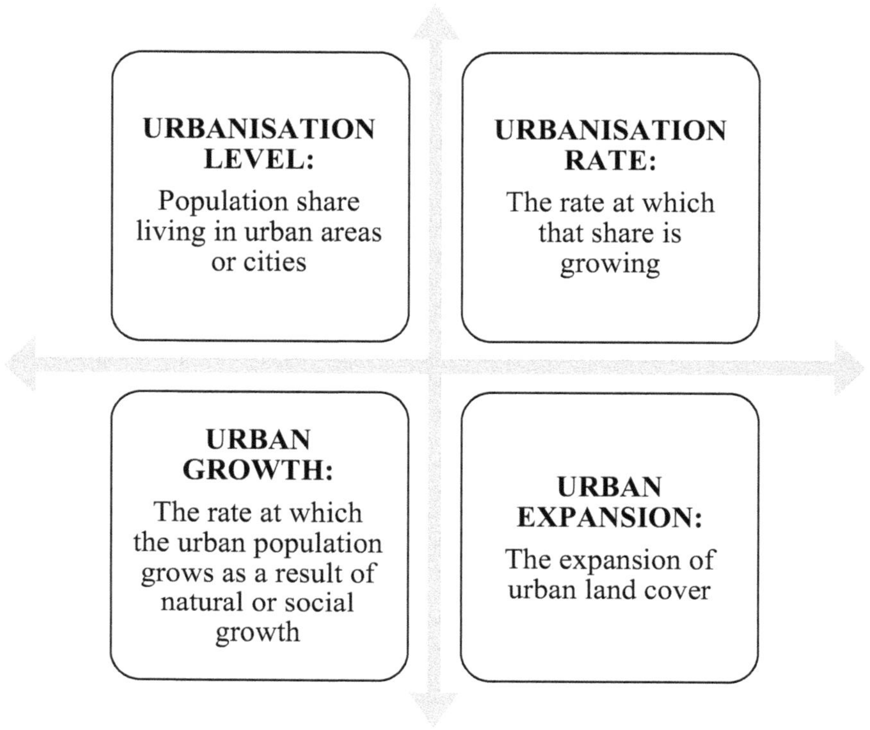

Figure 1.1 Urbanisation-related concepts

Source: Author's own elaboration.

Urbanisation, urban growth and urban expansion do not necessarily go hand in hand. Indeed, the problem with applying the same term to changes along these different dimensions is that they do not occur together. Moreover, shifts in any of these dimensions can have very different drivers and implications. According to McGranahan and Satterthwaite (2014), if urban and rural populations grow together at the same rate, urbanisation does not necessarily take place, and urbanisation does not involve urban expansion if land cover around the city remains the same, but increases in density. This is not the place to describe the diverse and complex ways in which these processes intertwine; however, as the terms are often used loosely it is important to highlight that the differences are analytically important if we are to understand the dynamics of urban change (Fox & Goodfellow, 2016). Finally, even though the demographic criterion is at the heart of the definition of urbanisation, important economic, spatial and social connotations of the phenomenon are implicit.

Drivers and explanations of urbanisation

Factors such as agricultural surplus, non-agricultural production, technological development, transport systems, specialisation and division of labour and the establishment of social and political power hierarchies appear frequently as factors explaining the appearance of cities (Mumford, 1966; Bourassa, 2007). The first towns that emerged, perhaps during or after the Neolithic Revolution (some of which were probably part of the Sumer culture in Mesopotamia), responded to primal technological advancements and economic specialisation, basic transport technologies and storage methods, the division of labour and technologies for the management of water and sewage. Emerging institutions in the form of cultural norms, governance structures and economic mechanisms were also necessary in the rise of urban concentrations. These institutional structures had to be sufficiently sophisticated to enforce internal rules and organise the protection of the city against external threats (OECD, 2015; Fox & Goodfellow, 2016). For instance, cities located close to the Tigris and Euphrates rivers, such as Ur, were characterised by a sociopolitical order that included divine kingship and developed basic state functions such as taxation, military conscription, policing and bureaucratic administration. Centuries later cities emerged independently in Phoenicia, India and China with more developed sociopolitical structures and diverse economic functions (Fox & Goodfellow, 2016).

It is more or less accepted that over time, urbanisation has been driven by a combination of key factors during different waves of urbanisation. Sectoral transformations and technological changes in production and transportation also play a prominent role in accounting for the dynamics of urbanisation and urban change by making cities of more than 10,000 inhabitants possible.

The Industrial Revolution set a first wave of urbanisation in motion. At the time, technical change, including the widespread introduction of the steam engine and improvements in iron and smelting techniques, allowed increases in agricultural productivity. Labour demand in this sector decreased, and workers were released and moved to cities. This helped to satisfy the demand for labour at a single location caused by the onset of larger-scale manufacturing. Additionally, with more efficient forms of transport such as shipping, road-based transport and the first railway line, which opened in 1836 in London, the transportation of larger quantities of goods into cities was made possible and port cities grew in importance. Other major innovations in production techniques and urban transport – such as underground steam, electric railways and horse-drawn omnibuses – occurred throughout the nineteenth century, feeding urbanisation and allowing cities such as London to reach a million or more inhabitants by 1900. At the onset of the twentieth century new construction technologies such as the development of steel-frame construction and the invention of reinforced concrete contributed to the reshaping of cities, as taller buildings allowed for greater population density. In brief, technological change led to increased productivity, reduced transport costs and new construction methods, and changes in productive structures and migration to cities supported the transformation of agricultural rural societies to industrialised urban areas and the urbanisation of countries benefiting from the impulse of the Industrial Revolution in the nineteenth century (Combes, Mayer & Thisse, 2008; OECD, 2015).

In the early twentieth century further changes in construction and transport technologies influenced not only urbanisation but also urban structure. Taller buildings and the rise of the car made suburban living possible. The adoption of the car in particular had fundamental effects on the nature of urban living and the shape of cities. It increased the feasible commuting distance and made it possible to develop single-purpose neighbourhoods in faraway locations. This led to the widespread development of low-density suburban residential locations and urban sprawl, which also was driven by a mix of cultural and economic factors. As urban and industrial change proceeded in the most developed countries, urban amenities and agglomeration economies became leading drivers of urbanisation. Prior to the Industrial Revolution the location of factor endowments and the role of natural advantage had been powerful forces that triggered the spatial concentration of economic activities and population (OECD, 2015).

These advances and the first wave of urbanisation mostly impacted Europe and North America. Since the second half of the twentieth century a second wave of urbanisation has taken place, mainly in less-developed countries. Even though it shares some of the characteristics of the earlier transition, some major factors distinguish urbanisation in developing nations from urbanisation in Europe and the US: (1) it is occurring faster, as it took more than a century for most developed countries to be 50 per cent urbanised, whereas today's developing economies are reaching this threshold in less than half the time; (2) larger numbers of people and countries are involved; and (3) urbanisation and income growth are less closely connected than they were in the developed countries, meaning than urbanisation does not necessarily imply that a country is developing (UN, 2014; OECD, 2015; Fox & Goodfellow, 2016).

One of the main concerns about the urbanisation transition in developing countries is that it does not resemble historical urbanisation based on industrialisation. In the poorest countries the manufacturing sector has not been the prime driver of urbanisation, and these developing countries, particularly in Africa and parts of Asia, have seen strongly growing levels of urbanisation without economic growth and development.

In the World Urbanization Prospects document the UN (2014) suggests that cities are still important drivers of development and poverty reduction and continue to concentrate much of their nation's economic activity. Big urban concentrations have higher levels of literacy and education, better health, greater access to social services and better cultural and political opportunities. However, fast, unplanned urban growth threatens economic productivity and development. As the world has continued to urbanise, the challenges of development are increasingly concentrated in cities, particularly in lower-middle-income countries where the pace of urbanisation is fastest. Accelerated urbanisation has imposed continuous social, economic and environmental challenges that hamper economic advantage.

Despite the differences between the first and the second waves of urbanisation, according to Yusuf (2013) a combination of both old and new forces has accounted for the structural characteristics and dynamics of recent urbanisation (Figure 1.2). First, the demographic transition, caused by a sharp decline in infant mortality, increasing life expectancy and a gradual reduction in fertility, has increased population size, especially in developing countries, and has led to rapid growth of urban populations and cities. Second, agricultural production has become less labour intensive and more capital intensive, with the result that the size of the agricultural labour force is dropping dramatically. This is a powerful pushing force for rural to urban migration. Furthermore, higher urban incomes and better amenities exert a pull effect towards cities. Third,

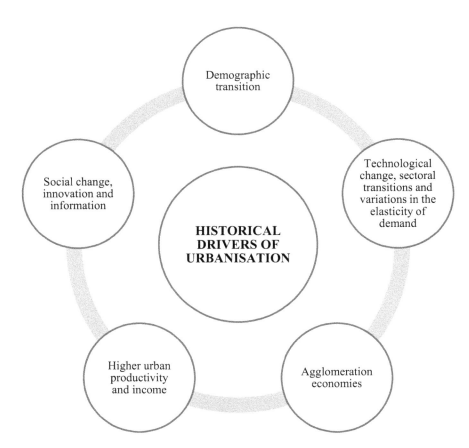

Figure 1.2 Drivers of urbanisation

Source: Based on Yusuf (2013).

technological advances and changes in the elasticity of demand have translated into structural changes which have enlarged the demand for urban services and the proportion of these services in GDP and employment. Fourth, localisation and urbanisation economies lead to significant productivity gains and higher average incomes in cities. Localisation economies are an important factor in the concentration of economic activity due to the productivity gains from dense and specialised labour markets, technological spillover and productive forward and backward linkages. On the other hand, urbanisation economies are agglomeration forces deriving from diversification, urban infrastructure and amenities that help firms to achieve economies of scale. Last, but not least, cities play a decisive role in stimulating social change, encouraging innovation and spreading information and ideas.

Depending on the balance of these forces, urbanisation and urban development are likely to evolve in different directions, with implications for growth and development. It is also important to emphasise that even though urbanisation is by no means historically specific to any mode of production, cities and urban agglomerations have played a significant part in the historical development of capitalism. In the current stage of globalisation in particular, cities hold a pivotal role in economic accumulation.

Urbanisation is relevant to and demands the engagement of a range of disciplines. As the phenomenon has been closely linked to modernisation, industrialisation and development, the field of economics has also a crucial place in urban studies. Economists as well as other scientists need to acknowledge and understand the roles of cities and metropolitan areas in national and the world economy and society. But the theoretical bases of urbanisation and urban development are far from conclusive. It is a more or less standard idea that the spatial concentration of people and jobs leads to productivity and efficiency gains, and these, in turn, explain the patterns and dynamics of contemporary cities. Economists, in particular, have focused on agglomeration economies – which are positive externalities in production and consumption – to explain the high concentration of people and jobs found in cities (Fujita, Krugman & Venables, 2001; Fujita & Thisse, 2002).

The idea of agglomeration economies continues to be powerful in explaining urban patterns and development, despite the problems cities increasingly face such as deindustrialisation, concentrated poverty, slums, insecurity, violence and crime, difficult access to housing and services, gentrification and many others (Fox & Goodfellow, 2016; Storper & Scott, 2016). The current context in which urbanisation is taking place has given way to a vigorous revival of debate related to the theoretical foundations of urban development. The role of agglomeration advantages has been at the core of those debates in urban theory, to which I will refer briefly. This book does not attempt to discuss the trends in urban theory in detail but rather defines the particular lenses through which it looks at urbanisation and development.

Attempts to provide alternative understandings of the empirical trends in urbanisation and international urban problems are found in some influential approaches to urban studies which claim to offer frameworks for disentangling the shifting geographies of urbanisation and interpreting the several problems that cities confront. Largely, some of these theories challenge the idea of the urban as a concept, as a scale and as a reality, and in so doing also contest the existence of a proper urban theory. They also regard explanations of cities based mainly on agglomeration advantages as ambitious economistic theories that neglect a number of the major forces that shape urban life (Storper & Scott, 2016). Some approaches date back to the 1970s, when intense critical scrutiny of urban orthodoxy deemed the city an ideology, a space of class struggle or an arbitrary geographic container of diverse economic, social and political phenomena (Scott & Storper, 2014).

More recent influential contentions about urban theory include postcolonial urban analysis, assemblage urbanism and the theory of planetary urbanism. Postcolonial urban theory questions the universality and intellectual parochialism of urban theory and defends the 'comparative gesture' as a basis for constructing knowledge about cities, whereas the assemblage theory calls for new methodological approaches to urban research (Scott & Storper, 2014) and planetary urbanism suggests that urban areas in the twenty-first century can no longer be distinguished from the rest of geographical space (Storper & Scott, 2016).

Concepts such as 'borrowed size' have also been used recently to explain contemporary urban dynamics that remain unaddressed by conventional urban theories. The 'borrowed size' idea refers to smaller cities that achieve performance levels normally associated with larger cities, enabled by interaction within networks of cities across multiple spatial scales, which serves as a substitute for the benefits of agglomeration (Meijers & Burger, 2017).

Storper and Scott (2016) and Scott and Storper (2014) argue that some of these approaches suffer from major flaws and fail to offer a meaningful analytical framework for the orientation of urban studies. Scott and Storper (ibid.) agree that contemporary cities exhibit considerable empirical variation across time and space, but suggest that it is possible to identify common denominators of urban analysis and that a theoretical framework can be constructed by which to understand cities and urbanisation in terms of the dynamics of agglomeration and the intrinsic interplay of location, land use and social interaction. Storper and Scott (2016) refer to the presence of common genetic factors that underlie urban processes wherever and whenever they occur.

Historically, all cities respond to dense local interaction, and major aspects of urbanisation are rooted in the spatial concentration of production. Hence, agglomeration remains important to understanding cities, regardless of space and time. Scott and Storper (2014) argue that it is the interplay between agglomeration advantages and the urban land nexus – the structure of intra-urban space intermingled with production and residential locations – that provides the rationale for any account of cities and urban processes. Whereas agglomeration advantages are mostly economic forces or forces driven by market mechanisms, the urban land nexus involves mechanisms of collective coordination supported by institutions that are able to implement planning and policy in the interests of economic efficiency and social wellbeing. Governance, moulded by government regulations, financing, and collective action, gives sense to rich urban variation. These are contextual circumstances that impose distinguishing features on urbanisation in different times and spaces. In short, spatial concentration, interacting with differentiated land uses and locations with institutional and political arrangements, is the essential force of the urbanisation process. Certainly, economic forces occupy a primary place in explanations of urban patterns and development and are important in the conceptualisation and understanding of the city and the urban as tangible phenomena.

I agree with this latter view that emphasises the relevance of contextual factors together with economic forces in the shaping of urbanisation and development. I also support the idea that in spite of diversity urban agglomerations in different countries face many similar challenges and have much to learn from one another. The urban land nexus idea inspires relevant cross-regional and cross-country comparative assessment because it is not necessary to put aside all concepts of European or North American urban theory or to invent a new vocabulary to provide an account of cities and urban development in the Global South.

A 'new' form of urbanisation: the metropolitan phenomenon

For many experts, the current reality of urbanisation is the increasing number of very large and intricate urban agglomerations. Cities are becoming extremely complex systems that are difficult to study and manage. The demographic concentration in cities is not in itself new. The demographic and industrial revolution that began in the second half of the eighteenth century propelled a progressive and constant urbanisation. The city became the target destination for growing numbers of the population who were in search of the wide-ranging conditions offered by urban life. Nonetheless, at some point between the nineteenth and the twentieth centuries a qualitative jump uncovered an emerging form of urbanisation known as metropolisation (Argullol, 2005).

Broadly speaking, metropolisation as a distinctive feature of urbanisation over the past 50 years is characterised by the expansion of urban settlements beyond official city limits. Metropolisation has intensified in the recent years and has generated significant changes in cities, and in the way we understand social and economic problems (Trejo, 2013). From a general standpoint, metropolisation has been regarded as an unprecedented phenomenon of global transformation (Gómez-Alvarez et al., 2017). However, manifold interpretations of metropolitan areas have emerged. According to Andersson (2015), the continuing urbanisation around the world has translated into the emergence of larger cities, particularly in developing countries. These cities are becoming spatially, functionally and economically interdependent with their surrounding territories, constituting metropolitan regions, each a single economy and labour market:

> The defining scope for metropolitan regions are their spatial dimensions based upon the functional relationships of resource cycles, regional

economic systems and formal as well as informal settlement structures. The linkages of metropolitan regions extend beyond administrative and political boundaries and usually include a number of local governments, peri-urban and rural lands, as well as neighbouring cities. The economic links between the core and the periphery may become so close that one part cannot succeed without the other, and thus they are perceived and behave as a single entity. Metropolitan areas are becoming 'the new normal'.

(ibid., p. 8)

Frey and Zimmer (2001) refer to the expansion of cities that has taken place in developed societies as the result of a deconcentration of population as individuals decide to move to live further away from the centre and locate in suburban areas. Improved transportation and communication technologies allow suburban residents to commute over longer distances to city centres. Ingram (1997) considers that the urban development of cities in both industrial and developing countries with market-based economies exhibits similar patterns of population and employment decentralisation. In both cases, this decentralisation has increased reliance on road-based transport for both passengers and freight. However, while industrial countries have experienced significant decreases in public transport use and increases in car ownership, in developing countries the use of public transport is still widespread.

Angel et al. (2016) suggest that most of the residential fabric of urban expansion areas, especially in less-developed countries, is unplanned, disorganised and occurs in defiance of municipal plans or regulations. Moreover, the proportion of expansion areas within walking distance of arterial roads is declining, failing to connect urban peripheries effectively to metropolitan labour markets, making cities less productive, less inclusive and less sustainable.

There is agreement on the need for flexibility in the definition of the term 'city' (Frey & Zimmer, 2001). This has resulted in the development of the concept of the 'metropolitan area' which has taken over as virtually the most dominant notion for defining the huge and complex urban areas of the twenty-first century. Moreover, metropolitan areas are becoming an increasingly important planning and policy territorial unit (Andersson, 2015).

Yet the diverse understandings of metropolisation translate into a variety of definitions. In the first place, metropolitan areas might be understood as cities that have become spatially, functionally and economically interdependent, with their less dense surrounding settlements and rural areas forming a single economy and labour market (Frey & Zimmer, 2001; Andersson, 2015). In principle, the definition of the metropolitan area is economic and territorial: the close economic links and interdependencies between the core and the periphery, to the extent that they behave as a single entity, characterise the formation and emergence of a metropolitan region. However, the political and administrative dimension of that territory adds complexity to the phenomenon. Because the jurisdictional boundaries of local governments tend to have a long history, a metropolitan region usually includes multiple independent jurisdictions, each with its own local government. The linkages of metropolitan regions extend beyond administrative and political boundaries and usually include a number of local governments, peri-urban and rural areas, and neighbouring cities (Andersson, 2015). Metropolitan areas represent a fusion of urban and regional development in which the distinction between what is urban and what is rural has become blurred as cities expand to include towns and villages (Drakakis-Smith, 2000).

A metropolitan region might arise as a result of the outward expansion of the city or of the gradual integration of various settlements, which at some point form an interdependent and agglomerated metropolitan area (Andersson, 2015). Such regions usually expand from the central city to beyond the municipal borders. Functional metropolitan areas disrupt the established administrative boundaries, their consumption of land rises rapidly, the social fragmentation of the territory grows, the needs and costs of infrastructure increase, fiscal imbalances intensify and coordination and planning become difficult (Argullol, 2005).

In practice the delimitation of a metropolitan area is diverse and complex. It is usually defined as a functional area according to city size or to the official limits of the municipalities that comprise the functional area. A functional economic area is determined by a 'commuting zone' whose labour market is highly integrated. This spatial labour market approach makes it possible to compare functional urban areas across countries. The methods and concepts used to define metropolitan areas in different countries differ or converge depending on the laws and regulations in force in each country, data availability and the purpose of the conceptualisation and measurement. Usually there are at least four common criteria: population size, urban expansion and contiguity, population density, and commuting and economic dependency. However, the definitional scope of metropolitan areas is manifold and changing and remains as a technical matter.

Economic interpretations of metropolitan areas as functional regions

From an economic perspective, metropolitan areas are largely understood as the by-product of externalities derived from a set of synergistic spatial effects that benefit economic activities and explain growth, structural change and innovation processes associated with economic development (Trejo, 2013). Cuadrado-Roura and Guell (2005) define the metropolitan area as territory or a set of territories with intense functional interdependencies, a broad labour market with a diversified professional supply, a spatial concentration of externalities and spillover effects and an ecosystem that shares natural resources. In a metropolitan area, the urban core and adjacent spaces are connected by strong economic links, forming a unified labour market linked by infrastructure for daily commuting. Metropolitan areas typically span a number of local authorities but are conceived as economically active territorial units and engines of development and wellbeing (Cochrane, McGree & Zandi, 2012). They offer significant opportunities for engendering wealth, investment, employment, added value and social welfare (Trejo, 2013). They are also natural spaces for the insertion of national economies into global markets. Hence, in an environment of increasing competitive pressures, interest in boosting the economic potentiality of metropolitan regions has also increased (Rionda-Ramírez, 2007).

According to Cochrane, McGree and Zandi (2012), metropolitan areas are key geographic units for understanding subnational economies because they fit the definition of functional economic regions. Metropolitan areas are intrinsically economic demarcations and are therefore better suited to regional economic analysis within countries and states than other subnational geographic units. De Mattos (2010) refers to metropolitan regions as productive concentrations located in a space in which externalities expand territorially from one city to other cities or municipalities with which it establishes a necessary economic interdependence.

De Mattos (ibid.) highlights the role of external economies located in cities and the intensification of their effects as a result of metropolisation. The enlarged scope of positive externalities due to urban expansion leads to agglomeration economies beyond the compact city to reach a regional scope. Economic growth and the territorial expansion of agglomerative effects result from intensification of the technical and functional articulation of different components of the metropolis.

Cochrane, McGree and Zandi (2012) point out that the combination of demographic trends, as defined by commuting patterns, and economic linkages accounts for most metropolitan dynamics because contemporary regional linkages are more commonly established via commuting patterns than by strictly input–output linkages. Commuting patterns reflect not only a region's common labour market but also a common pool of consumers of goods and services.

In this respect, in their chapter 'Living in the regional world' Calthorpe and Fulton (2001) describe how a century ago most American cities were self-contained so that their residents rarely had to leave their boundaries to perform their daily activities. In some cities residents could easily cover the city from north to south and from east to west on foot. In contrast, at the onset of the twenty-first century several urban spaces looked like a series of connected communities, often stretching across a vast geographical space; that is, a metropolitan area. There, people move daily from one town to another for work, shopping, and many other activities. These urban inhabitants become citizens of a region.

Work such as that of Suarez-Villa (1988), Knapp and Schmitt (2008), De Mattos (2010) and Jalomo Aguirre (2011) underscore the intimate link between metropolitanisation and structural economic transformation. The characteristics and changes of sectoral economic structures have important implications for the organisation of urban systems and the distribution of population between and within cities. Metropolitan economic change produces important transformations in the inter-urban spatial structure through the concentration or deconcentration of population and economic activity. The stages of metropolitan evolution are associated with different sectoral structures; likewise, sectoral adjustment occurs during metropolitan change (Suarez-Villa, 1988).

From a historical perspective, economic and technological transformation are also linked to the process of metropolisation (Jalomo Aguirre, 2011). At different stages the economic system produces a specific socio-spatial organisation in which territories and places are mobilised as productive forces (Knapp & Schmitt, 2008). In this sense, metropolitan areas have been the geographical structures serving as the framework for the productive process in the globalisation era. Méndez (2008) points out that in the process of metropolitan regions' conformation a series of economic transformations takes place, such as modification of the economic base towards services, inter- and intra-metropolitan rearrangement of labour markets, territorial reorganisation of productive activities, new policy fostering territorial development and a relative economic repositioning that increases the attraction capacity with respect to other regional spaces.

The strong association between metropolitanism and economic-productive processes explains why metropolitan regions have emerged as a subject of spatial economic analysis. Metropolitan areas are regarded as observatories for the analysis, description and interpretation of significant economic-spatial transformations. This nexus has also sustained the growing attention to metropolitan areas as territories from which economic growth and competitiveness should be promoted.

However, regardless of the overall processes and trajectories, metropolitan regions are highly heterogeneous, each performing differently. While they are territories of opportunity for economic growth and renewal, there is a potential for conflict in their competition with other regions for resources. Some metropolitan regions show special dynamism and greater capacity for building and maintaining competitive and productive spaces (ibid.).

Although the transformation of the economic base in the metropolis has resulted in an expanding service sector and the relative decline of industrial activity and employment, in some metropolitan areas this has represented their evolution towards more specialised and advanced services and knowledge-intensive activities, becoming developed economies with selective functional specialisation in competitive sectors. In other metropolises, by contrast, sectoral transformation takes the form of a predominant commercial sector combined with low-productivity services and a low-skilled public sector. In the latter situation, metropolitan economies diversify into less innovative activities (ibid.). In summary, the evolution of productive structures and specialisation is differentiated.

Metropolitan areas might follow uneven trajectories in terms of their labour markets or have different levels of attraction for productive activities and populations. Furthermore, metropolitan economies do not remain static but may experience continuous evolution towards progress or struggle with economic stagnation (Cuadrado Roura & Fernández Guell, 2005). It is essential to deepen knowledge and understanding of the spatial structuring of the population and economic activities, given their implications for the economic development of a country within the framework of intense urbanisation of a highly metropolitan nature. A comprehensive analysis with a metropolitan focus must address these and other significant aspects of metropolitan development.

Worldwide urbanisation trends in the midst of the metropolitan century

As mentioned earlier, at least two big waves of urbanisation have been identified historically, the first dating back to the early Industrial Revolution in Europe, and the second, which began in the second half of the twentieth century and spread from developed to developing countries, proceeding at a very fast pace. Even though the origins of cities can be traced back to Mesopotamia 8,000 years ago, the earliest civilisations had low levels of urbanisation. Over time, urban populations increased to reach a peak in the ancient Roman Empire, in which urbanisation accounted for between 10 and 30 per cent of the total population. The effects of the Industrial Revolution in the second half of the eighteenth century in Europe encompassed many processes that together led to substantial increases in urbanisation. By the end of that century, the average level of urbanisation in industrialised countries was above 50 per cent. This first wave of urbanisation took place over the course of two centuries from 1750 to 1950 (OECD, 2015).

The second wave of urbanisation has involved greater numbers and faster transitions in the less-developed world. In 2007, for the first time in history the global urban population exceeded the global rural population. Whereas in 1950 around 70 per cent of people worldwide lived in rural settlements, in the first decade of the new century more than half of the world's inhabitants made their homes in urban areas (UN, 2014). The absolute numbers of total urban population are substantial as the world's population crossed the 7 billion mark in 2011 (Yusuf, 2013). In accordance with UN data (2018), in 2018 the world urban population amounted to 4.22 billion people and global urbanisation was at 55.3 per cent, compared to 750 million and 29.6 per cent in 1950. Projections indicate that by 2050 the global urban population will have increased to 6.7 billion, with urbanisation accounting for 68.4 per cent (Table 1.2). OECD (2015) estimates that by the year 2100 the urban population will have increased to 9 billion inhabitants and will comprise 85 per cent of total population. Other estimations anticipate the addition of 20,000 new dwellings and 160 miles of road to existing stock each week. Accordingly, the built-up area will expand at a faster pace than the urban population: the latter could double by 2030, whereas the former could triple (Yusuf, 2013).

Thus, throughout history and across the world urbanisation has proceeded in a non-linear fashion, advancing in some regions while stagnating or declining in others at different times. In the first decades of the twenty-first century this non-linearity has been expressed in different global trends and patterns, with today's urbanisation significantly different from what we have experienced in the past.

Table 1.2 World urban indicators, 1950–2050

	1950	1960	1970	1980	1990	2000	2010	2020	2030	2040	2050
Total population (millions)	2,536	3,033	3,700	4,458	5,330	6,145	6,958	7,795	8,551	9,210	9,771
Urban population (millions)	750	1,023	1,354	1,754	2,290	2,868	3,594	4,378	5,167	5,938	6,679
Urbanisation %	29.6	33.8	36.6	39.3	43	46.7	51.7	56.2	60.4	64.5	68.4
Urban growth %		3.1	2.6	2.8	2.6	2.1	2.2	1.8	1.5	1.3	1.1
Urbanisation rate %		1.2	0.5	1	0.8	0.8	0.9	0.8	0.7	0.6	0.6

Source: United Nations (2018).

There is still considerable variation in the levels of urbanisation across regions and countries, depending on location and income levels. Similarly, there is great diversity in the characteristics of urban environments. In 2014, urbanisation in 16 countries was still below 20 per cent, while 59 countries were already more than 80 per cent urban. The most highly urbanised countries in that year were Belgium (98 per cent), Japan (93 per cent), Argentina (92 per cent) and the Netherlands (90 per cent). By 2050, 89 countries are expected to become more than 80 per cent urban (UN, 2014).

As of 2018, Hong Kong, Monaco and Singapore were 100 per cent urban. Regionally speaking, Latin America and the Caribbean, and North America have the highest levels of urbanisation at 81 and 82 per cent respectively. Sub-Saharan Africa and South Asia, in contrast, remain mostly rural, with urbanisation at 40 and 36 per cent each (Figure 1.3). Back in 1950, the most urbanised regions were North America (64 per cent) and Europe (51.7 per cent). Less than 50 per cent of the population of Latin America and the Caribbean lived in cities, but with an accelerated spurt of urbanisation, especially between 1940 and 1980, the region has become the second most urbanised region in the world, with levels similar to North America's. Whereas in the previous decades Latin America's rate of urbanisation was the fastest, over the coming decades Africa and Asia are expected to urbanise still faster. Population growth is projected to add 2.5 billion people to the global urban population by 2050, with nearly 90 per cent of the increase concentrated in Asia and Africa (UN, 2018). In that year all regions will be predominantly urban, and East Asia will be 81.4 per cent urban, similar to Europe.

Urbanisation also varies across income levels. While high-income countries have been highly urbanised for several decades, upper-middle-income countries have experienced the fastest pace of urbanisation since 1950. In 1950 high-income countries were 58.5 per cent urbanised, but only 22 per cent of the population lived in urban areas in upper-middle-income nations such as Brazil, China, Iran and Mexico (Figure 1.4). In 2016, high-income countries were 81.5 per cent urbanised, followed by upper-middle-income (66.6 per cent) and middle-income countries (52.6 per cent). Lower-middle-income and low-income countries remained mostly rural, at 40.6 and 32.2 per cent urban respectively. Compared to 1950, upper-middle-income countries had the largest increase in urbanisation. However, the pace of urbanisation in lower-middle-income and low-income countries is expected to be faster than that in other countries in the coming decades. By 2050, on average, their urban populations are expected to reach 59 and 50 per cent of the total respectively. This confirms that the urban transition in developing countries has proceeded much faster than that in developed countries. The current wave of urbanisation is taking place most intensely in developing and emerging non-OECD countries, in particular in Asia (OECD, 2015).

The world's urban population is highly concentrated in a few countries. Combined, China (758m) and India (410m) account for 30 per cent of the urban population. Together with a further five countries – the US (263m),

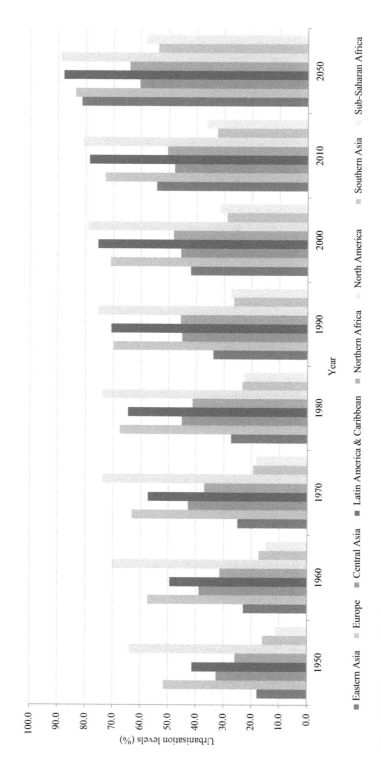

Figure 1.3 Urbanisation levels by region, 1950–2050 (%)

Source: United Nations (2018).

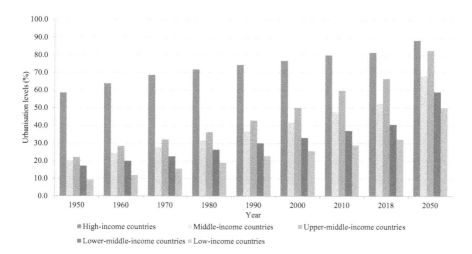

Figure 1.4 Urbanisation degree by countries' income level, 1950–2050 (%)

Source: United Nations (2018).

Brazil (173m), Indonesia (134m), Japan (118m) and Russia (105m) – they account for more than half of the world's urban population. In the future the urban population is also expected to be highly concentrated in a few countries in Asia and Africa, including China, India and Nigeria (UN, 2014).

Despite its lower level of urbanisation, South Asia was home to 18 per cent of the global urban population in 2018, second only to East Asia's 28 per cent. This means that nearly 47 per cent of the world's urban residents are concentrated in East and South Asia. The most urbanised region, North America, accounts for 8 per cent of world's urban population, only above North Africa and Central Asia (7 per cent). The second most urbanised region, Latin America and the Caribbean, has the fourth highest share, at 14.3 per cent (Figure 1.5). This distribution is in clear contrast to the allocation of urban populations in 1950, when Europe accounted for 40.4 per cent, followed by East Asia (17.2 per cent) and North America (15.7 per cent). At that time South Asia's urban population stood at around 11 per cent. Further changes in the size and spatial distribution of the global urban population are expected: in 2050, most will be concentrated in Asia (45.4 per cent) and Africa (25.7 per cent).

When classifying countries by income level, important rearrangements are identified (Figure 1.6). In 1950, high-income countries contained the largest urban populations (nearly 36 per cent), followed by middle-income countries (31.5 per cent) and lower-middle-income countries (12 per cent). In 2018, middle-income countries increased their share to 41.7 per cent and that of high-income countries decreased to 13.5 per cent. Concentration not only takes place in middle-income- but also in upper-middle- (24.3 per cent) and

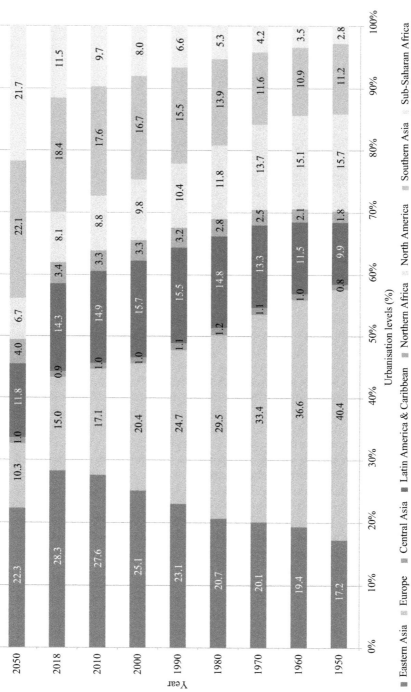

Figure 1.5 Distribution of global urban population by region, 1950–2050 (%)

Source: Based on United Nations (2018).

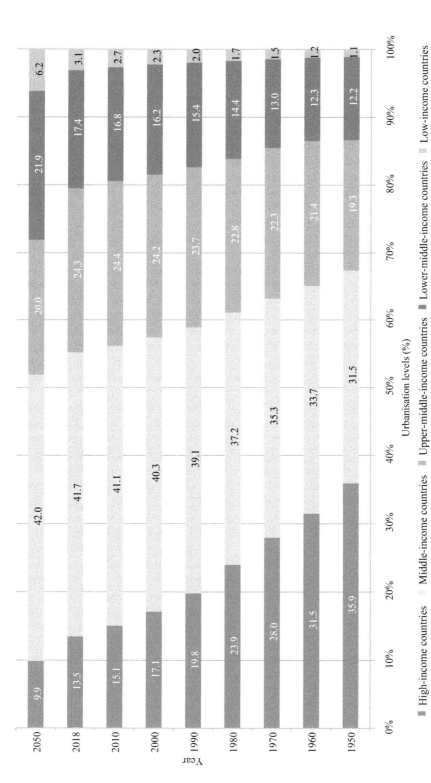

Figure 1.6 Distribution of global urban population by countries' income level, 1950–2056 (%)

Source: Based on United Nations (2018).

lower-middle-income countries (17.4 per cent). By 2050 the share of high-income countries will decrease further, middle-income countries will keep around 42 per cent of urban population, and lower-middle-income countries will have increased their share to almost 22 per cent, exacerbating the urban pressures on this group of countries.

The world's urban system has changed rapidly over the past seven decades. Another trend in the second wave of urbanisation was the emergence of megacities: urban agglomerations with more than 10 million inhabitants. In 1950 there were only two of these, providing homes for 23.6 million people, or less than 3 per cent of the global urban population (Table 1.3). In 2010 the number of megacities had increased to 25, housing to 387.1 million people, or 11 per cent of global urban population. By 2030 the number of megacities is expected to increase to 43 with 751.9 million inhabitants, or approximately 15 per cent of global urban population.

Cities with 5 to 10 million inhabitants are classified as 'large cities'. They account for a smaller but also growing proportion of total urban population. Most urban dwellers live in urban centres of less than 300,000 inhabitants, but these proportions have been decreasing. In 1950, 60 per cent of urbanites were concentrated in the smallest cities, and in 2050 this is expected to fall to only 38 per cent. Urban population is scarcely concentrated in small urban centres (300,000 to 500,000 inhabitants). Over time, the urban population has been absorbed mainly by megacities and cities with a population of 1 to 5 million (UN, 2018).

In 1950 the largest city in the world was New York, with a population of 12 million. Among the 30 largest urban agglomerations, all of which had at least 10 million inhabitants, 7 were in the US and only 10 were in the developing world. In contrast, in 2015 the largest urban agglomeration was Tokyo (37 million), and of the 30 largest cities only 6 were in in the developed world. It is expected that in 2035 Delhi will be the largest city (43 million), and this group will include only four cities in the developed world (in the US and Japan) (Table 1.4).

Table 1.4 shows that the location of megacities has followed geographical patterns which have evolved over time. In the past most of the world's largest urban agglomerations were in developed countries, whereas today most megacities and large cities are located in the Global South (Figure 1.7). In 2015 there were six megacities in China and four in India. Outside China and India, Asia had seven other megacities, and Africa contained Cairo, Kinshasa and Lagos, but more are expected. Latin America has four megacities, with Bogota and Lima projected to grow beyond the 10 million mark by 2030 to join Buenos Aires, Mexico City, Rio de Janeiro and São Paulo.

A striking feature of the contemporary trends in the US, Latin America and Asia, besides the emergence of megacities, is the proliferation of metropolitan regions (Yusuf, 2013). A quarter of the world's population lives in supersized metropolitan areas that cut across jurisdictional boundaries and bring one or more cities together with their surrounding areas (Ijjasz-Vasquez, et al., 2017).

Table 1.3 Number of cities, urban population and urbanisation by city size, 1950–2030

Size	1950	1960	1970	1980	1990	2000	2010	2020	2030
Number of cities									
10 million or >	2	3	3	5	10	16	25	34	43
5 to 10 million	5	9	15	19	21	30	39	51	66
1 to 5 million	69	93	127	174	243	325	380	494	597
500,000 to 1 million	101	132	190	247	301	396	510	626	710
300,000 to 500,000	129	184	225	297	416	524	645	729	827
Population (thousands)									
10 million or >	23,613	41,457	54,760	86,295	153,300	245,386	387,089	556,770	751,934
5 to 10 million	32,172	59,506	107,260	139,606	156,172	213,794	269,408	348,132	447,815
1 to 5 million	127,484	176,859	244,402	335,936	467,060	625,857	760,383	976,786	1,182,839
500,000 to 1 million	67,471	92,779	130,937	170,247	207,591	269,041	354,551	431,401	493,629
300,000 to 500,000	49,854	71,230	86,556	113,703	158,964	199,623	245,569	278,900	319,827
< 300,000	450,309	582,015	730,299	908,415	1147,140	1314,607	1577,869	1787,005	1,971,215
Percentage of urban population									
10 million or >	3	4	4	5	7	9	11	13	15
5 to 10 million	4	6	8	8	7	7	7	8	9
1 to 5 million	17	17	18	19	20	22	21	22	23
500,000 to 1 million	9	9	10	10	9	9	10	10	10
300,000 to 500,000	7	7	6	6	7	7	7	6	6
< 300,000	60	57	54	52	50	46	44	41	38

Source: United Nations (2018).

Table 1.4 The 30 largest urban agglomerations by population size, 1950, 2015 and 2035

1950			2015			2050		
Country	City	Pop. (m)	Country	City	Pop. (m)	Country	City	Pop. (m)
US	New York	12	Japan	Tokyo	37	India	Delhi	43
Japan	Tokyo	11	India	Delhi	26	Japan	Tokyo	36
United Kingdom	London	8	China	Shanghai	23	China	Shanghai	34
Japan	Osaka	7	Mexico	Mexico City	21	Bangladesh	Dhaka	31
France	Paris	6	Brazil	São Paulo	21	Egypt	Cairo	29
Russia	Moscow	5	India	Mumbai	19	India	Bombay	27
Argentina	Buenos Aires	5	Japan	Osaka	19	D. R. of the Congo	Kinshasa	27
US	Chicago	5	Egypt	Cairo	19	Mexico	Mexico City	25
India	Calcutta	5	US	New York	19	China	Beijing	25
China	Shanghai	4	China	Beijing	18	Brazil	São Paulo	24
US	Los Angeles	4	Bangladesh	Dhaka	18	Nigeria	Lagos	24
Mexico	Mexico City	3	Argentina	Buenos Aires	15	Pakistan	Karachi	23
Germany	Berlin	3	India	Kolkata	14	US	New York	21
US	Philadelphia	3	Pakistan	Karachi	14	China	Chongqing	21
India	Bombay	3	Turkey	Istanbul	14	India	Calcutta	20
Brazil	Rio de Janeiro	3	China	Chongqing	13	Pakistan	Lahore	19
Russia	Saint Petersburg	3	Brazil	Rio de Janeiro	13	Philippines	Manila	19
US	Detroit	3	Philippines	Manila	13	Japan	Osaka	18
US	Boston	3	China	Tianjin	13	India	Bangalore	18
Egypt	Cairo	2	US	Los Angeles	12	Turkey	Istanbul	18
China	Tianjin	2	Nigeria	Lagos	12	Argentina	Buenos Aires	17
United Kingdom	Manchester	2	Russia	Moscow	12	China	Guangzhou	17
Brazil	São Paulo	2	China	Guangzhou	12	China	Tianjin	16
Japan	Nagoya	2	D. R. of the Congo	Kinshasa	12	India	Chennai	15
United Kingdom	Birmingham	2	China	Shenzhen	11	China	Shenzhen	15
China	Shenyang	2	France	Paris	11	Brazil	Rio de Janeiro	15
Italy	Rome	2	Pakistan	Lahore	10	Angola	Luanda	14
Italy	Milan	2	Indonesia	Jakarta	10	India	Hyderabad	14
US	San Francisco	2	India	Bangalore	10	US	Los Angeles	14
Spain	Barcelona	2	Republic of Korea	Seoul	10	Indonesia	Jakarta	14

Source: United Nations (2018)

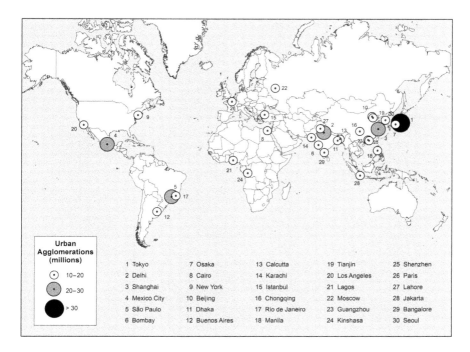

Figure 1.7 Top 30 largest cities of the world, 2015

Source: Based on United Nations (2018).

These urban areas have evolved from monocentric agglomerations to more complex systems that integrate urban centres and subcentres or are composed of cities and towns that have progressively linked up to form polycentric integrated areas (OECD, 2012).

Megacities and metropolitan areas offer economic and social benefits such as social interaction, amenities, diversity and productivity gains. Throughout the OECD, for instance, productivity and wages increase with city size, and their contribution to economic growth tends to be much higher than their initial population share. Some of the megacities in East Asia and South Asia account for a third or more of national GDP (OECD, 2015). Figure 1.8 shows the world's largest metropolitan regions in terms of economic activity, estimated by light-based activity (LBA). The largest metropolitan area is Greater Tokyo (including Kawasaki and Yokohama), which produces nearly $2 trillion dollars' worth of output, followed by Greater New York (including Philadelphia and Newark), Osaka-Kyoto-Kobe, Los Angeles and Nagoya. All the metropolitan areas in the top 20 are in the developed world, except for Seoul-Incheon. The economic weight of these metropolitan areas is substantially greater than their population size. The top 10 house just 2.6 per cent of the world's population but account for 21.2 per cent of global economic activity, and the top 20 are

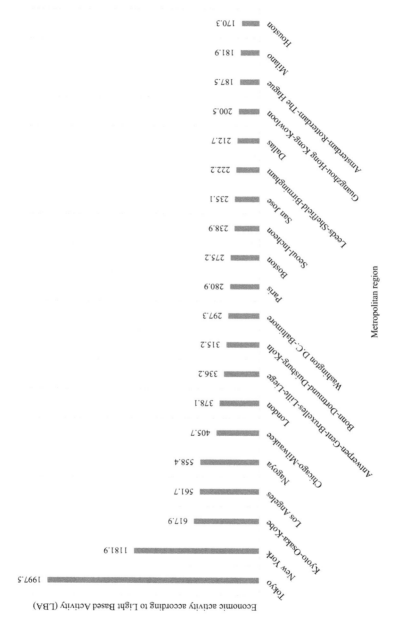

Figure 1.8 World's largest metropolitan regions by LBA (billions)

Source: Based on Florida, Mellander and Gulden (2009).

home to 4.4 per cent of the world's population and produce nearly 30 per cent of global economic activity.

The complex and evolving spatial organisation of urban centres and their wider territories impose a number of challenges that must be addressed. The quality of life of urban inhabitants must be assured, demand for transport and other infrastructure has to be satisfied and the environmental impacts of urbanisation need to be measured and taken care of (OECD, 2012). Effective coordination, planning, infrastructure development and service delivery across multiple jurisdictions is problematic (ibid.): land is scarce and subject to competing interests, and local income disparities are larger than in other contexts and create tension between poor and wealthy areas. These challenges affect a wide range of policy areas, and all reach beyond the limits of individual municipalities (Ahrend et al., 2014). This is particularly difficult in developing countries, which often lack the necessary legal, institutional and governance apparatus to undertake adequate planning and coordination. Since urban growth typically spreads beyond a single municipality, cities need to think beyond their boundaries and address challenges at the metropolitan level (UN, 2014). Recent metropolitan challenges have attracted increasing attention also in Europe. The following chapters will discuss urbanisation, metropolitan areas, development and governance issues, focussing on Mexico and the Latin American region with a number of international cases and comparative perspectives.

References

Ahrend, R., Farchy, E., Kaplanis, I. & Lembcke, A. C. (2014). *What makes cities more productive? Evidence on the role of urban governance from five OECD countries.* OECD Regional Development Working Papers, 2014/05, OECD Publishing, Paris. Available at: https://doi.org/10.1787/5jz432cf2d8p-en.

Andersson, M. (2015). *Unpacking metropolitan governance for sustainable development.* Discussion Paper. Berlin: GIZ–UN-Habitat. Available at: https://unhabitat.org/books/unpacking-metropolitan-governance-for-sustainable-development/.

Angel, S., Blei, A., Parent, J., Lamson-Hall, P. & Galarza, N. (2016). *Atlas of urban expansion (Vol. 1).* New York University, Nairobi: UN-Habitat, and Cambridge, MA: Lincoln Institute of Land Policy. Available at: www.lincolninst.edu/publications/other/atlas-urban-expansion-2016-edition.

Argullol, E. (2005). *Organización y funciones de las metrópolis: Estudio comparado.* Asociación Mundial de las Grandes Metrópolis, Barcelona. Available at: www.metropolis.org/sites/default/files/2005-c1-orgniz-funciones-metropolis.pdf.

Bouchet, M., Lius, S. & Parilla, J. (2018). *Global metro monitor 2018.* Washington, DC.: Metropolitan Policy Program at Brookings. Available at: www.brookings.edu/wp-content/uploads/2018/06/Brookings-Metro_Global-Metro-Monitor-2018.pdf.

Bourassa, S. C. (2007). 'Urban economics, 6th edition by Arthur O'Sullivan'. *Journal of Urban Affairs,* 29(5), 543–544. Available at: https://doi.org/10.1111/j.1467-9906.2007.00364.x.

Calthorpe, P. & Fulton, W. B. (2001). *The regional city: Planning for the end of sprawl.* Washington, D.C.: Island Press.

Cochrane, S., McGree, M. & Zandi, K. (2012). Global metropolitan areas: The natural geographic unit for regional economic analysis. *Economic and Consumer Credit Analytics:*

Moodys's Analytics. Available at: https://www.economy.com/home/products/samples/whitepapers/2012-06-20-Global-Metropolitan-Areas-The-Natural-Geographical-Unit-for-Regional-Economic-Analysis.pdf

Combes, P. P., Mayer, T. & Thisse, J. F. (2008). *Economic geography: The integration of regions and nations.* Princeton; Oxford: Princeton University Press.

Cuadrado Roura, J. R. & Fernández Guell, J. M. (2005). 'Las áreas metropolitanas frente al desafío de la competitividad'. In Rojas, E. (ed.). *Gobernar las metrópolis.* Washington, D.C.: Inter-American Development Bank, pp. 63–126. Available at: http://site.ebrary.com/id/10201140.

De Mattos, C. A. (2010). 'Globalización y metamorfosis urbana en América Latina'. *Revista de Geografía Norte Grande,* (47), 163–166. Available at: https://doi.org/10.4067/S0718-3402 2010000300010.

Dobbs, R., Smit, S., Remes, J., Manyika, J., Roxburgh, C. & Restrepo, A. (2011). *Urban world: Mapping the economic power of cities.* The McKinsey Institute. Available at: www.mckinsey.com/featured-insights/urbanization/urban-world-mapping-the-economic-power-of-cities.

Drakakis-Smith, D. W. (2000). *Third World cities.* London: Routledge.

Florida, R., Mellander, C. & Gulden, T. (2009). *The role of cities and metropolitan areas in the global economy.* Working Paper Series: Martin Prosperity Research MPIWP-002. Martin Prosperity Institute. Available at: www.creativeclass.com/rfcgdb/articles/Global%20metropolis.pdf.

Fox, S. & Goodfellow, T. (2016). *Cities and development.* 2nd edn. New York: Routledge.

Frey, W. H. & Zimmer, Z. (2001). 'Defining the city and urbanization'. In Paddison, R. (ed.). *Handbook of urban studies.* Thousand Oaks: SAGE Publications, pp. 14–35.

Fujita, M., Krugman, P. & Venables, A. (2001). *The spatial economy: Cities, regions, and international trade.* London: The MIT Press.

Fujita, M. & Thisse, J. F. (2002). *Economics of agglomeration: Cities, industrial location, and regional growth.* Cambridge: Cambridge University Press.

Gómez Alvarez, D., Rajack, R., López-Moreno, E. & Lanfranchi, G. (eds.) (2017). *Steering the metropolis: Metropolitan governance for sustainable urban development.* Washington, D.C.: Inter-American Development Bank. Available at: http://dx.doi.org/10.18235/0000875.

Hoornweg, D. & Pope, K. (2016). 'Population predictions for the world's largest cities in the 21st century'. *Environment and Urbanization,* 29(1), 195–216. Available at: www.researchgate.net/publication/308537126_Population_predictions_for_the_worlds_largest_cities_in_the_21st_century.

Ijjasz-Vasquez, E., Karp, P. E. & Sotomayor, M. A. (2017). *How to effectively manage metropolitan areas?* World Bank Blogs. Available at: http://blogs.worldbank.org/taxonomy/term/16578.

Ingram, G. K. (1997). 'Patterns of metropolitan development: What have we learned?' *Urban Studies,* 35(7), 1019–1035. Available at: https://doi.org/10.1080/0042098984466.

Jalomo Aguirre, F. (2011). *Gobernar el territorio entre descentralización y metropolización.* Colección Graduados, Serie Sociales y Humanidades, No. 13. Guadalajara, Jalisco: Universidad de Guadalajara. Available at: www.publicaciones.cucsh.udg.mx/pperiod/cgraduados/pdf/sin/1_Gobernar_el_territorio%20_entre_descentralizacion_y_metropolizacion.pdf.

Knapp, W. & Schmitt, P. (2008). 'Discourse on metropolitan driving forces and uneven development: Germany and the RhineRuhr Conurbation'. *Regional Studies,* 42(8), 1187–1204. Available at: https://doi.org/10.1080/00343400801932292.

McGranahan, G. & Satterthwaite, D. (2014). *Urbanisation: Concepts and trends.* Human Settlements Working Paper, 10709IIED. London: International Institute for Environment and Development. Available at: http://pubs.iied.org/10709IIED/.

Meijers, E. J. & Burger, M. J. (2017). 'Stretching the concept of "borrowed size"'. *Urban Studies*, 54(1), 269–291. Available at: https://doi.org/10.1177/0042098015597642.

Méndez, R. (2008). 'Procesos recientes en regiones metropolitanas: transformaciones económicas y reorganización territorial: Algunas interpretaciones y debates actuales'. Presented at Coloquio Ibérico de Geografía, Alcalá de Henares. Available at: www.gedeur.es/publicaciones/PUBLICACIONES_WEB/regionesmetropolitanastransformacionespacialesynueva%20economia/MENDEZ2008PONENCIAIBERICO.pdf.

Mumford, L. (1966). *La Ciudad en la historia: sus orígenes, transformaciones y perspectivas*. Buenos Aires: Infinito.

OECD. (2012). *Redefining 'urban': A new way to measure metropolitan areas*. Paris: OECD Publishing. Available at: https://doi.org/10.1787/9789264174108-en.

OECD. (2015). *Governing the city*. Paris: OECD Publishing. Available at: https://doi.org/10.1787/9789264226500-en.

Rionda-Ramírez, J. I. (2007). 'Dinámica metropolitana en México'. *Economía Sociedad y Territorio*, VII(25), 241–266. Available at: http://dx.doi.org/10.22136/est002007237.

Scott, A. J. & Storper, M. (2014). 'The nature of cities: The scope and limits of urban theory'. *International Journal of Urban and Regional Research*, 39(1), 1–15. Available at: https://doi.org/10.1111/1468-2427.12134.

Sellers, J. & Hoffmann-Martinot, V. (2008). *Gobernanza metropolitana: United cities and local governments*. Washington, D.C.: World Bank, pp. 226–293. Available at: www.cities-localgovernments.org/gold/Upload/gold_report/09_metropolis_es.pdf.

Storper, M. & Scott, A. J. (2016). 'Current debates in urban theory: A critical assessment'. *Urban Studies*, 53(6), 1114–1136. Available at: https://doi.org/10.1177/0042098016634002.

Suarez-Villa, L. (1988). 'Metropolitan evolution, sectoral economic change, and the city size distribution'. *Urban Studies*, 25(1), 1–20. Available at: https://doi.org/10.1080/00420988820080011.

Trejo, A. (2013). 'Las economías de las zonas metropolitanas de México en los albores del siglo XXI'. *Estudios Demográficos y Urbanos*, 28(3), 545–591. Available at: https://doi.org/10.24201/edu.v28i3.1447.

United Nations. (2018). *World urbanization prospects: The 2018 revision*. New York: United Nations. Available at: https://population.un.org/wup/Publications/Files/WUP2018-KeyFacts.pdf.

United Nations. (2014). *World urbanization prospects: The 2014 revision, highlights*. New York: United Nations, Department of Economic and Social Affairs and Population Division. Available at: http://esa.un.org/unpd/wup/highlights/wup2014-highlights.pdf.

Vargas, J., Brassiolo, P., Sanguinetti, P., Daude, C., Goytia, C., Álvarez, F., Estrada, R. & Fajardo, G. (2017). *RED 2017. Urban growth and access to opportunities: A challenge for Latin America*. Bogota: Banco de Desarrollo de América Latina, CAF. Available at: http://scioteca.caf.com/handle/123456789/1091.

Yusuf, S. (2013). 'Metropolitan cities: Their rise, role, and future'. In Bahl, R. W., Linn, J. F. & Wetzel, D. L. (eds.). *Financing metropolitan governments in developing countries*. Cambridge, MA: Lincoln Institute of Land Policy, pp. 31–56.

2 Urbanisation in Mexico and Latin America

A comparative assessment

Introduction

Although the region's urbanisation dates back to the pre-Columbian period, more than half a century ago Latin America remained predominantly rural. As a result of its explosive urbanisation in the second half of the twentieth century, Latin America is today one of the most urbanised regions in the world, with similar urbanisation levels as North America. In addition to the pre-Columbian and colonial legacy, national industrial policies, an urban bias and high demographic growth rates drove and shaped much of this urban explosion. Latin America is also the region with the highest urbanisation in the developing world and is home to three of the largest metropolises in the world: Sao Paulo, Mexico City and Buenos Aires. However, cities such as Mexico City, Buenos Aires, Sao Paulo, Rio de Janeiro, Quito, Lima and Bogota, to mention just a few of the largest region's urban centres, reveal an alarming reality: hours lost in traffic, poor-quality public services with little coverage, high inequalities, poverty and pollution. In spite of its high rate of urbanisation, incomes and productivity in Latin America are relatively low and, in general terms, the cities of Latin America face significant economic, social and environmental burdens. Urban primacy and hyper-urbanisation have had their effects on different dimensions of urban life. The recent trend of enlarging and reshaping urban centres has fostered additional problems.

It has been argued that the context in which urbanisation has occurred has generated chaotic urban patterns in most cases. Demographic, economic and political shifts have had major implications for addressing the urban challenge in these countries. Lack of adequate urban planning and policies in particular has been considered one of the main factors that slow the social and economic development of the region, affecting urban inhabitants' productive potential and quality of life.

Mexico especially has experienced the consequences of disordered, rapid and concentrated urbanisation accompanied by deficient urban planning and law-making. The growth and expansion of Mexico City Metropolitan Area, with its population of more than 20 million, offers opportunities for development but also puts stresses on the economy, the environment and the government.

Notwithstanding the recent deceleration in urban growth and urbanisation in Latin America and Mexico, less urbanised countries are currently facing fast transitions. In absolute numbers the size of the urban population in the region also remains problematic. Angotti (2013) considers that the basic questions about Latin American urbanisation lie not in population counts but in the relations that govern the city and the gigantic land grab that has produced urban Latin America. Yet an account of urban patterns and trends is still important, and this chapter offers an historical perspective and up-to-date data. This review is a useful contextual framework to discuss in some of the following chapters the land grab dynamics, its relation with social, political and economic forces and its consequences in Mexican urbanisation and the growing phenomenon of urban expansion.

In the following sections I identify the key urbanisation patterns and trends in Latin America, taking into consideration demographic, spatial and socioeconomic factors throughout the processes of historical-structural transformation. Within Latin America there is significant heterogeneity, and the regional trends are guided by a small number of countries, including some of the most urbanised, such as Mexico and Brazil. Even though many of the patterns and challenges of urbanisation across countries are similar, local and national structures may differ. Therefore, the general trends as well as cross-country differences are reviewed. Particular attention is paid to the urban transition on Mexico. The chapter concludes with a discussion on the flaws in Latin American urbanisation and the broken link to development.

Urbanisation and urban transitions prior to industrialisation: a historical outlook

Urbanisation and urban development have long been features of Latin American countries, with the Mayas, Incas and Aztecs – to name the best-known pre-Columbian societies – concentrating their population in large urban centres, even if none of these societies were urban *per se* (Rodgers, Beall & Kanbur, 2011). Latin America's long history of urbanisation stretches from its earliest towns to the huge metropolitan cities of today. Any concrete periodisation would fail to capture every nuance of the existing urban reality, but some geographical, political, technological and economic factors carry the greatest weight in characterising past and present conditions of Latin America's urbanisation.

According to Hardoy (1982), the flourishing of regional states during the first millennium B.C. marked the beginning of urban development in countries that make up present-day Latin America. Perhaps during the late formative period (600–0 B.C.) some cultures living in the Central Valley of Mexico and other regions of contemporary Mexico developed advanced technologies in answer to the demands of the growing populations of their larger villages. Similar, although less advanced, developments took place in Peru's coastal valleys during the early horizon period (900–200 B.C.). Between year 0 and A.D. 900 in Mesoamerica and the Andean region some organisational forms of the society had urban characteristics, with ruling technocracies beginning to organise economic institutions that helped trade and production and stimulated the formation of towns. Artisans were already engaged in producing a surplus for this ruling elite. Urban centres of unprecedented size, power and diversity started to emerge: Teotihuacan in the central highlands of Mexico, Tikal in Honduras, Monte Alban in Mexico's Oaxaca, Tianhuanaco in Bolivia, Pucara in the northern basin of Lake Titicaca and, centuries later, Huari in the highlands of Peru. Teotihuacan, for instance, reached a maximum size of some 2,200 hectares and a population of perhaps 85,000 inhabitants during the fifth and sixth centuries A.D. The origin of Tenochtitlan – one of the most important pre-Columbian cities, the Aztec capital city and today's Mexico City – is dated at around 1325, when it was established approximately 60 kilometres southwest of the already-abandoned city of Teotihuacan. When the conquistador Hernan Cortes arrived in 1519, Tenochtitlan probably covered 1,200 hectares and had some 220,000 inhabitants.

Almost all of the pre-Columbian Latin American cities flourished on the site of existing agricultural villages and religious centres and expanded due to favourable ecological factors which encouraged trade. Over time cities were used by the emerging elites to administer and control production, commerce and the religious and cultural life of vast territories. Thus, strategic location in relation to newly conquered territory became an important locational factor. Eventually some urban planning was undertaken at the highest level of government as the scope of a city required the organisation of labour, food and building supplies. Even though good organisation was needed to ensure a supply of water, food and basic consumer goods, we cannot talk of urban or housing policies; only of attempts to regulate the cities' physical growth. But the essential nature of pre-Columbian urban planning was not concerned with the housing of the lower classes, which was self-built on the peripheries (ibid.).

Rodgers, Beall and Kanbur (2011) suggest that although cities were an important feature of pre-Columbian societies, with some of their legacy remaining in some important cities of today, particularly Mexico City, the shape of contemporary urbanisation in Latin America and the Caribbean owes more to the common history and strong cultural roots laid during almost three centuries of European rule. Cities were planned and constructed to reflect the hierarchical, racial and political-economic organisation of colonial society itself. These cities were to be highly ordered, regular and governable, their streets uniform and their functions assigned to particular areas of the city, conforming to the ideal of rationality.

As soon as the Conquest began between 1520 and 1580, hundreds and even thousands of urban settlements of all types were officially founded. Urbanisation was a key element in the Spanish and Portuguese discovery, colonisation and administration of the region (Hardoy, 1982). Cities developed mainly in coastal areas and some strategic places in the interior in response to the political, commercial and military objectives of the colonial power. At times, colonial cities also replaced pre-Columbian sites (UN-Habitat, 2012). While the colonial city was the centre of power and domination (Hardoy, 1982), European colonialism was administered by means of a widespread network of cities from which power and control were projected (Rodgers, Beall & Kanbur, 2011).

In colonial Mexico, between 1521 and 1820 the Spaniards founded hundreds of cities and towns on and near established indigenous settlements and in new lands to create a territorial system for exploiting human, mineral and agricultural resources for the benefit of the Crown. Within this system the urban hegemony of Mexico City, the capital of New Spain, emerged, designed to expedite the flow of goods between the hinterlands, the capital, the port of Veracruz and finally, Spain. In addition to the Viceroyalty's capital the urban system consisted of a variety of settlement types: administrative-military cities (Guadalajara and Mérida), port towns (Veracruz, Acapulco and Mazatlan) and mining centres (Guanajuato, Pachuca, Zacatecas, San Luis Potosí and Taxco). The colonial urban system was almost completed by the middle of the eighteenth century, extending from Merida on the Yucatan Peninsula to San Francisco in Alta California in the northwest. A rank-size hierarchy could be identified: Mexico City had 113,000 inhabitants; the second city, Puebla, had 57,000; and the third, Guanajuato, had 32,000, although this hierarchy was changeable during the colonial and early independent period due to political-economic transformations (Kemper & Royce, 1979). Some of the predominant cities in the colonial urban network remain so in the current system.

The European powers that participated in the Conquest, especially the Spanish Crown,[1] brought to Latin America their own experience of urban planning and construction. Urban layout, land use patterns and location were similar to their own cities in Europe. Interestingly, few towns expanded physically during the colonial rule. The population density of major ports such as Havana (Cuba), Cartagena (Colombia), Veracruz (Mexico), Callao (Peru), Campeche (Mexico), Santo Domingo (Dominican Republic) and San Juan (Puerto Rico), where the Crown invested large sums in building defensive walls, was lower than that of their contemporary European towns and contained plenty of unbuilt areas. The colonial cities' populations grew very slowly: by the beginning of the nineteenth century only Mexico City and Rio de Janeiro had more than 100,000 inhabitants, and only Havana, Salvador, Lima, Buenos Aires and Santiago had over 40,000. Most of the growth was the result of internal migration because plagues undermined urban populations (Hardoy, 1982).

The postcolonial period saw an intensification of efforts to rationalise the urban landscape according to the commercial function of the city (Rodgers, Beall & Kanbur, 2011). It is estimated that some of the highest rates of urban growth occurred between 1840 and 1920 in major port cities, due to the construction of railway lines connecting mining areas and fertile land to ports. By 1900 Buenos Aires had around 800,000 inhabitants and Rio de Janeiro, 690,000. Twelve other cities had populations of more than 100,000: Mexico City (345,000), Santiago (333,000), Havana (329,000), Montevideo (309,000), Sao Paulo (240,000), Salvador (205,000), Valparaiso (162,000), Lima (142,000), Recife (113,000), Rosario (112,000), Guadalajara (101,000) and Bogota

(100,000). Most of these had been founded by the Spanish or the Portuguese between 1520 and 1580. The growth of some of these centres towards the end of the nineteenth century was exceptional. Buenos Aires, for instance, grew by 5.2 per cent annually between 1895 and 1900, and Sao Paulo by 12.5 per cent annually between 1886 and 1890. Several smaller cities emerged and grew rapidly as a consequence of foreign immigration. Buenos Aires and Rio de Janeiro also received massive immigration from Italy, Spain and Portugal (ibid.).

Independence from Spain brought Mexico neither political and economic stability nor important urban growth. The urban system was highly regionalised and weakly articulated. Mexico City kept its primacy due not to high dynamism but to the dispersion of economic and political power. For four decades, from 1821 to 1860, the country experienced few changes to its urban system except that several settlements in the northern territory disappeared from the network. The country suffered significant changes to its borders due to internal and external political conflict and unrest, losing more than 2 million square kilometres in the north, mainly in Alta California, Texas and Arizona, which were annexed to the United States (Kemper & Royce, 1979).

A number of noteworthy transformations began in the 1860s: the fall of Puebla as the second city in the hierarchy, with Guadalajara taking over; the decline of Guanajuato and a number of other cities in the Bajio; and the development of Tampico as the second major port. In the 1880s President Porfirio Diaz came into power, establishing a stable environment and promoting industrial and urban development (ibid.).[2] Incipient but important industrialisation was supported by foreign capital investment, mineral exploitation, the construction of a national railway system and rising exports. Of these, the development of the railways was particularly relevant to urban development. Railway lines benefited cities connected with the national capital and major ports and Mexico City, Guadalajara, Toluca and Aguascalientes grew rapidly as commercial and industrial centres. Torreon experienced an outstanding transformation due to the positive impact of the railway and became a major centre for cotton production, with an increase in population from 200 in 1892 to 34,000 by 1910, while Puebla, Morelia, Tlaxcala, Leon and Guanajuato shrank to become urban centres with limited local or regional markets. The most prominent cities grew at twice the national rate during Diaz's rule (Table 2.1). Guadalajara,

Table 2.1 Larger Mexican cities and demographic change during the Porfiriato era

City	Population, 1884	Population, 1910	Absolute variation 1884–1910	Annual variation rate %
Mexico City	300,000	471,000	171,000	2.19
Guadalajara	80,000	119,000	39,000	1.88
Puebla	75,000	96,000	21,000	1.07
Monterrey	42,000	79,000	37,000	3.39

Source: Based on Kemper and Royce (1979).

Monterrey, Merida, San Luis Potosi and Veracruz grew demographically faster than Mexico City, and Monterrey emerged as the most important industrial-manufacturing hub.

Social unrest due to wide inequalities and the concentration of political power during the Diaz dictatorship triggered a civil war, the Mexican Revolution, in 1910. The Revolution had important demographic impacts: total population dropped from 15.2 million in 1910 to 14.2 million in 1921; cities and towns in the Bajio experienced the debilitation of their populations; and Mexico City received a significant flow of refugees from the countryside, increasing its population to 662,000 inhabitants in 1921. The 1910–1940 period was an era of armed conflict with rural reform during the postrevolutionary regime of Lazaro Cardenas. This stage was characterised by slow demographic growth and varying rates of urbanisation across the country. Guadalajara (in the centre-west), Monterrey (in the north), Puebla (in the centre) and Tampico (on the east coast) became Mexico's second, third, fourth and fifth cities respectively (Kemper & Royce, 1979).

In addition to its pre-Columbian and colonial urban legacy, contemporary urban Latin America is very much a consequence of twentieth-century development. In 1900 most Latin Americans lived in the countryside and only three cities had more than half a million inhabitants. From the 1930s onwards a process of urbanisation led to the emergence of more than 40 cities with over a million inhabitants. This rapid urbanisation has not had parallel in history. Moreover, there is a particular quality and distinctiveness to the Latin American city: the unprecedented urban growth that characterised Latin America gradually promoted a negative general conception of cities and gave rise to the popular theory of over-urbanisation in the 1940s and 1950s (Rodgers, Beall & Kanbur, 2011).

The broader impulse to urbanisation came from the implementation of import substitution industrialisation (ISI) policies across most of Latin America from the 1930s onwards. This fuelled a massive movement of people from the countryside to urban settlements. In most cases cities created by colonial powers, which were heavily concentrated along the coast due to the strategic importance of maritime routes, prospered during the industrialisation process and maintained the competitive advantage of their coastal location. Although relatively few, there are examples of cities artificially created or planned for a specific purpose such as Brasilia and Ciudad Guyana (ibid.).

During the 1930s, 1940s and 1950s many cities established planning departments. Paradoxically, it was at this time that local governments lost much of their power to higher levels of government due to increasing centralisation. Legislation and ineffective government ministries could not solve urban problems rooted in centuries of exploitation. The urban population started to grow very rapidly, and after the Second World War many of the largest cities doubled their population every decade. New urban plans were prepared, but these were as ineffective as their predecessors. Urban planning across the region has largely failed to create a better human environment, with negative repercussions mostly for lower-income groups (Hardoy, 1982).

The region became demographically urban within less than two generations. Urban growth initially tended to concentrate in one or two cities per country, leading to a primacy effect whereby the populations of these principal urban centres far exceeded those of secondary urban centres. These are features of most developing countries, but Latin America stands out compared to other regions in the world, with several of its countries displaying the highest primacy indices in the world.

Contemporary urbanisation trends, patterns and disparities in Latin America

The rural-to-urban shift in the Latin American region occurred over 40 years of ISI policies, and due to this fast pace it has been qualified as an urban explosion. Today the region's urban transition is consolidated and the urban population is growing at a much slower pace. However, new phenomena are occurring, such as increased migration between cities, the growth of secondary cities and the emergence of megacities. Especially, we are witnessing significant expansion and urban sprawl, which present many challenges to the economic, social and environmental sustainability (UN-Habitat, 2012).

The urbanisation patterns and trends in the region are historically distinct. Urbanisation took place earlier and at a faster pace than in other developing regions and is now at the level of advanced economies. It accelerated significantly in the second half of the twentieth century, and 60 years later 80 per cent of Latin America's population now live in towns or cities. No other region in the world has urbanised so rapidly. However, rather than enjoying the benefits of urban life, most countries in the region are confronting economic, social and political pressures due to high population concentration and inequality. It is here that Latin America stands out: it is highly urbanised, and it is in the developing world.

If the two characteristics of the urbanisation of the Global South are urban primacy and over-urbanisation, this is truest in Latin America.[3] Firstly, it was the pace of its urbanisation, exceeding that of the whole of North America and Europe, that distinguished Latin America from other parts of the world in the twentieth century (Pinto da Cunha, 2002; Cerrutti & Bertoncello, 2003). At an aggregate level, the most intensive urbanisation took place between the mid-1920s and the 1970s (Lattes, 1995; Cerrutti & Bertoncello, 2003). Between 1925 and 1975 the pace of urbanisation was the second highest in the world, and in the 1940s the annual growth of the urban population reached the maximum observed historically in all regions at 5.1 per cent. This was the moment when the so-called 'Latin American urban explosion' took place (Lattes, 2000), declining to only 0.8 per cent between 1975 and 2000 (Cerrutti & Bertoncello, 2003). As a result of this rapid growth the degree of urbanisation in Latin America came close to that of the developed world (Lattes, 1995).

In the early twenty-first century urbanisation is slightly higher in Latin America than in Europe and very similar to that of North America, whereas it is around double that of Asia and Africa (Cerrutti & Bertoncello, 2003). In 1950 less than 42 per cent of the Latin American population lived in urban areas (Table 2.2) compared to nearly 81 per cent in 2018. By 2050 urbanisation will

Table 2.2 Latin America: urban indicators, 1950–2050

	1950	1960	1970	1980	1990	2000	2010	2020	2030	2040	2050
Total Population (millions)	168.9	221.0	288.1	364.3	445.9	525.8	597.6	664.5	718.5	757.0	779.8
Urban Population (millions)	69.8	109.3	165.0	235.2	315.3	397.1	469.6	539.4	600.5	649.6	685
Urbanisation %	41.3	49.4	57.3	64.6	70.7	75.5	78.6	81.2	83.6	85.8	87.8
Urban growth %		3.62	3.38	2.98	2.54	2.06	1.54	1.29	1.02	0.76	0.52
Urbanisation rate %		1.65	1.37	1.12	0.87	0.64	0.39	0.32	0.29	0.26	0.23

Source: United Nations (2018).

reach 87.8 per cent in the region, which is expected to be home to 685 million urban inhabitants. These numbers support the argument that urbanisation is and will continue to be a pressing issue in Latin America.

During the decades of the most intense urbanisation the economic model in Latin America went through a series of transformations, principally the implementation of industrialisation programmes via import substitution, which brought about profound demographic and spatial changes which contribute to explaining the urban explosion (Lattes, 1995; Cerrutti & Bertoncello, 2003; Montgomery, 2008; Martine & McGranahan, 2010; Stratmann, 2011). Rapid urbanisation took place in a context of very high demographic growth (Lattes, 1995, 2000) and the intense net transfer of the population from rural to urban areas (Lattes, 2000). The transformations in the economic model were reflected in the excessive concentration of population in just a few cities which defined the structure of national urban systems.

As with other, less-developed regions, two demographic factors accounted for the massive urban transformation of Latin America: (1) faster natural demographic growth in towns and cities and (2) migration, both of which were related to economic conditions and the demographic transition from high to low mortality and fertility (Chant & McIlwaine, 2009).

Since the start of the last century the total Latin American population has increased almost 10-fold from 60 million to nearly 652 million in 2018. The region now represents 8.5 per cent of the world's total population, a proportion that is projected to decline slightly through 2050. Total urban population in the region grew from 69 to 526 million between 1950 and 2018, and is expected to reach 685 million by 2050 (see Table 2.2). The very rapid population growth in Latin America over the last century has not been constant, however, and since the 1960s the trend has been towards moderate growth. At the regional level, the increase in the urban population has gradually approached stable rates and appears to be increasingly associated with natural growth. Yet, these rates represent absolute figures that continue to be considerable. Forecasts indicate that deceleration will continue in the future. Since the year 2000 the annual average urban population growth rate has been less than 2 per cent (UN-Habitat, 2012).

The second element, migration-driven urbanisation, is explained by the urban bias in state and private investment in economic activities, greater provision of welfare and services in town and cities and the development of transport and communications, among other factors (Chant & McIlwaine, 2009). The mass exodus of the rural population to cities took place during the most intense urbanisation (Jordan, Riffo & Prado, 2017). Subsequently rural–urban migration has declined and been displaced as the main migration pattern (IDB, 2015): most immigrants no longer come from the countryside but from other cities.

While rural–urban migration is still a factor of urbanisation in some countries, especially those undergoing a less-advanced urban transition, migration between cities is currently the most diverse and intense trend. It is also a characteristic that distinguishes Latin America from other emerging and developing countries. Urban–urban movement responds to the evolution of urban labour markets. Overall this type of migration occurs from expulsion areas (cities whose economic, employment and social conditions are less attractive) towards more economically dynamic recipient areas. However, this explanation of urban–urban migration fails to cover its full complexity. Most of the largest cities in the region still attract more people than they expel. In large metropolitan areas a proportion of the population has taken up residence in municipalities near the main city, and this, in turn, has continued to receive immigrants from other regions in the country (UN-Habitat, 2012).

The overall decrease in the intensity of urbanisation in the region may be due to already-high urbanisation, lower natural urban growth and decreased rural–urban migration (Cerrutti & Bertoncello, 2003). Despite the recent fall in urban growth and urbanisation rates, in absolute terms the size of the urban population continues to increase. As Lattes (2000) states, by 2025 the region will have virtually the highest level of urbanisation, while Asia and Africa will barely have reached 50 per cent, the level that Latin America had reached by the end of the 1950s. From a demographic perspective, urbanisation will be completed in the region by 2050. The decline in population growth rates should not hide the fact that in many cities absolute demographic increases remain very high and continue to exert pressure on urban infrastructure and services at a time when these are being affected by drastic decreases in capital resources and state expenditure.

Within the region there is great diversity; in fact, the demographic weight of some geographic areas would suggest the lack of a regional pattern. In 2018, more than 82 per cent of the total population is concentrated in the eight largest countries: Argentina, Brazil, Chile, Colombia, Ecuador, Mexico, Peru and Venezuela. Moreover, more than half of the regional population is concentrated in only two countries, Mexico and Brazil, with 20 and 32.3 per cent respectively. Brazil has a population of over 210 million, and Mexico one of over 120 million. In contrast, the populations of the smallest islands in the Caribbean are less than 100,000, and even countries such as Uruguay, Costa Rica and Panama have fewer than 5 million inhabitants. Thus, the aggregate tendencies observed in the region are guided by the trends of a small group of countries (Figure 2.1).

When countries are grouped into geographical subregions the variation is evident. In general there is a contrast between the high degree of urbanisation in the Southern Cone and Mexico, intermediate urbanisation in the Andean region, intermediate to low levels in Central America and wide variation across the Caribbean (UN-Habitat, 2012). Central America was the only subregion with a predominantly rural population at the beginning of this century, with urbanisation at 47.8 per cent, and was fast approaching the 50 per cent threshold (Lattes, 2000). In 2050 differences will persist, but all subregions will be highly urbanised: the Southern Cone will be 92 per cent, Mexico 88 per cent, the Andean region 86 per cent and Central America and the Caribbean 77.5

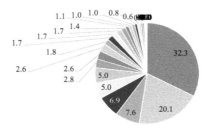

- Brazil
- Peru
- Ecuador
- Dominican Republic
- Nicaragua
- Uruguay
- Suriname
- Belize
- Curaçao
- United States Virgin Islands
- Saint Kitts and Nevis

- Mexico
- Venezuela
- Cuba
- Honduras
- Costa Rica
- Jamaica
- Guadeloupe
- French Guiana
- Saint Vincent and the Grenadines
- Antigua and Barbuda
- Sint Maarten (Dutch part)

- Colombia
- Chile
- Bolivia
- Paraguay
- Panama
- Trinidad and Tobago
- Bahamas
- Barbados
- Grenada
- Dominica
- Turks and Caicos Islands

- Argentina
- Guatemala
- Haiti
- El Salvador
- Puerto Rico
- Guyana
- Martinique
- Saint Lucia
- Aruba
- Cayman Islands
- British Virgin Islands

Figure 2.1 Countries by percentage of regional population, 2018

Source: United Nations (2018).

per cent urban (Table 2.3). However, there will be strong differences among the countries within all subregions except the Southern Cone (UN-Habitat, 2012).

While more than 50 per cent of the population lived in urban areas in only three inland countries, Uruguay, Argentina and Chile, in 1950, in 2018 all of the Latin American countries apart from the Caribbean and Belize were more than 50 per cent urbanised. However, differences across countries continue. In Central America, urbanisation ranges from 51 per cent in Guatemala to 79 per cent in Costa Rica; in the Caribbean, several islands have less than 50 per cent urbanisation, while territories such as Saint Martin and the Cayman Islands are considered entirely urban. In the Southern Cone, Argentina and Uruguay are more than 90 per cent and Ecuador and Paraguay are less than 65 per cent urbanised. Mexico seems to follow the overall regional tendency, while Brazil tends to surpass the average degree of urbanisation in Latin American (Figure 2.2).

The drivers of differences in urbanisation across Latin America are extremely complex. Variations in the implementation of economic models and differences in countries' demographic transitions may account for the disparity. Also, there appears to be some link between urbanisation and urban transitions, economic development and country size. Countries such as Argentina, Uruguay and Chile, whose urbanisation began earlier, are now highly urbanised, while countries such as Brazil, Mexico, Colombia, Peru and Venezuela, which started urbanisation after the 1930s, have urbanised very rapidly and are now in more advanced

Table 2.3 Urban indicators by subregion, 1950–2050

Mexico

	1950	1960	1970	1980	1990	2000	2010	2020	2030	2040	2050
Total population (millions)	28	38.1	52	69.361	85.3	101.7	117.3	133.9	147.5	157.7	164.3
Urban population (millions)	11.9	19.4	30.7	46	60.9	76	91.3	10.8	123.2	135.6	144.9
Urbanisation %	42.7	50.8	59	66.3	71.4	74.7	77.8	80.7	83.5	86	88.2
Urban growth %		3.83	3.69	3.33	2.45	1.98	1.67	1.55	1.23	0.92	0.64
Urbanisation rate %		1.6	1.4	1.1	0.71	0.44	0.4	0.36	0.33	0.29	0.25

Central America and the Caribbean

	1950	1960	1970	1980	1990	2000	2010	2020	2030	2040	2050
Total population (millions)	27.1	34.1	43.2	53.1	63.6	74.7	84.9	94.9	103.8	110.8	11.5
Urban population (millions)	9.2	12.9	18.6	25.7	34	42.9	52.7	62.9	73	82.1	89.5
Urbanisation %	33.8	37.8	43.2	48.4	53.5	57.4	62	66.3	70.3	74.1	77.5
Urban growth %		2.88	3.09	2.75	2.45	2.06	1.86	1.63	1.38	1.1	0.83
Urbanisation rate %		1.06	1.23	1.09	0.95	0.68	0.74	0.65	0.57	0.51	0.44

(*Continued*)

Table 2.3 (Continued)

Andean Region

	1950	1960	1970	1980	1990	2000	2010	2020	2030	2040	2050
Total population (millions)	32.1	42.9	57.6	74	93	111.8	129.2	145.9	159.4	169.9	176.8
Urban population (millions)	11.8	20.2	32.6	47.3	65	83	99.8	115.5	129.9	142.5	152.5
Urbanisation %	36.8	47.2	56.7	63.9	69.9	74.3	77.2	79.3	81.5	83.9	86.3
Urban growth %		4.17	3.8	3.1	2.72	2.17	1.68	1.36	1.11	0.88	0.66
Urbanisation rate %		2.2	1.68	1.13	0.85	0.59	0.38	0.26	0.27	0.28	0.28

Southern Cone, Brazil and Guyanas

	1950	1960	1970	1980	1990	2000	2010	2020	2030	2040	2050
Total population (millions)	81.7	105.9	135.272	167.8	203.9	237.6	266.1	290.1	307	318.6	323.2
Urban population (millions)	36.8	56.8	83	116.1	155.3	195.1	225.8	252.9	274.3	289.4	298.1
Urbanisation %	45.1	53.6	61.4	69.2	76.2	82.1	84.9	87.2	89.2	90.8	92.2
Urban growth %		3.51	3.16	2.85	2.52	2.04	1.36	1.07	0.78	0.52	0.29
Urbanisation rate %		1.59	1.27	1.13	0.92	0.73	0.32	0.27	0.22	0.18	0.15

Source: United Nations (2018).

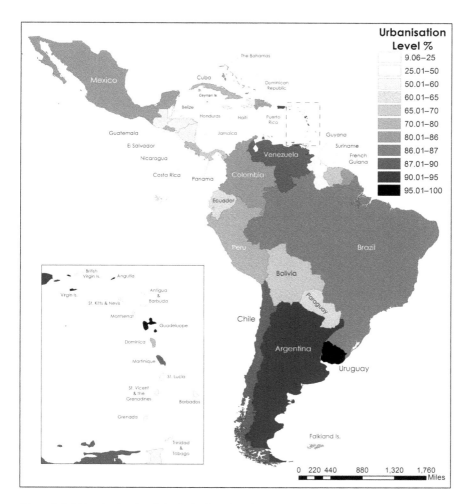

Figure 2.2 Urbanisation levels in Latin America, 2018
Source: United Nations (2018).

stages of this transition. Countries in moderate or incipient urban transitions have lower urbanisation but higher urban population growth, and the most urbanised countries are those that experienced an early demographic transition (Berquó, 2001; Dyson, 2011). Finally, another significant characteristic of urbanisation is its relationship to relative socioeconomic development, as the more-developed countries tend to be the most urbanised (Lattes, 1995; Cerrutti & Bertoncello, 2003). Urbanisation is also higher in large countries (Brazil, Mexico, Argentina and Colombia) and lower in small ones (Pinto da Cunha, 2002; Cerrutti & Bertoncello, 2003). For instance, Brazil and the Dominican

Republic are continuing to urbanise rapidly while El Salvador and Guatemala's urbanisation is very slow (Lattes, 2000). Relatively slow growth is expected in the future, although the trend is different in Central America, especially in Guatemala, Honduras and Costa Rica, which are in the full phase of urban growth (CEPAL, ONU-Habitat & MINURVI, 2016).

Historic and contemporary urbanisation in Latin America have been characterised by urban primacy; that is, the demographic, social, economic and political dominance of one city within an urban system. There is also a contemporary trend towards the emergence of megacities, with the population typically concentrating in one city which usually monopolises wealth, income, economic and administrative functions, and in most cases, political capital. In some countries such primacy is very marked. On average, primate cities are four times larger than the country's next-largest city. In other countries primacy is less acute, with two or a few major cities dominating the rest (Chant & McIlwaine, 2009).

Even though primacy has been decreasing in countries such as Mexico, Paraguay and Uruguay, the bicephalous or monocephalous urban pattern is still a dominant feature in the region.[4] Factors such as the economic model and economic activity, the maturity of the urbanisation process and historical conditions may account for the monopolistic weight of the primate city (UN-Habitat, 2012). The legacies of pre-Columbian or colonial urban development are noticeable in some countries' urban systems and primate cities, such as in the cases of Buenos Aires, Mexico City and Lima. The roles of industrialisation and the economic models of the twentieth century have been used as a powerful explicatory framework for urban primacy. Seeking an explanation for the huge metropolitan centres of the developing world and focusing particularly on Mexico City, Krugman and Livas (1996) find that this huge urban centre was the by-product of protectionist policy during the ISI. In a closed economy, strong forward–backward economic linkages and significant economies of scale derive from agglomeration in the main domestic market.

Primacy frequently involves the presence of megacities, which have been central components of the region's urbanisation process. In the first decades of the twentieth century large cities already existed despite the relatively low levels of urbanisation (Cerrutti & Bertoncello, 2003). High demographic, economic and political concentration in large cities is explained by a longer tradition of centralisation and concentration in one or a small number of cities (Angotti, 1996). Primacy and concentration led to the formation of huge urban agglomerations in the principal city, generally the capital city, followed by demographic concentration in a few other big cities in each country, with the number of Latin American cities of more than 1 million people increasing more than sixfold between 1950 and 1990, having almost tripled their population in that period. Therefore Latin America also stands out in comparison to other regions due to national urban systems that are dominated by gigantic cities (Pinto da Cunha, 2002; Cerrutti & Bertoncello, 2003).

Once urbanisation started to slow down from the end of the 1970s onwards there was a proliferation of medium-sized cities with populations of half a million to a million. This trend was linked to the end of import substitution and the widespread introduction of a new free-market approach, including the end of active industrial policy approaches. The rise of medium-sized cities also coincided with a decline in rural–urban migration flows and increased urban–urban migration. However these processes have not been homogeneous throughout Latin America (Rodgers, Beall & Kanbur, 2011). At the beginning of the twenty-first century the region's 16,000 cities included 8 with more than 5 million people and a growing number of medium cities. Altogether, these were home to 65 million inhabitants, half of them packed into medium-sized cities (Drakakis-Smith, 2000). In recent decades small and intermediate cities have grown somewhat faster than larger cities.

Whereas in 1950 Latin America had no megacities – that is, cities with over a 10 million people – six are projected for 2030: Buenos Aires, Mexico City, Rio de Janeiro, Sao Paulo, Bogota and Lima. Today the distribution of the urban population in the region according to city size is very similar to that in the rest of the world, with one important difference: the megacities account for more than 14 per cent of the total population, making Latin America the region with the largest proportion of its population living in this type of city. There is a relative lack of cities with populations of 5 to 10 million, but the number with 1 to 5 million is estimated to soon reach 65 (Table 2.4).

This latter group will include some capital cities (Caracas, Guatemala City, Panama City and San Salvador); some cities in border areas (Tijuana and Ciudad Juárez); a purposely established urban area where there was no previous urban settlement (Brasilia); and cities that have developed in an accelerated fashion (Belem and Manaus). In 2010 only four cities with more than a million people remained in the Caribbean (Havana, Port au Prince, San Juan and Santo Domingo) (UN-Habitat, 2012).

Thus, compared to other regions of the world, the distribution of the urban population by size is marked by the outstanding importance of megacities. Whereas cities with over 10 million inhabitants house around 15 per cent of Latin America's urban population, in Asia they house 13.4 per cent, in Africa 9.3 per cent and in North America 10.4 per cent (CEPAL, ONU-Habitat & MINURVI, 2016). In addition, Latin America's large cities (1 to 5 million inhabitants) accommodate more than a quarter of the urban population, also a higher proportion than in any other region. Finally, its smaller cities are relatively less significant.

Over time the urban population has deconcentrated from Latin America's larger cities. This has been observed in a few countries in the region since the 1950s and 1960s, but in most countries it is a more recent trend. Due to the increasing importance of inter-urban migration and large-scale industrial location, small and intermediate cities have seen accelerated growth. But frequently these cities have little room for negotiation in the national context and lack the technical capacity to lead a major urban development process (Jordan,

Table 2.4 Number of cities, urban population and urbanisation by city size in Latin America, 1950–2030

Size	1950	1960	1970	1980	1990	2000	2010	2020	2030
Number of cities									
10 million or more	0	0	0	2	3	4	4	6	6
5 to 10 million	1	2	4	2	2	3	4	3	5
1 to 5 million	7	9	13	24	36	44	54	65	77
500,000 to 1 million	4	10	20	27	41	53	57	58	60
300,000 to 500,000	11	19	21	32	44	48	69	83	101
Population (thousands)									
10 million or more	0	0	0	25,117	41,566	59,282	66,416	94,135	103,409
5 to 10 million	5,166	12,241	31,658	18,704	15,534	19,281	29,016	18,031	30,589
1 to 5 million	13,467	18,577	22,868	45,374	68,938	86,974	109,288	136,555	158,197
500,000 to 1 million	2,539	7,143	13,719	18,639	27,610	36,845	40,805	42,023	40,917
300,000 to 500,000	4,368	7,601	8,322	12,585	17,333	18,247	25,548	32,017	38,730
Percentage of urban population									
10 million or more	0	0	0	10.7	13.2	14.9	14.1	17.5	17.2
5 to 10 million	7.4	11.2	19.2	8	4.9	4.9	6.2	3.3	5.1
1 to 5 million	19.3	17	13.9	19.3	21.9	21.9	23.3	25.3	26.3
500,000 to 1 million	3.6	6.5	8.3	7.9	8.8	9.3	8.7	7.8	6.8
300,000 to 500,000	6.3	7	5	5.4	5.5	4.6	5.4	5.9	6.4
Fewer than 300,000	63.4	58.3	53.6	48.8	45.8	44.4	42.3	40.2	38.1

Source: United Nations (2018).

Riffo & Prado, 2017). Globalisation has also brought major changes to cities, especially border cities such as Ciudad Juarez, Tijuana and Nuevo Laredo in Northern Mexico. Exploitation of natural resources and tourism has stimulated the creation and/or growth of some urban areas. An emblematic case of urban growth in the tourism sector in Mexico is Cancun, which grew from a fishing village in the 1950s to a city of 30,000 inhabitants in the 1980s, and is now home to approximately 700,000 inhabitants (UN-Habitat, 2012).

Mexico's contemporary urbanisation in a nutshell

Even after industrial capitalism permeated its economy in the late nineteenth century, at the onset of the twentieth century Mexico remained characterised by a predominantly agrarian society. In 1900 it had only 33 cities of more than 15,000 inhabitants, totalling 1.4 million inhabitants. or 10.4 per cent of the national population (SEDESOL, CONAPO & INEGI, 2012). The 1940s were a critical point in Mexico's urbanisation process, with several contributing factors: the end of the Depression; the creation of the Bracero Program, an agreement with the US on migrant labour; the spread of health and education programmes; and above all a comprehensive set of governmental industrialisation policies (Kemper & Royce, 1979). Like several other developing countries, Mexico faced the problem of late industrialisation in the first half of the twentieth century because its economy was largely based on the production of primary products. The government implemented ISI as a development strategy in the 1940s, resulting in a transition from its largely rural society towards urbanisation and a sectoral shift from agriculture to manufacturing, and inducing the transfer of resources to industrial activities to the detriment of the primary sector. Investment in infrastructure channelled public funds directly into the development of urban areas. The constant transfer of resources from primary activities to industry and the high income expected in cities caused massive rural to urban migration, reinforcing the urban development bias (Trejo, 2007). Once activated, the most intense and accelerated stages of urbanisation took place between the 1940s and the 1980s (Garza, 1994).

Twentieth-century urbanisation may be divided into different stages of urbanisation intensity and urban growth. SEDESOL, CONAPO and INEGI (2012) identify three major stages: the first, from 1900 to 1940, is characterised by strong rural hegemony and relatively slow urban growth; the second, from 1940 to 1980, saw accelerated urbanisation and high levels of concentration; the third, from 1980 to the present, has been one of moderate and diversified urbanisation. Garza (1994) also divides the process of urbanisation in the last century into three stages: 'low urbanisation' (1900–1940), 'rapid urbanisation' (1940–1980) and 'metropolitan urbanisation' (1980 onwards), to which I refer in the next chapter. Ariza and Ramírez (2008) state that the biggest wave of urbanisation took place between the 1950s and 1970s, although Sobrino (1996) and Garza (2003) argue that the greatest amount of urban growth happened during the 1940s.

Demographic urbanisation did not occur in isolation from the broader trans-formation of Mexican society (Kemper & Royce, 1979), and several studies associate urban development with different stages in Mexico's economic devel-opment. Sobrino (2011) defines the years between 1900 and 1940 as those of the Revolution and the formation of the new nation-state and Garza (2003) as those of the Revolution, the World Wars and the Great Depression; 1940–1980 are associated with ISI (Sobrino, 2011), or the 'Mexican Miracle' (Garza, 2003). The period from 1980 onwards is linked to the liberalisation and opening up of the economy (Sobrino, 2011) and to neoliberal polycentric metropolitan concentration (Garza, 2003). Alternatively, Ruiz (1999) refers to the 1940–1970 period of 'stabilising development', the 'Mexican miracle'; the 'tragic decade' of 1970–1982; and the crisis–adjustment–crisis episode of 1982–1995. Garza (1999) also alludes to the prosperous period of high economic growth during ISI (1960–1980), the lost decade and the crisis (1980–1990), and the neoliberal model (1990–1995).

These different economic stages were accompanied by relatively well-defined urban tendencies and patterns (Figure 2.3). In 1900 Mexico's total population was 13.6 million, of which 1.4 million were urbanites, with urban-isation at just 10.5 per cent. According to Garza (1994), in the first decade of the last century the urban population grew faster than the total population. In 1910 urbanisation had increased to 11.7 per cent. The 1910s–1930s was a peculiar demographic stage due to the revolution against the Diaz dictator-ship. After the 1930s the population increased dramatically with profound modification of its internal distribution pattern. Urban growth was faster in large than in medium-sized and small cities. The most relevant feature was the primacy of Mexico City. Population tendencies and migration towards the prime city configured a highly concentrated spatial pattern of demographic distribution: in 1960 Mexico City's population was over 2 million people compared to that of Guadalajara (736,000) and Monterrey (596,000) (Snyder, 1966). In 1960 Mexico's urban population amounted to 12.7 million across 123 cities, each with over 15,000 people, and the country was 36.6 per cent urbanised.

Between 1960 and 1970 the bigger cities in the urban system saw the high-est growth (Ariza & Ramírez, 2008). The period 1960–1980 was accompanied by significant concentration in a few cities. In 1960 Mexico City had 5.4 mil-lion people and was 6.2 times the size of the second city, Guadalajara. This and Monterrey (third city) each had over half a million people. In 1970 Puebla's population passed the 500,000 mark and Guadalajara's and Monterrey's sur-passed a million. There was a considerable increase in the number of small and intermediate cities, although their contribution to the total urban popula-tion decreased. In 1978 Mexico became a predominantly urban country with more than 50 percent of its population living in localities with over 15,000 people. In 1980 Puebla surpassed a million inhabitants, and four other cities exceeded 500,000. Mexico City had a population of 13 million, but its growth rate began to decrease. A deceleration of the first-order primacy occurred with

Urbanisation stages and economic development

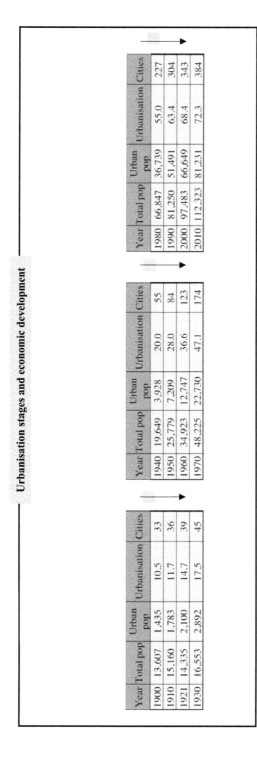

Year	Total pop	Urban pop	Urbanisation	Cities
1900	13,607	1,435	10.5	33
1910	15,160	1,783	11.7	36
1921	14,335	2,100	14.7	39
1930	16,553	2,892	17.5	45

Year	Total pop	Urban pop	Urbanisation	Cities
1940	19,649	3,928	20.0	55
1950	25,779	7,209	28.0	84
1960	34,923	12,747	36.6	123
1970	48,225	22,730	47.1	174

Year	Total pop	Urban pop	Urbanisation	Cities
1980	66,847	36,739	55.0	227
1990	81,250	51,491	63.4	304
2000	97,483	66,649	68.4	343
2010	112,323	81,231	72.3	384

Political conflict, Revolution and agrarian reform

Inward-looking development and import substitution industrialisation

Export-oriented industrialisation and neoliberal state

Figure 2.3 Mexico urbanisation and industrialisation stages, 1900–2010

Source: Based on SEDESOL, CONAPO and INEGI (2012).

the advancement of Guadalajara and Monterrey. The primacy index shows that Mexico City was 5.1 times the size of Guadalajara (Garza, 1999).

During 1970–1990 medium-sized cities grew at the fastest rate (Ariza & Ramírez, 2008). The government made little effort to stimulate the development of new towns or cities, exceptions including suburban developments such as Cuautitlan Izcalli in Mexico City Metropolitan Area and two significant industrial towns, Ciudad Sahagun in the state of Hidalgo, and Ciudad Lazaro Cardenas in the state of Michoacan. The development of specialised coastal tourist resort towns such as Cancun, Ixtapa and others was another important exception. Later, oil-related activity led to the creation of the so-called petrotowns (Kemper & Royce, 1979). Garza (2007) estimates that between 1980 and 1990 the fastest growth took place in cities neighbouring Mexico City: Puebla, Pachuca, Queretaro, Tlaxcala and San Juan del Rio. Some border cities (Tijuana, Ciudad Juarez, Mexicali, Matamoros, Nogales and Piedras Negras), port and tourist cities (Cancun, Puerto Vallarta, Acapulco, Oaxaca, Guanajuato and San Miguel de Allende) and manufacturing cities (Saltillo, Aguascalientes and San Luis Potosi) experienced high demographic dynamism.

These changes led to the relative decentralisation of the urban system. However, this implied not a more balanced urban hierarchy but rather just a moderate change in urban concentration and a decentralisation from the biggest city to a few other cities (Garza, 1999). Even though it did not substantially modify urban primacy, changes in the spatial pattern of the urban population in the 1970s signified a historical shift of the population away from the centre of the country to the northern border and to the west and east coasts (Kemper & Royce, 1979). Important shifts that started to gain force in the 1980s included increasing inter-urban and inter-regional migration, and the intensification of intra-metropolitan migratory flows (Sobrino, 1996).

With the onset of economic reforms in the 1980s and the 1990s the economy became relatively more open and liberalised, and Mexico became a largely urbanised country. In the 1990s the urbanisation rate was the slowest of the entire twentieth century. However, urban concentration and a well-defined urban system were reinforced. This decade saw a marginal increase in the share of small cities in the total urban population, from 10.4 to 10.8 per cent. Cities with populations of 500,000 to 1 million increased in number from 4 to 12, their share in the urban population standing at 16.3 per cent. In 1995 the number of small cities increased to 239, and of medium cities to 85, and there were 6 cities of over a million people (Garza, 1999). Cities around Mexico City continued to grow fastest, especially Toluca, Cuernavaca, Pachuca and Tlaxcala, as did the border cities Tijuana, Ciudad Juarez, Reynosa, Nuevo Laredo and Matamoros; the industrial cities Hermosillo, Saltillo and Aguascalientes; and the tourist cities Cancun and Puerto Vallarta (Garza, 2007).

According to UN data, Mexico's urban population stood at 104 million people in 2018, with 80 per cent urbanisation. By 2050 the country is expected to be 88 per cent urban (UN, 2018). By triggering fast urbanisation and urban growth the postrevolution industrialisation process created a long-lasting spatial and demographic pattern in the urban system. It promoted a vertical hierarchy and strong primacy, with all the associated problems observed in the urbanisation process across Latin America.

I argue in this and the previous section that the patterns of urbanisation in Latin America and Mexico have diverged significantly from historical trends in different ways. One of the most significant deviations is from the tight relationship between urbanisation and development, which seems to have broken down in much of the developing world, with Latin America the clearest example, as discussed in the final remarks for this chapter.

Final remarks: flaws in Latin American urbanisation and the broken link to development

The ideas that urbanisation in industrialised countries is closely linked to their socioeconomic development and that agglomeration favours cities' economic growth have been extremely powerful. Important empirical evidence on this has been delivered (see Bairoch, 1988). In general, regions in the world with higher economic growth tend to experience faster urbanisation, and vice versa. Urbanisation has been a forceful process with a positive evolution regardless of the economic cycle in which it takes place. However, more recent evidence is not conclusive. Whereas in the developed world significant urbanisation has been associated with industrialisation and economic prosperity, many developing countries and regions, although highly urbanised, lack significant social and economic progress. While the link between urbanisation and social and economic development seems to appear in some Asian regions, there is evidence that in Latin America this relationship is problematic (CEPAL, ONU-Habitat & MINURVI, 2016; Vargas et al., 2017). According to UN-Habitat (2012), while 60 to 70 per cent of regional GDP is generated in urban areas, it is concentrated in a few cities, in part due to the highly centralised economic model that has been adopted over many decades. Many major cities in the region have higher incomes per capita than their respective national figures, and their economic participation in the national economy has been greater than their demographic weight. In 2010 Latin America's 289 cities with more than 200,000 inhabitants produced more than three quarters of the region's GDP while comprising only half the population (Vargas et al., 2017).

Despite the relative importance of urban centres as engines of national economies, it has been particularly difficult to determine whether economic growth and urbanisation reinforce one another at the national level. Stylised facts suggest that Latin America's development has not been consistent with its rapid urbanisation trajectory. That is, the 'urban moment' in Latin America has hardly translated into an economic moment.

Compared to other regions, it seems that Latin America has become urban-ised without industrialising or benefiting from the economic advantages that cities offer. According to its urbanisation levels, Latin America lags half a cen-tury behind Europe and 70 years behind the US in terms of per capita income. The region's chaotic urbanisation has been guided by reasons other than the development of a strong and extensive manufacturing sector and high-value–added services (Vargas et al., 2017). For decades the low productivity of coun-tries in the region has been one of the reasons why its economic growth is even lower than that of other emerging economies. Its productivity has increased by just 1.4 per cent in the past 20 years, while India's has grown by 4.7 per cent and China's by 8.4 per cent. Structural economic factors such as widespread informality, lack of access to credit, macroeconomic volatility, the cost of trans-portation and low innovation may account for this (UN-Habitat, 2012).

The similarity between the level of urbanisation in the region and that in the developed world does not parallel other social and economic characteristics. In addition to, or as a result of, the broken positive link between urbanisation and development, recent urban trends disclose the presence of several problems and challenges in Latin American cities, which are regarded as the most unequal and often the most dangerous places in the world with social, economic and spatial divisions deeply rooted in urban society. Many Latin American cities have experienced traumatic transformations due to the fast and sometimes vio-lent processes of urbanisation marked by deterioration of the environment and deep social inequality (ibid.).

Low productivity, low capacity for collecting taxes, insufficient investment in infrastructure, high inequality compared to international standards, the informal economy, a shortage of services and housing, excessive commuting times, the high price of land and housing, irregular settlements, residential segregation, gentrification, poverty, insecurity, violence, environmental deterioration and vulnerability to natural disasters are some of the most severe problems cited in the literature (UN-Habitat, 2012; Klaufus & Jaffe, 2015; CEPAL, ONU-Habitat & MINURVI, 2016; Vargas et al., 2017; Jordan, Riffo & Prado, 2017).

UN-Habitat (2012) estimates that since 1970 Latin America's per capita income has nearly tripled and the region has made some progress in reducing poverty. However, per capita income hides income distribution problems, and the gains in poverty reduction have been modest compared to those of other developing regions. The richest 20 per cent of the population had an average per capita income nearly 20 times that of the poorest 20 per cent, and the aver-age Gini coefficient was higher than other regions of the world. The percent-age of people living in poverty in the region dropped from 48 to 33 per cent, or approximately by 180 million, between 1990 and 2009, but the absolute number of poor did not fall. Although urban areas account for much wealth generation, the vicious cycle of inequality appears stronger than the benefits of urbanisation. Higher income per capita in the major cities has not neces-sarily led to less inequality. There is also a strong correlation between income inequality and spatial fragmentation in cities, which have proved to be mutually reinforcing.

Jordan, Riffo and Prado (2017) underscore the huge contrasts, asymmetries, inequalities and poverty in urban Latin America, their calculations indicating that approximately 19 per cent of the population is settled in shanty towns and 122 million urban residents live in poverty. They also find that most countries are affected by the informal economy and associated lack of welfare coverage. Urban territories controlled by or at the mercy of organised crime illustrate the complexity of the challenge posed by the lack of security, which has become a major concern for most people in Latin America. Even though during the last decade of the twentieth century and the first of the twenty-first century there has been a socioeconomic diversification of the periphery, socioterritorial disparities remain elevated. High-income core areas are well-connected and dominant, whereas the periphery still constitutes the most dynamic space in demographic terms, but poverty prevails. The greatest lags in terms of socioeconomic development are found in the northeast of Brazil, southeast of Mexico and the Andean and Amazonian areas of Peru, Bolivia, Colombia and Ecuador.

Efforts have been dedicated to finding an explanation for the relatively weak economic power of urbanisation in Latin America. UN-Habitat (2012) suggests that the economic role of cities and urbanisation is closely related to each country's respective economic policy and production structure. Industrialisation strategies originally triggered urbanisation in the mid-twentieth century. Nonetheless, some failures in the implementation of the ISI strategy and the subsequent economic and trade liberalisation in the 1980s and 1990s onwards had a knock-on negative effect on cities and their economic performance. Although a long-standing phenomenon, the informal economy grew in the 1980s and 1990s with trade liberalisation, government downsizing and other reforms inspired by neoliberal reforms, leading to the dramatic contraction of the formal labour market, high unemployment and job insecurity.

Jordan, Riffo and Prado (2017) point out that productive structures in Latin American cities are characterised by relative deindustrialisation and the enlargement of the service sector on an even greater scale than in developed countries. The difference is the heterogeneity, the presence of a wide range of informal services, and their low productivity in Latin American urban centres. The predominance of the service sector can be seen in the composition of the workforce: on average, 70 per cent of urban populations work in the service sector, 24 per cent in industry and 6 per cent in agriculture (UN-Habitat, 2012). This invites a rethinking of the economic and productive structures of these urban areas.

Some authors have stressed that the excessive concentration of population in large cities has severely weakened the virtuous links between urbanisation and development. The positive benefits of the agglomeration of population and economic activities are accompanied by many negative externalities. Although cities present opportunities for economic growth, they also impose challenges that jeopardise the welfare of large segments of the population. The particular functioning of housing markets in the region, with poor-quality, unaffordable and expensive housing, as well as a housing deficit, the low availability of mortgage credit and the lack of cheap sources of finance, limit cities' ability to fully enjoy the benefits of agglomeration (Vargas et al., 2017).

Other important explanations for the lack of development despite high urbanisation are the political context, political governance, institutions, security and legal certainty. Although urbanisation is a key factor in development, this connection depends on appropriate planning and policy and adequate regulation: while urbanisation can be a catalyst for change and transformation, it should be led by a plan (UN-Habitat, 2012; CEPAL, ONU-Habitat & MINURVI, 2016;Vargas, et al., 2017). Political and technical lack of capacity to anticipate and manage urban growth and the problems it involves, in addition to shortcomings in productive and labour structures, have resulted in a more precarious and informal urbanisation and a less functional urban system for productivity and equality (Jordan, Riffo & Prado, 2017). Urban planning has been hindered by limited institutional capacity, strong stakeholders and a lack of resources, resulting in plans that are not implemented and laws that are not enforced. Most municipalities have planning responsibilities, but these are usually limited to basic regulation. They lack a conceptual understanding of urban problems and a holistic and comprehensive urban model (IDB, 2015).

Cities also need the support of efficient national governments. Organisations such as the Inter-American Development Bank, the Development Bank of Latin America, the Economic Commission for Latin America and the Caribbean and others have highlighted the need for a radical transition in urban management in the Latin American region to tackle urban issues, in response to which there has been a trend towards a recentralisation of urban policy. At the beginning of the year 2000 Latin America went through a phase in which active economic and social public policies resulted in the sustained reduction in structural heterogeneity (Jordan, Riffo & Prado, 2017). According to this trend, the importance of developing national urban policy lies in the fact that urbanisation plays a fundamental role in the transformation of developing countries. In recent years some Latin American countries have formulated this type of policy, including Mexico's 2015 National Urban and Housing Policy and its 2017 Human Settlements Act, Chile's 2014 National Urban Development Policy and Brazil's 2004 National Urban Development Policy. Other attempts include Peru's 2006–2015 National Plan of Urban Development and Colombia's 1997 Organic Law of Territorial Ordinance. In general, national urban plans are promoted by a sectoral ministry. In addition the international development agenda known as the 2030 Agenda establishes new objectives, among them one specifically dedicated to cities. The Habitat III Agenda seeks to rethink urban policy, promote urban planning at the national level and align and strengthen institutional mechanisms (CEPAL, ONU-Habitat & MINURVI, 2016).

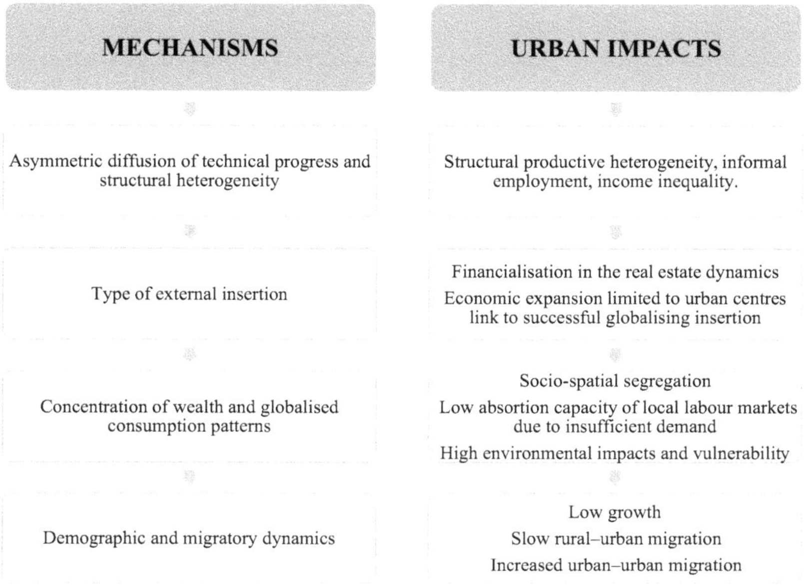

MECHANISMS	URBAN IMPACTS
Asymmetric diffusion of technical progress and structural heterogeneity	Structural productive heterogeneity, informal employment, income inequality.
Type of external insertion	Financialisation in the real estate dynamics Economic expansion limited to urban centres link to successful globalising insertion
Concentration of wealth and globalised consumption patterns	Socio-spatial segregation Low absorption capacity of local labour markets due to insufficient demand High environmental impacts and vulnerability
Demographic and migratory dynamics	Low growth Slow rural–urban migration Increased urban–urban migration

Figure 2.4 Peripheral dynamic insufficiency in urban contexts

Source: Based on Jordan, Riffo and Prado (2017).

'Peripheral dynamic insufficiency' has been used as an explanatory framework for urbanisation in Latin America (Figure 2.4), referring to factors that impede or hinder the transition to more balanced productive, social and spatial structures: (1) the asymmetric diffusion of technical progress and structural heterogeneity, (2) the type of external insertion, (3) the concentration of wealth and globalised consumption patterns and (4) demographic and migratory dynamics. These elements also explain informality, poverty and the reproduction of inequalities (Jordan, Riffo & Prado, 2017).

The urban challenge has evolved as new types of urban form have emerged in the region: urban expansion, peri-urbanisation and conurbation processes have resulted in new and differently shaped urban regions, blurring the urban–rural divide and imposing a new character on traditional urban problems. The process of metropolitan expansion, its causes and consequences are discussed in the following chapter.

Notes

1 The Spaniards built more settlements in America than the combined total of all the other European powers.
2 Diaz's rule eventually became a dictatorship from 1880 to 1910.

3 Over-urbanisation or hyper-urbanisation refer to a level of urbanisation that is out of proportion to the capacity of the urban economy, often with a heavy concentration of investment and economic activity.
4 In a number of countries the leadership of the main city has stabilized: for instance, the primacy of Panama City and Santo Domingo has remained the same or increased (Jordan, Riffo & Prado, 2017).

References

Angotti, T. (1996). 'Latin American urbanization and planning: Inequality and unsustainability in North and South'. *Latin American Perspectives*, 23(4), 12–34.

Angotti, T. (2013). 'Urban Latin America: Violence, enclaves, and struggles for land'. *Latin American Perspectives*, 40(2), 5–20. Available at: https://journals.sagepub.com/doi/pdf/10.1177/0094582X12466832.

Ariza, M. & Ramírez, J. (2008). 'Urbanización, mercados de trabajo y escenarios sociales en el México finisecular'. In Portes, A., Roberts, B. & Grimson, A. (eds). *Ciudades latinoamericanas*. México: Miguel Ángel Porrúa-Universidad Autónoma de Zacatecas, pp. 251–302.

Bairoch, P. (1988). *Cities and economic development: From the dawn of history to the present*. Chicago: University of Chicago Press.

Berquó, E. (2001). 'Demographic evolution of the Brazilian population during the twentieth century'. In Hogan, D. J. (ed.). *Population change in Brazil: Contemporary perspectives*. Campinas: Population Studies Center, pp. 13–33.

CEPAL, ONU-Habitat & MINURVI. (2016). *América Latina y el Caribe: desafíos, dilemas y compromisos de una agenda urbana común*. Documentos de Proyectos No. 716. Santiago, UN. Available at: https://repositorio.cepal.org/bitstream/handle/11362/40656/S1600986_es.pdf?sequence=1&isAllowed=y.

Cerrutti, M. & Bertoncello, R. (2003). Urbanization and internal migration patterns in Latin America. Paper prepared for Conference on African migration in comparative perspective, Johannesburg, South Africa, 4–7 June 2003.

Chant, S. & McIlwaine, C. (2009). *Geographies of development in the 21st century: An introduction to the Global South*. Cheltenham: Edward Elgar.

Drakakis-Smith, D. W. (2000). *Third World cities*. New York: Routledge.

Dyson, T. (2011). 'The role of the demographic transition in the process of urbanization'. *Population and Development Review*, (37), 34–54. Available at: https://doi.org/10.1111/j.1728-4457.2011.00377.x.

Garza, G. (1994). 'Dynamics of Mexican urbanization: Mexico City emerging megalopolis and metropolitan Monterrey'. *Urbana*, I(1), 29–42.

Garza, G. (1999). 'Global economy, metropolitan dynamics and urban policies in Mexico'. *Cities*, 16(3), 149–170. Available at: https://doi.org/10.1016/S0264-2751(99)00013-X.

Garza, G. (2003). *La urbanización de México en el siglo XX*. México, D. F.: El Colegio de México.

Garza, G. (2007). 'La urbanización metropolitana en México: normatividad y características socioeconómicas'. *Papeles de Población*, 13(52), 77–108.

Hardoy, J. E. (1982). 'The building of the Latin American cities'. In Gilbert, A., Hardoy, J. E. & Ramirez, R. (eds.). *Urbanization in contemporary Latin America: Critical approaches to the analysis of urban issues*. Chichester; New York: John Wiley, pp. 19–33.

IDB. (2015). *The experience of Latin America and the Caribbean in urbanization*. Discussion Paper No. IDB-DP-395. Inter-American Development Bank.

Jordan, R., Riffo, L. & Prado, A. (eds.) (2017). *Desarrollo sostenible, urbanización y desigualdad en América Latina y el Caribe: Dinámicas y desafíos para el cambio estructural*. Santiago: CEPAL.

Available at: www.cepal.org/es/publicaciones/42141-desarrollo-sostenible-urbanizacion-desigualdad-america-latina-caribe-dinamicas.

Kemper, R. V. & Royce, A. P. (1979). 'Mexican urbanization since 1821: A macro-historical approach'. *Urban Anthropology*, 8(3/4), 267–289.

Klaufus, C. & Jaffe, R. (2015). 'Latin American and Caribbean urban development'. *European Review of Latin American and Caribbean Studies*, (100), 63–72. Available at: https://doi.org/10.18352/erlacs.10127.

Krugman, P. & Livas, R. (1996). 'Trade policy and the Third World metropolis'. *Journal of Development Economics*, 49(1), 137–150. Available at: www.sciencedirect.com/science/article/pii/0304387895000550.

Lattes, A. E. (1995). Urbanización, crecimiento urbano y migraciones en América Latina. *Notas de Población*. Santiago: CEPAL, pp. 211–260 Available at: https://repositorio.cepal.org/bitstream/handle/11362/38594/NP62-06_es.pdf?sequence=1&isAllowed=y.

Lattes, A. E. (2000). 'Población urbana y urbanización en América Latina'. In Carrión, F. (ed.). *La ciudad construida: urbanismo en América Latina*. II Jornadas Iberoamericanas de Urbanismo sobre las Nuevas Tendencias de la Urbanización en América Latina. Quito: FLACSO-Ecuador, pp. 49–76. Available at: https://biblio.flacsoandes.edu.ec/catalog/resGet.php?resId=19146.

Martine, G. & McGranahan, G. (2010). 'A transição urbana brasileira: trajetória, dificuldades e lições aprendidas'. In Baeninger, R. (ed.). *População e Cidades: Subsídios para o planejamento e para as políticas sociais*. Brasilia: UNFPA, pp. 11–24. Available at: http://pubs.iied.org/X00048/?a=N.

Montgomery, M. (2008). 'The demography of urban transition'. In Martine, G. et al. (eds.). *The new global frontier: Urbanization, poverty and environment in the 21st century*. London: Earthscan, pp. 17–35.

Pinto da Cunha, J. M. (2002). *Urbanización, redistribución espacial de la población y transformaciones socioeconómicas en América Latina*. Serie Población y Desarrollo. Santiago: UN, CEPAL, CELADE. Available at: www.cepal.org/es/publicaciones/7168-urbanizacion-redistribucion-espacial-la-poblacion-transformaciones.

Rodgers, D., Beall, J. & Kanbur, R. (2011). *Latin American urban development into the 21st century: Towards a renewed perspective on the city*. WIDER Working Paper 2011/05, Helsinki: WIDER. Available at: http://hdl.handle.net/10419/54165.

Ruiz, C. (1999). 'La economía y las modalidades de la urbanización en México: 1940–1990'. *Economía, Sociedad y Territorio*, II(5), 1–24.

SEDESOL, CONAPO & INEGI. (2012). *Delimitación de las zonas metropolitanas de México 2010*. México, D. F.: Secretaría de Desarrollo Social, Consejo Nacional de Población, Instituto Nacional de Estadística y Geografía. Available at: www.conapo.gob.mx/es/CONAPO/Delimitacion_zonas_metropolitanas_2010_Capitulos_I_a_IV.

Snyder, D. E. (1966). 'Urbanization and population growth in Mexico'. *Revista Geográfica*, (64), 73–84.

Sobrino, J. (1996). 'Tendencias de la urbanización mexicana hacia finales del siglo'. *Estudios Demográficos y Urbanos*, 11(1), 101–137. Available at: https://doi.org/10.24201/edu.v11i1.965.

Sobrino, J. (2011). 'La urbanización en el México contemporáneo'. *Reunión de expertos sobre: Población, territorio y desarrollo sostenible* [online]. Santiago: CEPAL. Available at: www.cepal.org/es/eventos/reunion-expertos-poblacion-territorio-desarrollo-sostenible.

Stratmann, B. (2011). 'Megacities: Globalization, metropolisation, and sustainability'. *Journal of Developing Societies*, 27(3–4), 229–259. Available at: https://doi.org/10.1177/0169796X1102700402.

Trejo, A. (2007). *The evolving economic geography of production: Does globalisation matter?: Evidence from Mexican manufacturing activity and implications for regional development*. PhD thesis. University of East Anglia. Available at: https://ethos.bl.uk/OrderDetails.do;jsessionid=A52DEA0DE5407F8F2750D725AEAEF1F1?uin=uk.bl.ethos.439982.

UN-Habitat. (2012). *State of Latin American and Caribbean cities 2012: Towards a new urban transition*. Nairobi: UN-HABITAT. Available at: https://unhabitat.org/books/state-of-latin-american-and-caribbean-cities-2/.

United Nations. (2018). *World urbanization prospects*. Population Division–United Nations. Available at: https://esa.un.org/unpd/wup/Download/.

Vargas et al. (2017). *Urban growth and access to opportunities: A challenge for Latin America*. Bogota: Banco de Desarrollo de América Latina, CAF. Available at: http://scioteca.caf.com/handle/123456789/1091.

3   The spatial distribution of population

A study of metropolitan patterns and dynamics in Mexico

Introduction

At the end of the twentieth century, Latin America had 4 of the 15 largest cities in the world (Mexico City, Sao Paulo, Buenos Aires and Rio de Janeiro), plus 45 urban centres of more than 1 million inhabitants, 3 of which exceed 5 million (Bogota, Lima and Santiago) and many others with more than 1 million inhabitants. Most of these urban agglomerations occupied territories that exceeded the jurisdictional scope of a local authority, with labour markets that covered several municipalities, sometimes in different states or provinces. The internal structure of those large cities has experienced significant changes over the decades, including the displacement of population, industries and services from the central city to the periphery, as well as the creation of new centres. In many cases, this has represented a rupture of a traditional spatial structure of the city, compact and with a single centre (Rojas, Cuadrado Roura & Fernández Guell, 2005). The increasing emergence of metropolitan areas has created new conditions for the performance and organisation of urban and regional spaces. According to Lang and Knox (2009), because of their increasing importance metropolitan areas remain fundamental to understanding the spatial and economic organisation of advanced and developing countries.

In Mexico, the urban future is fundamentally being built on such significant territorial, economic and demographic shifts. In addition to its high urbanisation, which the United Nations and the World Bank estimate at 80 per cent, relatively recent urban processes including urban sprawl have involved the functional, morphological and qualitative transformation of several Mexican cities. These urban changes are largely associated to metropolisation: the physical expansion of cities beyond their administrative boundaries. Metropolitan areas are growing not just in number but also in significance as economic, political and social territorial entities. In 2015 national total population was nearly 120 million inhabitants of which 75 million (approximately 63 per cent) lived in metropolitan areas.

For a better understanding of the macrodynamics and patterns of Mexican metropolitan areas, this chapter provides a dedicated national outlook of the characteristics of the metropolitan system, an analysis of population distribution, urban growth and migration attraction, as well as inter-metropolitan disparities and urban hierarchies. Data from the 1990, 2000 and 2010 population and household censuses and a 2015 survey from INEGI (the national statistical office) are employed. The evaluation includes the 74 metropolitan areas identified in 2018 according to the official classification provided by the National Institute of Statistics and Geography (INEGI), the National Population Council (CONAPO) and the Ministry of Agrarian, Land, and Urban Development (SEDATU). As a preamble, the chapter presents a brief account of metropolitan origins and evolution in Latin America and Mexico. It also addresses the important empirical question of identifying and delimiting metropolitan areas and reviews how its conceptualisation and measurement have evolved over the decades in this country.

The metropolitan question and challenges to coherent development

While Latin America's urbanisation has slowed compared to its pace during the period of ISI, it has displayed new spatial forms (Jordan, Riffo & Prado, 2017). On a large scale, these new urban forms are increasing across the region. The physical expansion of cities and their economic transformation have led to the manifestation of urban forms such as metropolitan areas, megaregions and urban corridors. With the construction of new residential complexes and shopping centres, new industrial zones and new irregular settlements, Latin American cities are physically expanding at high speed. The urban footprint is growing up to twice or three times as fast as population growth. In Mexico, for example, the average city has geographically expanded three times faster than its population growth: currently the size of the urban footprint of a city such as Xalapa is doubling every five to six years. Urban expansion has meant that many cities have spilled over their municipal administrative boundaries, absorbing other urban centres in the conurbation process. The result is the emergence of urban areas with a large territorial size and multiple jurisdictions (UN-Habitat, 2012; IDB, 2015).

According to Parilla, Leal and Berube (2015), 22 of the 300 largest metropolitan economies in the world are in Latin America and account for 30 per cent of the region's population and 40 per cent of its economic output. Vargas et al. (2017) used the Extension of Metropolitan Areas (BEAM in Spanish) database to measure the expansion of cities and their metropolitan area as a cluster of stable nighttime luminosity pixels, captured through satellite imagery in 2000 and 2010. According to this estimation, Latin America had a total of 320 metropolitan areas in 2010, which was 113 more than in 2000 (Figure 3.1). In 2010 the largest metropolises were Sao Paulo (4,360 km^2), Buenos Aires (3,300 km^2) and Mexico City (3,180 km^2). Dedensification is increasing as cities expand spatially faster than their population growth. Cities in the region have become fairly dense compared to other urban areas around the world. Data from 2000 indicates that the average urban density in the region was 70 people per hectare, similar to that observed in Europe and Africa, but much greater than that

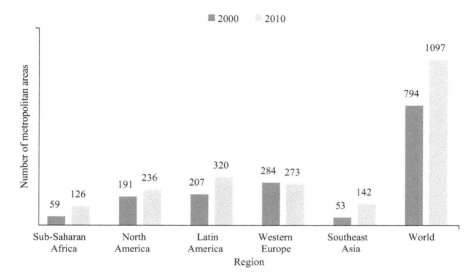

Figure 3.1 Estimated number of metropolitan areas with more than 100,000 inhabitants in selected regions, 2000 and 2010

Source: Based on Vargas et al. (2017).

Table 3.1 Total urban extension and average built-up area of selected cities by region, 2015

	Total urban extension			Built-up area		
	Total urban extension	Built-up area %	Urbanized open space	Urban (%)	Suburban (%)	Rural (%)
North American average	263,715	64	36	75	23	2
European average	82,909	66	34	78	21	1
Latin American average	47,977	72	28	84	15	1

Source: Based on Vargas et al. (2017).

of major cities in the United States and much less dense than large Asian cities with 200 to 400 inhabitants per hectare (UN-Habitat, 2012). Vargas et al. (2017) estimate that Latin America's metropolises are less extended than those in North America and Europe, but denser (Table 3.1). Finally, urban expansion is growing faster than population, mainly due to sprawl, which occurs when urban boundaries continuously expand beyond the existing limits of the built city (Figure 3.2).

The propensity of cities to urban expansion has complex origins and combines many forces, including planning control, urban plans, the supply of transport, housing needs, the dynamics of local real estate markets, the functioning of local labour markets, the quality of services, identity and lifestyle (UN-Habitat, 2012; IDB, 2015). In Latin America urban expansion is not limited to any social

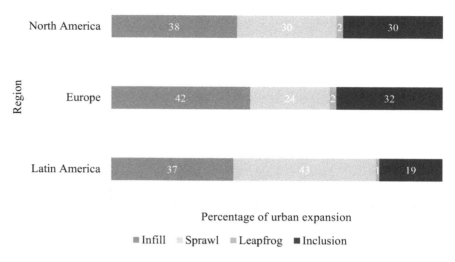

Region

North America

Europe

Latin America

Percentage of urban expansion

■ Infill   ▪ Sprawl   ■ Leapfrog   ■ Inclusion

Figure 3.2 Sources of urban expansion (%)

Source: Based on Vargas et al. (2017).

group or type of urban structure. It has included the development of closed-off housing projects for the upper- and middle-income classes, the construction of social housing projects and the proliferation of precarious and irregular settlements lacking in infrastructure and services. Each of these developments has its own dynamics, but they all contribute to the general trend of spatial dispersion with their consequential impacts and frequent environmental, social and economic costs (UN-Habitat, 2012).

The four largest metropolises in the region – Sao Paulo, Mexico City, Buenos Aires and Rio de Janeiro – are the centres of the economic and/or political power in their countries and have surpassed the limits of their immediate outermost periphery, expanding their boundaries and economic influence. Furthermore, Mexico City, but especially Sao Paulo, have established a strong connection with surrounding metropolises and cities to form urban regions. The metropolitan region of Sao Paulo, Campinas and Baixada Santista is an area of approximately 26 million people (UN-Habitat, 2012).

While these extended urban forms and networks have several advantages from an economic perspective, they also pose a range of new and intensified challenges to their management and sustainability. Unlike urban expansion in other urbanised regions, urban sprawl in Latin America has been rather chaotic as it has increased the abuse of land and other natural resources (UN-Habitat, 2012). Similarly, Angotti (2013) refers to the distinctive gigantic land grab in Latin America. Housing developments frequently proliferate without effective control to ensure consistency with environmental and social standards and effective cost-sharing. Moreover, the provision of physical infrastructure in these developments is problematic because it is often tied to subsidised tariffs. Such accelerated and disordered urban expansion increases both economic and social informality, inequality, poverty, low productivity, deteriorating competitiveness and poor access to social services and education. Sprawl can result in limited access to basic services, especially for those on the periphery, and high service–provision costs which usually affect lower-income groups most severely (IDB, 2015).

Urban planning enforcement, a key variable in managing urban footprint growth, has been poor in the region's cities. Most Latin American countries have failed to implement effective mechanisms that would allow the integrated governance of these urban areas, with consequential inefficiency and inconsistency in development strategies and service delivery. There is still little experience of managing metropolitan areas and harmonising the often-conflicting interests of institutional stakeholders at the municipal and local levels. Expansion without an integrated vision has translated into poor economic performance, segregation and poverty, failing to exploit the advantages offered by urbanisation. The urban expansion model has also been influenced by malfunctioning urban markets and social protection systems, with urban speculation a common trend in Latin America (UN-Habitat, 2012).

A variety of problems have been confronted in order to implement a more complex and efficient metropolitan planning framework. IDB (2015) refers to weak administrative information and coordination, obsolete plans, poor enforcement of planning instruments and regulations, limited tax collection, high public debt, losses in infrastructure cost recovery, limited governance and transparency, corruption and lack of commitment. UN-Habitat (2012) finds a tendency for non-state actors, private-interest groups and sometimes illegal groups to capture municipal institutions. Decentralisation has not always been accompanied by the transfer of capabilities and resources. Only a few municipalities manage to be self-financing, while others continue to depend heavily on central government. Low property tax collection, due to outdated land registers, deficient appraisal systems and inadequate revenue collection, prevent the achievement of adequate public financial capacity. The evolution of local authorities is heterogeneous. Fragmented and ad-hoc problem-solving cultures are persistent. Sectoral agendas and municipal secretariats are rarely coordinated. The debate on devolutionary and redistributive functions and the transfer of fiscal and other skills between different levels of government continues. Broadly, there is often no agreed spatial framework and articulation in the metropolitan space.

These elements create a very difficult environment for adequate planning and the provision of public services, impacting directly on the quality of life of inhabitants and on sustainability standards. Because many cities have outgrown their original political-administrative boundaries, there is a growing need for regional urban vision and coordination. Latin America seems to be in need of urban reforms and critical appraisal of institutional, operational, planning and legislative rules and procedures. Planning, management and government mechanisms need to be adapted to the new realities of urbanisation and urban expansion. The physical and functional expansion of cities and the strengthening of the tendency to metropolisation are the most outstanding characteristics of urbanisation also in contemporary Mexico, and we examine these in the next section.

Major aspects of the metropolitan transition in Mexico

Observable developments in several Mexican cities illustrate that, as in other developed and developing countries, Mexico in the twenty-first century is on its way to the 'metropolitan age'. Rather than remaining confined to their official administrative boundaries, cities are now covering neighbouring municipalities and extending as far as the reach of their everyday functional relations in the labour market and social interface. While metropolitan trends are more evident today, the origin of the metropolitan phenomenon in Mexico dates back to the 1940s, when the intense move to industrialisation fostered the acceleration of urbanisation. Cities such as Mexico City, Monterrey, Torreon, Tampico and Orizaba physically expanded, exceeding their administrative boundaries, with conurbations resulting from the integration of two or more municipalities which, in cases such as the Mexico City and Torreon metropolitan areas, belonged to different states (Moreno, 2005; SEDESOL, CONAPO & INEGI, 2007).

Unikel (2016) argues that this expansion was certainly the result of the relocation of both residential and industrial activities. Thereafter several cities underwent similar sprawl, including medium and small cities such as Colima, Cuernavaca, Toluca and Cuautla. For some decades urban sprawl had relatively little influence on urban growth. Metropolitan expansion accounted for 12.7 and 8.3 per cent of the total growth of the urban population in 1940–1950 and 1950–1960 respectively. In those periods, urban population growth due to metropolisation was greatest in Mexico City, Guadalajara, Monterrey and Puebla. In Puebla, for instance, 27 localities with 20,000 inhabitants were incorporated into the urban agglomeration.

Instruments for the regulation of phenomena related to metropolisation materialised in the 1970s in the General Law of Human Settlements, which included the legal recognition of conurbations, and later in reforms to Article 115 of the constitution which provided municipalities with a number of decentralised powers and autonomy (Jalomo, 2011; SEDESOL, CONAPO & INEGI, 2012). The General Law of Human Settlements defines 'conurbation' in Section IV of Article 2 as 'the physical and demographic continuity forming or tending to form two or more population centres'. This definition emphasises demographic and territorial criteria. Article 12 included some programmes intended as planning instruments for conurbations. Chapter IV of the article specified procedures for issuing a 'declaration of conurbation', for constituting a commission consisting of officials from the three levels of government responsible for defining a conurbation and for designing and implementing those programmes. Six conurbations, Mexico City, Puebla-Tlaxcala, Tampico, Orizaba, Monterrey and La Laguna, were officially recognised in 1976 (Moreno, 2005; SEDESOL, CONAPO & INEGI, 2012).

The territory covered by urban areas grew more rapidly from 1980 to 2000. For example, in Mexico City the urban area grew by 3.6 times, in Guadalajara by 3.8 times and in Monterrey by 4.9 times. A number of smaller metropolises experienced huge increases in their urban area, including Villahermosa (30.1 times), Toluca (26.3 times), Cancun (25.8 times), Pachuca (21.1 times) and Tuxtla Gutierrez (16.9 times). The largest increase took place in Cabo San Lucas, whose area extended by 76.4 times (SEDATU, CONAPO & INEGI, 2018).

In Mexico, as in other countries in Latin America, access to and the use of land has been a determining force of urban expansion. Historically, land allocation has remained a major area of social contention in the country. The land tenure regime framed by Article 27 of the national constitution recognises three types of land ownership: private, public and social. Of these, a large proportion of the national territory was under social land ownership in the twentieth century. Social land includes communal land, usually owned by indigenous communities or towns with indigenous origin, and *ejidos*, a unique form of collective ownership. *Ejidos* are pieces of land expropriated by the federal government from private owners after the Mexican Revolution for distribution among peasants. *Ejidatarios* (*ejido* collective owners) were entitled to use and work such land to their advantage, with agrarian laws prohibiting its rental or sale. A 1992 land tenure reform gave *ejidatarios* the formal titles to their land, enabling them to lease or sell their plots if the majority of members agreed (Payan & Correa-Cabrera, 2014). Due to the scarcity of private land, since the 1950s social land, and particularly *ejidos*, began to change hands to become, illegally or irregularly, forms of private property and were incorporated into the process of urban expansion in various ways. This particular feature of the land tenure regime in Mexico would represent the distinguishing feature on urbanisation giving shape to the urban land nexus.

The incorporation of urban land into metropolitan areas led to different forms of occupation not only in the peripheries, but also in places further away and disconnected from the central area. This expansion frequently began without planning, and resulted in significant loss of quality of life for the inhabitants (Legorreta, 1991; Ziccardi, 2016; SEDATU, CONAPO & INEGI, 2018). Referring to Mexico City, Legorreta (1991) suggests that for decades disordered and uncontrolled growth of urban peripheries, the occupation of land in inadequate areas and spontaneity and irregularity (or informality) have been essential characteristics of urban expansion. According to Ziccardi (2016), housing developments were the main engine of urban dispersal. However, while housing developments of a diverse nature have accounted for a substantial part of Mexico's urban expansion, the construction of other developments such as shopping centres, roads, industrial parks, etc. has also influenced the pattern of expansion (SEDATU, CONAPO & INEGI, 2018). In cases such as Mexico City and Torreon, the first form of urban expansion corresponded to the location or relocation of industrial activity, in particular when manufacturing businesses moved to occupy large plots of land on the peripheries.

Ziccardi (2016) underlines how in large Latin American cities the issue of urban peripheries inhabited by the so-called *sectores populares* (low-income population) is of the utmost importance, with poor urban dwellers driving substantial change in the city. Legorreta (1991) points out that illegality and irregularity have been fundamental characteristics of the land market in Mexico's urban peripheries. The commercialisation of land in a highly speculative environment and illegal occupation became the only access to housing for broad sectors of the population, given the growing need for housing and the lack of credit. Despite the land-ownership regime and regulations to control urban expansion,[1] irregular *ejido* land transactions and invasion by low-income residents were major factors of urban expansion. Another substantial part of urban sprawl was related to the construction of social housing; however, it is not only poor inhabitants who moved beyond the city perimeters, with expansion also including real estate developments for the middle and upper classes. Therefore, different types of housing developments on the Mexican peripheries have included exclusive high-class gated neighbourhoods, the mass production of social housing for the low- and middle-income population and informal and irregular housing for low-income population.

The relevance of the different factors shaping metropolitan expansion has changed over time, but some general sources refer to demographic, economic, political and policy factors, as well as the logic of the land and housing markets (Figure 3.3).

A significant difference between the housing industry in Mexico and that in developed countries is that a considerable segment of the residential construction industry began informally and, in many cases remains so. Similarly, many of the settlements on the periphery of various Latin American cities are the result of the irregular occupation tolerated by political structures and of rural workers migrating to the city in search of better work opportunities and living conditions, usually joining the informal workforce with no formal salary or social security and living in precarious housing conditions (Ziccardi, 2016). In Mexican cities the real estate market has been overseen by different political structures, and the prevailing legislation became a source of intricate corruption among these power structures with the political votes of the settlers sought by both the party in power and others. Hence, there was a close relationship between the market for land and illegal occupation on the one hand, and electoral cycles and periods of government on the other. In this sense urban growth and expansion have not followed an anarchic and spontaneous process but have been determined by the diverse economic and political interests of agrarian leaders, officials of the agrarian reform secretariat, housing promoters and real estate agents, and politicians (Legorreta, 1991).

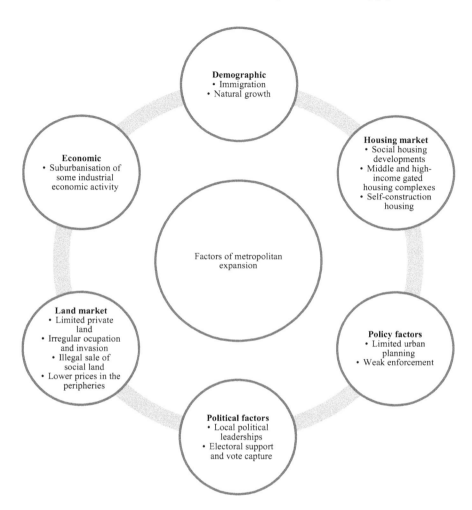

Figure 3.3 Factors in the expansion of Mexican cities

Source: Author´s elaboration.

Urban expansion based on the illegal real estate market had important social effects, including the gradual reduction of access to and quality of urban services. The city extended beyond its technical and financial capacity to provide the necessary services. This was urbanisation with minimal public investment. In addition, the irregular use of land slowed construction and consolidation processes (Legorreta, 1991).

The National Housing Policy of the late 1900s, based on deregulation and privatisation, led to important changes in the form and intensity of residential expansion in several cities. Mostly, it encouraged private housing developers to overbuild on the urban peripheries to maximise their revenue. Developers acquired sizeable territorial reserves and built large developments of identical, frequently small, tract houses. Many newly developed areas became peripheral to urban centres and lacked access to jobs, infrastructure, services and urban amenities. As a result many metropolitan areas emerged, while others expanded further. This transition in the land and housing market led to a changing political economy of urbanisation where national policy plus market forces reshaped the powers in the urban extension politics.

The delimitation of metropolitan areas

Due to the multifarious nature of metropolitan areas, classifying and delimiting them is problematical. They often incorporate urban cores, peri-urban areas and extensive tracts of mixed urban–rural land. However, their effective functional boundaries are beyond administrative definitions, although, usually due to data limitations, national official and statistical definitions respect local jurisdictions such as municipalities. There has been much discussion on how to delimit metropolitan areas, and international efforts have been made to identify them using comparable methodologies, including the OECD's delimitation in 29 countries (OECD, 2013). Various methods are used to delimit urban areas, and empirical definitions consist of a combination of criteria. The use of satellite imagery, the intensity of lights at night and spatial analysis are just some of the techniques used to delimit metropolitan areas, while size, conurbation and a single urban labour market are basic elements by which a metropolitan area can be recognised.

For several years there was a lack of systematic information by which to identify and analyse the characteristics and extent of metropolisation in Mexico (SEDESOL, CONAPO & INEGI, 2012). From the census data for 1960, Unikel identified 12 metropolitan areas: Mexico City, Monterrey, Guadalajara, Puebla, Orizaba, Veracruz, Chihuahua, Tampico, Leon, Torreon, Merida and San Luis Potosi (Figure 3.4). Following this pioneering work, other analyses attempting to identify metropolitan areas using different methodologies appeared sporadically. Negrete and Salazar identified 26 metropolitan areas using the 1980 census, and in 1993, Sobrino identified 37 metropolitan areas (SEDESOL, CONAPO & INEGI, 2012). Even though metropolisation was ongoing in many cities, the phenomenon and its measurement were ignored by governments and public policy for many decades.

Similarly, various economic, political and constitutional reforms to municipal powers and land regulation have underestimated the trend towards metropolisation. Despite its intensive and widespread expansion, there is no legal recognition of metropolitan areas, and in consequence there are no adequate instruments for their governability and governance (Zentella, 2007; Garza, 2010; Negrete, 2010; Jalomo, 2011). With the exception of conurbations, metropolitan areas are not recognised in Mexico's constitution, and juridical normativity does not consider the establishment of metropolitan governments; it only allows the formation of metropolitan commissions with limited powers (Moreno, 2005).

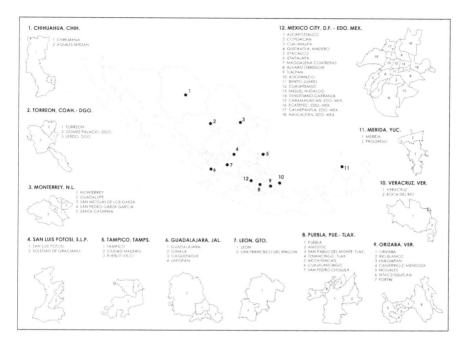

Figure 3.4 Metropolitan areas in Mexico in 1960

Source: Based on Unikel (2016).

In spite of the absence of an adequate institutional framework for coping with metropolitan expansion, in 2004, 55 metropolitan areas were identified by a group of central government agencies employing data from the 1990 census. Thereafter the government undertook more systematic delimitations, finding 56 metropolitan areas across the country in 2007 using data from the 2005 census, 59 in 2012 based on the 2010 census, and, using 2015 survey data, 74 in 2018 with a total of 75 million inhabitants, representing 63 per cent of the country's total population and 76 per cent of its urban population. Each of the Mexican states has at least one metropolitan area, and overall 417 Mexican municipalities belong to a metropolitan area.[2]

From 1960 to 2015 the number of metropolitan areas increased sixfold, its population multiplied by 800 per cent, the number of municipalities increased by 600 per cent and their participation in the national population more than doubled (SEDATU, CONAPO & INEGI, 2018). Figure 3.5 includes a number of indicators showing the evolution of the metropolitan phenomenon.

The latest delimitation of metropolitan areas in Mexico is based on several criteria: population size, functional (labour market and commuting) and

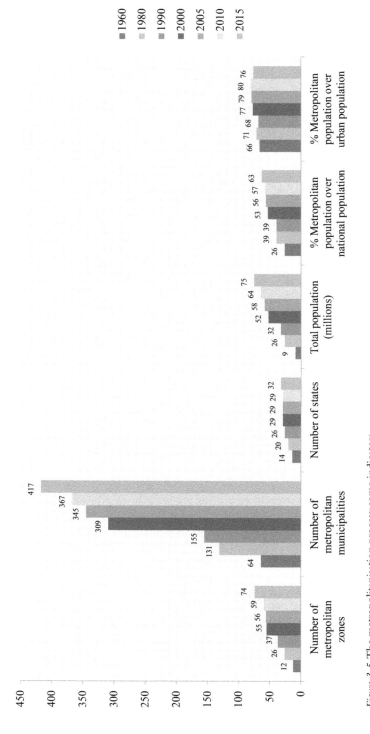

Figure 3.5 The metropolitanisation process: some indicators

Source: Based on SEDATU, CONAPO and INEGI (2018).

physical integration, productive structure, distance between population centres, density and public policy. It defines metropolitan areas (zones) as:

> Two or more municipalities where a city of 100,000 inhabitants or more is located, whose urban area, functions and activities exceed the limits of the municipality, incorporating directly within its area of influence neighbouring municipalities, predominantly urban, with which it maintains a high degree of socioeconomic integration. Also, it includes those municipalities that due to their particular characteristics are relevant to planning and urban policy in a given metropolitan area.[3]
>
> (SEDATU, CONAPO & INEGI, 2018, p. 34)

In addition, metropolitan areas incorporate municipalities with a city of more than 500,000 inhabitants, those with cities of 200,000 or more inhabitants located on the Mexico's northern and southern borders or in a coastal zone and cities with a state capital (ibid.). Overall, central and outer (contiguous and non-contiguous) municipalities are part of the 74 metropolitan areas (Figure 3.6).

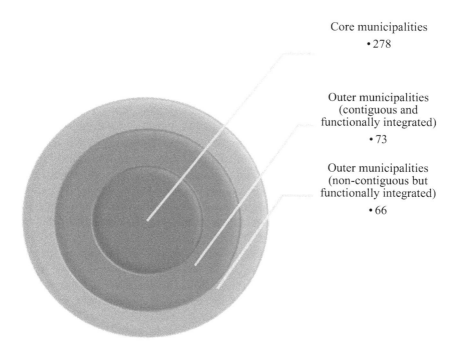

Core municipalities
• 278

Outer municipalities
(contiguous and
functionally integrated)
• 73

Outer municipalities
(non-contiguous but
functionally integrated)
• 66

Figure 3.6 Number of metropolitan municipalities in Mexico by category

Source: Based on SEDATU, CONAPO and INEGI (2018).

Metropolitan size and inter-metropolitan population distribution

Metropolitan areas involve a twofold tendency: the general concentration of people and the economy in a few big cities, and the deconcentration of population and economies activities via a sprawl from the central city to its periphery and going beyond the administrative limits (Douay, 2008). As argued earlier, the worldwide process of metropolisation has been relatively more rapid and uncontrolled in developing countries, where high and rapid urbanisation have contributed to the over-concentration of economic, political and administrative functions. In these countries metropolisation and increased spatial inequalities are seen in close interaction, hindering not only overall economic growth but also having a debilitating impact on the stability of their social and political development (Bronger, 1984). These disparities are perceptible at various levels: intra-urban, inter-urban and international.

Unbalanced patterns of development among a country's metropolitan areas are a common trait. Regardless of the overall urbanisation of a country, its cities and urban agglomerations are highly heterogeneous. Whereas metropolitan areas are places of economic opportunity, there is both real and potential national and international competition with other cities for resources. Only some metropolitan areas show greater dynamism and ability to build competitive and productive spaces (Méndez, 2007).

As far as Mexico is concerned, important asymmetries across metropolitan areas are uncovered. This section discusses the organisation of the system of metropolitan areas, taking into consideration population size and its spatial distribution over the past 25 years. The following section will address population dynamics and migration attraction across metropolitan areas. In order to be able to make comparisons across time, I use the metropolitan areas identified in 2015 and apply this delimitation to census data from 1990, 2000 and 2010.

In 2015 Mexico had a total population of 119.5 million. Of these, 63 per cent (roughly 75 million) lived in 74 metropolitan areas. The country had one huge metropolitan area with a population of more than 10 million concentrating 28 per cent of Mexico's metropolitan population; 12 'millionaire' metropolitan areas with over a million residents accounting for 34 per cent of the national metropolitan population; 23 medium-sized metropolitan areas representing 24 per cent; and 38 small metropolitan areas comprising 14 per cent of the total metropolitan population (Table 3.2).

Figure 3.7 shows the geographic location of the 74 metropolitan areas by population size. Eight metropolitan agglomerations are located at the border with the US: Tijuana, Mexicali, Nogales, Ciudad Juarez, Piedras Negras, Matamoros, Nuevo Laredo and Reynosa-Rio Bravo. Some metropolitan areas, for instance Guaymas, Puerto Vallarta, Tecoman, Acapulco, Cancun, Coatzacoalcos, Veracruz and Tampico, are near seaports and coastal tourist developments. The rest are located inland, and of these a large proportion lie in a belt across the centre of the country.

Table 3.2 Population distribution in Mexico, 2015

	Inhabitants (000)	% of total population	Number of metropolitan areas
National	119,531	100	
Non-metropolitan	44,434	37.2	
Metropolitan	75,097	62.8	
Metropolitan	75,097	100	74
Mega metropolis (≥ 10,000,000)	20,893	27.8	1
Millionaire (9,999,999 ≥ 1,000,000)	25,735	34.3	12
Medium (999,999 ≥ 500,000)	17,890	23.8	23
Small (≤ 500,000)	10,576	14.1	38

Source: Based on INEGI (2015).

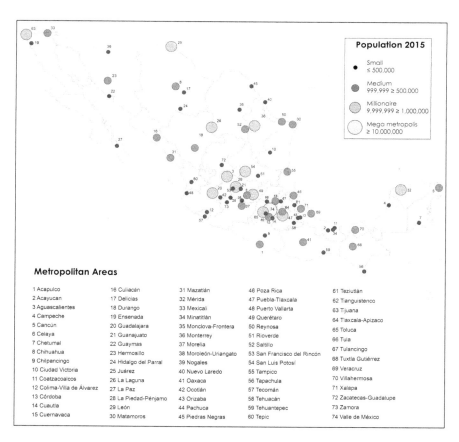

Figure 3.7 Metropolitan areas according to population size, 2015

Source: Based on INEGI (2015).

A pattern of overconcentrated population in a few urban agglomerations was evident over the twentieth century. Much of the concern with urbanisation has focused on the growth of the primate city and a few others. A significant proportion of the national population has concentrated in Mexico City, Guadalajara and Monterrey, the main Mexican cities. An important reorganisation of the urban system occurred in the 1980s, partly due to changes in demographic dynamics, and partly in response to various government measures to restructure the economy. However, the population remains concentrated in the biggest metropolitan areas. In 2015 the population of the largest metropolitan area, Mexico City, was slowly approaching 21 million and contained 27.8 per cent of the metropolitan population and 17.5 per cent of the national population (see Table 3.5 in the Annex). The 12 millionaire metropolitan areas, Guadalajara, Monterrey, Puebla-Tlaxcala, Toluca, Tijuana, Leon, Ciudad Juarez, La Laguna, Queretaro, San Luis Potosi, Merida and Aguascalientes, homed 25.7 million people altogether.

The average population of the metropolitan area increased to more than a million in 2015. However, demographic concentration in Mexico City and the millionaire cities on the one hand, and the small metropolitan areas (the smallest with a population of 113,000 inhabitants in clear contrast to Mexico City's almost 21 million) on the other hand, makes the average population a biased indicator. In contrast to the mean, the median population in 2015 was 481,000.

Some authors have argued that even though the Mexico City Metropolitan Area continues to hold a significant proportion of the Mexican population, the strong verticality in the spatial distribution of population has reduced over time (Rionda-Ramírez, 2007). The relative weight of Mexico City has decreased over the past three decades from 33 per cent of total metropolitan population in 1990 to 28 per cent in 2015. In contrast, the populations of the metropolitan areas Tijuana and Monterrey in the north of the country, Toluca and Queretaro in the centre of the country and Cancun, a coastal tourist city, have increased. According to the coefficient of variation, the differences in population sizes across metropolitan areas decreased between 1990 and 2015, and there has been some rearrangement at the top of the population distribution. While in 1990 the Mexico City Metropolitan Area was 5 times bigger than the second metropolitan area, Guadalajara, in 2015 this had dropped to only 4.1 times bigger. Similarly, Mexico City was 5.8 times larger than Monterrey, the third most populated metropolitan area, in 1990, but only 4.5 times larger in 2015. Although the demographic weight of many cities has increased, there remain significant disparities in the distribution of the population, since the metropolitan area of Mexico City and the 12 millionaire metropolitan areas contain 62 per cent of the metropolitan population.

I examined the size distribution of metropolitan areas in Mexico to check whether it shows an important primacy. I used a simple and straightforward tool, Zipf's law, which establishes that if we consider n cities from a country and sort them according to their size from 1 to n, the city in rank i will have a population equal to that of the largest city divided by i. Thus, the second-rank city will have half the population of the first; the third, a third; and so on (Vargas et al., 2017).

Zipf's law is also known as the 'rank-size rule' and describes an empirical regularity which is useful for identifying the primacy of a country's main cities. The law is satisfied when the coefficient that correlates the logarithm of the rank of each city with the logarithm of its population is equal to −1. If the coefficient is greater than −1 (i.e. the absolute value is less than 1), this suggests that cities of lower rank than the first city also have a large population and there is no primacy. On the other hand, if the coefficient is less than −1 (or its absolute value is greater than 1), the populations of the lower-order cities are small relative to the Zipf prediction, and there is a primacy of the main city in the city-size distribution within a country (ibid.). Empirical evidence and examples of the stability of Zipf's law can be found in the cities of the US in 1970–1990, in France in 1831–1982, and in general in Russia, England, China and India (Batten, 2001).

According to the rank-size rule, in Mexico the metropolitan area of Guadalajara will have half and Monterrey a third of the population of Mexico City, and so on. According to estimations for 1990, 2000, 2010 and 2015, the empirical size distribution of Mexican cities complies with Zipf's law. The coefficient is very close to −1 in all periods (Figure 3.8); at least the data for

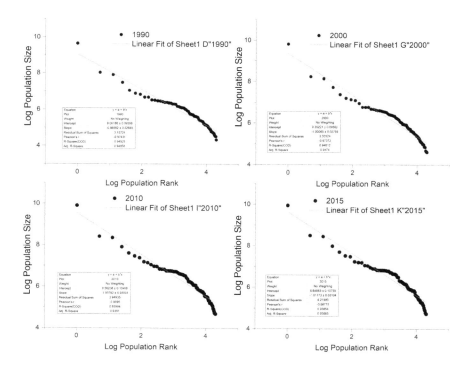

Figure 3.8 Zipf's law in Mexican metropolitan areas, 1990, 2000, 2010 and 2015

Source: Based on INEGI (1991, 2001 & 2011).

those years confirms the presence of a size distribution in which Mexico City retains significant primacy.

Population growth and migration attraction

Population growth can exhibit high heterogeneity because cities' growth prospects reflect very different demographic paths and dynamics. According to Garza (2003), between 1990 and 1995 population growth was concentrated in Mexico's cities and metropolitan areas. The cities of Tijuana and Ciudad Juarez had the highest population growth rates, which was related to the presence of a large maquiladora industry. The industrial cities Cuernavaca, Queretaro, Toluca, Aguascalientes and Leon also saw relatively high population growth.

Following the change in the economic model, in the 1990–2000 period the biggest metropolitan areas started to grow more slowly while medium-sized metropolitan areas with seaports and at the US border grew more rapidly. These urban centres' expanding labour markets attracted immigrants (Rionda-Ramírez, 2007; see also Table 3.5). Cancun, a tourist city, and Tijuana, a border city, were the most dynamic metropolitan areas with population average annual growth rates (AAGR) of over 4 per cent, compared to the metropolitan average of 2.0 per cent. Other tourist and industrial border cities such as Puerto Vallarta (AAGR 3.8 per cent), Ciudad Juarez (3.5 per cent) and Nogales (3.3 per cent) also saw high demographic growth, and another 35 metropolitan areas grew at above average rates. However, Mexico City's AAGR during this period was only 1.5 percent, below average metropolitan growth. The populations of the two other biggest metropolitan areas, Guadalajara and Monterrey, grew at 1.9 and 2.1 per cent respectively, slightly below the AAGR, confirming the decelerating population growth in the largest metropolitan areas.

Between 2000 and 2010, Mexico's total metropolitan population experienced a demographic slowdown, with the AAGR falling to 1.6 per cent, with a declining AAGR recorded in 48 metropolitan areas. Among these, the population of Ciudad Juarez dropped dramatically from 3.5 per cent average growth in the previous decade to 0.9 per cent. From the 1960s the promise of maquiladora jobs had attracted people from other parts of Mexico. Regardless of the economic and industrial attractiveness of Ciudad Juarez, in the 1990s the city started to have acute problems with violence and crime, which were uncontrolled due to the drug market. Tijuana, another big metropolitan area at the US border, underwent a similar demographic slowdown associated with issues of violence and lack of security. Cancun, Matamoros and Cuernavaca's AAGRs dropped by more than 1 percentage point.

Despite this, Cancun remained the most dynamic city, with an AAGR of 4.5 per cent, followed by Puerto Vallarta at 4.4 per cent. These two tourist cities boomed in the 1990s, increasing their attraction for migrant workers in search of jobs. Nogales and Reynosa at the US border and Pachuca and Queretaro in Mexico's Central Region had high growth rates. Mexico City ranked among the 10 least dynamic cities, with an AAGR of less than 1 per cent; Guadalajara and Monterrey kept growing at almost the same rate as in the previous period. Overall, tourist and border cities were highly dynamic.

Data for 2010–2015 reveals a reversal of trends. The AAGR in the metropolitan population dropped to 1.4 per cent. Nogales and Reynosa experienced a reduction in their AAGR of almost 2 percentage points and were growing at below the metropolitan AAGR. However, while Puerto Vallarta and Cancun's AAGRs also fell by 2 per cent, they remained among the 10 most dynamic metropolitan areas. Tehuacan and Queretaro in the central region and Mazatlan and Hermosillo in the northwest had the highest population growth. Of the largest metropolitan areas, Mexico City grew at only 0.8 per cent annually, Guadalajara's AAGR dropped to 1.3 per cent, and Monterrey continued to grow at 2.2 per cent.

In Table 3.3 the metropolitan areas are grouped according to their growth rates. In 1990–2000 some metropolitan areas were growing dynamically at rates

Table 3.3 Metropolitan areas by population growth rate

1990–2000	2000–2010	2010–2015
3.1–5.7%	3.1–5.7%	3.1–5.7%
Cancun, Tijuana, Puerto Vallarta, Ciudad Juarez, Nogales, Tehuacan	Cancun, Puerto Vallarta, Reynosa, Nogales, Pachuca	Tehuacan
2.1–3.0%	2.1–3.0%	2.1–3.0%
Tuxtla Gutierrez, Ensenada, Nuevo Laredo, Toluca, Queretaro, Reynosa, Oaxaca, Matamoros, Cuernavaca, Villahermosa, Chilpancingo, Tianguistenco, Hermosillo, Pachuca, Teziutlan, Aguascalientes, Tlaxcala-Apizaco, Cuautla, Saltillo, Tulancingo, Piedras Negras, Leon, Colima-Villa de Álvarez, Puebla-Tlaxcala, San Luis Potosi Xalapa, Tepic, Zacatecas-Guadalupe, Monterrey, Merida, Mexicali, Chihuahua, Ciudad Victoria, San Francisco del Rincon	Queretaro, Tuxtla Gutierrez, Tijuana, Saltillo, Hermosillo, Aguascalientes, Zacatecas-Guadalupe, La Paz, Leon, Ensenada, Toluca, Villahermosa, Tepic, San Francisco del Rincon, Monterrey, Nuevo Laredo, Tehuacan, Chilpancingo, Tulancingo, Tianguistenco	Mazatlan, Queretaro, Hermosillo, Saltillo, Cancun, Durango, Chilpancingo, Aguascalientes, Puerto Vallarta, Zacatecas, Guadalupe, Monterrey, Tuxtla Gutierrez

(Continued)

Table 3.3 (Continued)

1990–2000	2000–2010	2010–2015
1.1–2.0%	1.1–2.0%	1.1–2.0%
Morelia, Campeche, Tehuantepec, Guadalajara, Culiacan, Veracruz, Mazatlan, Tapachula, La Paz, Tula, Acapulco, Celaya, Chetumal, Ocotlan, Durango, Guanajuato, Mexico City, Orizaba, Cordoba, Zamora, Tecoman, Tampico, La Laguna, Coatzacoalcos, Acayucan, Delicias	Mexicali, Chihuahua, Morelia, Tlaxcala-Apizaco, Ciudad Victoria, San Luis Potosi, Oaxaca, Colima-Villa de Álvarez, Tula, Guanajuato, Guadalajara, Puebla-Tlaxcala, La Laguna, Merida, Xalapa, Celaya, Durango, Campeche, Piedras Negras, Teziutlan, Veracruz, Tapachula, Chetumal, Matamoros, Cuautla, Delicias, Cuernavaca, Tampico, Culiacan, Mazatlan, Zamora, Cordoba, Coatzacoalcos, Guaymas, Orizaba, Monclova-Frontera, Tehuantepec, Ocotlan	Leon, Veracruz, Morelia, Tepic, Cordoba, Toluca, Cuautla, Campeche, Tula, San Francisco del Rincon, San Luis Potosi, Villahermosa, Pachuca, Tapachula, Merida, Oaxaca, Tlaxcala-Apizaco, La Paz, Guadalajara, Puebla-Tlaxcala, Chihuahua, Xalapa, Tianguistenco, Tecoman, Monclova-Frontera, Colima-Villa de Álvarez, Ciudad Victoria, Tulancingo, Piedras Negras, Guanajuato, Ocotlan, Teziutlan, Tampico, Cuernavaca, Reynosa, Matamoros, Orizaba, Zamora, Nogales, Tehuantepec, Acayucan, Celaya, Delicias, Tijuana, La Laguna, Mexicali, Culiacan, Coatzacoalcos, Guaymas
0–1.0%	0–1.0%	0–1.0%
Monclova-Frontera, Hidalgo del Parral, Rioverde, MoroLeon-Uriangato, Poza Rica, Minatitlan, La Piedad-Penjamo, Guaymas	Tecoman, Mexico City, Ciudad Juarez, Poza Rica, Minatitlan, Acayucan, Acapulco, La Piedad, Penjamo, MoroLeon-Uriangato, Rioverde, Hidalgo del Parral	Poza Rica, Ciudad Juarez, Ensenada, Minatitlan, MoroLeon-Uriangato, Mexico City, Nuevo Laredo, Acapulco, Rioverde, Hidalgo del Parral, La Piedad-Penjamo, Chetumal

Source: Based on INEGI (1991, 2001 & 2011).

as high as 5.7 per cent, although most were closer to 2.1 to 3 per cent. After 2000, the majority of metropolitan areas grew at 1.1 to 2 per cent, but increasingly metropolitan areas are growing at less than 1 per cent.

Regarding the other relevant driver of urbanisation and metropolisation, Romo, Téllez and López (2013) find that the composition of Mexico's internal migration has changed according to the country's urban context. Rural–urban migration has fallen and urban–urban flows have intensified, in line with changes in migration trends in Latin America's most urbanised countries. Intra-metropolitan migration has also been gaining ground. Based on the previous delimitation of metropolitan areas (59 metropolises in 2012), they estimate that between 1995 and 2000 the largest net migration rate (the difference between the number of immigrants and the number of emigrants divided by the total population and expressed per thousand inhabitants) occurred in the metropolitan areas of Cancun (27.3 migrants per thousand inhabitants), Reynosa-Rio Bravo (17.1) and Ciudad Juarez (13.8), followed by Tijuana, Puerto Vallarta and Toluca. Veracruz (−12.1), Acayucan (−11.1) and Minatitlan (−10.2) metropolitan areas, all in the state of Veracruz, had net negative migration rates.

Between 2005 and 2010, Puerto Vallarta (11.7 migrants per thousand inhabitants), Cancun (10.9) and Colima-Villa de Álvarez (9.5) had the largest net migration rates, followed by Reynosa-Rio Bravo, Pachuca and Queretaro; Tehuantepec (−5.5) and Acapulco (−4.0) had negative rates. The five largest metropolitan areas had the largest number of migrants in 2005–2010, and the rank according to population matches the rank according to the volume of migrants. Overall, some cities located at the US border, in the centre of the country and in coastal tourist developments attracted the most migrants. Over time some metropolitan areas have lost their migrant attraction, while that of tourist and metropolitan areas near Mexico City has increased (Romo, Téllez & López, 2013).

Data on migration status at the level of municipalities from 2000 and 2010 includes the 417 metropolitan municipalities according to the 2015 delimitation. In this data, municipalities are grouped into five different categories of attractiveness to migrants: high attraction, intermediate attraction, equilibrium, intermediate expulsion and high expulsion. In both periods the category that predominates in most of the municipalities is high attraction, followed by intermediate attraction. In 2000 almost 66 per cent of all metropolitan municipalities had a positive migratory balance, 7 per cent were in equilibrium and 27 per cent were expulsion municipalities. In 2010, the percentage of metropolitan municipalities with high and intermediate attraction had fallen (Table 3.4).

High-attraction municipalities are mainly located in the centre and northeast of the country. The largest metropolitan areas are important attraction centres for immigrants, although in 2000 Monterrey and Mexico City had a high proportion of expulsion municipalities, as did Ciudad Juarez, Acapulco, Tapachula, Nogales and Guanajuato (Figure 3.9).

In 2010 the number of attraction municipalities increased in Mexico City, Monterrey, Tijuana and Reynosa. Ciudad Juarez, Matamoros and Nogales changed from high-expulsion to high-attraction metropolitan areas, while La Laguna and Monclova-Frontera (in the state of Coahuila), Cuernavaca and

Table 3.4 Distribution of metropolitan municipalities according to migration category

	2000		2010	
	Number of municipalities	*% of total*	*Number of municipalities*	*% of total*
High attraction	182	43.6	156	37.4
Intermediate attraction	92	22.1	98	23.5
Equilibrium	29	7	27	6.5
Intermediate expulsion	42	10.1	71	17
High expulsion	72	17.3	65	15.6
Total	417	100	417	100

Source: Based on CONAPO (2017).

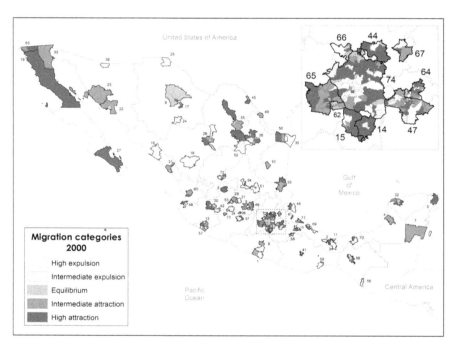

Figure 3.9 Metropolitan municipalities by migration category, 2000

Source: Based on CONAPO (2017).

Cuautla (Morelos), Veracruz, Minatitlan and Coatzacoalcos (Veracruz), and Tehuantepec (Oaxaca) and Merida (Yucatan) became expulsion metropolitan areas (Figure 3.10).

According to population growth and migration trends, some metropolitan areas are experiencing little or no dynamism. Mazatlan and Ensenada in the

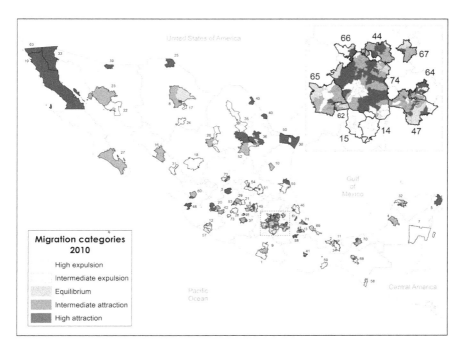

Figure 3.10 Metropolitan municipalities by migration category, 2010

Source: Based on CONAPO (2017).

northwest of the country, Veracruz in the east and Cuautla in the centre became metropolitan areas of migratory expulsion in 2015. In addition to becoming cities of net emigration, Celaya, Poza Rica, Coatzacoalcos, Cuernavaca, Acapulco, Colima, Monclova, La Laguna, Tampico, Chetumal, Tehuantepec, Delicias and Guanajuato grew very slowly between 2000 and 2010.

Concluding comments

Mexico's urbanisation and metropolisation have been rooted in its economic development models and industrialisation, but also in pre-existing concentrations of population and political power. Its metropolitan dynamism was initially driven by large rural migratory flows to big cities, with migration often contributing to cities' peripheral expansion as immigrants settled farther from the urban core. These peripheral settlements contributed to the consolidation of a pattern of metropolitan expansion. Even though early metropolitan growth was nourished by rural–urban migration and peripheral expansion, more recently migration patterns have changed both quantitatively and qualitatively. A large proportion of migration is now intra-metropolitan, usually from the centre to the periphery (Cerruti & Bertoncello, 2003).

A feature of metropolisation in Mexico which generally differs from that in the developed world is that its metropolitan areas are typically populated by medium- and low-income dwellers. Low-income groups who could not afford to live in the central city moved to the peripheries. These economically disadvantaged peripheries have become a common feature of large metropolitan areas in Latin America, although more recently they have become a more complex social environment due to the presence of different income groups which, however, tend to be segregated.

Even though metropolisation in Mexico has been similar in several ways to that in other Latin American countries, the specific context determines how urban and metropolitan developments are experienced. In Brazil, for instance, due to its huge territory four times the size of Mexico, the urban structure is more complex but also less centralised. Whereas the main population concentration in Mexico is found in only one city, in Brazil there are two cities of comparable importance: Rio de Janeiro, with approximately 11 million inhabitants, and Sao Paulo, with more than 19 million, and explicit efforts have been made to decentralise the urban system, including the construction of the new capital city, Brasilia.

Their legal recognition of metropolitan areas has made a fundamental difference to countries such as Colombia and Brazil. Brazil's institutionalisation of metropolitan areas dates back to a complementary act of 1973 which recognised nine such in the country. Brazil defines metropolitan areas as regional entities and recognises them in its constitution, while the Mexican constitution only recognises conurbations, and its so-called metropolitan zones have no legal status in the political-administrative structure of the country. In practical terms, the lack of a clear and homogeneous institutional definition of the metropolitan area is a common issue in Latin America. There are no specific criteria for how it should be measured, managed or planned, and most countries do not recognise metropolitan areas in their constitution.

Summing up, historical patterns of concentration, economic models, and local governance and regulation structures help to explain the development of large metropolitan areas such as Mexico City, Sao Paulo and Rio de Janeiro. However, the diversity of local and national factors requires closer inspection in specific countries. In particular, understanding how the interplay of factors including market forces and public policies, regulations and the political economy determine the internal structure of cities is fundamental. The absence of adequate planning and governance, for instance, challenges the viability of metropolitan territories in such varied contexts as those that exist across both the region and the less-developed world.

Annex

Table 3.5 Mexico's population, distribution and growth in 1990, 2000, 2010 and 2015

Metropolitan Area	Total population (thousand)				% of total metropolitan population				Annual average growth rate (%)		
	1990	2000	2010	2015	1990	2000	2010	2015	1990–2000	2000–2010	2010–2015
Total MAs	47,481	59,484	70,165	75,097	100	100	100	100	2	1.6	1.4
Mexico City	15,564	18,397	20,117	20,893	32.8	30.9	28.7	27.8	1.5	0.9	0.8
Guadalajara	3,058	3,773	4,522	4,887	6.4	6.3	6.4	6.5	1.9	1.8	1.6
Monterrey	2,704	3,426	4,226	4,690	5.7	5.8	6	6.2	2.1	2.1	2.2
Puebla–Tlaxcala	1,777	2,270	2,729	2,942	3.7	3.8	3.9	3.9	2.2	1.8	1.6
Toluca	1,156	1,606	2,014	2,203	2.4	2.7	2.9	2.9	2.8	2.2	1.9
Tijuana	799	1,352	1,751	1,841	1.7	2.3	2.5	2.5	4.1	2.5	1.1
Leon	983	1,269	1,610	1,768	2.1	2.1	2.3	2.4	2.3	2.3	2
Ciudad Juarez	798	1,219	1,332	1,391	1.7	2	1.9	1.9	3.5	0.9	0.9
La Laguna	929	1,054	1,271	1,342	2	1.8	1.8	1.8	1.2	1.8	1.1
Queretaro	628	873	1,161	1,324	1.3	1.5	1.7	1.8	2.8	2.8	2.8
San Luis Potosi	678	873	1,065	1,160	1.4	1.5	1.5	1.5	2.2	1.9	1.8
Merida	689	873	1,054	1,143	1.5	1.5	1.5	1.5	2.1	1.8	1.7
Aguascalientes	547	728	932	1,044	1.2	1.2	1.3	1.4	2.5	2.4	2.4
Mexicali	602	765	937	988	1.3	1.3	1.3	1.3	2.1	2	1.1
Cuernavaca	587	799	925	983	1.2	1.3	1.3	1.3	2.7	1.4	1.3
Saltillo	487	637	823	924	1	1.1	1.2	1.2	2.4	2.5	2.5
Chihuahua	552	696	853	918	1.2	1.2	1.2	1.2	2.1	2	1.6
Tampico	649	746	859	917	1.4	1.3	1.2	1.2	1.3	1.4	1.4
Veracruz	580	708	834	915	1.2	1.2	1.2	1.2	1.8	1.6	2

(Continued)

Table 3.5 (Continued)

Metropolitan Area	Total population (thousand)				% of total metropolitan population				Annual average growth rate (%)		
	1990	2000	2010	2015	1990	2000	2010	2015	1990–2000	2000–2010	2010–2015
Morelia	543	679	830	912	1.1	1.1	1.2	1.2	2	2	2
Culiacan	601	746	859	905	1.3	1.3	1.2	1.2	1.9	1.4	1.1
Acapulco	654	792	863	887	1.4	1.3	1.2	1.2	1.7	0.8	0.6
Hermosillo	449	610	784	884	0.9	1	1.1	1.1	2.6	2.5	2.6
Villahermosa	438	601	755	823	0.9	1	1.1	1.1	2.7	2.2	1.8
Tuxtla Gutierrez	398	566	738	814	0.8	1	1.1	1.1	3	2.6	2.1
Reynosa	377	525	727	773	0.8	0.9	1	1	2.8	3.2	1.3
Xalapa	461	591	711	768	1	1	1	1	2.2	1.8	1.6
Cancun	187	431	677	763	0.4	0.7	1	1	5.7	4.5	2.5
Celaya	480	578	690	732	1	1	1	1	1.7	1.7	1.2
Oaxaca	366	509	619	671	0.8	0.9	0.9	0.9	2.8	1.9	1.7
Durango	414	491	582	655	0.9	0.8	0.8	0.9	1.6	1.7	2.5
Pachuca	277	375	512	557	0.6	0.6	0.7	0.7	2.6	3.1	1.8
Tlaxcala-Apizaco	304	408	500	540	0.6	0.7	0.7	0.7	2.5	2	1.7
Poza Rica	446	467	514	538	0.9	0.8	0.7	0.7	0.4	0.9	1
Matamoros	303	418	489	520	0.6	0.7	0.7	0.7	2.8	1.5	1.3
Mazatlan	314	381	438	503	0.7	0.6	0.6	0.7	1.8	1.4	2.9
Ensenada	260	371	467	487	0.5	0.6	0.7	0.6	3	2.3	0.9
Cuautla	280	372	434	475	0.6	0.6	0.6	0.6	2.5	1.5	1.9
Tepic	268	343	429	471	0.6	0.6	0.6	0.6	2.2	2.2	2
Orizaba	331	384	430	457	0.7	0.6	0.6	0.6	1.4	1.1	1.3
Puerto Vallarta	151	245	380	426	0.3	0.4	0.5	0.6	3.8	4.4	2.4
Nuevo Laredo	219	311	384	399	0.5	0.5	0.5	0.5	3	2.1	0.8
Zacatecas-Guadalupe	206	263	336	376	0.4	0.4	0.5	0.5	2.2	2.4	2.4
Minatitlan	311	323	356	372	0.7	0.5	0.5	0.5	0.4	0.9	0.9
Coatzacoalcos	272	308	347	365	0.6	0.5	0.5	0.5	1.2	1.2	1.1
Monclova-Frontera	282	303	339	364	0.6	0.5	0.5	0.5	0.7	1.1	1.5

Colima–Villa de Álvarez	212	276	334	359	0.4	0.5	0.5	0.5	2.3	1.9	1.5
Tapachula	222	272	320	348	0.5	0.5	0.5	0.5	1.8	1.6	1.8
Cordoba	238	277	316	348	0.5	0.5	0.5	0.5	1.4	1.3	2
Ciudad Victoria	208	263	322	346	0.4	0.4	0.5	0.5	2.1	2	1.5
Tehuacan	165	241	297	345	0.3	0.4	0.4	0.5	3.2	2.1	3.2
Chilpancingo	169	233	288	324	0.4	0.4	0.4	0.4	2.7	2.1	2.5
Campeche	174	217	259	283	0.4	0.4	0.4	0.4	2	1.7	1.9
La Paz	161	197	252	273	0.3	0.4	0.4	0.4	1.8	2.4	1.7
Zamora	185	216	250	266	0.4	0.4	0.4	0.4	1.4	1.4	1.3
Tulancingo	147	194	240	257	0.3	0.3	0.4	0.4	2.4	2.1	1.5
La Piedad-Penjamo	219	229	250	254	0.5	0.4	0.3	0.3	0.4	0.8	0.4
Nogales	108	160	220	234	0.2	0.3	0.3	0.3	3.3	3.2	1.3
Tula	140	170	206	225	0.3	0.3	0.3	0.3	1.8	1.9	1.9
Chetumal	173	208	245	224	0.4	0.3	0.3	0.3	1.7	1.6	-1.8
Guaymas	175	180	203	214	0.4	0.3	0.3	0.3	0.3	1.2	1.1
San Francisco del Rincon	114	145	182	199	0.2	0.3	0.3	0.3	2.1	2.2	1.9
Tehuantepec	130	163	183	195	0.3	0.3	0.3	0.3	2	1.1	1.3
Piedras Negras	115	151	181	194	0.2	0.3	0.3	0.3	2.4	1.7	1.5
Delicias	139	156	182	193	0.3	0.3	0.3	0.3	1.1	1.5	1.2
Guanajuato	119	141	172	184	0.3	0.2	0.2	0.2	1.6	1.9	1.5
Ocotlan	121	146	164	176	0.3	0.2	0.2	0.2	1.7	1.1	1.5
Tianguistenco	93	127	158	170	0.2	0.2	0.2	0.2	2.7	2.1	1.6
Tecoman	110	128	141	153	0.2	0.2	0.2	0.2	1.4	1	1.6
Rioverde	121	129	135	140	0.3	0.2	0.2	0.2	0.6	0.5	0.6
Teziutlan	76	103	123	132	0.2	0.2	0.2	0.2	2.6	1.7	1.5
Acayucan	91	103	113	120	0.2	0.2	0.2	0.2	1.2	0.9	1.3
Hidalgo del Parral	100	107	112	115	0.2	0.2	0.2	0.2	0.7	0.4	0.5
MoroLeon–Uriangato	95	100	109	113	0.2	0.2	0.2	0.2	0.5	0.8	0.9
Mean	642	804	948	1,015					2.1	1.8	1.6
Median	281	374	436	481							
Variation coef.	2.9	2.7	2.5	2.5					0.4	0.4	0.5

Source: Based on INEGI (1990, 2000 & 2010).

Notes

1   Some regulations and programmes have to delimit urban expansion by means of physical limits and imposing civil and legal sanctions. In particular, the illegal sale and purchase of *ejido* land were sanctioned.
2   Mexico is divided into 32 states and 2,474 municipalities.
3   My translation.

References

Angotti, T. (2013). 'Urban Latin America: Violence, enclaves, and struggles for land'. *Latin American Perspectives*, 40(2), 5–20. Available at: https://journals.sagepub.com/doi/pdf/10.1177/0094582X12466832.
Batten, D. F. (2001). 'Complex landscapes of spatial interaction'. *The Annals of Regional Science*, 35(1), 81–111. Available at: https://doi.org/10.1007/s001680000032.
Bronger, D. (1984). 'Metropolisation in China?' *GeoJournal*, 8(2), 137–146. Available at: https://doi.org/10.1007/BF00231492.
Cerrutti, M. & Bertoncello, R. (2003). Urbanization and internal migration patterns in Latin America. Paper prepared for Conference on African migration in comparative perspective, Johannesburg, South Africa, 4–7 June, 2003.
CONAPO. (2017). *Categoría migratoria municipal 1995–2000 y 2005–2010, Datos abiertos* [online]. Available at: https://datos.gob.mx/busca/dataset/migracion-interna/resource/04a76ab7-0581-4066-be6d-3a1caf3dc3e1.
Douay, N. (2008). 'From urban corridor to Megalopolis: The Taiwanese metropolisation'. Presented at the 5th Congress of the European Association of Taiwan Studies, Prague. Available at: www.soas.ac.uk/taiwanstudies/eats/eats2008/file43175.pdf.
Garza, G. (2003). *La urbanización en México en el siglo XX*. México, D. F.: El Colegio de México.
Garza, G. (2010). 'La transformación urbana de México, 1970–2020'. In Garza, G. & Schteingart, M. (eds.). *Los grandes problemas de México: Desarrollo urbano y regional. T-II*. Mexico, D. F.: El Colegio de Mexico, pp. 31–86. Available at: www.jstor.org/stable/j.ctt1657tf2.5.
IDB. (2015). *The experience of Latin America and the Caribbean in urbanization*. Discussion paper No. IDB-DP-395. Inter-American Development Bank.
INEGI. (1991). *XI Censo General de Población y Vivienda 1990* [online]. Available at: www.beta.inegi.org.mx/proyectos/ccpv/1990/default.html.
INEGI. (2001). *XII Censo General de Población y Vivienda 2000* [online]. Available at: www.beta.inegi.org.mx/proyectos/ccpv/2000/default.html.
INEGI. (2011). *Censo de Población y Vivienda 2010* [online]. Available at: www.beta.inegi.org.mx/proyectos/ccpv/2010/.
INEGI. (2015). Encuesta intercensal 2015 [online]. Available at: www.beta.inegi.org.mx/proyectos/enchogares/especiales/intercensal/.
Jalomo Aguirre, F. (2011). *Gobernar el territorio entre descentralización y metropolización*. Colección Graduados, Serie Sociales y Humanidades, No. 13. Guadalajara, Jalisco: Universidad de Guadalajara. Available at: www.publicaciones.cucsh.udg.mx/pperiod/cgraduados/pdf/sin/1_Gobernar_el_territorio%20_entre_descentralizacion_y_metropolizacion.pdf.
Jordan, R., Riffo, L. & Prado, A. (eds.) (2017). *Desarrollo sostenible, urbanización y desigualdad en América Latina y el Caribe: Dinámicas y desafíos para el cambio structural*. Santiago: CEPAL. Available at: www.cepal.org/es/publicaciones/42141-desarrollo-sostenible-urbanizacion-desigualdad-america-latina-caribe-dinamicas.
Lang, R. & Knox, P. K. (2009). 'The new metropolis: Rethinking megalopolis'. *Regional Studies*, 43(6), 789–802. Available at: https://doi.org/10.1080/00343400701654251.

Legorreta, J. (1991). 'Expansión urbana, mercado del suelo y estructura de poder en la ciudad de México'. *Revista mexicana de ciencias políticas y sociales*, 36(145), 45–76.

Méndez, R. (2007). 'El territorio de las nuevas economías metropolitanas'. *Revista EURE*, XXXIII(100), pp. 51–67. Available at: www.eure.cl/index.php/eure/article/view/1370.

Moreno, O. (2005). 'Reestructuración económica y refuncionalización territorial en México: Su impacto en el sistema regional y el urbano en México 1980–2000'. *Revista Electrónica de Geografía y Ciencias Sociales*, IX(194). Available at: www.ub.edu/geocrit/sn/sn-194-78.htm.

Negrete, M. E. (2010). 'Las metrópolis mexicanas: Conceptualización, gestión y agenda de políticas'. In Garza, G. & Schteingart, M. (eds.). *Los grandes problemas de México: Desarrollo urbano y regional: T-II*. México, D. F.: El Colegio de México, pp. 173–212. Available at: www. jstor.org/stable/j.ctt1657tf2.8.

OECD. (2013). *Definition of Functional Urban Areas (FUA) for the OECD metropolitan database*. Paris: OECD. Available at: www.oecd.org/cfe/regional-policy/Definition-of-Functional-Urban-Areas-for-the-OECD-metropolitan-database.pdf.

Parilla, J., Leal, J. & Berube, A. (2015). *Latin America's stagnating global cities* [online]. Available at: https://www.brookings.edu/blog/the-avenue/2015/03/05/latin-americas-stagnating-global-cities/.

Payan, T. & Correa-Cabrera, G. (2014). *Land ownership and use under Mexico's energy reform. Issue Brief*, October 29, 2014, Rice University's Baker Institute for Public Policy. Available at: https://scholarship.rice.edu/handle/1911/92489.

Rionda-Ramírez, J. I. (2007). 'Dinámica metropolitana en México'. *Economía, Sociedad y Territorio*, 7(25), 241–266. Available at: https://est.cmq.edu.mx/index.php/est/article/view/237/243.

Rojas, E., Cuadrado Roura, J. R. & Fernández Guell, J. M. (2005). *Gobernar las metropolis*. Washington, D.C.: Inter-American Development Bank. Available at: http://site.ebrary.com/id/10201140.

Romo, R., Téllez, Y. & López, J. (2013). 'Tendencias de la migración interna en México en el periodo reciente'. In CONAPO (ed.), *La situación demográfica de México, 2013*. México, D. F.: CONAPO, pp. 83–106. Available at: www.conapo.gob.mx/work/models/CONAPO/Resource/1734/1/images/5_Tendencias_de_la_migracion_interna_en_Mexico_en_el_periodo_reciente.pdf.

SEDATU, CONAPO & INEGI. (2018). *Delimitación de las zonas metropolitanas de México 2015*. Secretaría de Desarrollo Agrario, Territorial y Urbano, Consejo Nacional de Población, Instituto Nacional de Estadística y Geografía. Mexico City. Available at: www.gob.mx/conapo/documentos/delimitacion-de-las-zonas-metropolitanas-de-mexico-2015.

SEDESOL, CONAPO & INEGI. (2012). *Delimitación de las zonas metropolitanas de México 2010*. México, D. F.: Secretaría de Desarrollo Social, Consejo Nacional de Población, Instituto Nacional de Estadística y Geografía. Available at: www.conapo.gob.mx/es/CONAPO/Delimitacion_zonas_metropolitanas_2010_Capitulos_I_a_IV.

SEDESOL, CONAPO & INEGI. (2007). *Delimitación de las Zonas Metropolitanas de México 2005*. México, D. F.: Secretaría de Desarrollo Social, Consejo Nacional de Población, Instituto Nacional de Estadística y Geografía. Available at: http://internet.contenidos.inegi.org.mx/contenidos/productos/prod_serv/contenidos/espanol/bvinegi/productos/geografia/publicaciones/delimex10/multi_archivo/702825003884/DZM20101.pdf.

UN-Habitat (2012). *State of Latin American and Caribbean cities 2012: Towards a new urban transition*. Nairobi: UN-HABITAT. Available at: https://unhabitat.org/books/state-of-latin-american-and-caribbean-cities-2/.

Unikel, L. (2016). *El desarrollo urbano de México: Diagnóstico e Implicaciones Futuras*. México, D. F.: El Colegio de México.

Vargas, et al. (2017). *Urban growth and access to opportunities: A challenge for Latin America*. Bogotá: Banco de Desarrollo de América Latina, CAF. Available at: http://scioteca.caf.com/handle/123456789/1091.

Zentella, J. C. (2007). '¿Cómo gobernar las zonas metropolitanas en México?' *Este País*, (194), 30–37.

Ziccardi, A. (2016). 'Poverty and urban inequality: The case of Mexico City metropolitan region'. *International Social Science Journal*, 56(217–218), 205–2019.

Part II

Metropolitan economic development in Mexico

Patterns, trends and drivers

4 The economic significance of metropolitan areas

Patterns of economic performance and disparities

Introduction

It is widely recognised that cities are the key social and economic organising units of our time and the most powerful engines of growth and development. They bring together people, economic activity and many of the inputs required for human wellbeing. As they have grown bigger, many are morphing into metropolitan areas, which, in turn, are now the most symbolic spaces for innovation and creativity and for maximising social interaction, the foci for integration with the rest of the world through globalisation and the heart of economic competitiveness. Simultaneously, these metropolitan areas, especially in the developing world, face significant challenges. They confront growing territorial, social, political and economic internal divides. Many experience high levels of poverty, crime and environmental degradation. Several metropolises also have difficulties with maximising wealth and income generation. Moreover, metropolitan areas and the presence of pronounced inequalities are seen in close interaction, especially in the developing countries (Bronger, 1984). The international economic environment has led to a growing need and aspiration of territories – both cities and regions – to increase their productive capacity, attract new economic activity and create new jobs. However, some urban agglomerations perform better than others, and this has led to the emergence of 'successful' and 'losing' cities, and the reinforcement of spatial heterogeneity.

While in the last decade the general academic and policy interest has returned to metropolitan governance issues – why and how the new metropolitan reality is planned, governed and defined – and new problems such as sustainable development, international migration, violence, social transformation and other issues are of great concern, the economic significance of urbanisation has not lost ground. Because metropolitan areas hold such a concentration of people, businesses, jobs and opportunities, their economies matter more than ever. Furthermore, the relationship between urbanisation and economic development has become more complex as rapidly urbanising countries in the Global South experience enormous difficulties generating economic growth, prosperity and wellbeing. Moreover, Florida, Mellander and Gulden (2009) argue that while the general process and patterns of urbanisation are well-known, we know a great deal less about the global level of economic activity produced by cities and metropolitan areas, and about their role in the global (and I would add national) economy. It is therefore essential to continue discussing the economic relevance of metropolitan areas, the functions they perform in the national and global urban systems and the differences that emerge among them if we want to appraise the real benefits and advantages of contemporary urbanisation in the light of all the challenges and problems that cities increasingly face.

As argued in Chapter 2, on average, metropolitan areas are the most productive and wealthiest territories in Latin America; however, they are growing more slowly than cities of similar size in other parts of the world. Latin America was the only global region to experience declines in per capita gross domestic product (GDP) in recent years. The relative backwardness of metropolitan areas and cities in the region manifest as an array of economic, social and environmental problems, as well as in various intra-urban inequalities. Similar patterns of inequality emerge in the region's national urban systems.

In this chapter I emphasise the role of metropolitan areas as heterogeneous economic spaces and examine the dynamics and patterns of variables that offer an approximation to metropolitan economic development. The analysis deals with spatial patterns of economic performance, the distribution of economic activity, specialisation, efficiency and productivity, labour supply, and with inter-metropolitan disparities. The discussion focuses on metropolitan areas in Mexico, with references to international examples. Knowledge about metropolitan economic development and evolution is valuable for defining economic hierarchies across urban systems and the positioning of urban spaces in both the national and the global economy.

A remainder of the economic interpretation of metropolitan areas

In contrast to the traditional notion of cities characterised by a unique and differentiated centre, well-defined territorial limits and a well-established area of economic influence, in the twentieth and twenty-first centuries metropolitan areas have been characterised by more diffuse limits, a more extensive area of economic influence, high diversification and often the presence of multiple centres of activity. Historically, the reasons driving these urban dynamics have been wide-ranging, including different strategic functions such as military defence, industrial production, commercial exchange, religious centres and political complexes. However, big contemporary cities exercise functions of greater complexity (Cuadrado-Roura & Fernández, 2005).

From an economic perspective, a metropolitan area is defined as an integrated urban labour market and can be conceptualised as a functional economy that does not correspond to state or local political boundaries because its functional urban labour market extends beyond the municipal boundaries of the city. According to Lefévre (2010), metropolitan areas have become the new spatial fix of capitalism where the most salient societal issues are taking place:

economic growth and wealth, social distress, environmental degradation, cultural (dis)integration and so on. Méndez (2007) argues that large metropolitan agglomerations constitute a significant observatory for the description, analysis and interpretation of several transformations associated with capitalist development. The evolution of both their internal structure and morphology and their external limits and interactions with the environment affect the functioning of their firms, the volume and quality of employment, and the lives of their citizens.

Assessing the economic relevance of metropolitan areas is equivalent to examining the effects of urbanisation on development and economic growth. For economists, cities are concentrations of economic activity and population that generate a broad set of cumulative synergistic effects such as economies of scale derived from the presence of positive factors such as greater density, the quality of the infrastructure, human resources, labour markets and agglomeration economies. However, various theoretical interpretations of agglomeration economies identify different sources of such external economies of scale. Although agglomeration effects are quantitatively important and pervasive, the productive advantage of large cities is constantly eroded and must be sustained by new job creation and innovation: dynamic agglomeration effects (Duranton, 2015). Metropolitan areas are a consequence of extended externalities derived from this set of synergistic effects in space that benefit economic activities and explain growth, structural change and innovation processes – in short, economic development (Cuadrado-Roura & Fernández, 2005; De Mattos, 2010; Vargas et al., 2017).

Metropolitan areas are territories that exhibit intense functional interdependencies, a broad labour market with a diverse professional supply, and a spatial concentration of externalities and spillover effects (Cuadrado-Roura & Fernández, 2005). In these spatial concentrations of production and population, externalities expand territorially from the central city to other cities or municipalities, with which it establishes a necessary economic interdependence (De Mattos, 2010). These definitions highlight the role of the extensive external economies of scale (agglomeration economies) located in cities. The expanded field of externalities caused by urban expansion allows the benefits of agglomeration economies to spread beyond the central city. The trend towards the greater concentration of population and economic activities in metropolitan areas is explained by the perceived greater opportunities for generating wealth, investment, employment, added value and social welfare. Metropolitan areas are also conceived as spaces for the insertion of national economies into global markets. Hence, within the globalisation paradigm, where competition for investment and specialised labour is promoted intensely, interest in boosting the economic dynamism of metropolitan regions has increased (Rionda-Ramírez, 2007).

Independently of their general economic advantages, metropolitan areas behave and perform very differently. Although they are territories of opportunity and economic revitalisation, there is potential conflict associated with their competition with other regions for resources. Some metropolitan regions have a special dynamism and greater capacity to build competitive and productive spaces (Méndez, 2007). As Duranton (2015) mentions, agglomeration benefits are not monoliths that apply equally to all cities depending only on their overall size; instead, there is great heterogeneity. Thus, some generic and specific advantages can be identified in metropolitan areas. Their specific advantages explain the differentiated performance of metropolitan areas (Figure 4.1).

While transformation of the economic base in metropolitan areas has given way to an increasing weight of services and the relative decline of industrial production and employment, their productive structures and specialisations are diverse. Some metropolitan areas specialise in advanced services for producers and knowledge-intensive activities (i.e. developed economies with a selective functional specialisation in competitive sectors). Other metropolitan areas specialise in services, commerce and activities of public administration of low-productivity/unskilled employment (Méndez, 2008).

Uneven metropolitan trajectories are also evident in the evolution of labour markets, in the attraction of productive activities and population and, in general, in their unequal economic performance. Metropolitan economies do not remain static but experience continuous evolution towards progress or stagnation with respect to their original position (Cuadrado-Roura & Fernández, 2005). Garza (2010) points out that it is essential to deepen knowledge of the type of spatial structuring of not only the population but also economic activities, because of their implications for the economic development of countries within the framework of a metropolisation process.

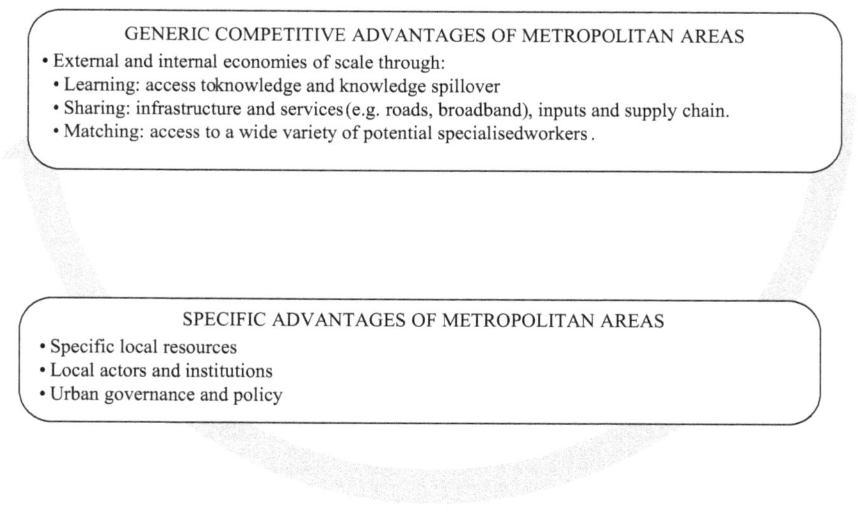

GENERIC COMPETITIVE ADVANTAGES OF METROPOLITAN AREAS
• External and internal economies of scale through:
  • Learning: access to knowledge and knowledge spillover
  • Sharing: infrastructure and services (e.g. roads, broadband), inputs and supply chain.
  • Matching: access to a wide variety of potential specialised workers.

SPECIFIC ADVANTAGES OF METROPOLITAN AREAS
• Specific local resources
• Local actors and institutions
• Urban governance and policy

Figure 4.1 Generic and specific economic advantages of metropolitan areas

Source: Author's elaboration.

International evidence on the relevance of metropolitan areas

The world's 300 largest metropolitan areas (based on the size of their economies) account for nearly half of all global output. Interestingly, they also account for less than a quarter of employment, indicating their weaker power to generate employment but extremely high relative levels of productivity. In 2016 a third of these largest metropolitan areas were located in China, 57 in North America and 43 in Western Europe. However, recently a significant network of large metropolitan economies has emerged in Asia, the Middle East and Africa. Only 14 of the largest metropolitan areas are located in Latin America: in Argentina, Brazil, Chile, Colombia, Dominican Republic, Mexico and Peru. In this sample, 160 metropolitan economies are in emerging economies and 140 in advanced economies (Bouchet, Lius & Parilla, 2018). Between 2014 and 2016, GDP growth averaged 3.3 per cent annually and employment growth 1.9 per cent, surpassing the global average of 2.6 and 1.2 per cent respectively (Figure 4.2).

The WEF (2018) calculates that 600 cities generate close to 60 per cent of the world's output. While in the coming years the concentration of economic activity is expected to remain more or less steady, the geographical mix of the top urban areas will continue to change significantly as economic power shifts towards Asia – thanks to the legacy of the developmental state in which economic development is centralised and directed by the government – and other emerging regions.

Florida, Mellander and Gulden (2009) estimate the world's largest metropolitan areas in terms of their economic activity based on light intensity. They note that the economic activity produced by these metropolitan areas is substantially greater than their population size. The top 10 metropolitan areas house 2.6 per

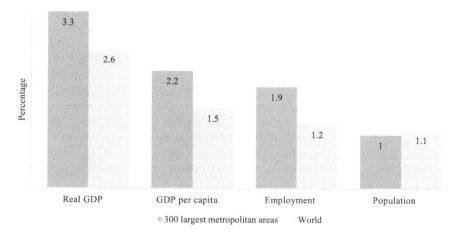

Figure 4.2 Compound annual growth rates in the world's largest metropolitan areas, 2014–2016 (%)

Source: Based on Bouchet, Lius and Parilla (2018).

cent of the world's population but produce more than 21.0 per cent of global economic activity. The world's 50 largest metropolitan economies account for almost 40 per cent of global economic activity. The largest metropolitan area is Greater Tokyo. Most of the metropolitan areas in the top 20 are in North America and Western Europe, the exceptions being Tokyo, Kyoto and Nagoya (Japan); Seoul (South Korea); and Guangzhou (China). Table 4.1 present the largest metropolitan areas by region. Some of those in Latin America appear in the top 10 in the BRICS (Sao Paulo, Rio de Janeiro, Belo Horizonte and Porto Alegre) and emerging economies regions (Buenos Aires and Mexico City).

In the OECD countries, metropolitan areas that include the capital of the country tend to be the richest, with a GDP per capita on average 37 per cent higher than the national value. Capital metropolitan areas such as Bratislava (Slovak Republic), Warsaw (Poland), Paris (France), Prague (Czech Republic), Budapest (Hungary) and London (the UK) have a GDP per capita 50 per cent higher than that of the average of the country in which they are located. Metropolitan areas in general contribute to 51 per cent of annual GDP per capita growth in the OECD countries (OECD, 2018).

These figures illustrate how urbanisation has helped lift the productive potential of countries and how cities continue to be engines of economic growth and opportunity. The GDP of some of the largest metropolitan areas is greater than that of a number of countries, and they rank among the top worldwide economies: Seoul, Paris and Mexico City, for instance, have each overtaken the economies of countries including Sweden, Austria and Chile (Fernández, 2017). Other metropolitan areas perform as global cities that are internationally connected. However, the capacity of metropolitan areas for prosperity should not be overestimated, as they are not always synonymous with success. Furthermore, despite the generic advantages that they offer as spaces of opportunity, the distribution of those opportunities among and within cities remains uneven.

Metropolitan areas experience differing economic trajectories, and a subset of high-performing ones are driving growth and performing remarkably well. The fastest-growing economies (relatively high growth in GDP and employment) include Dublin (Ireland), San Jose (US), Chengdu (China), San Francisco (US), Beijing (China), Delhi (India), Manila (Philippines) and Fuzhou, Tianjin and Xiamen (China). Yet, the bottom quintile, that exhibited lower performance, include many Latin American metropolitan areas, particularly those in Brazil (Rio de Janeiro, Porto Alegre, Brasilia, Belo Horizonte, Curitiba and Sao Paulo). Latin America was the region with the weakest economic performance across all regions with an annual decrease in employment and GDP per capita (0.5 and 1.3 per cent respectively) (Bouchet, Lius & Parilla, 2018).

In most OECD countries spatial differences remain significant, with the inter-regional range of GDP per capita revealing large discrepancies. On average, GDP per capita was more than four times higher in the top than in the bottom region within a country. In 2016, the top 10 per cent of regions in a country recorded an average GDP per capita more than twice the size of that of the bottom 10 per cent in the same country. Moreover, in the last decade regional differences have increased in several countries (OECD, 2018).

Table 4.1 Largest metropolitan economies by region (light-based activity)

North America	LBA (billions)	Europe	LBA (billions)	Asia	LBA (billions)	BRICS	LBA (billions)	Emerging economies	LBA (billions)
New York–Philadelphia–Newark	$1,181.90	London	$378.10	Tokyo–Kawasaki–Yokohama	$1,997.50	Guangzhou–Hong Kong–Kowloon	$200.50	Buenos Aires	$143.20
Los Angeles	561.7	Antwerpen–Gent–Bruxelles–Lille–Liege	336.2	Kyoto–Osaka–Kobe	617.9	Sao Paulo	114.3	Mexico City	139.4
Chicago–Milwaukee	405.7	Bonn–Dortmund–Duisburg–Koln	315.2	Nagoya	558.4	Beijing	46.9		
Washington D.C.–Baltimore	297.3	Paris	280.9	Seoul	238.9	Shanghai	45.8	Jerusalem–Tel Aviv–Yafo	104.6
Boston	275.2	Leeds–Sheffield–Birmingham	222.2	Guangzhou–Hong Kong–Kowloon	200.5	Rio de Janeiro	42.1	Bangkok	75.4
San Jose	235.1	Amsterdam–Rotterdam–The Hague	187.5	Fukuoka-Kita Kyushu	105.8	New Delhi–Delhi	31.6	Pretoria–Johannesburg	62.9
Dallas	212.7	Milano	181.9	Singapore	91.9	Tianjin	17.3	Jakarta	45.9
Houston	170.3	Manchester–Liverpool	134.3	Sapporo	79.4	Belo Horizonte	16.5	Cairo–El-Giza	44.3
Detroit	168.3	Berlin	96	Bangkok	75.4	Calcutta	14.9	Kuala Lumpur	39.5
Atlanta	164.5	Frankfurt am Main	93	Fukuyama	53.1	Porto Alegre	14.5		

Source: Based on Florida, Mellander and Gulden (2009).

In the same vein, within the OECD a number of metropolitan areas lag behind their national average, including Berlin (Germany), Fukuoka (Japan), Lille (France), Naples (Italy) and Pittsburgh (US). Some megacities experience diseconomies of agglomeration (e.g. Seoul, Mexico City, Istanbul and Tokyo) because of high congestion costs due to traffic, pollution and environmental degradation. Several metropolitan areas have unemployment rates above the national average with lower activity. Social exclusion and poverty in most OECD countries have become urban phenomena, not only in less-advanced metropolitan areas such as Mexico City, but also in cities that have undergone strong industrial restructuring such as Rotterdam (the Netherlands), Lille (France), and Detroit (US). Socioeconomic inequalities, poverty and social exclusion are becoming common problems (OECD, 2006).

Latin America's economic activity is highly concentrated in a relatively small number of urban centres. The 36 major cities in the region generate approximately 30 per cent of GDP, half of which is produced by Sao Paulo, Mexico City, Buenos Aires and Rio de Janeiro. The main political, socioeconomic and administrative functions are also highly concentrated in a few cities (Montero & García, 2017). Table 4.2 shows the main metropolitan economies

Table 4.2 Main metropolitan economies in Latin America, 2007

	Total GDP (2007)[1]	Share of national GDP (%)	GDP per capita (2007)	Annual average growth in per capita GDP (2004–2007) (%)
Mexico City	230,401	22.5	11,504	7.1
Sao Paulo	177,360	14	5,944	13
Buenos Aires	100,517	38.3	8,329	13.1
Río de Janeiro	64,242	5.1	5,498	11.7
Santiago	51,796	31.6	8,162	11.9
Monterrey	48,237	4.7	13,144	8.3
San Juan	44,362	49.1	18,484	7.9
Guadalajara	34,205	3.3	8,364	6.5
Lima	26,662	26.8	3,433	9
Bogota	23,591	11.6	3,233	8.1
Curitiba	19,799	1.5	6,486	12.7
Caracas	18,222	8	4,753	9.4
Queretaro[2]	13,688	1.3	14,732	27.4
Santo Domingo[2]	10,862	26.5	3,657	13.5
Montevideo	8,340	36.1	5,817	10.8
Ciudad de Guatemala	7,838	23.4	2,539	5.5
San Jose	7,155	27.3	4,462	3.4
Quito	4,284	9.9	2,692	1.9
Asuncion	2,316	19.4	1,245	5.1
Santa Cruz de la Sierra	1,784	13.6	1,269	3.1
La Paz	1,559	11.9	961	2.8

Source: Based on Manzano (2009).

1 Current USD.
2 GDP growth 2006–2008.

in Latin America. The largest urban economy is Mexico City; San Juan (Puerto Rico) and Queretaro and Monterrey (Mexico) have the highest GDP per capita; and Queretaro is the most economically dynamic metropolitan area. San Juan, Buenos Aires and Montevideo concentrate a large proportion of their respective national GDP (49, 38 and 36 per cent respectively).

Metropolitan areas in Latin America have evolved within widely diverse physical, economic, social and political contexts, which influence their dynamics and production structures (Cuadrado-Roura & Fernández, 2005). They have also experienced comparatively high economic, social and environmental costs, selective relocation, unemployment, poverty, exclusion, insecurity and congestion (Méndez, 2008). As explained in Chapter 2, they have particular characteristics in terms of spatial and socioeconomic structures as a result of the historical genesis of the region. The main particularities include the excessive concentration of the urban system (i.e. primacy in cities such as Buenos Aires, Sao Paulo and Mexico City), a dichotomy in the productive apparatus between innovative high technology companies integrated with international markets and unproductive and rather undynamic enterprises, high informality, dual labour markets, strong segregation and spatial fragmentation. Globalisation and productive technological restructuring have also contributed to defining spaces and metropolitan performance in Latin America (Cuadrado-Roura & Fernández, 2005).

Thus, the geographic distribution of resources and economic activities, and the characteristics of labour markets, productive structures, economic growth and productivity, are fundamental elements that reveal territorial disparities. These factors also have significant meaning in terms of large-scale development processes.

Despite its fundamental relevance, there is relatively little systematic study and monitoring of the economy of metropolitan spaces in Mexico. The following sections examine a number of economic variables and inter-urban disparities in its metropolitan areas.

Spatial distribution of economic activity and specialisation in Mexico's metropolitan areas

Economic activity is very unevenly distributed across the Mexico's urban system. Generally, there has been a significant geographical concentration of population and production in the largest metropolitan areas: Mexico City, Monterrey and Guadalajara. Economic policies have had a significant impact on urban development and have led to important changes in Mexico's economic geography. As discussed earlier in this book, Mexico's economic model underwent a deep transformation in the 1980s and the 1990s, with privatisation, deregulation, economic liberalisation and the promotion of exports, after the crisis, with the import substitution industrialisation (ISI) strategy implemented between the 1940s and the 1970s. For more than three decades the geographical distribution of economic opportunities in Mexico has been closely linked to the industrialisation model, which shifted from market protection to the opening of the economy via structural measures of trade liberalisation and export promotion (Trejo, 2016). As a result of these policy changes, industrial production increasingly located in the north and north-central regions nearer to the US border and highway systems as opposed to around Mexico City and domestic consumers, as had been the case under ISI. Oil-producing areas in the states of Campeche, Tabasco and Veracruz grew quickly during the commodities boom in the 1970s and have remained centres of industrial production. Government policies encouraging tourism led to the rapid urbanisation of places such as Cancun, Zihuatanejo and Puerto Vallarta, all of which were sparsely settled until the second half of the twentieth century (Alix-García & Sellars, 2018).

Moreno (2005) argues that macroeconomic patterns and adjustments influenced cities' urban system and economic performance. The economic and demographic overconcentration in the main urban centres began to decline in the 1980s in favour of medium-sized cities. Trade liberalisation and productive restructuring led to a spatial change resulting in a group of winning metropolitan areas versus a group of disadvantaged cities. The successful and winning metropolitan areas were located in the northeast due to its linkages with the US economy, in the Mexican Gulf with its oil-related activity and in the Bajio region in the centre and centre-west, owing to its more concentrated and specialised productive infrastructure. Despite this spatial redistribution of economic activity, production and employment are still concentrated in the largest metropolitan areas.

The size distribution of metropolitan areas measured by gross production, as reported in the Mexican economic census, correlates with population size by more than 98 per cent. Data reveals the economic primacy of Mexico City Metropolitan Area which, with the highest population, accounted for 32 per cent of total metropolitan production in 2013, three times more than the second-ranking city. Guadalajara, which ranks second on population, is the third largest metropolitan economy (5 per cent); Monterrey, the third most-populated metropolis, is the second largest economy (11.3 per cent). Puebla-Tlaxcala and Toluca are also among the largest metropolitan economies. These top 5 metropolitan areas accounted for 55.2 per cent of total gross metropolitan production in 2013, and the top 15 for almost 76 per cent (see Table 4.3). The concentration of production in the largest metropolitan areas has decreased over time, with the top 5 dropping by 6.6 percentage points between 1998 and 2013, and the top 15 by 2.2 percentage. The Herfindalh index of geographic concentration and the entropy index indicate a slight deconcentration of production between 1998 and 2008 before stabilising until 2013 (Table 4.3). The share in production of the largest metropolitan economy, Mexico City, gradually dropped by 6.8 percentage points between 1998 and 2013. Two of the top three largest economies, Mexico City and Guadalajara, saw the largest drop in their shares in metropolitan production between 1998 and 2013. This suggests some losses to the comparative advantages of these cities, and others such as Toluca, Juarez, Monclova and Morelia. In contrast, Monterrey saw the largest increase. In spite of such readjustments, the data shows persistent economic agglomeration in the largest metropolitan areas (Figure 4.3).

Table 4.3 Largest metropolitan economies in Mexico (share in metropolitan gross production) and geographic concentration indices, 1998, 2003, 2008 and 2013

Metropolitan area	1998		2003		2008		2013	Change 1998–2003 (%)
Valle de México	39.08	Valle de México	36.65	Valle de México	32.77	Valle de México	32.33	−6.75
Monterrey	9.2	Monterrey	10	Monterrey	10.18	Monterrey	11.31	2.11
Guadalajara	6.99	Guadalajara	6.16	Guadalajara	5.46	Guadalajara	5.03	−1.96
Puebla–Tlaxcala	3.37	Puebla–Tlaxcala	3.5	Puebla–Tlaxcala	3.4	Puebla–Tlaxcala	3.61	0.24
Toluca	3.17	Toluca	2.56	Toluca	3.05	Toluca	2.88	−0.28
Saltillo	2.37	Leon	2.55	Saltillo	2.5	Saltillo	2.86	
Leon	2.25	Saltillo	2.54	Tampico	2.05	Queretaro	2.39	
Tijuana	1.71	Juarez	1.79	Queretaro	1.96	Leon	2.38	
Queretaro	1.7	La Laguna	1.72	La Laguna	1.93	Hermosillo	2.07	
San Luis Potosi	1.68	Queretaro	1.69	San Luis Potosi	1.88	Tehuantepec	1.93	
La Laguna	1.54	Tampico	1.63	Leon	1.76	San Luis Potosi	1.9	
Juarez	1.51	San Luis Potosi	1.6	Coatzacoalcos	1.72	Tampico	1.88	
Hermosillo	1.2	Tijuana	1.6	Hermosillo	1.7	Tula	1.88	
Aguascalientes	1.18	Aguascalientes	1.35	Tijuana	1.69	La Laguna	1.87	
Chihuahua	1.15	Chihuahua	1.29	Reynosa	1.66	Aguascalientes	1.56	
Accumulated	78.1		76.63		73.71		75.88	
Herfindalh index	**0.17**		**0.16**		**0.13**		**0.13**	**−0.04**
Entropy index	**0.64**		**0.61**		**0.55**		**0.56**	**−0.08**

Source: Based on INEGI (1999, 2004, 2009 & 2014).

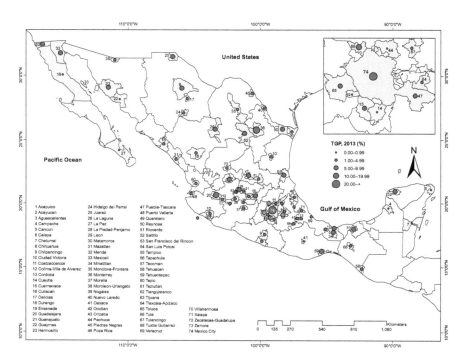

Figure 4.3 Metropolitan share of total gross production, 2013 (%)

Source: Based on INEGI (1999, 2004, 2009 & 2014).

In 1998 some metropolitan areas which specialise in oil-related economic activities (Tehuantepec, Tula, Minatitlan and Coatzacoalcos) had the highest production per capita. This estimation about average wellbeing, however, is misinforming in the sense that the oil profits are distributed across the country because they are administered by a parastatal company. A group of industrial cities (Saltillo, Hermosillo, Monterrey, Tampico, Monclova-Frontera, Queretaro, San Luis Potosi, Piedras Negras, Aguascalientes, La Laguna, Leon, Reynosa and Toluca) and Mexico City were also in the uppermost quartile. This group is mainly of metropolitan areas in the north and the centre of the country and the Bajio (Table 4.4).

In 2013 the geographic pattern of production per capita is less clear-cut. The top quartile continues to include some cities with chemical and oil-related industries (Tula, Tehuantepec, Coatzacoalcos and Minatitlan), a number of industrial cities in the north (Saltillo, Monclova-Frontera, Monterrey, Hermosillo and Chihuahua), some cities in the centre (Mexico City, Toluca, Tianguistenco, Queretaro and Puebla-Tlaxcala) and other cities in Bajio (San Luis Potosi, Guadalajara, Leon and Aguascalientes) (Figure 4.4). With the exception of oil-producer cities, the south of the country remains behind. This is a historical trend that has not been overcome.

Table 4.4 Per capita production in metropolitan areas, 1998, 2003, 2008 and 2013

	1998	*2003*	*2008*	*2013*	*Change*
Mean	121,551.89	125,133.38	88,887.70	79,357.44	−42,194.5
Standard deviation	168,153.77	138,074.29	75,039.50	53,969.42	−114,184.4
Coefficient of variation	1.38339085	1.10341693	0.84420576	0.68008019	−0.7

Source: Based on INEGI (1999, 2004, 2009 & 2014).

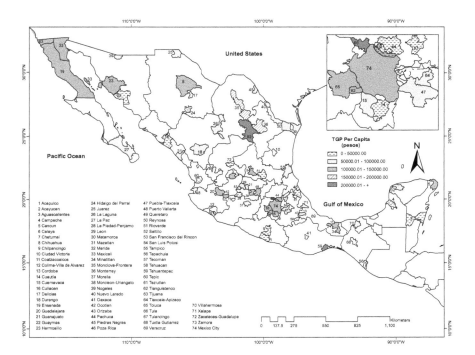

Figure 4.4 Total gross production per capita, 2013

Source: Based on INEGI (1999, 2004, 2009 & 2014).

In the literature on economic convergence, a drop in the standard deviation of GDP per capita over time is interpreted as a process of sigma convergence (Sala-i-Martin, 1996). The calculations of the standard deviation and the coefficient of variation in metropolitan per capita production indicate decreases over time, signalling a reduction in disparities between metropolitan areas. However, it is important to mention that the average per capita production in metropolitan Mexico has fallen overall (Table 4.4).

An urban economy consists of the city's economic base, or the mix of economic functions that create value and employment. These functions can be continually in transformation or can remain. Normally metropolitan areas transit through different stages of economic development to which their local

Table 4.5 Specialisation in metropolitan areas and economic function, 2013

Most specialised			Intermediate			Least specialised		
MA	Specialisation	Economic function	MA	Specialisation	Economic function	MA	Specialisation	Economic function
Coatzacoalcos	83.1	Chemical industry	Cancun	33.9	Temporary accommodation and food and beverage preparation services	Tapachula	22.6	Retail
Saltillo	67.1	Manufacture of transport equipment	La Laguna	33.4	Basic metal industries	Pachuca	22.3	Retail
Hermosillo	64.7	Manufacture of transport equipment	Veracruz	33.2	Basic metal industries	Oaxaca	22.2	Retail
Tampico	58.1	Chemical industry	Guaymas	32.1	Manufacture of transport equipment	Hidalgo del Parral	22.1	Retail
Aguascalientes	55.6	Manufacture of transport equipment	Rioverde	31.4	Wholesale	La Paz	21.6	Retail
Monclova-Frontera	53.2	Basic metal industries	Minatitlan	30.4	Chemical industry	Xalapa	21.4	Food industry
Cordoba	52.3	Food industry	Acayucan	29.9	Retail	Zacatecas-Guadalupe	21.4	Retail
San Francisco del Rincon	48.1	Manufacture of leather	Toluca	28.9	Manufacture of transport equipment	Matamoros	21	Manufacture of transport equipment
Puebla–Tlaxcala	45	Manufacture of transport equipment	Reynosa	27.5	Mining	Celaya	21	Food industry
Chilpancingo	44	Mining	Nuevo Laredo	27.4	Transportation and mailing services	Ciudad Victoria	20.9	Retail

City	Value	Industry	City	Value	Industry	City	Value	Industry
Zamora	42.1	Food industry	Chetumal	27.3	Retail	Tuxtla Gutiarrez	20.3	Manufacture of transport equipment
Teziutlan	41.8	Manufacture of clothing	Poza Rica	26.4	Chemical industry	Queretaro	19.9	Manufacture of transport equipment
Leon	40.6	Manufacture of transport equipment	Tecoman	26.4	Food industry	Guanajuato	19.7	Construction
Tianguistenco	40.6	Chemical industry	Cuautla	26.2	Manufacture of products based on non-metallic minerals	Chihuahua	19.7	Manufacture of transport equipment
La Piedad–Penjamo	39.4	Food industry	Tulancingo	26.2	Retail	Mexico City	19.2	Financial services
Cuernavaca	39.4	Manufacture of transport equipment	Acapulco	25.4	Retail	Culiacan	18.9	Food industry
Villahermosa	39	Chemical Industry	Tehuantepec	24.7	Wholesale	Campeche	18.2	Retail
Puerto Vallarta	38.8	Temporary accommodation and food and beverage preparation services	Mazatlan	24.5	Food industry	Tijuana	16.8	Manufacture of transport equipment
Merida	38.5	Information in mass media	Moroleon-Uriangato	24.2	Retail	Morelia	16.8	Retail
Piedras Negras	37.8	Beverages and tobacco industry	Mexicali	23.9	Manufacture of transport equipment	Durango	16.7	Retail
Tehuacan	37	Food industry	Tlaxcala-Apizaco	23.1	Basic metal industries	Tepic	16.5	Food industry
Ocotlan	36.3	Food industry	Colima-Villa de alvarez	23	Retail	Guadalajara	15.8	Food industry

(*Continued*)

Table 4.5 (Continued)

	Most specialised		Intermediate			Least specialised		
MA	Specialisation	Economic function	MA	Specialisation	Economic function	MA	Specialisation	Economic function
Tula	35.5	Manufacture of products based on non-metallic minerals				Ensenada	15.4	Retail
Juarez	35.3	Manufacture of transport equipment				San Luis Potosi	14.4	Manufacture of transport equipment
Orizaba	35	Food industry				Nogales	14.3	Manufacture of computer equipment
Delicias	35	Food industry				Monterrey	12.9	Manufacture of transport equipment

Source: Based on INEGI (2014).

productive structures have to adjust (Suarez-Villa, 1988). Larger cities tend to be more diversified, with an increasing weight of service activities in the more advanced stages of metropolisation (Suarez-Villa, 1988).

Cities often establish their national and global position through a distinct economic specialisation. However, being specialised does not mean lacking in diversity, and a city can include multiple specialisations. The most specialised Mexican metropolitan areas are heavily reliant in one single economic activity, such as Saltillo, Hermosillo, Aguascalientes and Puebla, medium-sized or large urban agglomerations that are highly dependent on the manufacture of transport equipment (Table 4.5). However, most of the metropolitan areas in the highly specialised category are small and rely on more traditional industries, such as food, leather, clothing, beverages, tobacco or mining. The three largest metropolitan areas, Mexico City, Monterrey and Guadalajara, have low levels of specialisation but seem to develop specific functions in the urban system: Mexico City specialises in financial services, Monterrey in the manufacture of transport equipment and Guadalajara in the food industry. Mexico City therefore functions at a higher and more sophisticated level than the rest of the metropolitan areas, which mainly rely on traditional manufacturing activities, retail, wholesale or low-order services.

Labour supply, poverty and informality

For most urban residents, economic success is determined by income generated in the labour market. Employment remains their primary source of income, and in developing economies it represents the means by which they can access social protection, status, self-respect and social mobility. Inclusion in the labour market contributes to reducing the risk of poverty because people can expand their individual opportunities and self-realisation. All metropolitan areas face the challenge of creating and maintaining jobs while at the same time generating conditions for increased productivity. However, the most mobile factors of production, many forms of labour included, are dominated by a few urban centres, leaving some others with obsolete physical capital and less-qualified labour, which in turns translates as a heterogeneous metropolitan distribution of productivity, profits and efficiency.

In a number of metropolitan areas labour supply has been highly dynamic. Here the working-age population, which is an indicator of the potential labour supply (i.e. the total population considered able and likely to work based on the number of people in a predetermined age range), the economically active population (EAP; i.e. the fraction of the population that is employed or actively seeking employment and represents the actual labour force in the economy) and the occupied population (i.e. the fraction of the population actually in employment) grew by more than 3 per cent per annum between 2010 and 2015. A second group of cities grew by 2 and 3 per cent a year (Table 4.6). However, in some metropolitan areas, for instance Puerto Vallarta and Mazatlan, the working-age population grew more than the EAP and the occupied population, while the

Table 4.6 Metropolitan areas by average annual growth rates, 2010–2015 (%)

Working-age population	*Economically active population*	*Occupied population*
3.1–3.9%	3.1–3.6%	3.1–3.8%
Tehuacan, Queretaro, Puerto Vallarta, Cancun, Durango, Mazatlan, Hermosillo	Durango, Tehuacan, Cancun, Queretaro, Saltillo, Hermosillo	Durango, Saltillo, Tehuacan, Aguascalientes, Cancun, Queretaro, Hermosillo, San Luis Potosi
2.1–3%	2.1–3%	2.1–3%
Aguascalientes, Chilpancingo, Zacatecas–Guadalupe, Reynosa, Saltillo, Veracruz, Morelia, Monterrey, San Luis Potosi, Toluca, Leon, Xalapa, Pachuca, San Francisco del Rincon, Tuxtla Gutierrez, Juarez, Cuautla, Villahermosa, Puebla–Tlaxcala, Cordoba, Guanajuato, Nuevo Laredo, Oaxaca, Guadalajara, Chihuahua, Tlaxcala–Apizaco, Tepic, Nogales, Merida, La Paz, Tula, Colima–Villa de Alvarez, Cuernavaca, Tianguistenco, Tulancingo, Matamoros, Teziutlan, Piedras Negras	Aguascalientes, San Luis Potosi, San Francisco del Rincon, Chilpancingo, Leon, Mazatlán, Merida, Juarez, Puerto Vallarta, Monterrey, Colima–Villa de Alvarez, Zacatecas–Guadalupe, Chihuahua, Tepic, Villahermosa, Morelia, Cuautla, Veracruz	Juarez, Leon, San Francisco del Rincon, Mazatlan, Puerto Vallarta, Chilpancingo, Merida, Monterrey, Chihuahua, Pachuca, Colima–Villa de Alvarez, Cuautla, Morelia, Tepic, La Paz, Zacatecas–Guadalupe, Tula
1.1–2%	1.1–2%	1.1–2%
Tapachula, Campeche, Celaya, Mexicali, Tampico, Orizaba, La Laguna, Ocotlan, Monclova–Frontera, Ciudad Victoria, Delicias, Tijuana, Tehuantepec, Tecoman, Mexico City, Zamora, Acayucan, Moroleon–Uriangato, Culiacán, Poza Rica, Coatzacoalcos, Guaymas, Ensenada, Minatitlan, Acapulco	Campeche, La Paz, Tuxtla Gutierrez, Pachuca, Toluca, Tlaxcala–Apizaco, Xalapa, Puebla–Tlaxcala, Tula, Guanajuato, Tapachula, Reynosa, Piedras Negras, Tianguistenco, Cordoba, Cuernavaca, Ciudad Victoria, Monclova–Frontera, Celaya, Oaxaca, Guadalajara, Zamora, Nuevo Laredo, Nogales, Teziutlán, Tijuana, Mexicali, La Laguna, Mexico City, Acayucan	Campeche, Piedras Negras, Monclova–Frontera, Veracruz, Villahermosa, Toluca, Tlaxcala–Apizaco, Tianguistenco, Puebla–Tlaxcala, Celaya, Tuxtla Gutierrez, Guanajuato, Xalapa, Nogales, Tijuana, La Laguna, Cuernavaca, Ciudad Victoria, Zamora, Nuevo Laredo, Cordoba, Teziutlan, Oaxaca, Guadalajara, Reynosa, Guaymas, Tapachula, Mexicali, Mexico City, Tulancingo, Tehuantepec, Acayucan, Tampico, Ocotlan

(*Continued*)

Table 4.6 (Continued)

Working-age population	Economically active population	Occupied population
< 1.1%	< 1.1%	< 1.1%
Rioverde, Hidalgo del Parral, La Piedad–Penjamo, Chetumal	Ocotlan, Tampico, Guaymas, Tehuantepec, Matamoros, Culiacan, Tulancingo, Delicias, Tecoman, Hidalgo del Parral, Ensenada, Poza Rica, Orizaba, Coatzacoalcos, Minatitlan, Acapulco, Rioverde, Moroleon–Uriangato, La Piedad–Penjamo, Chetumal	Matamoros, Delicias, Culiacan, Hidalgo del Parral, Ensenada, Coatzacoalcos, Orizaba, Tecoman, Minatitlan, Rioverde, Acapulco, Poza Rica, La Piedad–Penjamo, Moroleon–Uriangato, Chetumal
Average	Average	Average
2.2%	1.5%	1.7%

Source: Based on INEGI (2011 & 2015).

opposite occurred in Saltillo and San Luis Potosi. EAP and occupied population grew by between 1 and 2 per cent a year in Mexico City and Guadalajara, whereas the labour supply in Monterrey was more dynamic.

Average years of schooling is a factor of differentiation in metropolitan development and competitiveness. It can be interpreted as a more qualified workforce and a generator of local advantages and economic attractiveness. It may also indicate improved population wellbeing. The mean average years of schooling in Mexico, which was 6.1 years in 1990 and 9.2 years in 2015 (Table 4.7), is very low compared to other countries (e.g. Switzerland's 13.9 years), yet it has been increasing across metropolitan areas. A number of cities in the north of the country such as Hermosillo, Ciudad Victoria and La Paz, among others, have the highest average years of schooling, while small metropolitan areas tend to have low average years of schooling.

In many cities in developing countries, the informal economy is the main area of production, employment and income generation. For instance, it ranges from 25 to 40 per cent of GDP in developing economies in Asia and Africa (UN-Habitat, 2016). In Mexico there are not estimations of labour informality by metropolitan area, but the National Survey of Occupation and Employment includes estimations for 33 of the most important cities in the country (Figure 4.5). All together, these cities exhibit an informality rate of 45.5 per cent; cities in the north of the country have lower rates (Monterrey, Chihuahua, Saltillo and La Paz); Mexico City has a relatively high informality rate (50 per cent); Puebla, Acapulco, Oaxaca and Cuernavaca have the highest labour informality with rates as high as 67.8 per cent in the case of Tlaxcala.

Poverty has become one of the most relevant social and economic problems in metropolitan areas. Urban poverty is a complex problem due to the concentration of population and the spatial heterogeneity in metropolitan areas. In

Table 4.7 Highest and lowest average years of schooling by metropolitan area, 1990, 2000, 2010 and 2015

	1990		2000		2010		2015	
1	Hermosillo	8.4	Ciudad Victoria	9	Ciudad Victoria	10.5	Hermosillo	11.1
2	Ciudad Victoria	8.3	Hermosillo	9	Hermosillo	10.4	Ciudad Victoria	10.9
3	La Paz	8.2	La Paz	9	La Paz	10.2	La Paz	10.7
4	Nogales	7.9	Mazatlan	9	Culiacan	9.9	Culiacan	10.6
5	Mexicali	7.8	Nogales	9	Mazatlán	9.8	Tepic	10.5
70	Puebla–Tlaxcala	4.9	Acayucan	6	Rioverde	7.2	Teziutlan	7.6
71	Tuxtla Gutierrez	4.9	La Piedad–Penjamo	6	Morelon–Uriangato	7.2	Zamora	7.6
72	Rioverde	4.7	Merida	5.9	La Piedad–Penjamo	7.2	Morelen–Uriangato	7.6
73	San Francisco del Rincon	4.6	San Francisco del Rincon	5.5	Tecomán	7	Tecoman	7.4
74	Aguascalientes	4.1	Teziutlan	5.5	San Francisco del Rincon	6.8	San Francisco del Rincon	7.4
Mean		6.1		7.4		8.7		9.2

Source: Based on INEGI (1991, 2001, 2011 & 2015).

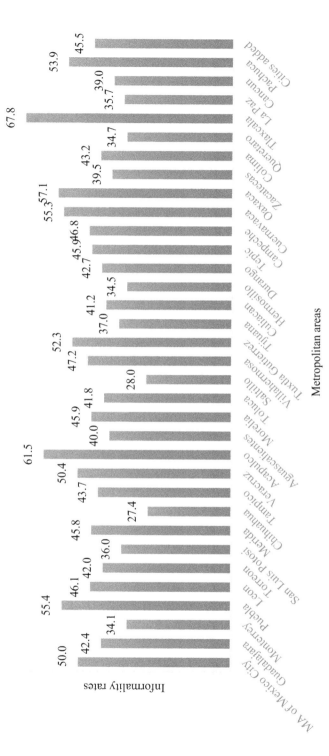

Figure 4.5 Labour informality rate, fourth quarter 2017 (%)

Source: INEGI (2018).

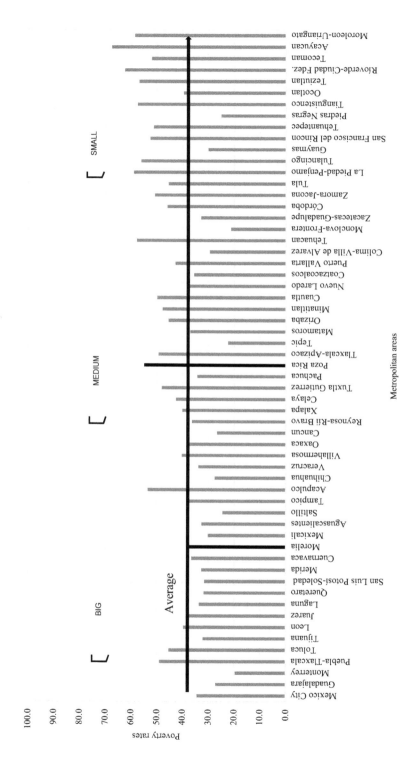

Figure 4.6 Poverty rates by metropolitan area by population size, 2010 (%)

Source: Based on CONEVAL (2014).

addition to insufficient income, the inhabitants of metropolitan spaces face difficulties associated with accessing housing, precarious housing conditions and irregular settlements where the lack of education, health and urban services and equipment affects their daily lives.

Significant poverty incidence is revealed in the set of municipalities that comprise the metropolitan areas of Mexico. The territorial pattern of poverty in metropolitan areas is not well defined, yet most with poverty above the metropolitan average of 41 per cent are in the south and south-east of the country (Acapulco, Tuxtla Gutierrez, Orizaba, Minatitlan, Cordoba, Acayucan, and Tehuantepec), in states in the centre of the country (State of Mexico, Puebla, Tlaxcala and Hidalgo) and in the state of Guanajuato.

The highest percentages of the population in poverty are found in the smallest metropolitan areas (under 500,000 inhabitants), whereas the largest metropolitan areas tend to have poverty rates lower than the average (Figure 4.6). Some exceptions to this pattern are Puebla and Toluca, where the poverty rate is close to 50 per cent. On the other hand, a number of small metropolitan areas have below-average poverty. The lowest poverty rate is observed in Monterrey, whereas Mexico City had a rate of 34.4 per cent and Guadalajara 27.1 per cent in 2010. The high percentages of poverty observed in metropolitan areas translate as large numbers of urban poor. Labour market conditions, and particularly labour informality, contribute to explaining this high and increasing metropolitan poverty.

Productivity and economic efficiency

Economic efficiency is strategic in boosting metropolitan and national wellbeing and competitiveness. Its measurement is informative of a number of aspects of urban development and contributes to a fundamental diagnosis with the aim of creating better practices and incentives for urban performance. From the economic point of view, efficiency is a concept that can be employed to evaluate the productive performance of a territory. Technical efficiency, in particular, indicates how close a territory is to its optimal production levels, given a production technology and factor endowments. Efficiency in metropolitan areas means reasonable resource allocation, appropriate management and the coordinated development of various urban social, political and economic aspects, and therefore strong competitiveness (Guo, He & Dong, 2011). Therefore there is increasing interest in the economic efficiency of cities, metropolitan areas, regions and countries.

According to the OECD (2015), Mexican cities do not exhibit a productivity corresponding to their potential, and their productivity levels per worker are significantly lower than those of cities in other OECD countries. Mexican cities have not taken advantage of their potential for economic growth due to serious structural problems that prevent them from translating urbanisation into economic development. One of these problems has been the widespread urban expansion. According to the OECD, in the last decade Mexican cities had the third-highest rate of urban expansion among member countries. Patterns of expansion have moved people away from jobs and urban services, resulting in losses of productivity and lower levels of wellbeing. The economic centralities remain strongly circumscribed to the central cities.

Data envelopment analysis (DEA) and the Malmquist index are non-parametric methods used for evaluating economic efficiency and productivity change. DEA uses linear programming and principles of frontier analysis to build an efficient frontier or empirical production function using a data set of similar economic units or decision-making units (DMUs). DEA compares metropolitan areas' input–output relations by assuming that they use the same kinds of inputs (e.g. labour and capital) to produce the same kinds of outputs (e.g. product or value added). The metropolitan areas with the best practices determine the maximum output achievable. The distance to the efficient production frontier sets the efficiency score for all other metropolitan areas. In other words, estimated efficiency is a relative score obtained by using the metropolitan areas with the best technological practices as references. The Malmquist index measures changes in total factor productivity (TFP) and allows the decomposition of TFP change into the change attributable to technical efficiency and that brought about by technical progress.

Table 4.8 presents efficiency indicators by year. According to estimates of technical efficiency in 2013 we observe a heterogeneous performance that would be better described as polarised efficiency: there is a small group of only five efficient metropolitan areas with more than 60 per cent of such areas below average efficiency, with some below 20 per cent. Average efficiency decreased over from 1998 to 2013. In 2013 mean efficiency was only 44 per cent.

Only Mexico City and Tehuantepec, which specialises in oil production, remained in the group of efficient metropolitan areas throughout the period. Monterrey, the second-largest metropolitan economy which is highly

Table 4.8 Efficient metropolitan areas and mean efficiency, 1998, 2003, 2008 and 2013

	1998	*2003*	*2008*	*2013*
1	Monclova–Frontera	Saltillo	Mexico City	Mexico City
2	Saltillo	Juarez	Tula	Monterrey
3	Mexico City	Mexico City	Monterrey	Tehuantepec
4	Leon	Leon	Tehuantepec	Teziutlan
5	San Francisco del Rincon	La Piedad–Penjamo	Acayucan	Acayucan
6	Tula	Monterrey		
7	Toluca	Tehuantepec		
8	Tehuantepec	Teziutlan		
9	Rioverde	Rioverde		
10	Acayucan	Acayucan		
Mean efficiency	**61.70%**	**64.20%**	**37.90%**	**44.10%**

Source: Based on INEGI (1999, 2004, 2009 & 2014).

Table 4.9 Summary of total factor productivity changes, 1998–2013

	Technical efficiency change index	Technological change index	Total factor productivity change index
1998–2003	1.067	0.888	0.948
2003–2008	0.262	3.409	0.894
2008–2013	1.856	0.51	0.946
All years mean	**0.804**	**1.156**	**0.929**

Source: Based on INEGI (1999, 2004, 2009 & 2014).

industrialised and located in the north, exhibited full efficiency from 2003. A group of small metropolitan areas achieved full efficiency, yet due to the nature of the methodology this group compares with metropolitan areas with similar characteristics, particularly in terms of size. At the other end of the spectrum Puerto Vallarta, Acapulco, Chilpancingo, Chetumal and Zacatecas were the most inefficient metropolitan areas in 2016. Puerto Vallarta, Acapulco and Chetumal are coastal tourist metropolitan areas where insecurity levels have increased considerably. Chilpancingo is another city with insecurity problems. These results are an indication of the ample room for improvement in the performance of the whole metropolitan area system and of most of the individual metropolitan areas which do not reach the optimal production frontier.

An assessment of changes in productive performance and productivity in Mexico's metropolitan areas, based on estimation of technical efficiency and TFP, is shown in Table 4.9. Changes in TFP and its components, technical change and efficiency change, provide us with significant information about the productive trends and potentiality of economic growth. Indices above 1.0 indicate positive change, and below 1.0, negative change. The whole group of metropolitan areas experienced a negative average change in TFP of 7.1 per cent per year between 1998 and 2013. Even though technological change increased productivity by 15.6 per cent, technical efficiency had a negative impact, reducing productivity by 19.6 per cent. Thus, the negative change in productivity in metropolitan areas is the result of increasing inefficiency in the use of resources, despite their technological advancement. The means of all the years are strongly influenced by changes in TFP between 2003 and 2008, when technical efficiency fell dramatically.

A review by individual metropolitan area reveals their very different trajectories. Only a third saw positive changes in TFP (Figure 4.7). Many of these areas' expansion was the result of technological changes implemented with the transformation of their inputs into outputs. In a few cases this was combined with some improvement in technical efficiency.

Figure 4.7 indicates important levels of inefficiency in most of the metropolitan economies. Moreover, their capacity to generate and maximise their material wealth is deteriorating, endangering their economic stability and cohesion. Productive efficiency problems are not limited to the local level; the country as

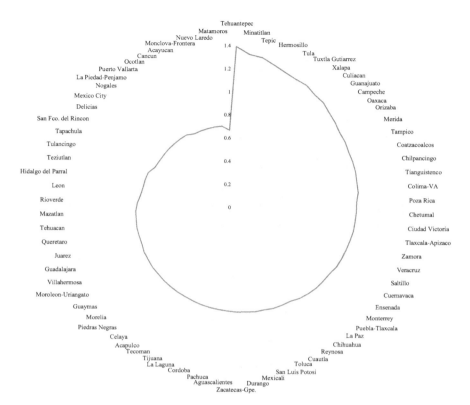

Figure 4.7 Malmquist total factor productivity index by metropolitan area, 1998–2013
Source: Based on INEGI (1999, 2004, 2009 & 2014).

a whole has significant problems with productivity. Apart from further analysis, productivity and efficiency issues require attention and a private and a public policy strategy.

Concluding remarks

While the economy is just one component of the complex running of cities, it deserves close attention due to its implications for and relationships to other urban dimensions. The economic activity that drives growth is heavily concentrated in cities, with metropolitan areas in particular seen as the engines pulling the economy. It is not uncommon for individual metropolitan areas to account for more than a quarter of national GDP in both developing and developed countries. Growth and higher productivity are not limited to the largest cities, as medium–sized cities are increasingly emerging as economic powers. International evidence has showed the economic significance of metropolitan areas and urban agglomerations.

Certainly, size and agglomeration economies can influence urban fortunes through productivity gains, but there are too many examples of metropolitan areas that are not realising their potential. In some of them growth is stagnating, productivity and efficiency are low, their labour market is not dynamic and their productive economic base is weak. These cities are deriving few advantages from their size and instead are suffering from diseconomies of agglomeration. This is mainly happening in developing regions such as Latin America but also in metropolitan areas of the developed world.

Understanding the economic performance of metropolitan economies brings valuable insight into the development of these territories that national assessments tend to obscure. Urban performance can be assessed across diverse economic and social aspects using a variety of indicators. This chapter is an attempt to pinpoint some of the patterns and trends which appear to be crucial to assess how metropolitan economies in Mexico are performing. By analysing the spatial concentration of economic activities, productivity, efficiency, specialisations, informality, poverty and labour markets, a highly differentiated economic performance and unstable patterns and tendencies are identified across metropolitan areas.

A few metropolitan areas, such as Mexico City and Monterrey, have remained as the most relatively efficient over time. These two metropolises have been true engines of economic development in both their regions and the country by concentrating and, in some years, attracting new activity. Nevertheless, trends in spatial concentration of production indicate relatively small but gradual losses in Mexico City. Guadalajara has experienced similar reductions in its share in economic activity, whereas Monterrey has increased its relative relevance and has consolidated its position as the second metropolitan economy in the country. Deterioration in spatial concentration of production is observed in a number of traditional maquiladora and manufacturing centres in the north of the country, including Ciudad Juarez and Tijuana; Puebla, Toluca and especially Queretaro have consistent progress; tourist poles such as Cancun, Puerto Vallarta and Acapulco are decreasing in relevance; metropolitan areas with oil-related activity are a special group with high gross production but also high instability in their economic variables; and a series of small metropolitan islands exhibit variable behaviour.

In Queretaro and Monterrey production per capita is relatively high and increasing. In contrast to these economic successes and improvements to average wellbeing, poverty rates are variable but high in general across metropolitan areas. In addition, there are unequal metropolitan trajectories in terms of the evolution of labour markets and different production structures are configured, in different regional contexts. Overall the heterogeneous metropolitan performance brings about the challenge of extending economic benefits to all metropolitan areas.

The variability of the results across variables and periods makes it difficult to identify stable categories and trends. Therefore, special caution is needed to measure and interpret the performance in particular metropolis. In this respect, the task of generating economic information in greater detail remains fundamental. Last, but not least, whether from the perspective of the metropolitan system or of individual metropolitan areas, it is essential to identify the driving factors of economic development to deepen the metropolitan economic debate in Mexico and elsewhere. Chapter 6 deals with the task of pinpointing those elements that contribute to the improved economic performance of cities. In the following chapter, I develop an analysis of local public finances which, I suggest, is a significant determinant of the functioning and performance of metropolitan economies.

References

Alix-García, J. & Sellars, E. (2018). Locational fundamentals, trade, and the changing urban landscape of Mexico. Selected Paper prepared for presentation at the 2018 Agricultural & Applied Economics Association Annual Meeting, Washington, DC. Available at: https://EconPapers.repec.org/RePEc:ags:aaea18:274238.

Bouchet, M., Lius, S. & Parilla, J. (2018). *Global Metro Monitor 2018*. Washington, D.C.: Metropolitan Policy Program at Brookings. Available at: www.brookings.edu/wp-content/uploads/2018/06/Brookings-Metro_Global-Metro-Monitor-2018.pdf.

Bronger, D. (1984). 'Metropolisation in China?' *GeoJournal*, 8(2), 137–146. Available at: https://doi.org/10.1007/BF00231492.

CONEVAL. (2014). *Pobreza urbana y de las zonas metropolitanas en México* [online]. México: Consejo Nacional de Evaluación de la Política de Desarrollo Social. Available at: www.coneval.org.mx/Informes/Pobreza/Pobreza%20urbana/Pobreza_urbana_y_de_las_zonas_metropolitanas_en_Mexico.pdf.

Cuadrado-Roura, J. R. & Fernández Guell, J. M. (2005). 'Las áreas metropolitanas frente al desafío de la competitividad'. In Rojas, E. (ed.). *Gobernar las metrópolis*. Washington, D.C.: Inter-American Development Bank, pp. 63–126. Available at: http://site.ebrary.com/id/10201140.

De Mattos, C. A. (2010). 'Globalización y metamorfosis urbana en América Latina: de la ciudad a lo urbano generalizado'. *Revista de geografía Norte Grande*, (47), 81–104. Available at: www.redalyc.org/articulo.oa?id=30015379005.

Duranton, G. (2015). 'Growing through cities in developing countries'. *World Bank Research Observer*, 30(1), 39–73. Available at: https://openknowledge.worldbank.org/bitstream/handle/10986/24808/wbro_30_1_39.pdf?sequence=1&isAllowed=y.

Fernández, A. (2017). *Metropolises addressing the global agendas*. Issue Paper 02. Barcelona: Metropolis Observatory. Available at: www.metropolis.org/sites/default/files/metropolis-observatory_issue-paper-2_en.

Florida, R., Mellander, C. & Gulden, T. (2009). *The role of cities and Metropolitan areas in the global economy*. Working Paper Series: Martin Prosperity Research MPIWP-002. Martin Prosperity Institute. Available at: www.creativeclass.com/rfcgdb/articles/Global%20metropolis.pdf.

Garza, G. (2010). 'La transformación urbana de México, 1970–2020'. In Garza, G. & Schteingart, M. (eds.). *Los grandes problemas de México: Desarrollo urbano y regional: T-II*. Mexico, D. F.: El Colegio de Mexico, pp. 31–86. Available at: www.jstor.org/stable/j.ctt1657tf2.5.

Guo, T., He, S. & Dong, G. (2011). 'Metropolitan resources efficiencies, change trends and causes in China under the goal to build an international metropolis'. *Journal of Geographical Sciences*, 21(4), 746–756. Available at: https://link.springer.com/article/10.1007/s11442-011-0877-y.

INEGI. (1991). *XI Censo General de Población y Vivienda 1990* [online]. Available at: www.beta.inegi.org.mx/proyectos/ccpv/1990/default.html.

INEGI. (1999). *Censos Económicos 1999* [online]. Available at: www.inegi.org.mx/est/conte nidos/proyectos/ce/ce1999/default.aspx.

INEGI. (2001). *XII Censo General de Población y Vivienda 2000* [online]. Available at: www.beta.inegi.org.mx/proyectos/ccpv/2000/default.html.

INEGI. (2004). *Censos Económicos 2004* [online]. Available at: www.inegi.org.mx/est/conte nidos/proyectos/ce/ce2004/default.aspx.

INEGI. (2009). *Censos Económicos 2009* [online]. Available at: www.inegi.org.mx/est/conte nidos/espanol/proyectos/censos/ce2009/default.asp?s=est&c=14220.

INEGI. (2011). *Censo de Población y Vivienda 2010* [online]. Available at: www.beta.inegi.org. mx/proyectos/ccpv/2010/.

INEGI. (2014). *Censos Económicos 2014: Resultados definitivos* [online]. Available at: www.inegi.org.mx/est/contenidos/proyectos/ce/ce2014/default.aspx.

INEGI. (2015). *Encuesta intercensal 2015* [online]. Available at: www.beta.inegi.org.mx/proyectos/enchogares/especiales/intercensal/.

INEGI. (2018). *Encuesta Nacional de Ocupación y Empleo (ENOE)* [online]. Available at: www.beta.inegi.org.mx/proyectos/enchogares/regulares/enoe/.

Lefèvre, C. (2010). 'The improbable metropolis: Decentralization, local democracy and metropolitan areas in the Western world'. *Análise Social*, XLV(197), 623–637.

Manzano, N. (2009). 'Competitividad entre metrópolis de América Latina'. *Revista EURE*, XXXV(106), 51–78. Available at: https://scielo.conicyt.cl/pdf/eure/v35n106/art04.pdf.

Méndez, R. (2007). 'El territorio de las nuevas economías metropolitanas'. *Revista EURE*, XXXIII(100), 51–67 Available at: www.eure.cl/index.php/eure/article/view/1370.

Méndez, R. (2008). 'Procesos recientes en regiones metropolitanas: transformaciones económicas y reorganización territorial: Algunas interpretaciones y debates actuales'. Presented at Coloquio Ibérico de Geografía, Alcalá de Henares. Available at: www.gedeur.es/publicaciones/PUBLICACIONES_WEB/regionesmetropolitanastransformacionesespa cialesynueva%20economia/MENDEZ2008PONENCIAIBERICO.pdf.

Montero, L. & García, J. (2017). *Panorama multidimensional del desarrollo urbano en América Latina y el Caribe: Documentos de proyectos.* Santiago: ONU, CEPAL. Available at: https://repositorio.cepal.org/bitstream/handle/11362/41974/1/S1700257_es.pd.

Moreno, O. (2005). 'Reestructuración económica y refuncionalización territorial en México: Su impacto en el sistema regional y el urbano en México 1980–2000' [online]. *Revista Electrónica de Geografía y Ciencias Sociales*, IX(194). Available at: www.ub.edu/geocrit/sn/sn-194-78.htm.

OECD. (2006). *OECD territorial reviews: Competitive cities in the global economy.* Paris: OECD Publishing. Available at: www.oecd.org/cfe/regional-policy/oecdterritorialreviewscom petitivecitiesintheglobaleconomy.htm.

OECD. (2015). *OECD urban policy reviews: Mexico – transforming urban policy and housing finance.* Paris: OECD Publishing. Available at: https://read.oecd-ilibrary.org/urban-rural-and-regional-development/oecd-urban-policy-reviews-mexico-2015_978926422 7293-en#

OECD. (2018). *OECD regions and cities at a glance 2018.* Paris: OECD Publishing. Available at: https://doi.org/10.1787/reg_cit_glance-2018-en.

Rionda-Ramírez, J. I. (2007). 'Dinámica metropolitana en México'. *Economía Sociedad y Territorio*, VII(25), 241–266. Available at: http://dx.doi.org/10.22136/est002007237.

Sala-i-Martin, X. X. (1996). 'The classical approach to convergence analysis'. *The Economic Journal*, 106(437), 1019–1036.

Suarez-Villa, L. (1988). 'Metropolitan evolution, sectoral economic change, and the city size distribution'. *Urban Studies*, 25(1), 1–20. Available at: https://doi.org/10.1080/00420 988820080011.

Trejo, A. (2016). 'Nuevas Dinámicas Económicas Metropolitanas y Regionales en México y los Problemas de la Política Territorial'. In Negrete, M. E. (ed.). *Urbanización y Política Urbana en Iberoamérica: Experiencias, Análisis y Reflexiones.* Ciudad de México: El Colegio de México, pp. 107–144.

UN-Habitat. (2016). *Urbanization and development: Emerging futures: World Cities Report 2016.* Nairobi: UN-Habitat. Available at: www.unhabitat.org/wp-content/uploads/2014/03/ WCR-%20Full-Report-2016.pdf.

Vargas et al. (2017). *RED 2017. Urban growth and access to opportunities: A challenge for Latin America.* Bogota: Banco de Desarrollo de América Latina, CAF. Available at: http://sci oteca.caf.com/handle/123456789/1091.

WEF. (2018). Cities and urbanisation: Urban economies [online]. World Economic Forum. Available at: https://toplink.weforum.org/knowledge/insight/a1Gb0000000LiPhEAK/ explore/dimension/a1G0X000004Pz5WUAS/summary.

5 Public financing in metropolitan areas

Introduction

Contemporary urbanisation has progressively been defined by patterns of urban expansion and metropolisation, the functional boundaries of cities becoming informal and always changing, whereas their political and administrative divisions have rigid boundaries. Several difficulties are caused by such ever-expanding cities that function as a single urban area but are governed by multiple jurisdictions. The major role assigned to local governments is the provision of goods and services to residents within a particular geographic area that is defined from an administrative standpoint; however, by their very nature metropolitan areas are not suited to administrative jurisdictions such as municipalities. Jurisdictional fragmentation usually disconnects the territorial scope of urban needs from the public resources required to fulfil those needs. Increasingly, this mismatch occurs in an overall context of constrained public budgets and local authorities being asked to do more with less. This is a growing and increasingly daunting challenge for metropolitan areas, because the availability, allocation and management of public financial resources determine the possibility of achieving economic and social objectives for development (i.e. reducing poverty; ensuring competitiveness, environmental sustainability and human capital formation; the provision of public services; and an adequate supply of urban equipment and infrastructure).

While not the only aspect, the underlying legal and administrative arrangements relating to public finances and their performance contribute to explain substantive problems in metropolitan areas, and should be analysed with a view to making public finances more supportive of metropolitan objectives (OECD, 2001). Inefficient public finances can become a critical threat to the performance of metropolitan economies. A major problem confronting most local governments, especially in less-developed countries, is the widening gap between the availability of financial resources and spending needs. Metropolitan areas in Latin America and the Caribbean, for instance, face critical pressure to overcome underfunding for the betterment and expansion of infrastructure and services. Despite various improvements to the management of metropolitan finances around the world, comprehensive metropolitan area fiscal reforms remain largely non-existent or inadequate. Governments have not developed the ability to effectively manage metropolitan wide fiscal issues: the delivery of most services is inefficient, large infrastructure deficits persist, revenues remain scarce and appropriate transfer systems have not been implemented (Bahl, Linn & Wetzel, 2013). As the OECD (2001, p. 94) puts it, 'Local government structures are often unwieldy, tax and transfer systems are ill adapted to the form and function of modern city-region economies, and government policies, in general, seldom recognise or address the particular needs of cities'.

While developed countries have paid more attention to financing their metropolitan areas by granting special revenue-raising powers, instituting special intergovernmental transfer arrangements and granting metropolitan governments state-level status, metropolitan areas in less-developed countries, whose expenditure and revenue regimes are highly centralised, depend less on local taxation and more on transfers. In these countries, the replacement of revenue regimes and the provision of increased powers of taxation to local governments is frequently hindered by political competition and the pain associated with imposing taxes at the local level (Bahl, 2010).

Like several countries in the less-industrialised world, Mexico lacks fiscal and transfer systems that reflect the differences between metropolitan areas and other local contexts. The allocation of responsibilities, functions and financial resources is based on the prevailing political-administrative structures. These confer on the municipal government the function of providing basic urban services to the population without distinguishing between metropolitan, urban and rural environments or between small and big municipalities.

This chapter draws attention to the critical need for a more metropolitan-sensitive approach to public finances. It identifies a number of general guidelines for a normative model of metropolitan public finances, describes the decentralisation process and the institutional and legal frameworks that define public local budgets in Mexico and presents an empirical analysis of metropolitan areas in the country with a focus on the macroevolution and structure of public budgets, as well as their performance and disparities. Metropolitan areas are classified based on indicators of financial performance.

A metropolitan approach to public finances

Metropolitan areas face common and daunting fiscal and financial challenges of increasing scope and complexity. Bahl, Linn and Wetzel (2013) see the basic challenge as one of capturing a sufficient share of local economic growth to finance necessary expenditure and deliver public services in a cost-effective and inclusive way. The OECD (2001) argues that many metropolitan areas need to cope with and adjust to an environment of decentralisation and fiscal federalism, weak local autonomy, significant financial and fiscal disparities, difficult access to capital for investment and the necessary participation of the private sector in the provision of services.

The metropolitan approach to public finance claims that to overcome a variety of financial and fiscal challenges, the distinctive characteristics of metropolitan areas – some of which relate to formal government structures and others to particularities of revenue and spending – must be recognised. Metropolitan areas involve a more complex urban environment, a high concentration of population and production, and often problematic legal and government arrangements. These particularities imply mounting pressures on the efficient use of resources, increase the need for innovative financial tools that promote efficiency and demand mechanisms to stimulate the tax payment of non-residents for the services they consume within a given metropolitan area (Bird & Slack, 2005).

Without fiscal metropolitan structures, governmental fragmentation adversely affects the behaviour of public finances, economic performance and the effective provision of public services (Chernick & Reschovsky, 2006). It is also assumed to imply high heterogeneity (Bahl, Linn & Wetzel, 2013). Fragmentation involves not only the possibility of little or no horizontal or vertical intergovernmental coordination and cooperation, but also weak technical or administrative capacity on the part of local governments, especially in the poorest and smallest jurisdictions. In addition to the presence of multiple uncoordinated and fragmented local governments in metropolitan areas, the overlapping functions of different tiers of government make the administration, distribution and execution of public resources more problematic than in other local environments.

Economic and demographic factors also have significant implications for public finances. Concentrated population and growth create an ever-increasing demand for social services such as housing, transportation and cultural activities, as well as for infrastructure and urban amenities. Per capita expenditure in metropolitan areas is usually higher than in other cities because of the number of non-residents who regularly use services and infrastructure. In addition, the demographic concentration involves greater social and economic heterogeneity and more diversified demand for services (Bird & Slack, 2005). Similarly, expenditure needs increase in volume and complexity, and sufficient revenue is needed to meet those needs.

A number of guidelines have been suggested for a metropolitan revenue and expenditure model. The most general rule refers to the allocation of greater metropolitan control not only in the provision of services but also in their financing and accountability mechanisms, and in the formulation of policies. If services are provided locally while financing and accountability are implemented by, or strongly dependent on, higher levels of government, inefficiencies can emerge that compromise the fiscal health of the metropolitan area and can lead to the need for financial rescue. Regarding allocation for expenditure the magnitude and objectives of subsidies deserve careful attention to avoid overspending. Excessive subsidies can imply efficiency costs that impact the economic competitiveness of the metropolis. However, it is desirable to align spending on social and economic policy so that the one is not detrimental to the other (Chernick & Reschovsky, 2006).

Bird and Slack (2005) suggest allocating a share of current revenue to a reserve fund to avoid financing capital investment through debt. They argue that whereas operating expenditure tends to increase over time according to population growth, inflation and other factors that can be anticipated, the evolution of capital investment is more volatile. The wide irregularity of capital investment generates acute synchronisation problems, especially in metropolitan areas. Governments need to protect themselves from these effects to safeguard the availability of funds (Figure 5.1).

In addition to the wider capacity of the tax base, the metropolitan revenue model should consider the different scales and natures of the services provided. As a rule, metropolitan agglomerations should be given greater fiscal autonomy with greater capacity and responsibility for levying their own taxes and collecting their own revenues (Bird & Slack, 2005). Designing a revenue model for metropolitan areas entails an adequate choice of financial instruments and the setting of both tariffs and tax rates in order to be able to implement efficient decisions about the quantity of public services. However, such fiscal and financial reforms and reorganisation are complex because no 'one size fits all' approach across metropolitan areas can adequately accommodate all of the varying circumstances. Which models of fiscal governance can best account for the particular characteristics of, and problems in, metropolitan areas is an issue of great debate and remains as an empirical question (Bird & Slack, 2007).

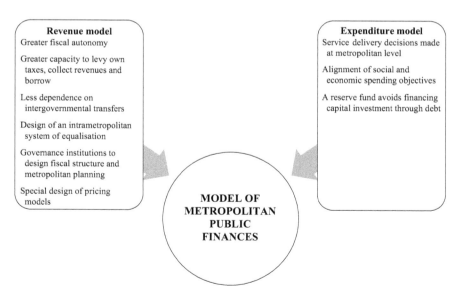

Figure 5.1 General guidelines for a model of metropolitan public finances

Source: Author's elaboration.

While supplying governments or metropolitan institutions with greater fiscal powers is extensively practiced in developed countries, international responses to the need for a structure and special arrangements for metropolitan finances are diverse. A variety of metropolitan governance institutions exist around the world, reflecting both the complexity and the context-specificity of the issues to be resolved (Bird & Slack, 2007). Largely, when metropolitan governments exist they have been given a limited range of responsibilities and functions and operate in a similar way to the lowest tiers of government. Functional specialisation – where the metropolitan area is served by general-purpose metropolitan institutions (districts) and public or semi-public companies with specific responsibilities and functions – has been an alternative approach of metropolitan fiscal structure (Slack, 2007; Bahl, 2010).

The reform of public finances with a metropolitan approach is often held back by political factors that explain both national governments' reluctance to extend the decentralisation of tax revenues and the weak use of revenue authority granted to local governments. The search for a balance between metropolitan efficiency and the preservation of local control is also influenced by local interests that hinder the formation of governments and metropolitan institutional structures (Bahl, 2010). Hence, any fiscal and financial reform requires capacity and political will on the part of local authorities and the marshalling of national political support to introduce the necessary legal and institutional changes. Each situation is unique, and the design and process of reform must be adjusted to reflect both local and national circumstances (UN-Habitat, 2015).

In some cases where political factors have hindered the formation of metropolitan fiscal structures, voluntary cooperation, association or special districts by service have been employed to meet local demand and implement integrated financial schemes. Metropolitan-level fiscal and financial organisational structures are possible without necessarily creating a metropolitan government. It is compulsory, however, to move forward with institutional arrangements of a financial nature to improve metropolitan financial capacity and performance, and especially the capacity for self-financing (Bird & Slack, 2005).

The supra-municipal institution whose geographic scope covers the entire service region is another mechanism for coordinating services such as public transport, water, the collection and treatment of solid waste, etc., that offer opportunities for significant economies of scale and reductions in the cost of negative externalities. Therefore, municipal associations need to be institutionalised in national constitutions (Bahl, 2010). Alternatively, two-tier metropolitan structures allow the formation of metropolitan districts for the development of infrastructure in services that lend themselves to coordination, planning and regional pricing, the regional district performing as a funding and service-delivery area while the fiscal or tax system is structured according to the two-tier government structure. Taxes at the lower level of government are adjusted to meet the basic rules of efficiency and specially to eliminate the export effect. On the other hand, a metropolitan- or district-level organisation would guarantee better balance between the allocation of spending and the allocation of revenue. This arrangement also requires the adoption of legislative changes by a higher level of government. Any of these pathways would create substantial changes in the tax bases assigned to metropolitan areas. Chapter 8 contains more in-depth analysis of metropolitan governance organisation to address the provision of public services and financing. Next, we examine metropolitan public finances in metropolitan areas in Mexico.

Decentralisation, fiscal federalism and the broader context of local public finances in Mexico

The ability of metropolitan areas to deal with the issues and problems of public finance needs to be evaluated in light of the decentralisation processes that have been a part of national restructuring, adjustment programs and fiscal federalism in many countries. Most cities in developing countries have depended largely on central government transfers, with less revenue from local taxes and fees. In contrast, central governments in those countries continue to control the most profitable sources of revenue, which are potentially suitable for financing urban areas. Fiscal reform is necessary, yet it is not an easy task, especially in developing nations where, according to UN-Habitat (2015), political economy issues are critical for understanding central governments' refusal to decentralise significant amounts of tax revenue on the one hand, and local governments' refusal to use the tax revenue authority that they are granted efficiently on the other. The local political economy determines the success of any fiscal reform. Local authorities require political will and need to develop their capacity to generate local political support in order to be able to make the legal and institutional adjustments necessary for improved financial and fiscal situations in cities and metropolitan areas (Smoke, 2015).

Decentralisation reform in Latin America and the Caribbean has been ongoing for more than three decades, based on two streams of thought. The first is associated with neoliberal thinking, which argues that decentralising state powers makes services more efficient. The second holds that political and administrative decentralisation bring social policies closer to the community and boost democratisation (Antunez & Galilea, 2003). Fiscal and administrative decentralisation, in particular, have important implications for local and metropolitan public finances. Most countries in the region have experienced the increasing decentralisation of spending responsibilities. Subnational governments have been given a much larger share of the public-sector budget, although not as large as that in most industrial countries. However, the rapid devolution of spending responsibilities has not been mirrored on the revenue side. With the exception of Brazil, and to a much lesser extent Argentina, Bolivia and Colombia, subnational own revenue accounts for only a small share of total tax revenue, creating large vertical imbalances (Brosio & Jiménez, 2012). Smoke (2015) argues that fiscal decentralisation has been particularly disappointing, with weak own-revenue generation one of the most problematic fiscal concerns in developing countries.

Mexico is governed under a federal system in which powers and functions are distributed between central, intermediate and municipal governments, although historically the country has seen significant political, administrative and financial centralisation. Between the 1940s and 1970s intergovernmental relations in the country were characterised by the federation's dominance over the states, also reproduced in the relationship between the states and their municipalities. In the 1980s formal decentralisation was initiated based on the subsidiarity principle, which sees local government as the most suitable level to exercise revenue and spending functions due to its proximity to the population (Sobarzo, 2004), while redistributive and stabilisation functions were the responsibility of the central government (Rosales, 2012).

Mexico's decentralisation included multiple constitutional reforms granting greater power to municipalities (Jalomo, 2011). On paper, it was conceived as the basic driving force to boost local development and the rational use of public resources. Under this premise, the main legal foundation of the process was reforms in 1983, 1987, 1999 and 2009 to Article 115 of the national constitution that placed the municipality at the core of the administrative and political organisation of the national state. Article 115 stipulates municipal autonomy, municipal sources of revenue (property tax, fees and tariffs) and municipal functions (provision of local public services and local development) (Meza, 2004). In practice, decentralisation responded to the macroeconomic context of the moment: fiscal and administrative crises in the federal government (ibid.) and high inflation (Rosales, 2012). Certainly decentralisation was one of the various state reforms – which included trade liberalisation, privatisation and deregulation – aiming to reduce the size of the federal administration, eliminate the fiscal deficit and strengthen a free-market approach. Regardless of its origin, decentralisation had an important impact on the nature of intergovernmental relations, federalism and the structure of public finances (Sobarzo, 2004).

In addition to the constitutional reforms to Article 115, other legal and financial reforms were implemented in the move to fiscal federalism.[1] In 1980 the second Law of Fiscal Coordination (LFC) created the National System of Fiscal Coordination (NSFC) to bolster ongoing efforts towards fiscal decentralisation. The NSFC was the institutional framework for the allocation of federation, states and municipalities' fiscal powers and spending responsibilities via laws, regulations and formulas for distribution. Paradoxically, as part of this fiscal system Mexico's states subscribed to an adhesion agreement handing over broader powers of taxation to the federal government while states and municipalities participated in the administration of federal revenues (Courchene & Diaz-Cayeros, 2000; Meza, 2004). Thus, the federal government centralised tax rights, leaving subnational governments to collect only small fees and other minor taxes. The federal government collected sales and income taxes; the states, payroll taxes, vehicle tax and fuel tax; and the municipalities, property tax (Sobarzo, 2004).

On the expenditure side, until 1997 the most important component of the transfer system was unconditional revenue-sharing – the so-called Item 28.

In that year federal transfers to municipalities were expanded via Item 26 – Social and Productive Development in Poverty Regions. In 1998 the LFC created five funds under the new Item 33. Item 33 includes conditional funds transferred to states and municipalities to finance expenditure programmes that had been decentralised to states, that is, for education and health, and to municipalities for basic local infrastructure (Moreno, 2003).

Article 115 of the Constitution of Mexico specifies that municipalities are responsible for freely managing their finances. However, the municipalities do not have their own legislative bodies, and the state-level congresses issue the different laws that govern the municipal budget, inhibiting local autonomy. Hence, in addition to the LFC, municipal public finances are regulated by a set of legal and administrative rules – the federal expenditure budget, state-level constitutions, organic municipal laws, municipal finance laws, state public debt laws, laws of municipal revenue and the municipal expenditure budget. Additionally, the decree issuing the financial discipline law for the states and municipalities was published in the Official Gazette of the Federation in April 2016 to promote the sustainable management of public finances by the Mexican Federation and its states, municipalities and capital city (Palomera & Bojórquez, 2015).

The various constitutional, tax and fiscal reforms throughout the 1980s and 1990s have transformed the volume and composition of local government revenue and expenditure. The general macroeconomic environment of the recurrent economic crises (Aguilar, 2010) and declining oil revenues (Mendoza, 2010) has also delineated the fate of local public finances. Decentralisation has resulted in a major challenge to build up solid alternatives that meet the demands of the population adequately (Diaz, 2015), and the scarcity of financial resources has become one of the main obstacles attending the most pressing social problems in the country.

Mexico faces a number of challenges that limit its capacity for healthy and sustainable public finances. It is one of the countries in the region with the lowest tax revenue in proportion to its GDP, and its tax intake is the lowest of all Latin American countries. Many of the main fiscal and financial weaknesses of the Mexican federal system manifest at the local level. According to Castañeda and Pardinas (2012) the 1997 reforms to the LFC largely contributed to increasing state and municipal expenditure authority without fostering responsibilities or capacity for revenue collection.

According to Mexico's constitution, local governments must provide infrastructure and a variety of services including transportation, water, sewage, waste collection and disposal, police and fire, parks, recreation, culture, housing and social assistance. Governments need enough resources to finance all of these functions. However, the type of legal and institutional structure in place in the country has had significant consequences for the quantity and quality of the services provided, their efficiency and how they are financed.

Several problems with municipal finances in Mexico have been extensively analysed and discussed: the uniform allocation of revenue and expenditure responsibilities for all municipalities regardless of size or administrative capacity (Rosales, 2012); the lack of financial discipline arising from the greater decentralisation of spending accompanied by limited powers of taxation (Sobarzo, 2004); poor financial capacity, inadequate financing policies, low payment of citizens with strong preference for subsidised services, lack of political will to strengthen local tax-collection capacity, fiscal laziness and few incentives to collect local taxes (Rosales, 2012); significant dependence on federal transfers, distribution mechanism failures and recurrent operational deficits (Meza, 2004); poor collection of property tax and high heterogeneity in administrative and resource management (Sobarzo, 2004); limited financial autonomy and inefficiency in property tax collection, differing considerably depending on the size of the municipality (Rosales, 2012), as well as among municipalities of similar size (Cabrero & Martinez-Vazquez, 2000); the excessive decentralisation of total public spending (Sobarzo, 2004); the growing expansion of current and administrative expenditure in relation to investment spending (Cabrero & Martinez-Vazquez, 2000); the boom in borrowing (Kinto, 2009); and inefficient provision local public services (Rosales, 2012).

To sum up, municipalities have exhibited poor fiscal and financial performance, strong dependence on federal transfers, strong municipal heterogeneity and high municipal inefficiency. Figure 5.2 summarises the general trends in municipal public finances before and after the municipal reforms of 1983 and 1999: growing current expenditure in relation to investment spending, scarce

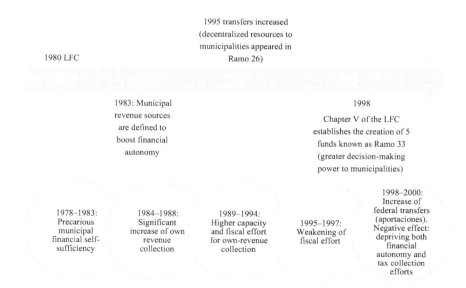

Figure 5.2 Municipal public finances, 1978–2000

Source: Based on Cabrero and Martinez-Vazquez (2000).

autonomy due to the high percentage of expenditure financed by conditional transfers (Cabrero, 2004) and the high budget underrun (Meza, 2004).

Over the years, financial and fiscal decentralisation have revealed a precarious federal design in terms of vertical balance, competition and autonomy, as well as a lack of coordination mechanisms. States and municipalities' own-revenue bases remain weak; subnational governments are heavily dependent on federal transfers and less reliant on own revenues. Municipalities in particular are maintained in a subordinate position and have developed very little in the way of administrative, technical and human capabilities (Diaz, 2015). For the most part, they face severe financial and fiscal constraints as well as increasing devolution of responsibilities to the local level.

Trends, composition and dynamics of public finances in metropolitan areas

An empirical tradition is starting to emerge in studies of the public finances of metropolitan areas, particularly in developed countries. Despite the difficulties of comparing very dissimilar structures (OECD, 2001), common patterns include metropolitan areas' efforts to reinforce their own resources, reduce their strong dependency on transfers and grants from central government, improve their capture of value-added and transfer part of their financing and the operation of infrastructure and public services to the private sector. Studies particularly call attention to the increasing involvement of the private sector in infrastructure services.

Moya (2014) and others tackle the issue of the functioning and impact of the Metropolitan Fund (MF), a relatively small federal subsidy designed to fund metropolitan projects and to complement state resources. However, few studies of local public finances in Mexico analyse metropolitan areas. Aguilar (2010), for instance, examines the factors determining the tax capacity of three metropolitan areas. This work presents three main findings: with few exceptions, municipal governments show a decreasing fiscal effort; there is high dependence on intergovernmental transfers with a harmful effect on fiscal effort; and fiscal capacities are spatially differentiated. The first two findings are in clear contradiction to the emerging trends identified in OECD countries. On the other hand, the literature on municipal finances reveals a couple of stylised facts about local public spending; that is, the expansion of current expenditure in relation to investment spending and the boom in borrowing.

Speaking of metropolitan public finances in Mexico is problematic, because there is no formal public budget at that level. The MF is the only dedicated federal fund for metropolitan areas. It was established in 2008 by the Ministry of Finance as a federal subsidy designed for the country's officially identified metropolitan areas to finance studies, plans, evaluations, programmes, projects and infrastructure. However, the MF has very limited resources given the scale of metropolitan projects; its size varies from year to year depending on federal government revenue; it accounts for only a small fraction of the public budgets;

the projects that it funds are typically on a local rather than a metropolitan scale; it has had a limited impact on encouraging cooperation, joint planning and the implementation of projects; and its administrative management and legal framework are complex (OECD, 2015).

IMCO (2010) calculates metropolitan areas' public finances by adding up the municipal budgets. The public budget of the Mexico City Metropolitan Area, for instance, aggregates the data from all municipalities in the metropolitan area and Mexico City. By using the same aggregation criterion, public finances in metropolitan areas are estimated and analysed.[2] Local public financing is strongly concentrated in metropolitan areas. In 2015, 72 per cent of total municipal revenue and 89 per cent of own revenue was concentrated in metropolitan municipalities. Differences in the amount of revenue items in metropolitan and non-metropolitan municipalities are presented in Figure 5.3. In both cases, absolute revenues increase over time; however, the evolution of different revenue items varies. Conditional transfers soared in all municipalities in 1997 and have become the most important source of revenue for non-metropolitan municipalities, but have remained below own revenue and unconditional transfers in metropolitan areas. In metropolitan areas own revenue and unconditional transfers tend to converge over time, while in the case of non-metropolitan municipalities conditional and unconditional transfers also converge over time and have exceeded own revenue since 1999.

Conditional transfers, especially in non-metropolitan municipalities, exhibit the highest growth rates of over 20 per cent between 1989 and 2016, in opposition to own revenue and unconditional transfers (Figure 5.4).

A general problem that hampers the adequate provision of services and public investment in Mexico and Latin America is the weak collection of own revenue and local taxes. Local tax revenue contributes an average of 3.8 per cent of national GDP in OECD countries and 0.8 per cent in those of the Latin America and the Caribbean, but barely 0.3 per cent in Mexico (Figure 5.5). Gómez and Jiménez (2012) argue that, in practice, the decentralisation of taxing authority to subnational government has been relatively weak in most Latin American countries. Local tax collection in the region has remained stagnant for years due to limitations to the level and structure of subnational taxation and the tax bases available to these governments. The taxes collected by local governments are generally taxes on assets, primarily real estate.

Traditional federalism theory prescribes a very limited fiscal base for subnational governments, arguing that the most adequate local tax is property tax: easy to administer, it has a relatively immobile tax base, does not involve conflicts of harmonisation nor competition between subnational governments or with central government, is relatively stable and predictable and has a visible fiscal base which facilitates accountability (Kitchen, 2005; Bird & Slack, 2005). Nonetheless, compared to municipal governments, the sources of metropolitan government revenue should be varied and more similar to those available to states and provinces (Kitchen, 2005; Bird & Slack, 2005; Bahl, 2010). In practice, there is considerable variability across federalist countries in the OECD with

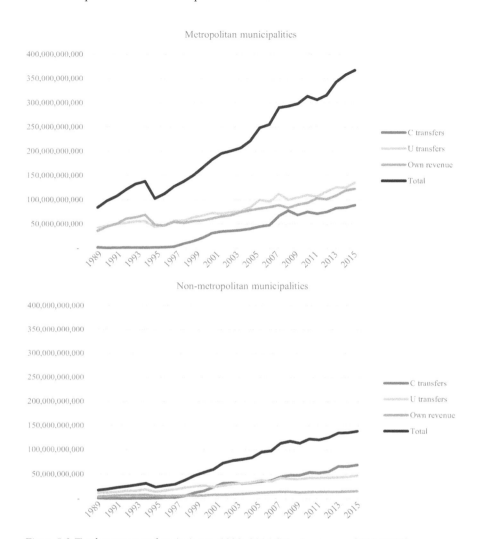

Figure 5.3 Total revenue and main items, 1989–2016 (Mexican pesos, 2010 = 100)

Note: C transfers refers to Conditional transfers, U transfers refers to Unconditional transfers

Source: Based on INEGI (2018).

reference to local government dependence on property tax, from 100 per cent in Australia to 14 per cent in Germany. In Latin America and the OECD countries this tax accounts for 46 per cent of local taxation. However, the percentage can be as high as or close to 100 per cent in unitary and federal countries (Australia, the UK, Canada, Israel and Greece). In contrast, property tax makes up only 2 per cent of total local taxation in Sweden, where, according to Stenkula

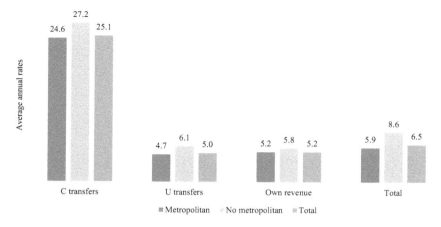

Figure 5.4 Average annual revenue variation, 1989–2016 (%)
Source: Based on INEGI (2018).

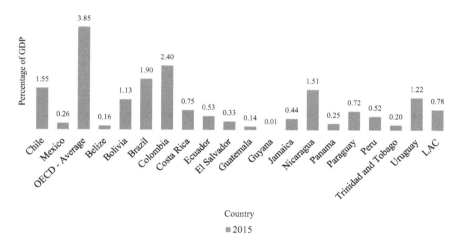

Figure 5.5 Local government tax revenue as a percentage of GDP, 2015
Source: Based on OECD (2018b).

(2015), it was initially intended to provide municipalities with a stable tax base; however, following a tax reform in 1990 property was taxed exclusively at the national level, and in 2008 part of the tax was changed to a local fee. In Mexico, 75 per cent of all local taxes come from property taxation (Figure 5.6).

As a result of their differentiated fiscal capacity and autonomy, revenue structures vary widely between cities and countries. Figure 5.7 shows the revenue structure of local governments in OECD federations. Whereas Mexico is

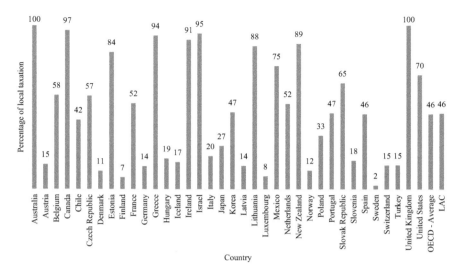

Figure 5.6 Property tax as a percentage of local taxation, 2015
Source: Based on OECD (2018a).

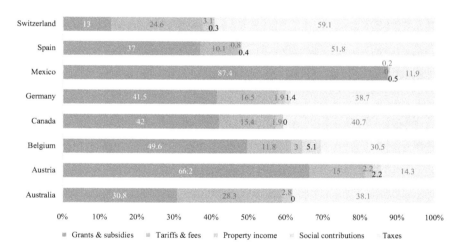

Figure 5.7 Revenue structure in federal OECD countries, 2015 (%)
Source: Based on OECD (2018c, Table 8).

heavily dependent on federal transfers (87.4 per cent of total revenue), Switzerland relies mostly on own revenue collected through local taxes (59 per cent).

Property tax is the main source of local own revenue in Mexico. However, under the NSFC transfers from higher levels of government make up the most substantial proportion of total local revenues. The most important revenue items for municipalities within the Mexican tax-sharing system are unconditional transfers (Item 28) that include eight funds and conditional transfers with compensatory objectives (Item 33) that include two funds. Transfers to municipalities come from federal assignable taxation, a large source of the federation's fiscal resources from which transfers are distributed to the territorial entities. Federal transfers are the basis of local revenue in all municipalities, and their percentage increases over time (Figure 5.8). Metropolitan areas in Mexico do not follow the OECD countries' trend of decreasing dependence on transfers over time. On the contrary, the contribution of transfers to their total revenue rose from around 45 per cent in 1997 to more than 60 per cent in 2016. Dependence on federal transfers is markedly higher in non-metropolitan

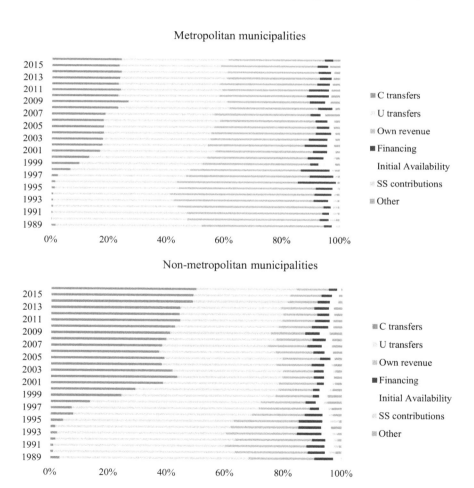

Figure 5.8 Revenue composition by item, 1989–2016 (%)

Note: U (Unconditional), C (Conditional), SS (Social Security)

Source: Based on INEGI (2018).

municipalities, where total transfers contribute to more than 80 per cent of revenue, with unconditional transfers alone representing almost 45 per cent of this.

As a result of these trends, own revenue tends to show a relative decrease within the structure of local financial resources, which has been slower in metropolitan areas (Figure 5.8). At the onset of decentralisation metropolitan own revenue had been increasing, reaching a peak in 1994 at more than 50 per cent. However with the appearance of Item 26 (unconditional transfers) this percentage dropped. In non-metropolitan municipalities the contribution of own revenue has fluctuated between 12 and 15 per cent in the 1989–2016 period, showing that metropolitan municipalities rely more than other local governments on own resources.

Spending budgets have grown in Mexico over time. The evolution of individual items in non-metropolitan municipalities is not the same as those in metropolitan municipalities. In metropolitan areas current expenditure has expanded, especially since 1998, mirroring total spending. Transfers and subsidies and public investment have exhibited similar trends. They also have comparable sizes, but at lower levels than current spending. Public debt has also seen an important increase, beginning in 2002. In contrast, current spending in non-metropolitan municipalities has increased in a linear fashion in volumes similar to those of public investment. Levels of public debt, transfers and subsidies are the lowest, with a smooth trend over time (Figure 5.9).

Transfers and subsidies have the highest average annual variation rate in metropolitan areas while public investment has been the most dynamic expenditure component in non-metropolitan municipalities. Public debt grows faster in metropolitan areas and current spending grows faster in non-metropolitan municipalities (Figure 5.10).

While metropolitan areas around the world tend to provide similar services, the allocation of expenditure may differ significantly across cities and metropolitan areas. In some countries the allocation of spending responsibilities depends on the size of their urban areas, whereas in countries such as Mexico responsibilities are uniform across all local governments (Bird & Slack, 2005). Figure 5.11 shows the variation in local government expenditure structures across OECD countries. While this data includes all local expenditure in federations and subnational expenditure in unitary countries and does not refer exclusively to metropolitan areas, it illustrates how subnational spending is distributed very differently for different purposes. Federations allocate a higher proportion of spending to health (16.6 per cent) and general public services (16.8 per cent) than subnational governments in unitary countries. Among federal countries, however, there are differences. A high proportion of spending in Germany, Belgium and Austria is allocated to social protection, in Austria and the US to health, in Switzerland and the US to education, in Spain to general public services and in Australia to economic affairs. These differences may be explained by the countries' different decentralisation structures.

In Mexico current spending predominates, accounting for an average of approximately 50 per cent of total expenditure in both metropolitan and

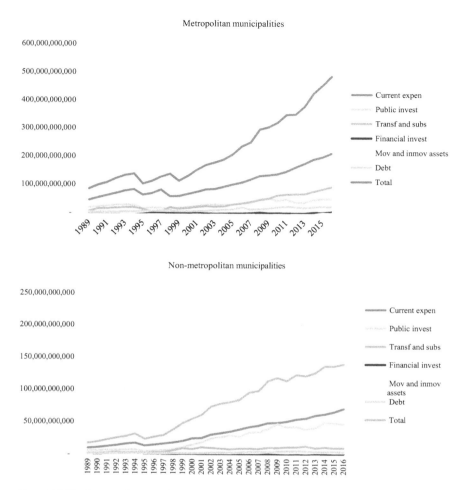

Figure 5.9 Total expenditure and main items, 1989–2016 (2010 = 100)
Source: Based on INEGI (2018).

non-metropolitan municipalities. The level of public investment is very similar in both settings, but in relative terms public investment occupies a more prominent position in the spending structure of non-metropolitan municipalities. In contrast, transfers and subsidies make up a higher proportion of spending in metropolitan areas (Figure 5.12). On average 3.7 per cent of spending is on public debt.

The wide-ranging trends reported in previous studies on Mexico's municipal finances are largely confirmed: increasing federal transfers and declining own revenues in contrast to the trends observed in OECD countries,

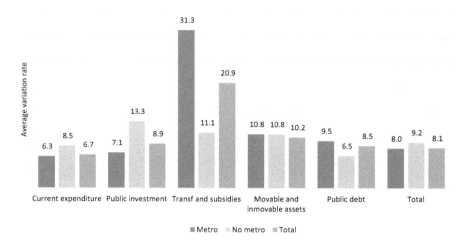

Figure 5.10 Average annual expenditure variation rates, 1989–2016 (%)
Source: Based on INEGI (2018).

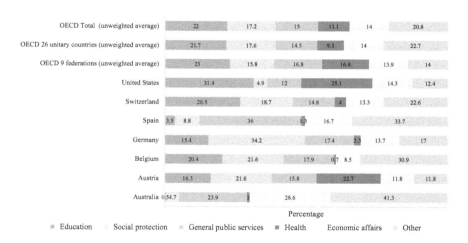

Figure 5.11 Structure of public expenditure in OECD countries, 2015
Source: Based on OECD (2018c, Table 5).

growing current and administrative expenditure in relation to investment spending and a boom in public debt. Nonetheless, the data reveals clear differences between metropolitan and non-metropolitan contexts, mainly in the relative composition of revenue and spending and the dynamism of their different items.

Figure 5.12 Spending composition by item, 1989–2016 (%)

Source: Based on INEGI (2018).

Performance and fiscal disparities in metropolitan areas

The empirical approaches taken for the study of local finances and their performance are diverse. Some interest has focused on analysing the fiscal health of local governments, and on horizontal and vertical disparities. Attempts to assess the performance of local public finances have included aspects such as local governments' self-financing ability, their degree of dependence on transfers, the capacity to save and use of borrowing, among others. Another line of work emphasises the analysis of local government management structures to determine its capacity for administering local finance. Financial pressure and vulnerability also uncover the performance of local public finance (Mendoza, 2010). Other factors involved in the efficiency and performance of local budgets include fiscal autonomy and efficiency in spending (IMCO, 2010). And Schwarcz (2002, cited in Mendoza, 2010) points out that subnational debt is an acute and growing problem in public finances that accompanies decentralisation.

In the field of federal intergovernmental relations, fiscal health is the ability to cover spending based on the capacity to generate tax revenues. Poor fiscal health has a significant impact on socioeconomic development and sustainability. There can be considerable spatial variation in fiscal health within and between countries. When these differences are due to factors over which local governments exercise little control, they are called fiscal disparities. The presence of wide fiscal disparities translates into differentiated provision of public services, even where citizens face identical tax burdens.

Differences in fiscal health generate externalities that motivate both citizens and businesses to move to a metropolitan area with better fiscal health. Companies and population leaving a metropolitan area with weak fiscal health generates reductions in its capacity and fiscal base, which, in turn, reduces its financing capacity and increases the concentration of low-income population and the average cost of service provision. This type of dynamic precipitates a vicious circle of cumulative deterioration in which poor territories deteriorate (i.e. physical decline of infrastructure, loss of population and economic activity, scarce housing and high crime levels), while the richest cities become better off. In brief, strong fiscal disparity is inequitable and inefficient (Chernick & Reschovsky, 2006; Heng, 2008).

In several cases fiscal and financial disparities have led to the implementation of national equalisation programs to reduce horizontal and vertical imbalances, diminish incentives that generate inefficient competition, correct fiscal externalities and ensure at least the minimum provision of services in all jurisdictions (Capello, Airaudo, & Degiovanni, 2014). Equalisation programs generally take the form of transfer systems from central government to subnational governments. The results of such systems have been widely questioned. In the case of Mexico, most municipalities are highly dependent on transfers, placing them in a fragile fiscal and financial situation (IMCO, 2010). Similarly, in countries such as China fiscal transfers have rarely promoted fiscal equalisation or reduced regional gaps (Heng, 2008). Argentine, Brazil and India allocate a considerable proportion of public resources via discretionary transfers, and in the specific case of Argentina it appears that the allocation criteria discriminate against the poorest provinces (Capello, Airaudo, & Degiovanni, 2014). Chernick and Reschovsky (2006) point out that equalisation systems generate political competition for transfers and reduce both the effective fiscal capacity of local governments and citizens' willingness to pay for public services. In addition, depending on their design and volume, transfers can significantly reduce the efficiency and competitiveness of national and subnational territories by inducing excessive or inefficient spending, the 'flypaper effect'.

Concerns about disparities and fiscal gaps between intermediate and local governments emerged in the 1970s and 1980s, mainly in the US (Yilmaz et al., 2006). A different approach looks at vertical disparities and the role of intergovernmental transfers in the elimination of fiscal gaps (Heng, 2008). In the analysis of horizontal disparities, the representative tax-system approach has often been used to quantify differences and compare revenue capacity and spending needs across jurisdictions. The concept of a fiscal gap, defined as the difference between spending needs and fiscal capacity, is used to define the fiscal health of each jurisdiction. The representative tax system has largely been used to measure fiscal gaps (Chernick & Reschovsky, 2006; Yilmaz et al., 2006).

Despite the informative nature of the representative tax system, lack of information frequently reduces the possibility of estimating it (Sour, 2008). In the absence of adequate data from which to estimate horizontal fiscal disparities, other approaches have been used. Heng (2008) uses the Gini coefficient, the coefficient of variation and generalised entropy indexes to measure disparities in per capita revenue and expenditure among Chinese provinces. In his study, fiscal capacity and spending needs are measured as per capita public revenues and expenditure. Heng compares the disparities before and after the implementation of intergovernmental transfers to assess their effect on fiscal equalisation and analyse the long-term persistence of inequalities.

Per capita revenue and expenditure provide an approximation of tax capacity and spending needs in metropolitan areas. Figure 5.13 shows the average per capita public budgets from 1989–2016. At first glance, greater per capita variation is observed in spending and its different items (especially current spending). On the one hand, this suggests differences across metropolitan areas' structure of spending; on the other, differences in investment per capita can also reveal disparities in development and wellbeing. In 2016 per capita own revenue ranged from 3,677 Mexican pesos in Mexico City Metropolitan Area to 259 Mexican pesos in the small metropolitan area of Tianguistengo. These differences usually translate into substantial asymmetries in the provision of services.

Whether these fiscal and financial disparities will remain a persistent problem is a critical question. Trends over time in the coefficient of variation in per capita revenue suggest decreasing disparities up to 2002, but further analysis is necessary to confirm the persistence of inter-metropolitan disparities in, say, fiscal capacity. The trend in spending is one of increasing disparities in current expenditure from 2001 onwards, with no clear trend in public investment and public debt and declining disparities across transfers and subsidies (Figure 5.14).

Indicators of financial dependence, financial capacity and financial leverage (Table 5.1) provide a perspective on metropolitan areas' relative financial performance, taking aggregated metropolitan performance as a benchmark. These indicators are informative regarding key aspects of public finances such as the collection of own revenues to cover operating expenses, the propensity for finance total spending through intergovernmental transfers and the extent to which borrowing is used.

The three indicators in Table 5.1 allow us to propose a categorisation of metropolitan areas according to five criteria (Table 5.2). This categorisation is

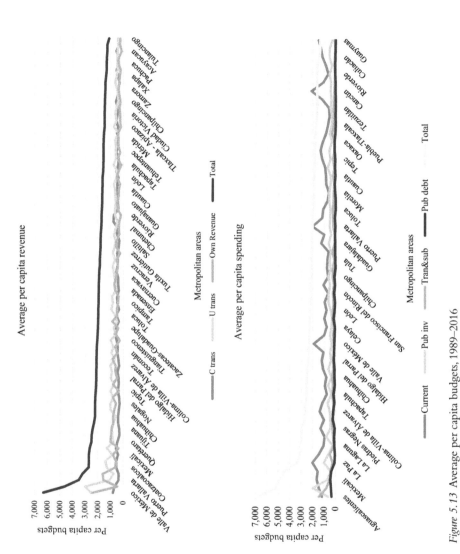

Figure 5.13 Average per capita budgets, 1989–2016

Source: Based on INEGI (2018).

Figure 5.14 Evolution of disparities, 1989–2016

Source: Based on INEGI (2018).

Table 5.1 Indicators of public finances of metropolitan performance

Performance Measure	Definition	Formula
Financial dependency (FD)	How far the municipality covers its total expenditure through federal transfers.	$FD = unconditional\ transfers/total\ expenditure$
Financial capacity (FC)	The extent to which own revenue covers current expenditure. Shows the capacity for self-sufficiency to keep the municipal administrative apparatus in operation.	$FC = own\ revenue/current\ expenditure$
Financial leverage (FL)	The proportion of debt with respect to the total revenue.	$FL = debt\ finance/total\ revenue$

Source: Author's own elaboration.

Table 5.2 Criteria for the categorisation of metropolitan areas

Category	Criteria
High vulnerability	Low capacity, high dependency, high leverage
Financial weakness	Low capacity, high dependency, low leverage
Propensity for instability	Low capacity, low dependency, high leverage
Stability	Low capacity, low dependency, low leverage
	or
	High capacity, high dependency, low leverage
Financial health	High capacity, low dependency, low or high leverage

Source: Author's own elaboration.

Table 5.3 Classification of metropolitan areas based on performance indicators, 1989–2016

Category	No. of metropolitan areas	Percentage (%)	Metropolitan area
High vulnerability	10	14.7	Tecomán, Tianguistenco, Tepic, Tehuantepec, Guaymas, Ciudad Victoria, Matamoros, Tampico, Acayucan, Orizaba
Financial weakness	20	29.4	Campeche, Monclova–Frontera, Piedras Negras, Colima–Villa de Álvarez, Tuxtla Gutiérrez, Hidalgo del Parral, Ocotlán, Cuautla, Oaxaca, Rioverde, Nogales, Villahermosa, Tlaxcala – Apizaco, Coatzacoalcos, Córdoba, Minatitlán, Veracruz, Xalapa, Mérida, Zacatecas–Guadalupe
Propensity for instability	6	8.8	Ensenada, La Paz, Durango, Celaya, La Piedad–Pénjamo, Zamora
Stability	11	16.2	Aguascalientes, Mexicali, La Laguna, Moroléon–Uriangato, Tula, Tulancingo, Toluca, Cuernavaca, Chetumal, San Luis Potosí, Poza Rica
Financial health	21	30.9	Tijuana, Saltillo, Chihuahua, Delicias, Juárez, Valle de México, Guanajuato, León, San Francisco del Rincón, Acapulco, Pachuca, Guadalajara, Puerto Vallarta, Morelia, Monterrey, Querétaro, Cancún, Culiacán, Mazatlán, Hermosillo, Reynosa

Source: Author's own elaboration.

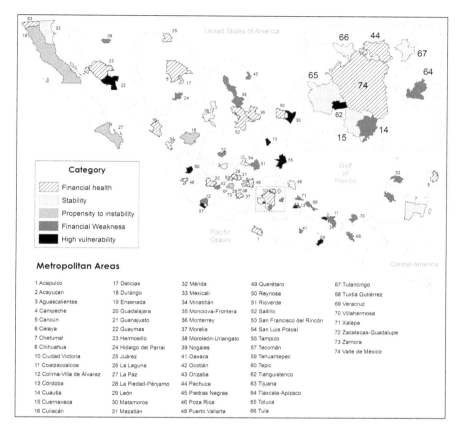

Figure 5.15 Metropolitan areas by public finance performance, 1989–2016

Note: Tapachula, Chilpancingo, Puebla–Tlaxcala, Tehuacan, Teziutlan and Nuevo Laredo have been omitted due to lack of information.

Source: Author's own elaboration.

useful as a basis for preliminary identification of the problems that metropolitan areas face.

Among the 74 metropolitan areas in the country 10 are in the worst position with 'high vulnerability', which describes a situation with low financial capacity, high dependency and high leverage (Table 5.3 and Figure 5.15). 'Financial weakness' and 'propensity for financial instability' indicate the presence of important challenges in metropolitan areas. 'Stability' and 'financial health' describe the best financial positions in this classification, and nearly 47 per cent of metropolitan areas position in these two groups. At first glance, the bigger a metropolitan area is, the better its financial and fiscal situation, yet this relationship is not linear because a number of small cities such as Acapulco do not fit the size–financial health rule.

Concluding comments

In this chapter I argue that the financial and fiscal situation have a significant effect on the overall economic development of metropolitan areas. Even though the examination of metropolitan areas' public finances in Mexico faces various theoretical and empirical challenges, this exploratory review has shed some light on the characteristics and performance of these complex urban environments. Mexico's local public finances in general, and metropolitan finances in particular, increasingly depend on federal transfers with weakened fiscal capacity and rising local debt. This is in clear contrast to emerging trends in OECD countries. However, metropolitan areas in Mexico exhibit relatively less dependence and more capacity than non-metropolitan municipalities. They also have a higher proportion of public debt with, paradoxically, lower relative of public investment in total spending. Two likely explanations for this are (1) a decreasing number of infrastructure projects and (2) increasing private financing of infrastructure projects. Important fiscal and financial disparities have remained, but the persistence of such inequalities requires further analysis.

The three suggested financial performance measures – financial dependency, financial capacity and financial leverage – were used as a basis for grouping Mexican metropolitan areas into five different categories. Less than half fall into the 'financial health' and 'stability' categories, demonstrating the problematic financial situation of the rest of Mexico's metropolitan areas and their heterogeneity. In light of these findings, the questions of the best fiscal reform and metropolitan-area-sensitive fiscal structure for Mexico remain of critical importance. Santos (2013) argues that technical and apolitical approaches to the study of tax reform have inhibited full understanding of the political factors that underlie tax reforms. As the metropolitan model suggests, to improve their financial and fiscal metropolitan areas require more diversified sources of income, such as a portfolio of assets combining instruments that generate stability with other forms of taxation that provide the elasticity necessary to cover the expected instability of investment spending. This is in clear contrast to the revenue model that is available to local governments, especially in countries where revenue sources are highly centralised, restricted by historical norms and, in some cases, by the national constitution. In addition to property taxes, other taxes and revenue sources should be devolved to metropolitan areas (e.g. a consumer charges for non-residents, motor vehicle license taxes, taxes that contribute to intra-metropolitan equalisation, service fees and tariffs). Metropolitan cities, especially in developing countries, also need to increase their own revenue and mobilise resources by improving their administrative capacity and being more willing to collect local taxes and more efficient at collecting them

(Bahl, 2010). However, such changes are often hindered by the local political economy, since any reform is likely to entail high political costs.

A feasible and responsible fiscal future requires novel financing mechanisms such as financial investment and land value capture. Martinez-Vazquez (2015) suggests some innovative approaches to financing urban development, and in particular infrastructure projects as used in international practice, including developer exactions, the acquisition and sale of excess land, the sale or lease of publicly held land and different public–private partnership modalities. In Mexico little has been done to develop such innovative instruments. Moreover, a land value capture proposal in Mexico City failed following a significant lobbying opposition by the real estate industry. The implementation of an effective metropolitan model in each particular metropolitan area will depend on a series of macro and local factors, but the dynamics of the local political economy will be decisive.

Notes

1 Fiscal federalism attempts to determine the optimal structure of the public sector by means of a system of governmental functions and financial relations between the national, intermediate and local levels of a non-unitary government (Oates, 1997). Theoretically these intergovernmental fiscal arrangements include at least four approaches: (1) empowerment of local governments to manage their own tax systems, (2) withholding tax on the part of central government and the subsequent distribution of revenues to intermediate governments through transfers, (3) the selective assignment of taxation powers to local governments and (4) the distribution of revenues collected centrally to specific funds. In practice, most systems are hybrids of these schemes (UN-Habitat, 2015).
2 Based on National Institute of Statistics and Geography (INEGI) annual series of state and municipal public finances 1989–2016.

References

Aguilar, G. (2010). 'Capacidad tributaria y finanzas públicas metropolitanas en México'. *Estudios Demográficos y Urbanos*, 25(1), 103–132. Available at: https://estudiosdemograficosyurbanos.colmex.mx/index.php/edu/article/view/1369/1362.

Antunez, I. & Galilea, S. (2003). *Servicios públicos urbanos y gestión local en América Latina y el Caribe: problemas, metodologías y políticas.* Serie medio ambiente y desarrollo No. 69. Santiago: CEPAL. Available at: http://200.41.82.27/cite/media/2016/02/Antunez_I_et_al_2003_Servicios_publicos_urbanos_y_gestion_local_en_America_Latina_y_el_Caribe_problemas_metodologias_y_politicas1.pdf.

Bahl, R. (2010). 'Financing metropolitan cities'. In United Cities and Local Governments (ed.). *Local government finance: The challenges of the 21st century: Second global report on decentralization and local democracy.* Northampton, MA: Edward Elgar, pp. 285–307. Available at: www.uclg-localfinance.org/sites/default/files/GOLD%20II_ENG.pdf.

Bahl, R. W., Linn, J. F. & Wetzel, D. L. (2013). 'Governing and financing metropolitan areas in the developing world'. In Bahl, R. W., Linn, J. F. & Wetzel, D. L. (eds.). *Financing metropolitan governments in developing countries.* Cambridge, MA: Lincoln Institute of Land Policy, pp. 1–30.

Bird, R. M. & Slack, E. (2005). 'Aspectos fiscales de la gobernabilidad metropolitana'. In Rojas, E. (ed.). *Gobernar las metrópolis*. Washington, D.C.: Inter-American Development Bank, pp. 263–347. Available at: http://site.ebrary.com/id/10201140.

Bird, R. M. & Slack, E. (2007). 'An approach to metropolitan governance and finance'. *Environment and Planning C: Government and Policy*, 25(5), 729–755. Available at: https://doi.org/10.1068/c0623.

Brosio, G. & Jiménez, J. P. (2012). 'The intergovernmental allocation of revenue from natural resources: Finding a balance between centripetal and centrifugal pressure'. In Brosio, G. & Jiménez, J. P. (eds.), *Decentralization and reform in Latin America: Improving intergovernmental relations*. Massachusetts: ECLAC, pp. 290–320.

Cabrero, E. & Martinez-Vazquez, J. (2000). 'Assignment of spending responsibilities and service delivery'. In Guigale, M. & Webb, S. B. (eds.). *Achievements and challenges of fiscal decentralization: Lessons from Mexico*. Washington, D.C.: World Bank Publications, pp. 139–176.

Cabrero, E. (2004). *Los municipios y sus haciendas locales: Un escenario de carencias y oportunidades*. Premio Gobierno y Gestión Local México, 2005. Available at: www.premiomunicipal.org.mx/Premio2004/articulos.php.

Capello, M. L., Airaudo, F. S. & Degiovanni, P. G. (2014). Sistema de transferencias y nivelación fiscal: Una comparación internacional [online]. *IV Jornadas Iberoamericanas de Financiación Local*. Santiago: CEPAL. Available at: https://webcache.googleusercontent.com/search?q=cache:NvNtvDpJkdwJ:https://dialnet.unirioja.es/descarga/articulo/5696470.pdf+&cd=1&hl=es&ct=clnk&gl=be&client=safari.

Castañeda, L. C. & Pardinas, J. E. (2012). *Sub-national revenue mobilization in Mexico*. IDB Working Paper No. IDB-WP-354, Washington, D.C.: Inter-American Development Bank. Available at: https://papers.ssrn.com/sol3/papers.cfm?abstract_id=2234313.

Chernick, H. & Reschovsky, A. (2006). 'Local public finance: Issues for metropolitan regions'. In *Competitive cities in the global economy*. Paris: OECD Publishing, pp. 415–432. Available at: http://dx.doi.org/10.1787/9789264027091-18-en.

Courchene, T. & Diaz-Cayeros, A. (2000). 'Transfers and the nature of the Mexican Federation'. In Giugale, M. & Webb, S. (eds.). *Achievements and challenges of fiscal decentralization: Lessons from Mexico*. Washington, D.C.: World Bank, pp. 200–236.

Diaz, A. (2015). 'La oportuna fragilidad del municipio en México: Capacidades institucionales en el marco de un federalismo disfuncional'. *Revista Iberoamericana de Estudios Municipales*, (11), 145–172. Available at: www.revistariem.cl/index.php/riem/article/view/22.

Gómez, J. C. & Jiménez, J. P. (2012). 'The financing of subnational governments'. In Brosio, G. & Jiménez, J. P. (eds.). *Decentralization and reform in Latin America: Improving intergovernmental relations*. Northampton, MA: Edward Elgar, pp. 140–171. Available at: https://repositorio.cepal.org/handle/11362/2030.

Heng, Y. (2008). 'Fiscal disparities and the equalization effects of fiscal transfers at the county level in China'. *Annals of Economics and Finance*, 9(1), 115–149. Available at: https://pdfs.semanticscholar.org/37b4/9fbf13b53c0c66952a54340651ff6479b05d.pdf.

IMCO. (2010). Competitividad urbana 2010. Acciones urgentes para las ciudades del futuro. México, D. F.: IMCO, pp. 166–183. Available at: https://imco.org.mx/ciudades2010/.

INEGI. (2018). *Finanzas públicas estatales y municipales* [online]. Available at: www.beta.inegi.org.mx/proyectos/registros/economicas/finanzas/.

Jalomo Aguirre, F. (2011). *Gobernar el territorio entre descentralización y metropolización*. Colección Graduados, Serie Sociales y Humanidades, No. 13. Guadalajara, Jalisco: Universidad de Guadalajara. Available at: www.publicaciones.cucsh.udg.mx/pperiod/cgraduados/pdf/sin/1_Gobernar_el_territorio%20_entre_descentralizacion_y_metropolizacion.pdf.

Kinto, M. (2009). 'Intermunicipalidad metropolitana y finanzas públicas: Un análisis de los determinantes del gasto público municipal en México'. *Urban Public Economics Review*, (11), 13–39.

Kitchen, H. (2005). 'Local and metropolitan finance'. In Shah, A. & Shen, C. (eds.). *Local public finance and governance*. Washington, D.C.: CITIC Publishing House, pp. 134–175.

Martinez-Vazquez, J. (2015). 'Mobilizing financial resources for public service delivery and urban development'. In UN-Habitat (ed.). *The challenge of local government financing in developing countries*. Nairobi: UN-Habitat, pp. 32–52. Available at: https://unhabitat.org/the-challenge-of-local-government-financing-in-developing-countries/.

Mendoza, A. (2010). 'Indicadores de desempeño, presión y vulnerabilidad de las Finanzas Públicas Estatales en México'. *El Trimestre Económico*, 77(307), 603–647. Available at: www.scielo.org.mx/scielo.php?script=sci_arttext&pid=S2448-718X2010000300603.

Mendoza, A. (2011). *Las finanzas públicas locales en México*. México, D. F.: Miguel Ángel Porrúa.

Meza, J. (2004). La coordinación intergubernamental para el desarrollo metropolitano en el Estado de México: El caso de la zona metropolitana del Valle de México. *Congreso Internacional del CLAD No. 09*. Madrid. Available at: https://cladista.clad.org/handle/123456789/3219.

Moreno, C. (2003). *Fiscal performance of local governments in Mexico: The role of federal transfers*. Working Paper 127, México, D. F.: Centro de Investigación y Docencia Económicas.

Moya, L. A. (2014). *Implementación e impacto del fondo metropolitano: Análisis comparado de las zonas metropolitanas de Guadalajara y Valle de México*. México, D. F.: Instituto Nacional de Administración Pública.

Oates, W. (1997). 'On the welfare gains from fiscal decentralization'. *Journal of Public Finance and Public Choice*, 2(3), 83–92.

OECD. (2001). *Cities for citizens: Improving metropolitan governance*. Paris: OECD Publishing. Available at: https://doi.org/10.1787/9789264189843-en.

OECD. (2015). *OECD territorial reviews: Valle de México*. Paris: OECD Publishing. Available at: http://dx.doi.org/10.1787/9789264245174-en.

OECD. (2018a). *Global revenue statistics database* [online]. Available at: www.oecd.org/tax/tax-policy/global-revenue-statistics-database.htm.

OECD. (2018b). *Revenue statistics: Latin American countries: Comparative tables* [online]. Available at: https://stats.oecd.org/index.aspx?DataSetCode=RSLACT.

OECD. (2018c). *Subnational government structure and finance, Table 5* [online]. Available at: https://stats.oecd.org/Index.aspx?DataSetCode=SNGF.

Palomera, B. & Bojórquez, C. (2015). Se publicó la ley de disciplina financiera de las entidades federativas y los municipios. Boletín Especial, Indetec.

Rosales, M. (2012). *Descentralización del Estado y finanzas municipales en América Latina*. México, D. F.: Instituto Nacional para el Federalismo y el Desarrollo Municipal.

Santos, S. (2013). *The political economy of tax reform in Latin America: A critical review*. Washington, D.C.: Woodrow Wilson Center, Latin American Program. Available at: www.wilsoncenter.org/sites/default/files/Political%20Economy%20of%20Tax%20Reform.pdf.

Slack, E. (2007). *Managing the coordination of service delivery in Metropolitan cities: The role of metropolitan governance*. Policy Research Working Paper, No. 4317. Washington, D.C.: World Bank. Available at: https://openknowledge.worldbank.org/handle/10986/7264.

Smoke, P. (2015). 'Urban government revenue: Political economy challenges and opportunities'. In UN-Habitat (ed.). *The challenge of local government financing in developing countries*. Nairobi: UN-Habitat, pp. 34–53. Available at: https://unhabitat.org/the-challenge-of-local-government-financing-in-developing-countries/.

Sobarzo, H. (2004). 'Federalismo fiscal en México'. *Economía, Sociedad y Territorio*, Special Issue, 103–121. Available at: www.uv.mx/personal/clelanda/files/2014/09/Sobarzo-2005-Federalismo-Fiscal-en-Mexico.pdf.

Sour, L. (2008). 'Un repaso de los conceptos sobre la capacidad y esfuerzo fiscal, y su aplicación en los gobiernos locales mexicanos'. *Estudios Demográficos y Urbanos*, 23(2), 271–297. Available at: https://estudiosdemograficosyurbanos.colmex.mx/index.php/edu/article/view/1312/1305.

Stenkula, M. (2015). *Taxation of real estate in Sweden (1862–2013)*. IFN Working Paper No. 1018. Stockholm: Research Institute of Industrial Economics.

UN-Habitat. (2015). 'Introduction'. In *The challenge of local government financing in developing countries*. Nairobi: UN-Habitat. Available at: https://unhabitat.org/the-challenge-of-local-government-financing-in-developing-countries/.

Yilmaz, Y. et al. (2006). *Measuring fiscal disparities across the US states: A representative revenue system/representative expenditure system approach, fiscal year 2002*. New England Public Policy Center Working Papers. Boston: The Urban Institute. Available at: www.bostonfed.org/publications/new-england-public-policy-center-working-paper/2006/measuring-fiscal-disparities-across-the-us-states-a-representative-revenue-systemrepresentative-expenditure-system-approach-fiscal-year-2002.aspx.

6 Exploring the driving forces of metropolitan economic development

Introduction

Rapid urbanisation and urban expansion in the world have changed the locus of economic power. At the onset of the twenty-first century metropolitan areas are perceived as the engines of development with vast potential for economic growth. They provide an environment where productivity and efficiency gains can be achieved. High concentration of people and businesses in metropolitan areas offers more opportunities for interaction, communication and learning and creates a propitious setting for innovation and specialisation due to the possibility of more extended knowledge and technological spillovers. Metropolitan areas also provide consumers with greater variety of goods, services and infrastructure. These territories can certainly take the lead to address many of the global and national developmental challenges, and evidence has shown their central role in the world economy and in national economies, especially in developing countries. However, there is also evidence showing that the productivity gains and the myriad of development opportunities metropolitan areas provide cannot be taken for granted. The persistence of slow national economic growth in several urbanised countries and the presence of economic asymmetries across metropolitan areas in the world or within countries raise the question of why some metropolitan areas grow and are able to boost living standards while others stagnate or decline.

The economic development debate has revolved, on the one hand, around identifying the patterns and trends in a series of economic performance indicators such as economic growth, productivity change, sustainability, liveability, living conditions or wellbeing. Chapter 4 in this book addressed the dynamics and patterns of metropolitan economic development in Mexico according to different performance indicators and shows the variability across metropolitan areas and across time. On the other hand, the debate attempts to uncover the driving forces that contribute to improving urban economic performance and development. What makes a city or a metropolitan area grow and develop remains a major enigma in empirical research. Disentangling the key factors driving economic development is clearly more problematic because forces and processes behind economic development are intricate, interpretations are not straightforward and history and path-dependence processes are usually involved. The evidence is mixed, and further discussion and empirical work is needed.

This chapter assesses the drivers of economic development of metropolitan areas in Mexico. For practical purposes, economic development reduces to productivity and output per capita. Agglomeration economies, specialisation, infrastructure, human capital, innovation and institutions are regarded as influential variables in the economic performance of regions and cities. While several factors can affect economic development, I argue that a number of variables related to the functioning of institutions, especially in contexts of poor governmental performance and weak institutional structures, as in Mexico, are essential elements of economic behaviour. In urban agglomerations such as metropolitan areas the internal spatial structure and territorial organisation must be included as a meaningful influence on economic and social efficiency.

I ask the specific question of which group of factors best explains metropolitan economic performance: traditional factors, such as physical capital, human capital, economic structure and specialisation, or other factors, such as innovation, the creative class, institutions, metropolitan governance and urban structure. Addressing this interrogation can contribute to start resolving some of the fundamental problems in the field of metropolitan economic development in the country.

The chapter incorporates a review of the theoretical approaches that explain urban economic development. The theoretical review is followed by a section that summarises some international evidence on the determinants and factors of economic development in metropolitan areas. Afterwards a model to test a number of variables that I identify as relevant to account for economic performance in Mexico's metropolitan areas in 2008 and 2013 is estimated. The chapter concludes with some final remarks.

Theoretical approaches to urban economic development

Economic development became a major macroeconomic concern after World War II in view of the clear variation in income levels and growth across countries. Over time several approaches have emphasised how development is an intrinsically geographic phenomenon. Spatial development is a process that lies in localised structural change associated with permanent progress towards improving the living standards of the local population. In the development process entrepreneurs use their capacity to organise local productive factors to achieve high levels of productivity and market competition, and to create a favourable economic environment (Vázquez-Barquero, 1988).[1]

Discussion of metropolitan economic development is guided by different notions and understandings of what economic development represents, and by the manifold geographical scales – local, urban, metropolitan, regional or national – at which it takes place. From these different perspectives, metropolitan economic development involves the underlying idea that every city has a series of economic, social, human, institutional, cultural, etc. assets. Each city has its own structure and productive system, labour market, entrepreneurial capacity and technological knowledge, natural resources and infrastructure, and social and political systems to articulate the processes of local economic development.

The literature on macroeconomic and local development has sought to explain development factors, relationships, mechanisms and processes, and to understand disparities in spatial development. In so doing it offers different bodies of explanation. Each of these approaches has a different starting point; different assumptions, epistemologies and ontologies; and a different impact on development policy. Pike, Rodríguez-Pose and Tomaney (2006) summarise approaches to growth and development, grouping them as shown in Figure 6.1.

Among those approaches the most ideologically and politically influential has been the neoclassical theory, according to which economic growth equates to development and wellbeing. Economic growth is explained by physical capital accumulation, which, in turn, determines the level and growth rate of per capita income while population growth and technological progress influence economic growth as exogenous variables. Development disparities are explained by cities' different rates of capital accumulation. Neoclassical theory postulates that an economy starting from a low level of capital per worker ratio and low per capita income accumulates more capital and runs through a process with the growth rate initially increasing, then declining, and finally approaching zero when it arrives at a steady state. The model predicts convergence in the sense that poorer economies will tend to grow faster than richer economies. As a result, all economies eventually converge in terms of per capita income. The implication for development policy is that while intervention could accelerate convergence and correct market failures, a free-market approach eliminates spatial differences in the long run.

Endogenous growth theory is an approach with neoclassical roots that has at its core technical change based on knowledge and learning as a determinant variable. In contrast to neoclassical theory, technical progress is seen as

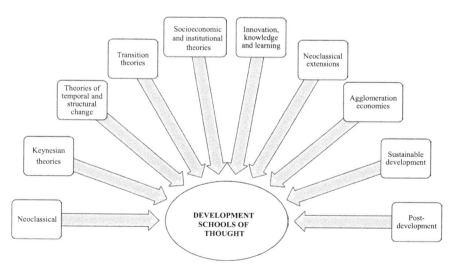

Figure 6.1 Theoretical approaches to economic development

Source: Based on Pike, Rodríguez-Pose and Tomaney (2006).

endogenous to the economic system; that is, technological change and innovative activity take place within the production process in response to the decisions of economic agents. Knowledge is a cumulative factor of production and is the source of positive externalities and productivity gains. It generates innovation and technological change, producing localised spillovers that improve performance and specialisation. A research and development sector in the economy is also a source of innovation that, in turn, increases total productivity.

Keynesian theories have been also influential in development policy. They offer demand-side explanations of development with external demand (exports) and specialisation as the engines of economic growth. Likewise, these theories also integrate a policy program of explicit government intervention to provide infrastructure, promoting decentralisation, and assisting backward regions (Table 6.1).

The competitive advantages and clusters paradigm postulates that industrial sectors gain in productivity when there is vigorous competition between companies that belong to the same sector and are concentrated territorially. Cluster theory gives great importance to geographical proximity, firm interdependence, and public and private institutions to foster the creation of knowledge, innovation and spillovers for growth. Thus, competitive advantage derives from the location of companies and sectors and their interrelations within spatial clusters.

Table 6.1 Keynesian theories of development

Theory	Measure of development	Factors of development	Mechanisms	Disparities
Export-based theory	Growth in income	External demand: exports Specialisation in the basic sector Competitiveness in the basic sector	Specialisation in production and export of goods that are intensive in the abundant factor of production Multiplier effects	Different specialisations and competitiveness
Cumulative causation theories	Growth in per capita income	Specialisation in manufacturing Economies of scale	Productivity gains based on manufacturing specialisation Cumulative positive or negative spirals of development	Divergence as a natural tendency Agglomeration economies Presence of trickle-down effects
Growth pole theory	Growth in income	Inter-industry linkages	Presence of propulsive industries that generate economies of scale Production linkages	Core–periphery patterns

Source: Based on Pike, Rodriguez-Pose and Tomaney (2006).

According to the theories of temporal and structural change, development is a historical and evolutionary process. They conceptualise the unequal character of development in relation to production, technology, consumption, institutions and government. This approach is used mainly at the macroeconomic level and includes stage theories, the theory of cycles, the theory of waves, Marxism and radical political economy.

Transition theories include flexible specialisation, new industrial spaces and regulationist theory (Table 6.2). These approaches introduce the importance

Table 6.2 Transition theories of development

	Development mechanisms	*Policy*	*Critic*
Flexible specialisation	Importance of industrial agglomerations of small and medium enterprises. Specialisation. Flexibility and adaptability. Vertical disintegration and agglomeration reduce transaction costs.	Decentralisation of production networks. Economies of local agglomeration. Local cooperation networks. Local capacity to promote learning, adaptation, innovation and entrepreneurship. Reproducible policies and models.	Emphasis on change and role of broad structures. They ignore or downplay the role of big companies.
New industrial spaces	Marshallian externalities (localisation economies) reduce transaction costs. Territorial production complexes. Spatially concentrated production systems. Cities and regions enclose the causal elements and active development.		
Regulationist theory	Flexible accumulation determines the development. Neo- and post-Fordist systems of production. Growth depends on the degree of correspondence between the organisation of production and the social and institutional structures that regulate it. Flexible, innovative and competitive productive complexes.		

Source: Based on Pike, Rodríguez-Pose and Tomaney (2006).

of localised economies of scale, positive externalities and regulatory institutional organisation to promote networks of innovative and competitive small and medium-sized firms in a flexible production environment.

Socioeconomic and institutional theories seek to explain the processes, forms and characteristics of development. Particular attributes, local assets and economic capacities, both endogenous and exogenous, are the basis of competitiveness and development. These approaches refer specifically to the institutional and social factors that stimulate development, including formal and informal institutions that reduce risk, increase confidence in economic relationships and affect cities' ability to absorb or create technological progress. When the socio-institutional context is highly differentiated in its nature and form, disparities emerge.

Theories that emphasise the importance of innovation, knowledge and learning as factors contributing to development have grown in significance. Development is understood here as improvement in a city's capacity to produce, absorb and use innovation and knowledge through learning processes. The knowledge economy, local innovation systems and learning territories are models that enable these processes, and are based on sustainable institutional networks capable of lasting and adapting over time given adequate physical and technological infrastructure.

In contrast to most approaches that emphasise economic growth, there has been growing awareness of social inequalities, environmental and ecological problems and adequate use of resources. The paradigm of sustainable development, for instance, brings with it a new conception of development as long-term, durable, sustained and less-harmful economic growth. From this perspective, development symbolises the integration of economic, social and environmental outcomes. Significant principles such as energy efficiency, efficient use of resources, environmental regulation, environmental justice, remediation of environmental degradation, recycling and action from below are at the centre of the sustainable development paradigm. However, there are varied interpretations of sustainable development, and they are not clearly explicit about the factors that contribute or activate development.

From these theoretical frameworks, a myriad of factors has been identified and surveyed in the quest to understand the economic prosperity and the unequal economic development and performance of cities and metropolitan areas around the world: capital accumulation, specialisation, competitiveness, agglomeration economies, social, institutional and regulatory structures, innovation and knowledge, and education and human capital.

International assessments and evidence

As I have highlighted, the economic performance and dynamics of metropolitan areas is uneven both among and within countries. Even the world's largest metropolitan areas show significant variation in their economic performance, and the economic advantages are distributed asymmetrically. Leal and Parrilla's (2016) typology of global cities groups the world's top 123 metropolitan economies into seven categories: (1) Global Giants are wealthy hubs with concentrations of the world's largest companies' corporate headquarters; (2) Asian Anchors are very large business and financial nodes anchoring inward investment into Asia-Pacific and Russia; (3) Emerging Gateways include large business and transport entry points for major national and regional emerging markets in Africa, Asia, Eastern Europe and Latin America; (4) Factory China includes second- and third-tier Chinese cities that are distinctly reliant on export-intensive manufacturing; (5) Knowledge Capitals are highly productive knowledge-creation centres in the US and Europe with talented workforces and research universities; (6) American Middleweights are midsized US metropolitan areas striving for a postrecession niche in the global economy; and (7) International Middleweights are cities in Australia, Canada and Europe that are globally connected by investment flows and whose growth has lagged since the financial crisis (Table 6.3). The relative economic development of global metropolitan areas according to this classification depends on city size, competitiveness factors (economic performance, trade, innovation, talent and infrastructure), and the industrial or sectoral structure of each city. Governance also matters in competitiveness, because government, public and civic groups can

Table 6.3 Seven categories of global cities, 2015

Category	Metropolitan areas	Number of metropolitan areas
Global Giants	London, Los Angeles, New York, Osaka–Kobe, Paris and Tokyo	6
Asian Anchors	Beijing, Hong Kong, Moscow, Seoul–Incheon, Shanghai and Singapore	6
Emerging Gateways	Ankara, Brasilia, Busan–Ulsan, Cape Town, Chongqing, Delhi, East Rand, Guangzhou, Hangzhou, Istanbul, Jinan, Johannesburg, Katowice–Ostrava, Mexico City, Monterrey, Mumbai, Nanjing, Ningbo, Pretoria, Rio de Janeiro, Saint Petersburg, Santiago, Sao Paulo, Shenzhen, Tianjin, Warsaw, Wuhan and Xi'an	28
Factory China	Changchun, Changsha, Changzhou, Chengdu, Dalian, Dongguan, Foshan, Fuzhou, Haerbin, Hefei, Nantong, Qingdao, Shenyang, Shijiazhuang, Suzhou, Tangshan, Wenzhou, Wuxi, Xuzhou, Yantai, Zhengzhou and Zibo	22
Knowledge Capitals	Atlanta, Austin, Baltimore, Boston, Chicago, Dallas, Denver, Hartford, Houston, Minneapolis, Philadelphia, Portland, San Diego, San Francisco, San Jose, Seattle, Stockholm, Washington D.C. and Zurich	19

(Continued)

Table 6.3 (Continued)

Category	Metropolitan areas	Number of metropolitan areas
American Middleweights	Charlotte, Cincinnati, Cleveland, Columbus, Detroit, Indianapolis, Kansas City, Miami, Orlando, Phoenix, Pittsburgh, Riverside, Sacramento, San Antonio, St. Louis and Tampa	16
International Middleweights	Brussels, Copenhagen–Malmö, Frankfurt, Hamburg, Karlsruhe, Köln–Düsseldorf, Milan, Munich, Nagoya, Rome, Rotterdam–Amsterdam, Stuttgart, Vienna–Bratislava, Athens, Barcelona, Berlin, Birmingham, Kitakyushu–Fukuoka, Madrid, Melbourne, Montreal, Perth, Sydney, Tel Aviv, Toronto and Vancouver	26

Source: Based on Leal and Parrilla (2016).

mobilise investment from a wide variety of domestic and international sources to trigger new growth dynamics.

The literature has made some progress towards identifying the determinants of economic development. These include various assessments of the economic performance of metropolitan areas. Ahrend et al. (2014) evaluate metropolitan areas in five OECD member countries (Germany, Mexico, Spain, the UK and the US); Martin, Gardiner and Tyler (2014) assess the empirical significance of various factors of the economic performance of UK cities; Bluestone (2014) estimates the factors that influence firms' choice of location and their economic growth in US cities; Gagliardi and Percoco (2012) analyse the determinants of European cities' economic performance (Metropolitan NUTS 3 regions); and Blumenthal, Wolman and Hill (2009) and Donegan et al. (2008) examine the drivers of economic performance in metropolitan areas in the US.[2] These authors employ predominantly quantitative approaches using performance indicators as dependent variables that are explained by different sets of factors.

Bluestone (2014) argues that most cities and towns' economic prosperity rests on their ability to attract and retain business investment, and the jobs and tax revenue that such investment generates. In empirical research, standard measures of economic performance include the level and growth of income, production, productivity and employment. Another measure of performance associated with average welfare is GDP per capita. A more social and inclusive evaluation of the economic success of metropolitan areas would also review the incidence and levels of poverty. Emerging paradigms such as the Smart City and the Sustainable City associate economic success with the use of innovations that exploit information and communication technologies (ICT) to improve the quality of life, efficiency of operations and urban services, and competitiveness, or to satisfy the needs of present and future generations.

The theories and approaches summarised in the previous section have been adapted for the analysis of metropolitan growth and change (Storper, 2009). Frameworks that drive empirical research tend to be based on ad hoc combinations of explanatory factors that are present in the theoretical approaches and a set of control variables. Some strands of research incorporate complementary aspects to explain the performance of cities and regions. The main forces at the heart of the empirical literature are city size and agglomeration economies (demographic and economic geographic concentration), specialisation and economic structure (the industrial mix), human capital and the creative class, innovation, knowledge and technology, and institutions. Some studies also address the importance of urban spatial structure and connectivity (Blumenthal, Wolman & Hill, 2009; Gagliardi & Percoco, 2012), whereas others refer to the relevance of governance structures as specific forms of institutional arrangement (Ahrend et al., 2014; Martin, Gardiner & Tyler, 2014). Control variables usually include demographic characteristics and migration, the natural and the business climates, regional dummy variables and other contextual variables. These are controls for unspecified differences among metropolitan areas; that is, they are a measure of our ignorance (Blumenthal, Wolman & Hill, 2009).

All approaches emphasise how differences in the set of variables translate into divergence in inter-urban economic performance, and therefore explain why some cities prosper more than others. Agglomeration is a key variable that explains productivity gains, economic growth and productive transformation in metropolitan areas. Usually it is assumed that the economic productivity of a city increases with its size, the size of a metropolitan area affecting urban fortunes by increasing not only productivity but also wages (Gagliardi & Percoco, 2012). This is in part a result of sorting, as better-educated individuals tend to live and work in larger cities, and the evidence suggests that the productivity of a given individual increases with the size of the city in which he or she works (Ahrend et al., 2014). Thanks to urbanisation, location and development theories we know that the decisions and interactions of co-located economic agents produce emergent effects – in particular, various forms of positive externality and spillovers – that appear and operate at the level of the city as a whole, but which are not simply reducible to those underlying micro-behaviours, and which enhance the competitive advantages of the activities that cities contain. As I have pointed out, the effects of increasing returns generated by the spatial agglomeration of economic activity in cities relate to various attributes that arise at the level of a city as a whole from the myriad actions and interactions of spatially proximate individual economic agents – firms, workers and consumers. Traditionally, the building up of a pool of specialised and skilled labour on which local firms can draw, the emergence of specialised suppliers and intermediaries serving those firms and the creation of a local pool of knowledge and know-how – which has been called an 'industrial atmosphere' and 'something in the air' and shapes production processes and business practices – form

Marshall's well-known triad of externalities, which explains agglomeration economies (Martin, Gardiner & Tyler, 2014).

However, the spatial concentration of population and economic activity in cities may also lead to various diseconomies such as pollution, congestion costs, high prices for land and increasing house prices and wages, all of which may impose limits on not just the growth of cities, but also their productivity and competitive advantages. Moreover, as some examples such as Detroit testify, cities can go into relative and even absolute decline.

Specialisation stands out as an important driver of growth. Some activities have higher rates of growth than others, and this translates into divergences in inter-urban growth and income. However, the effects on development of economic structure and specialisation are in dispute, and no magical combination of sectoral structures can ensure economic success (Blumenthal, Wolman & Hill, 2009). Generally, geographic concentration and agglomeration benefits are present in newer and more innovative activities, and in those sectors that depend on hard-to-imitate skills or knowledge. Cities can also specialise in a way that makes them poorer than the average. Activities with none of the locational processes that generate positive externalities locate in a city simply because it has the basic factor supply (Storper, 2010).

There is debate about Marshallian externalities (localisation economies) and Jacobsian externalities, which have to do with the scope and opportunities for interaction and knowledge spillover between diverse industries and sectors (urbanisation economies). According to Ahrend et al. (2014) agglomeration benefits are industry specific given the importance of sharing and specialisation in the context of Marshallian externalities. But urbanisation economies can emerge in a diversified economic structure.

Another debate raises the problem not only of how to measure specialisation, but also of how to predict its likely relationship with economic performance. To nuance the specialisation–diversification controversy, other concepts have emerged to explain economic development. In a diversified specialisation, a city or metropolitan area specialises in a few (related) sectors but is otherwise diversified. There is also the idea of related variety, where a city or metropolitan area has a group or groups of economic activities that share or have overlapping or related features such as inputs, markets, specialised knowledge, skills or technologies.

More consensus has been reached over the positive importance of human capital. Lately some scholars have pointed to the importance of the ability of cities to attract the so-called creative class (Martin, Gardiner & Tyler, 2014). The relevance of educational attainment is consistent with human capital as a driver of urban growth. However, formal education is not the only route to sustained higher incomes: training and knowledge spillovers also positively increase productivity. There is similar agreement on the positive impact of innovation, technology and the knowledge economy on productivity and growth, as evidence has been found of a direct relationship between increasing productivity and science, research and development activities and research universities (Gagliardi & Percoco, 2012).

Researchers across a wide range of disciplines are increasingly resorting to analysing institutions for a better grasp on how economic development takes place. The presence of effective institutions that improve the provision of collective and public goods, address market failures and increase efficiency is essential for development. The concept of institutions, however, is very broad, subjective, controversial and difficult to operationalise and measure, and for that reason major gaps remain in our understanding of how institutions affect growth and development (Storper, 2010; Gagliardi & Percoco, 2012; Rodríguez-Pose, 2013). Understanding institutions is critical for the design and implementation of efficient development strategies, and researchers are seeking to identify which types of institution matter, whether these are high-order societal rules and formal institutions, or informal institutions and social capital (Rodríguez-Pose, 2013).

Institutional arrangements work better at both the local and the regional scales, as the national scale can be too distant, remote and detached to local needs in order to be effective. With regards to urban and metropolitan economic success, a strong emphasis has been placed on the role of local institutional arrangements and governance structures. In the process of development local institutions are the most important force for adjustment (Storper, 2009). Importantly, institutions can play a huge part in local political economy (Storper, 2010). The attitudes of local public and private bodies towards growth and development, the local presence of pro-business groups and associations, the degree of local autonomy over raising tax revenues and over expenditure and the presence of strong local leadership with vision, all these can contribute to the perception and reality of a city as a place to locate and expand businesses, and to attract and retain workers (Martin, Gardiner & Tyler, 2014).

Metropolitan governance structures are a specific aspect of institutions and political economy issues. Such structures include factors that help to increase cities' economic performance and that are shaped by local actors: leadership by key institutions and individuals; competition, collaboration or cooperation among the various constituencies of the metropolitan area; policy and planning frameworks; and action supporting new and existing industries (Bluestone, 2014).

The influence of governance failures on metropolitan outcomes is generally thought to be pervasive. Because we are faced with a patchwork of fragmented competing and cooperating authorities at the metropolitan level (Storper, 2010), the mismatch between administrative and functionally defined city boundaries can result in failure to implement growth-promoting policies, as spillovers from these policies are not fully internalised by their managing (and funding) administrative bodies. Problems particularly arise in areas that require not only vertical coordination of different levels of government but also horizontal coordination across numerous local governments. In metropolitan areas, cooperation and coordination among horizontal governments substitute for the administrative consolidation required to enhance urban productivity (Ahrend et al., 2014).

Urban structure plays an essential role in metropolitan economic performance. Gagliardi and Percoco (2012) suggest that it is key to understanding modern metropolitan spatial imbalances and disparities. Sparsely populated areas reduce the probability of social interaction and result in a lower stock of social capital, increasing transaction costs and lowering economic efficiency. There are, however, arguments for a beneficial effect of well-functioning dispersed cities.

Overall, the empirical literature finds evidence that productivity tends to increase with city size; human capital appears to play a strong direct role in increasing productivity; specialisation in certain types of activities appears to affect productivity levels with cities with a larger share of high-tech manufacturing, finance and business services found to have higher levels of productivity; there is lower productivity in cities with fragmented governance structures; and sprawl reduces efficiency and productivity. Yet the empirical evidence on the significance of the various factors believed to influence urban economic performance is mixed and inconclusive. Findings cannot be taken as fact, or at least they are much more complex or nuanced than is normally assumed (Martin, Gardiner & Tyler, 2014).

Despite increasing research, the problem with most existing quantitative analyses of urban growth is that while they may identify certain structural determinants of growth, they have difficulty identifying the net effect of forces and explaining the processes that shape cities' different pathways and growth experiences (Storper, 2010). Although often discussed and analysed separately in the literature, in reality the various determinants interact in complex ways. In the dependent and independent variables there is a strong degree of two-way causation and endogeneity. Many variables that affect economic development are in part also the outcome of economic development: they are both the cause and the consequence of development, and are mutually reinforcing. In addition to problems of endogeneity there are strong path-dependence processes in economic development that require explanation (Storper, 2010; Rodríguez-Pose, 2013; Martin, Gardiner & Tyler, 2014). It is this complexity that makes it difficult to formulate any single comprehensive model of urban economic development.

An exploratory assessment of factors that shape economic development in metropolitan areas in Mexico

While the disparities in development factors translate into diverging inter-urban economic performance, explaining why some cities thrive while others fail or stagnate, empirical evidence is varied and inconclusive (Martin, Gardiner & Tyler, 2014). Due to the complexity of the factors underlying economic performance, the formidable statistical problems at play and data limitations assessing the drivers of development becomes a daunting task. Moreover, there are significant gaps in our knowledge about urban economic performance in developing and emerging economies, because much of the research on the economic development of cities and metropolitan areas has been carried out in and for developed countries. These lacunae in the empirical literature justify an exploratory look at the sources of development and growth in developing countries.

Most empirical analysis of urban, regional or local development assesses the interpretative capacity of one or several theoretical approaches. The questions about economic development are frequently presented from a relative point of view. Rather than asking what factors determine the development or growth of a specific city, the commonly asked question is why some cities grow faster, develop more or have better living conditions than others. I employ data on productivity and production per capita, as dependent variables, and a number of independent variables to explore what elements are most related to the economic performance of Mexico's metropolitan areas. This provides an approximation of the factors that seem to be necessary for economic performance and are decisive in broader metropolitan development. It also offers some indication of the extent to which territories can influence their own economic destiny, in the sense of assets and endowments that are not just determined by nature. From the onset it is pertinent to question whether conventional factors such as physical capital accumulation, human capital and specialisation can explain metropolitan economic performance in this country better than urban and territorial variables (e.g. city size, the presence of the creative class, local institutions, fragmentation, etc.).

Based on information availability, I employ a data set that includes only 65 of the 74 official metropolitan areas and a simple panel for the years 2008 and 2013. Because the time period (t) is small, the simplest approach to analysing this panel is to omit the space and time dimensions of the pooled data and estimate only the usual OLS regression. This model is expressed as:

$$Y_{it} = \alpha + \beta_1 X_{1it} + e_{it} \tag{6.1}$$

where i is the ith cross-section unit (metropolitan area) and t the time period (year).

Given the methodological difficulties, which usually include endogeneity problems, adequate specification and measurement errors in the proxies for the different dependent and independent variables, this estimation is a basic attempt to modelling economic performance in metropolitan areas. Two alternative measures of economic success (Y_{it}) are used: productivity (product per hour worked) and production per capita. The independent variables (X_{it}) include a combination of traditional and urban-specific factors associated with the set of development factors enumerated in the literature: capital accumulation, human capital, specialisation, productive structure, local institutions, agglomeration economies, connectivity, territorial fragmentation and governance, and local political economy. The dependent variables are GDP pc (gross production per inhabitant, 2014 = 100) and productivity (production per hour worked, 2014 = 100). All the independent variables initially incorporated in the model are described in Table 6.4.

Table 6.4 Independent variables used to study metropolitan economic development

	Development factors	Variable	Indicator	Expected effect
	Capital accumulation	Physical capital investment	Investment (K/L)	(+)
	Human capital	Schooling levels	Mean years of schooling ★A	(+)
		Presence of high-quality schools	% of schools with good or excellent performance ★B	(+)
		Higher education	% Population with higher education (25 years old and over) ★C	(+)
	Specialisation	Labour specialisation ★A	Krugman index based on labour	(+)
		Productive specialisation ★B	Krugman index based on gross production	
	Productive structure	Relative importance of financial services employment in the local economy	LQ: financial and professional services (labour) ★A	(+)
		Relative importance of cultural services employment in the local economy	LQ: culture, entertainment and tourism services (labour) ★A	(+)
		Relative importance of financial services production in the local economy	LQ: financial and professional services (production) ★B	(+)
		Relative importance of cultural services production in the local economy	LQ: culture, entertainment and tourism services (production) ★B	(+)
Independent variables	Institutions	Formality	Formal employment	(+)
		Public finances autonomy	Own revenue/total revenue	(+)
		Public debt leverage	Public debt/total expenditure	Ambiguous
		Violence	Homicide rate	(-)
	Agglomeration economies	City size	% of population in total metropolitan population	(+)
	Connectivity	Airline connections	Number of airlines operating from city airport	(+)

(Continued)

Table 6.4 (Continued)

Territorial fragmentation and governance	Horizontal fragmentation	Number of local governments	(–)
	Territorial fragmentation	Local governments per 100,000 inhabitants ⋆A	(–)
	Rate of territorial fragmentation	Average population per local government ⋆B	(–)
Local political economy	Electoral competition	Difference in no. of votes between 1st- and 2nd-place candidates for local government as % of total vote	(–)

K= capital; LQ = location quotients; ⋆A, B, C are variants of the same factor measured by different indicators.

After controlling for heterogeneity within the panel, the model with productivity as a dependent variable has an adjusted R-squared of 96 per cent and is significant according to the F statistic (Table 6.5). Despite this, only 4 of the 14 independent variables are significant at 95 per cent confidence: capital accumulation, human capital (mean years of schooling), specialisation in cultural services and entertainment, and formal employment. Two additional variables become significant at 90 per cent confidence: financial autonomy and labour specialisation. What is striking is that formal employment and the greater presence of cultural and entertainment services have a negative impact on productivity. On the other hand, productivity seems to be positively and significantly related to traditional development factors such as physical capital, human capital according to the average level of formal education and labour specialisation. An additional factor that relates positively to productivity and denotes better local institutional frameworks is financial autonomy. The city-size variable is not significant, meaning that metropolitan areas are not exploiting agglomeration economies. This is very much in line with the OECD's findings regarding the relatively low productivity of Mexican cities compared to other cities in member countries due to urban expansion and inefficient urban structures. The fragmentation and local political economy variables are not significant either. One possible explanation for this is that they impact all metropolitan areas to the same extent, and so are not good predictors of inter-metropolitan differences in economic performance.

Table 6.5 Estimation of the model for productivity

Variable	Coef.	Std. Err.	t	P > t
Constant	−29.29108	16.12429	−1.82	0.072
Investment★	0.0020897	0.0000454	46.06	0
Mean years schooling★	7.118406	2.01295	3.54	0.001
Specialisation Labour★★	23.46691	12.70431	1.85	0.067
Financial services (Labour LQs)	−2.218812	8.974479	−0.25	0.805
Culture and entertainment services (Labour LQ★)	−11.67034	3.717425	−3.14	0.002
Formal employment★	−0.6899188	0.2358589	−2.93	0.004
Local financial autonomy★★	0.3140812	0.1637385	1.92	0.058
Public debt leverage	0.0818813	0.4113651	0.2	0.843
Violence	0.0204653	0.0939837	0.22	0.828
City size	0.2153712	1.271007	0.17	0.866
Connectivity	0.0765497	0.3070026	0.25	0.804
Number of local governments	−0.1884478	0.4140448	−0.46	0.65
Territorial fragmentation	−2.294829	2.981037	−0.77	0.443
Electoral competition	0.110382	0.152346	0.72	0.47
Number of observations	130			
Prob > F	0			
R-squared	0.9695			
Adjusted R-squared	0.9658			

★ Significant at 95% of confidence; ★★ significant at 90% of confidence.

Table 6.6 Estimation of the model for GDP pc

Variable	Coef.	Std. Err.	t	P > t
Constant	−304321.4	312833.2	−0.97	0.333
Investment★	2.081781	0.9061936	2.3	0.023
Presence of high-quality schools	−7032.095	2561.669	−2.75	0.007
Specialisation Production	−8199.624	124748.9	−0.07	0.948
Financial services (Production LQ)	−18926.57	160139.4	−0.12	0.906
Culture and entertainment services (Production LQ)	11067.55	26942.3	0.41	0.682
Formal employment	695.1393	3055.41	0.23	0.82
Local financial autonomy	317.8936	3096.457	0.1	0.918
Public debt leverage	−4158.596	7769.645	−0.54	0.594
Violence	204.5257	1745.586	0.12	0.907
City size★	81151.43	24398.28	3.33	0.001
Connectivity	−5138.847	5626.998	−0.91	0.363
Number of local governments	−1546.714	6067.741	−0.25	0.799
Rate of territorial fragmentation	−0.0454799	0.1529364	−0.3	0.767
Electoral competition	102.2341	2822.849	0.04	0.971
Number of observations	130			
Prob > F	0			
R-squared	0.5465			
Adjusted R-squared	0.491			

★ Significant at 95% of confidence; ★★ significant at 90% of confidence.

The model with GDP per capita as a dependent variable has an adjusted R-squared of just 49 per cent, but is significant according to the F statistic (Table 6.6). In this estimation only capital accumulation and city size are significant at 95 per cent confidence. Scale, rather than sectoral structures, institutions, human capital or metropolitan structure, contributes to average income. The rest of the variables lose their predictive capacity to explain any difference in production per inhabitant across Mexico's metropolitan areas. This and the previous model might be affected by measurement error in the independent variables, but productivity rather than production per inhabitant seems to be better explained by the variables included in the model according to the results provided.

Concluding comments

In this book I have highlighted how metropolitan areas are an essential spatial scale of economic development for various reasons. They are dense economic and demographic concentrations that produce agglomeration effects: economic concentration allows labour-market pooling and input sharing; the frequent and relatively low-cost face-to-face contact that is possible at the metropolitan scale enables rich human interaction and permits the exchange of many forms of information and knowledge. Such exchanges also foster knowledge production and innovation, which can power the economy by reducing average costs.

Importantly, metropolitan areas are the scale at which spatial labour markets are best delineated.

While the economy is only one component of the complex functioning of metropolitan areas, it deserves particular attention due to its implications and relationships with other metropolitan dimensions. Analysis of the economic performance of metropolitan areas provides valuable information about different aspects of the development of these territories that national evaluations tend to obscure. Identifying the driving mechanisms and forces of economic prosperity is a significant step towards better understanding of the patterns, processes and functioning of metropolitan performance, which, in turn, is essential for effective planning and policies.

Some knowledge has developed about how metropolitan economies grow and perform. Whereas the theoretical literature has identified development factors such as capital accumulation, human capital, specialisation, institutions, agglomeration effects, urban structure and governance, the empirical literature on the significance of variables that influence urban economic performance is mixed and inconclusive. Largely, the evidence shows that city size, human capital, specialisation in certain types of economic activities and solid institutions have a positive impact on productivity, while sprawl and fragmented governance structures reduce efficiency and productivity.

The existing literature, however, has shown that there is no automatic route by which less-developed metropolitan areas catch up with wealthier metropolises, and there is no conclusive evidence about what puts a metropolitan economy on a trajectory of higher growth, increased firm and worker productivity and improved living standards, thus achieving deeper prosperity. Moreover, despite studies investigating urban and metropolitan economic patterns and mechanisms, the dynamics of the driving forces and the disparities are well-documented in only a few countries, especially in the developed world.

This chapter has reviewed the most prominent ideas, theories and evidence on the drivers of economic development and performance in cities and metropolitan areas. It has also discussed and examined development factors in Mexico's metropolitan areas. As discussed in Chapter 4, in contrast to some economic successes and improvements, economic functioning in a good number of metropolitan areas in Mexico has experienced slowdown, declining performance and high instability.

Economic disparities and deteriorating metropolitan performance across the country pose the challenge of increasing and extending the economic benefits to all metropolitan areas, for which deep and systematic evaluation of their economic performance and disparities is necessary. In this exploratory analysis of the variables that foster economic performance, the important role of traditional factors such as physical capital accumulation, human capital and specialisation to increase productivity untangled. The presence of cultural and entertainment services does not seem to contribute to the best metropolitan economic performance in Mexico, but plays a role against urban productivity. City size, the presence of financial services, public debt leverage, connectivity, violence and fragmentation are not statistically significant. It is particularly odd that fragmentation is not significant. On the other hand, the model to explain GDP per capita has a relatively weak capacity, and only capital accumulation, human capital and city size seem to be significantly related to average income.

Development is a fundamental question that requires consideration of metropolitan areas in their particular context, which is politically and administratively different to that of cities. Metropolitan economic strategies must differ from uncoordinated city development policy, because the lack of coordinated efforts in the former is often a key factor contributing directly to economic decline. Naturally every metropolitan area experiences economic development or decline regardless of the existence of comprehensive strategic plans or public policy. Yet metropolitan areas that function as fully integrated economies in terms of their production and distribution of goods and services need a coherent economic strategy.

Explaining the performance, the drivers of development and inter-metropolitan differences in Mexico, and many other countries, is a pending task that is linked to the need of generating adequate information and deepening the metropolitan analysis and debate. Further work in terms of modelling and data production is needed in order to be able to inform better policies and strategies for improving economic performance and positively affecting metropolitan development.

Notes

1 Boisier (1997) points out that territorial development increased in relevance as a result of the expansion of trade liberalisation and globalisation because regions, cities and local economies were obliged to engage in international competition to succeed.
2 The nomenclature of territorial units for statistics, abbreviated as NUTS (from the French 'nomenclature des unités territoriales statistiques') is a geographical classification that subdivides EU territories into regions at three different levels as NUTS 1, 2 and 3 respectively, moving from larger to smaller territorial units.

References

Ahrend, R. et al. (2014). *What makes cities more productive? Evidence on the role of urban governance from five OECD countries.* OECD Regional Development Working Papers, No. 2014/05, Paris: OECD Publishing. Available at: https://doi.org/10.1787/5jz432cf2d8p-en.

Bluestone, B. (2014). *What makes working cities work? Key factors in urban economic growth.* Community Development Issue Briefs. Available at: www.bostonfed.org/publications/community-development-issue-briefs/2014/what-makes-working-cities-work-key-factors-in-urban-economic-growth.aspx.

Blumenthal, P., Wolman, H. L. & Hill, E. (2009). 'Understanding the economic performance of metropolitan areas in the US'. *Urban Studies*, 46(3), 605–627. Available at: https://journals.sagepub.com/doi/pdf/10.1177/0042098008100997.

Boisier, S. (1997). 'El vuelo de una cometa: Una metáfora para una teoría del desarrollo territorial'. *Revista EURE*, XXIII(69), 7–29. Available at: www.eure.cl/index.php/eure/article/view/1159/260.

Donegan, M., Drucker, J., Goldstein, H., Lowe, N. & Malizia, E. (2008). 'Which indicators explain metropolitan economic performance best? Traditional or creative class'. *Journal of the American Planning Association*, 74(2), 180–195. Available at: www.tandfonline.com/doi/full/10.1080/01944360801944948?needAccess=true.

Gagliardi, L. & Percoco, M. (2012). Understanding European urban development: A review of selected issues. [online]. Available at: www.unibocconi.it/wps/wcm/connect/5be94778-216d-4866-bfd9-9d25dd88d93c/Gagliardi-Percoco+Revdocx.pdf?MOD=AJPERES&useDefaultText=0&useDefaultDesc=0.

Leal, J. & Parrilla, J. (2016). *Redefining global cities: The seven types of global metro economies.* The Brookings Institution Metropolitan Policy Program. Available at: www.brookings.edu/research/redefining-global-cities/.

Martin, R., Gardiner, B. & Tyler, P. (2014). *The evolving economic performance of UK cities: City growth patterns 1981–2011.* Future of cities, Working Paper. Foresight, Government Office for Science. Available at: http://pie.pascalobservatory.org/sites/default/files/14-803-evolving-economic-performance-of-cities.pdf.

Pike, A., Rodríguez-Pose, A. & Tomaney, J. (2006). *Local and regional development.* London: Routledge.

Rodríguez-Pose, A. (2013). 'Do institutions matter for regional development?' *Regional Studies*, 47(7), 1034–1047. Available at: https://doi.org/10.1080/00343404.2012.748978.

Storper, M. (2009). *Local economic development: Some cities develop more than others: specialization, human capital and institutions.* CAF Working paper, 2009/08, Caracas: CAF. Available at: http://scioteca.caf.com/handle/123456789/201.

Storper, M. (2010). 'Why does a city grow? Specialisation, human capital or institutions?' *Urban Studies*, 47(10), 2027–2050. Available at: https://journals.sagepub.com/doi/abs/10.1177/0042098009359957.

Vázquez-Barquero, A. (1988). *Desarrollo local: Una estrategia de creación de empleo.* Madrid: Pirámide.

Part III

Local experiences

Metropolisation, governance and public policies

7 The metropolisation process and spatial structure in Mexico City

A giant's tale

Introduction

As a global phenomenon metropolisation is not only transforming national and international urban systems and hierarchies, but is also involved in the inner spatial restructuring of the functional urban space though the reorganisation of land use, economic behaviour and political structure. Along with population and economic restructuring, metropolisation reshapes the urban territory through the materialisation of diverse spatial structures. Land markets become strong determinants of this territorial reorganisation and of the development patterns of metropolitan areas (Ingram, 1998), and thus the land market becomes inherent to economic development itself (Alix-García & Sellars, 2018). The intra-urban restructuring is reflected usually by the fragmentation of urban functions, also affecting the economic development of metropolitan areas. Therefore, a closer look at the internal structure and spatial organisation of individual metropolises is needed.

The aim of this chapter is to examine a specific case of the metropolisation process, exemplified by Mexico City Metropolitan Area (MCMA), where the national capital city seats, to observe how it adjusts to general forms or models of urban structure. This metropolitan area is the most important demographic urban nucleus in the national urban system, and Mexico's main political, economic, financial, business and cultural centre. Sometimes categorised as a global city, MCMA is one of the largest urban centres in Latin America and the world. The population in the capital city is around 9 million inhabitants. Yet, due to significant urban expansion, its metropolitan area has approximately 21 million inhabitants, making it the world's third largest urban agglomeration, the biggest on the American continent and the most populous Spanish-speaking city in the world. Spatially, it has spilled over into 60 municipalities in the states of Hidalgo and State of Mexico, more than doubling its size in the process. As a result of its expansion, significant spatial divisions have taken place in the labour market, in the political-administrative framework and in the socioeconomic composition of the metropolitan area. Whereas expansion led to an enlarged urban landscape, at the same time the urban structure was disconnected and the metropolis developed socially differentiated and administratively fragmented.

The chapter starts by recounting the foundation and historical evolution of Mexico City. This historical overview emphasises the shifts taking place in the second half of last century when metropolisation began as a conurbation process with the intense integration of smaller urban centres in the neighbouring State of Mexico. Intense industrialisation, high demand for labour – particularly in manufacturing – that attracted population from the countryside, higher salaries and natural population growth were reflected in the displacement of industrial activities and housing to the urban periphery extending to different municipalities. In addition, the political economy of territorial transformation and its relationship with peripheral urbanisation is discussed. Particularly, the widely established idea that the urban expansion of Mexico City was the result of an anarchic occupation and land invasion is contested.

The economy and productive structure of this metropolis is depicted to show its relative position and function in the national and global urban systems. Yet a more detailed analysis concentrates on the recent spatial patterns of the labour force and economic activities within the metropolitan area in order to identify the prevailing urban structure which has been blamed for much of its social and economic inefficiency. Exploratory spatial data analysis (ESDA) techniques allow identification of location and clustering patterns of economic activity (place of work) and population (place of residence) and determination of a statistical magnitude of the existing spatial mismatch in the metropolitan labour market. Overall, a well-defined monocentric economic structure in the city centre is contrasted with a more dispersed concentration of population in the faraway urban periphery.

The chapter also reviews the governance and political frames in which metropolitan evolution and functioning take place. Lastly, the most pressing economic, social, political and environmental challenges brought by the metropolitan transition are identified. Such challenges are complex and manifold. In spite of their significance, an in-depth analysis of such issues is beyond the scope of the chapter and the book.

The underlying territorial evolution of Mexico City Metropolitan Area

The conformation of every metropolitan area depends closely on comparative advantages or historical accidents. A city will more probably emerge as a metropolitan area if it is well placed within the national hierarchy of cities, and this is especially so if the city is a national capital with a high urban primacy. Perhaps more important, at later stages metropolisation depends on a number of necessary conditions. Metropolitan functions will develop only if positive agglomeration externalities extend widely over the territory. However, in addition to urban sprawl, metropolisation implies, in numerous cases, the formation of a discontinuous and heterogeneous internal structure, which leads to formation of ever more fragmented urban spaces. Interpretations diverge as to varying logics underlying the metropolisation process.

Metropolisation depends essentially on specific agglomeration forces. The intensity of these forces, in turn, depends on the size and composition of the city. Yet the phenomenon is complex and non-linear. We can imagine the process unfolding over time and over the territory in a cumulative or circular fashion. Complexity of issues in metropolitan areas along with intricacy and a number of influential factors in metropolisation necessitate careful approaches.

MCMA has been the outcome of the explosive urban growth and expansion of the original urban centre (that included the historic and colonial districts of Mexico City). Urban ordering in this huge metropolitan area has been determined by the historical, economic and political processes that have taken place over time. In recent decades, international influences have also acquired great relevance, situating the city as a strategic player in the global urban system.

Tenochtitlan, the ancient capital of the Aztec Empire and the site of modern Mexico City, was located in the middle of a large lake system that was used for trade with hinterland areas to feed city residents and accumulate wealth. When the Spanish conquistador Hernan Cortes arrived to Tenochtitlan in 1519, the magnificent city was home to more than 200,000 people. As such, it was one of the largest in the world, and certainly bigger than any in Europe. Actually, at the time of the Spanish Conquest, the whole Aztec Empire was a large and urbanised society. However, the Conquest was accompanied by one of the most dramatic demographic collapses in history due to disease, drought and famine.[1] During the colonial rule the Spanish maintained Mexico–Tenochtitlan as the political capital. Yet, they destroyed and rebuilt the city according to their own conventions, with grand churches and palaces on a grid pattern based around a central square, or Zocalo. After independence from Spain in 1810 and the many subsequent years of civil conflict, the economic and political preeminence of Mexico City was enhanced, particularly during the Porfirian dictatorship from 1870 to 1910 when the nation's capital was endowed with strong advantages in terms of infrastructure (Alix-García & Sellars, 2018).

Until the end of the nineteenth century, Mexico City reduced to what is known as the 'first square', which comprises an area of about 20 km^2 around Zocalo. This period was characterised by the great polarisation between the residential areas of the elite, located within the first square, and the precarious houses, usually remote, of the poor. Later, the elite of the city centre began to move towards new developments in the physically more attractive areas of the periphery. Among the main causes of this mobilisation were the traffic in the centre of the city, which was becoming problematic, as well as the fear of being exposed to dangerous diseases. For their part, working-class families began to inhabit the unoccupied houses that remained in the centre of the city (Sánchez, 2012). The neighbourhoods and districts, which have their origin in the period of the Porfiriato in the nineteenth century, had a boom from the mid-1920s until about the mid-1940s. They underpinned the political will and economic logic of modernisation promoted by the Mexican State. Mexico City was once again a privileged place during the postrevolution period, at least until the 1930s (Carrillo, 2004). It was in the aftermath of the Mexican Revolution, in the 1930s, when the city population began its decisive upsurge to become the archetypical Latin American primate city (Connolly, 2003). Since then, Mexico City has been often highlighted as a canonical example of a primate megacity (Alix-García & Sellars, 2018).

In the mid-twentieth century Mexico City developed as a result of numerous political (e.g. the centralisation of power and one-party rule) and economic (e.g. ISI policies) factors. This programme of highly centralised industrialisation changed the city irrevocably. Industrialisation as a state policy for economic development originated in the 1940s and influenced the economic-territorial configuration of the national capital (Carrillo, 2004; Sánchez, 2012). Between the 1940s and 1970s during the phase of economic miracle and stabilising development,[2] Mexico City became the spatial gravitational core of the industrialisation model (Carrillo, 2004).

Metropolisation of Mexico City began as a conurbation process which defined a territorial restructuring and a transformation characterised by the suburbanisation of different activities and the intense integration of smaller urban centres (Carrillo, 2004). From the 1940s Mexico City began its expansion to other jurisdictions outside its administrative boundaries. Urban expansion took place under the modality of different forms of land occupation and housing production (Legorreta, 1991; Carrillo, 2004). The presence of different economic and demographic forces (intense industrialisation; high demand for labour, particularly in manufacturing, that attracted masses of population from the countryside; higher salaries; and natural population growth) was reflected in the displacement of industrial activities and vast housing developments to the urban periphery extending to municipalities of the State of Mexico (Sánchez, 2012).

As described in Chapter 3 the land surrounding the city, under their different forms of property (collective, public and private), was transformed into a commodity or a place of occupation mainly for housing purposes. The land market, through both irregular and legal mechanisms, became an inseparable part of the growth and expansion of the city (Legorreta, 1991).

From the 1950s, regulations and norms to prevent new human settlements in Mexico City started to be implemented, a situation that stimulated the occupation of land for housing purposes in an irregular manner. These regulations reinforced the move to metropolisation, through the conurbation of an increasing number of neighbouring municipalities of the State of Mexico where such land occupation rules were not applied (e.g. Naucalpan, Netzahualcoyotl and Ecatepec). In this process, the conurbated municipalities of the State of Mexico were transformed into areas of industrial location, middle-class housing and, above all, popular sectors housing[3] (Sánchez, 2012).

Subsequently, urban expansion took place quickly through continuous land occupations and long-term constructive processes of mainly individual housing carried out by low-income sectors (Legorreta, 1991). A significant part of the city expansion was the product of invasions, illegal occupations and uncontrolled sales of parcels for housing uses. In most cases, the occupation took place in self-construction housing, and often in irregular settlements in a process that was reinforced by the natural increase of the population and, notably, by large flows of immigrants from the countryside and lagging areas from the country (Carrillo, 2004).[4]

Yet, virtually all social classes were engaged in land acquisition processes. In general terms, higher-income groups moved to the south and west, while the poor moved to the north and east. During the 1950s, extensive areas of urban land began to be privatised into residential subdivisions that were also achieved illegally through the inadequate dissolution of ejido lands,[5] and were later converted into properties of the elite and higher-income classes. Ejidatarios also sold smaller parcels of land to low-income families. Similarly, real estate brokers privatised government lands ceded for agricultural improvement purposes to convert them and sell them to the poor as land without services. Landowners in the east of the city also saw the opportunity to capitalise on their low-quality properties by selling lots with minimal investment capital (Sánchez, 2012). The need for land for productive and housing activities, and a consequent increase in price led to the occupation, for urban uses, of vast agricultural and forestry areas, mountains and hills. Facing the exhaustion of flat land in the Valley of Mexico, and because of the land monopolised by better organised real estate interests, popular sectors demanding housing began to massively occupy difficult terrains (hills, ravines and mountains) (Legorreta, 1991).

The physical evolution of the city was also derived from the opposing processes of deindustrialisation and expansion of trade and services (Sánchez, 2012). Similarly it became necessary and profitable to establish commercial, banking and service areas, private and public, in the new housing areas, which formed, temporarily, urban subcentres in different parts of the metropolis (Pradilla, 2005). Important commercial developments were produced in the south of the city and in the northwest, and relocation of industry in the north of the city took place (Unikel, 2016).

The so-called process of invasion–succession that began in the 1940s and intensified until the 1970s was the product of the substantial increase in the needs and real demand for land for housing, industry and services, the scarcity of land, significant increases in the value of the land in the central areas of the city and of the difficult mobility in the central city (Unikel, 2016). The increase of income of some population groups, the increase of the vehicular fleet and use of private cars, the development of vehicular roads towards the periphery, the availability of large areas of undeveloped land in the periphery and social preferences more inclined to new lifestyles towards a horizontal urbanism in an environment of relatively low population density became contributing factors of urban expansion (Unikel, 2016; Legorreta, 1991; Carrillo, 2004; Pradilla, 2005).

Between 1970 and 1990 the city multiplied its extension almost twice. The most outstanding cases of incorporation of new urban areas were municipalities at the east and north of the central city: Chimalhuacan (713 per cent increase),

Chicoloapan (563 per cent), Chalco (473 per cent), Cuautitlan Izcalli (518 per cent) and Tultitlan (529 per cent). In the Federal District the peripheral delegations of Milpa Alta (168 per cent), Cuajimalpa (155 per cent) and Tlalpan (147 per cent) had important increases. The 17 conurbated municipalities of the State of Mexico recorded population growth rates of 7.3 per cent in the 1950s, 11.8 per cent in the 1960s and 8.1 per cent in the 1970s, while the Federal District reached only 4.6, 3.4 and 2.2 per cent growth rates respectively (Legorreta, 1991).

New housing policies and financial markets deregulation in the 1990s redefined the housing and land markets. Since the early 2000s, contrary to previous periods when peripheral urbanisation in Mexico meant primarily the expansion of informal settlements under limited public control, contemporary housing policies have focused on market-driven housing provision where the real estate developers and the mortgage financing agents became the leading actors. Financial markets have received important stimuli through the securitisation of these mortgages. The market-oriented rationalities have strongly incentivised private real estate.

The main feature of the new housing model consists in settling and implementing a strategy that aims at 'enabling markets to work'. This means a reorientation of housing policies by shifting responsibilities from the state to private actors: the public sector provides only the legal and administrative framework for different kinds of subsidies and loans, which are granted either to construction companies or to dwellers. In this new scheme, housing policies do not necessarily satisfy the needs of the poorest sectors, but focus on those who have formal employment (Janoschka & Salinas, 2017; Valenzuela, 2017).

According to Janoschka and Salinas (2017) homeownership has become increasingly normalised to those on lower incomes, mainly through market-driven housing policies. Through the implementation of large-scale housing programmes subsidising part of the construction costs and providing households with state-backed mortgages, public administrations have been assuring private investment in affordable housing in Mexico, and in many other developing countries. The massive production of low-income housing in urban peripheries demonstrates the capacity of those market-driven programmes to provide quantitative solutions to housing deficits, particularly in middle-income economies.

However, market-driven schemes have displaced the poor to ever more peripheral locations where land is available and cheap. The provision of social housing[6] stimulated the move of hundreds of thousands of households to the northern and eastern periphery. Most of the new low-income housing spread into urban peripheries that typically lack sufficient infrastructure to satisfy the basic needs of new residents. The insufficient quality and small size of housing units have been commonly reflected in deficient public infrastructure, urban services and transportation and the abandonment of housing units. Public policies targeting the densification of central areas of the city contributed to the peripheral expansion as they provoked a 'selective modernisation' and substantial house price increases, because urban renovation and housing replacement chiefly targeted the middle and upper-middle classes, triggering widespread gentrification (ibid.).

This territorial organisation of a centrifugal character continues in the second decade of the twenty-first century, integrating an increasing number of residential developments, which usually function as dormitory zones, and advancing also on natural reserves and rural areas (Sánchez, 2012). The irregular settlements continue to define some of the expansion to the municipalities of the State of Mexico, with a disorderly urbanisation and great spatial and demographic complexity (Carrillo, 2004). Table 7.1 summarises different stages of the metropolitan transformation of Mexico City.

Table 7.1 The stages of metropolisation of Mexico City

Period	Characteristics
1940s: Intense industrialisation and manufacturing conurbation	Intense industrialisation of Mexico City.
	Continuous territorial expansion of industrial activity to the north and northwest of the city.
	Location of industrial plants in the neighbouring municipalities of Mexico.
	Formation of small industrial conglomerates that began to join spatially.
	Industries such as the automobile assembly (Chrysler and General Motors) and tire manufacturing (Euskadi) relocated to those areas.
1950s–1960s: Polarised residential conurbation	Housing started to develop more intensely towards the neighbouring municipalities of the State of Mexico.
	Low-income population located in low-cost territories, far from the centre of Mexico City, particularly to the east and north of the city.
	Middle-income population accessed new housing projects, such as Ciudad Satelite (State of Mexico), that were well-connected through the peripheral ring road with the city centre.
	Around 1960, the total population of the metropolitan area was estimated at 5.1 million inhabitants who lived in an urbanized area of 417 km².
1970s–1980s: Accelerated expansion	Accelerated and uncontrolled expansion. In 1980 the population was almost 14.5 million inhabitants, around twice the population registered in 1970.
	Deconcentration policies, the 1985 earthquakes and price increases in urban land, especially in the central boroughs of Cuauhtemoc, Benito Juarez, Venustiano Carranza and Miguel Hidalgo, prompted greater displacement of population and some economic activity towards the metropolitan periphery.
	Most of the industry moved gradually towards the municipalities of Ecatepec, Cuautitlan, Cuautitlan Izcalli and Tepotzotlan in the State of Mexico.
1990s–2000s: Peripheral extended expansion	Population in the metropolitan area surpassed 15.5 million inhabitants in 1990.
	Towards the end of the century, the process of metropolitan expansion and demographic growth intensified, mainly in further municipalities of the State of Mexico.
	Population exceeded 18 million inhabitants in 2000.

Source: Based on Sánchez (2012).

The political economy of a territorial transformation and peripheral urbanisation

Critical reflections about the dilemmas of metropolisation and the role of public policies, real estate and the financial markets have recently acknowledged the importance of political economy factors to analyse those urban processes that have become paradigmatic in many cities in and beyond Latin America. The link between politics, territorial transformation and peripheral urbanisation has taken the form of a set of interrelated processes that entangle multiple public and private actors. One important dimension of the political economy of peripheral urbanisation in Mexico City has been land and low-income housing policies, which also have dramatically shaped peripheral urban expansion in several countries of Latin America and the 'Global South' (Janoschka & Salinas, 2017).

MCMA experienced complex and a seemingly chaotic growth from the 1940s to the 1980s. The metropolisation process was characterised by weak planning and regulation, was strongly determined by speculative interests (Legorreta, 1991; Carrillo, 2004) and the gradual expansion of the metropolis did not follow any formal rationality. But the real estate developers have been always linked to economic and political power. Also, strong clientelist practices, preserved by political parties and other political groups, were operating to allow, especially, land occupation by the low-income population (Carrillo, 2004).

The widely established idea that the urban expansion of Mexico City was the result of an anarchic occupation and land invasion is challenged by the notion of a land market in illegal areas of the urban periphery being part of a real estate sector made up of powerful and strategic local structures. Initially, this segment of the market was unstable, lacked formal financial channels and was not very profitable. However, the significant power structures, including public (the state and local governments) and private actors (developers and local leaders), have preserved the operation of the land and housing markets through different forms of urban corporatism. These have included the appropriation and commercialisation of land and housing by different actors by means of established political relationships (Legorreta, 1991; Janoschka, 2011; Connolly, 2003).

Between the 1940 and 1990s two aspects predominated in these relationships: the control of social discontent caused by urban deprivation, and the support of the population to the local governments in turn. Counting on the economic advantages offered by the illegal real estate market, the promoters needed to have the support of some political power. Hence, a close relationship between the sale processes and the illegal occupation developed in accordance to electoral periods (Legorreta, 1991; Connolly, 2003). Figure 7.1 summarises the cycle of urban corporatism regarding the land market.

Although they operated mostly at the local level, large numbers of agents maintained political relations in other nearby municipalities or neighbourhoods; in fact, they acted as a regional force, exceeding their local scope in the State of Mexico. Thus, growth and urban expansion in MCMA was not an

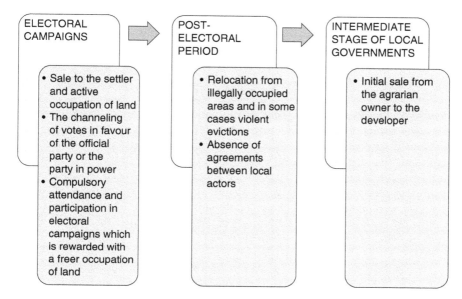

Figure 7.1 The cycle of the urban corporatism and the land market

Source: Based on Legorreta (1991).

anarchic and spontaneous process, but rather was determined by economic and political interests of great diversity (Legorreta, 1991).

The organisational structure of the political powers around the expansion processes depended on the origin and form of land ownership, the type of public intervention and the links established. Ejido and communal lands were the most complex structures to deal with. The rural and urban spheres combined to form an intricate network of relationships. When agrarian structures predominated, important public entities, such as the Secretariat of Agrarian Reform, and the local authorities in the municipalities of the State of Mexico and the boroughs of Distrito Federal enabled the acquisition and occupation processes (ibid.).

A redefinition of power relations in Mexican and Latin American cities occurred as neoliberal policies and a reordering of political power through public–private cooperation were implemented (Janoschka, 2011). New low- and medium-income housing schemes may be considered as a regime that is fundamentally based upon vigorous alliances between public administrations, especially on the federal level, and actors from the real estate industry (Janoschka & Salinas, 2017). Locally, the replacement of the traditional one-party corporativist clientelism by competitive electioneering has altered the unwritten rules governing access to benefits and basic necessities such as housing credits, urban services, regularisation programmes and social subsidies. The role of political intermediaries –the 'official' trade unions, community leaders, professional invaders and other grassroots organisation representatives – has been undermined; however, in many cases similar practices and the political cultures persist, with different – or sometimes the same – social actors on the scene (Connolly, 2003).

The urban economy and the productive structure

MCMA is home to 17 per cent of the national population and contributes almost a fourth (23 per cent) of national GDP. One explanation of the significant degree of economic and demographic concentration in Mexico City has been the competitive advantage of cumulative investment in productive infrastructure, inherited from previous centuries and enhanced throughout the twentieth century. Economic, political and educational opportunities, as well as markets, were overwhelmingly concentrated in the capital. The influence of the politically centralised postrevolutionary presidential regimes and the consolidation of a one-party state, in power until 2000, are equally important (Connolly, 2003).

Between 1900 and 1940, the share of Mexico City in national GDP went from 9 to 30 per cent (annual average growth rates of 5.4 per cent, while for the country it was 2.3 per cent), which evidences the growing economic significance of this urban economy with respect to the national economy (Sánchez, 2012).

Between the 1940s and 1970s Mexico City and its metropolitan area became the engine of industrialisation, capitalist development and cultural modernisation (Pradilla, 2005). The major part of economic growth during the ISI stage took place in Mexico City, at first due to the World War II bonanza for already existing industries, and subsequently because of the increasing national and foreign direct investment by multinational companies, all nurtured by a variety of macroeconomic policies. Mexico City's contribution to the national economy, already dominant, continued to increase until 1970 (Connolly, 2003). In 1970, the Federal District generated 27.6 per cent of the national GDP and MCMA produced 36.2 per cent (Pradilla, 2005). Between 1940 and 1970 the annual growth rate was 7 per cent and the national growth rate was 6.2 per cent (Sánchez, 2012).

Because the critical effects of world recession were delayed in Mexico (due to oil revenues and public expenditure financed by an escalating national debt), public spending included ambitious projects for Mexico City, such as the subway system, roads and deep drainage. Mexico City's economic preeminence began to moderate, coincident with the crisis of the ISI model at the end of the 1970s. The national crisis in 1982 particularly affected Mexico City because many industries oriented to the domestic market went out of business (Connolly, 2003). The city started to lose population and certain types of economic activities to a number of medium-sized cities in the country (Graizbord, Rowland & Aguilar, 2003). As a consequence, unemployment, informality and street vending soared.

Economic stagnation, deindustrialisation and informal tertiarisation started to characterise MCMA's economy in the 1980s (Connolly, 2003; Pradilla, 2005; Sánchez, 2012). The change in the national economic model, environmental problems, traffic congestion and pollution undermined Mexico City's comparative advantages (Connolly, 2003). Some diseconomies of agglomeration engendered by the relatively higher cost of land, the higher average wages in relation to other regions, the higher rate of unionisation of workers, the shortage of water, the cost-time of transportation of raw materials and final products due to road saturation and the environmental regulations imposed to deal with the high level of pollution counteracted the advantages of the metropolitan area and caused the exit of industries to other locations. Large companies, such as automotive assemblers, moved to other cities in the centre of the country and cities in the north, in order to appropriate the advantages of localisation with respect to the North American market (Pradilla, 2005).

Despite the relative industrial decline of MCMA the implementation of the new national development strategy in the 1980s accentuated the importance of the national capital as a centre of high-level financial and specialised service activities. The city kept the country's highest-paid jobs and high-skilled labour. It also offered opportunities for unskilled workers to find employment as low-paid support to service industries, as well as in personal services, primarily in the informal sector (Graizbord, Rowland & Aguilar, 2003). Its industrial structure is concentrated in high-value-added services, especially financial services and insurance, with transport and communications, real estate and business services accounting for a relatively high share of value added (OECD, 2015).

This situation reveals the two sides of the coin in the recent past of MCMA with regard to the process of integration into the international economy: one side of the coin reveals the presence of high-paid jobs and specialised services, whereas the opposite side consists of the prevalence of poverty, low wages, unproductive services and informality (Graizbord, Rowland & Aguilar, 2003). Tertiarisation, in particular, has been very polarised: the formal and modern service sector increased its participation in the GDP, but created very little highly qualified employment and more or less adequate salaries. Meanwhile, the informal and traditional commercial and service sector grew rapidly in the number of precarious and unstable jobs with very low remuneration and no social benefits (Pradilla, 2005).

Although MCMA is among the most productive and efficient metropolitan areas in the country, it is also located among the metropolitan areas with the greatest deterioration in its labour productivity (Trejo, 2016). OECD metropolitan areas with a comparable population share, such as London and Paris, produce around 30 per cent of the national GDP, whereas MCMA produces less than 25 per cent. Likewise, MCMA is well below the economic potential of an urban agglomeration of its size in an emerging economy. Its labour productivity (GDP per worker) is not significantly higher than the average among the 33 Mexican metropolitan areas (per the OECD definition). Of all 275 OECD metropolitan areas, MCMA remains among the 10 per cent with the lowest

GDP per capita (OECD, 2015). Accordingly, MCMA does not seem to generate enough agglomeration benefits relative to its size.

One explanation that has been proposed to explain the deteriorating productivity in MCMA is the significant job-housing imbalance or, in other words, the mismatch between the location of jobs and housing. The OECD's estimations indicate that more than 40 per cent of metropolitan residents commute across municipalities to go to work or to school. Moreover, the transport system has not been able to match the rapid urban development. The problem is exacerbated by the lack of strategic regional planning frameworks at the metropolitan level, insufficient financial backing, ambiguous constitutional definitions of metropolitan areas and weak coordination and collaboration among state and municipal level governments for urban development (ibid.).

Urban structure and the spatial mismatch of the labour market

Metropolisation implies the intra-urban relocation of population and economic activities to areas far from the central city and involves the spatial redistribution of the labour market within the functional city (Sobrino 2003 cited in SEDESOL et al., 2012). One method to delimit metropolitan areas is by defining the spatial structure of the urban labour market, that is, the economically integrated geographical area within which individuals can reside and find employment within a reasonable distance or can change jobs easily without changing residence. The relationship between the place of residence (location of workers) and the location of workplaces (location of companies and businesses) defines centralities and peripheries from an economic-territorial perspective (Isunza & Soriano, 2008).

Throughout its history Mexico City has experienced several stages of expansion and spatial restructuring which have led to different economic and residential location patterns (Sánchez, 2012). According to Unikel (2016), in 1960 MCMA included four municipalities in the State of Mexico (Naucalpan, Tlalnepantla, Ecatepec and Chimalhuacan) and the Federal District (excepting two boroughs, Milpa Alta and Tlahuac). In the 1970s it covered the Federal District (except Tlahuac) and 10 conurbated municipalities in the State of Mexico (Naucalpan, Tlalnepantla, Ecatepec, Tultitlan, Coacalco, La Paz, Cuautitlan, Chimalhuacan, Huixquilucan and Nezahualcoyotl). As reported by the latest official delimitation, MCMA consists of 16 territorial demarcations (boroughs which are the administrative divisions within Mexico City proper,[7] formerly the Federal District) and 60 conurbated municipalities (59 in State of Mexico and one in the state of Hidalgo). It covers approximately 7,866 km^2 (SEDATU, CONAPO & INEGI, 2018), which is almost five times the size of the Greater London region and three times the size of Luxembourg (OECD, 2015). Data from the 2015 intercensal survey indicates that its population amounted 20.9 million people, most of whom lived outside Mexico City proper (57.3 per cent). The four most populated municipalities and boroughs each exceed 1 million inhabitants: Iztapalapa (Mexico City), Ecatepec (State of Mexico), Gustavo A. Madero (Mexico City) and Nezahualcoyotl (State of Mexico) (Figure 7.2).

Between 2010 and 2015 the municipalities with the highest population growth were located mainly in the north of the metropolitan area and away from the central city. In some of them, such as Tizayuca, Huehuetoca, Tecamac and Zumpango, the largest developments in social housing in the metropolis have been established, increasing the pressure for the provision and delivery of basic services, urban infrastructure and public transport. In contrast, the central boroughs present very low growth and even loss of population. According to the OECD (2015), the high rate of growth in the commuting zone is fairly exceptional among OECD metropolitan areas.

In Mexico, the strong functions of economic centrality of historic centres has showed important contrasts with the peripheral urban expansion of significant residential nature. The balance of agglomeration and deagglomeration forces has been reflected in the displacement of workers towards the periphery. Metropolisation has involved the territorial decentralisation of population that has been accompanied by the poor development of infrastructure in the peripheries and the scarcity of urban services, or less access to them due to

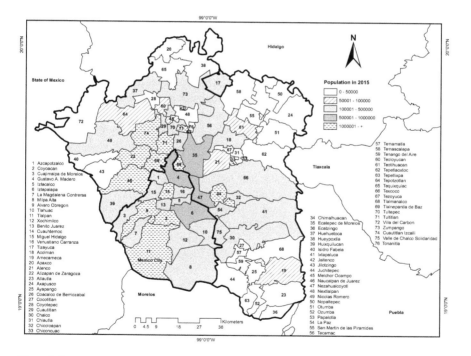

Figure 7.2 Mexico City Metropolitan Area's municipalities and boroughs by population, 2015

Source: Based on SEDATU, CONAPO and INEGI (2018).

their price or distance. Socially and functionally disintegrated population centres emerge, as well as spaces of segregation and remoteness, which limit the social networks of the inhabitants. The population faces a fundamental restriction: distance from jobs and poor access to employment. This urban structure, in turn, is detrimental to living conditions and favours poverty and vulnerability.

The spatial balance between work and residence location – the jobs–housing balance – suggests that proximity and accessibility to jobs from place of residence are translated into greater urban efficiency, high productivity and welfare. When there is physical remoteness and limited spatial accessibility to jobs, the traditional mechanisms of social and economic insertion are impaired. Distance to jobs causes high mobility needs which are limited by poor infrastructure, high cost of travel and elevated travel times.

Comparably, the spatial mismatch hypotheses (SMH) describes the existence of the spatial separation between labour demand and supply, revealing a necessity for daily mobility and an uneven accessibility to jobs, depending on the location and other socioeconomic features of different population groups. The SMH is regarded as a useful framework for addressing the spatial definition and organisation of urban labour markets. Furthermore, the literature suggests that the extent of the spatial mismatch can have negative effects on the efficiency and competitiveness of the city if it does not develop adequate accessibility. This idea assumes that the mismatch increases transportation costs and reduces disposable income which, in turn, translates into an unequal access to employment between different social groups within cities (Martin & Morrison, 2003). The spatial mismatch between workplace and residence location has been a prominent idea for several decades in urban economics, and recently has enjoyed renewed interest due to many recent transformations of urban structure in cities worldwide, for instance, the tendency towards polycentrism.

Changes in the urban structure of MCMA have resulted from a readjustment in housing and labour markets via changes in residence and job location. Decentralisation of residential areas mainly, but also of employment in the high-income sectors, has led to longer journeys to work for large segments of the population. While jobs have concentrated primarily in the central boroughs, the workforce concentrates predominantly in the municipalities of State of Mexico, increasingly farther away. The main economic centrality can be clearly defined, while the presence and the number of urban subcentres is insignificant. Population can spend on average 16 hours per week in commuting to their schools or workplaces, implying important mobility restrictions (Graizbord, Rowland & Aguilar, 2003). Journeys usually involve additional problems and risks such as insecurity and crime.[8]

Univariate and bivariate local indicators of spatial association (LISAs) and Moran's indexes allow for the identification and visualisation of the location and concentration of employment and workers in the city and co-location between jobs and place of residence. Moran's index is a global spatial correlation coefficient that measures the overall spatial autocorrelation in a data set. It is similar to correlation coefficients and evaluates whether the spatial pattern of a variable is clustered, dispersed or random. It has a value from −1 to 1: −1 is perfect dispersion, 0 is no autocorrelation (perfect randomness) and +1 indicates perfect clustering of similar values. However, the Moran index does not inform the location of a cluster. LISAs are the map representations of global Moran's indexes and indicate the location of clusters. According to the univariate Moran's index, MCMA exhibited a statistically significant trend towards the concentration of labour supply in specific areas of the city in 2010 (Figure 7.3).

As for LISAs, the results are shown as a map in Figure 7.4. Cold spots (areas of low concentration) of labour supply are located mainly in the central city and some faraway areas (AGEBS)[9] in the north, northeast, east and southeast outer peripheries. The main concentrations of workers, or hot spots, are big and well-defined clusters located in the east and southwest periphery (mainly in the municipalities of La Paz, Chimalhuacan, Ixtapaluca, Nezahualcoyotl, Ecatepec and Tecamac in the State of Mexico), as well as the boroughs of Cuajimalpa,

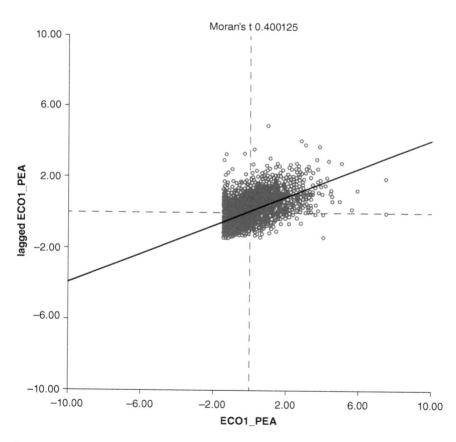

Figure 7.3 Global Moran's index of labour supply, 2010

Source: Based on INEGI (2010).

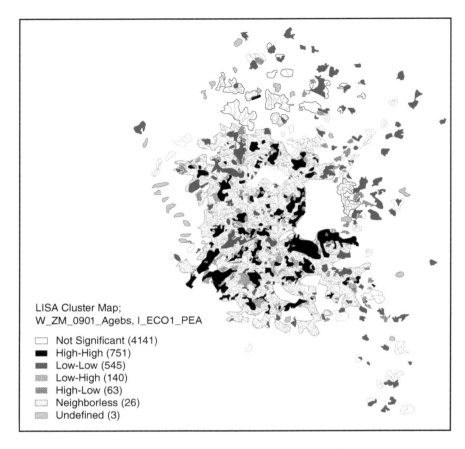

Figure 7.4 Local indicators of spatial association of labour supply, 2010

Source: Based on INEGI (2010).

Tlalpan and Magdalena Contreras. Other clusters of high concentration occur in the boroughs of Coyoacan, Azcapotzalco and Venustiano Carranza. Smaller clusters occur in the north and northeast periphery. As discussed earlier, these are peripheral zones of the metropolitan area that have registered the highest population growth rates.

The univariate Moran index also reveals a statistically significant trend towards the concentration of labour demand (Figure 7.5), although in this case the spatial correlation has a lower value (0.19)

LISAs show a very well-defined and consolidated cluster of employment in the central city and a corridor down the city (Figure 7.6). Mexico City's north–south axis of high-end commercial and office development runs mainly along the well-known Insurgentes Avenue, which stretches approximately 15

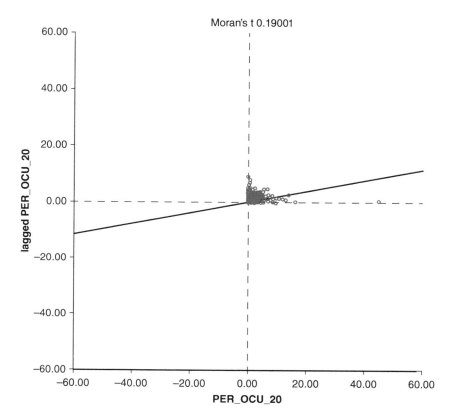

Figure 7.5 Global Moran's index of labour demand, 2008

Source: Based on INEGI (2009).

kilometres from the central city to the most important and consolidated high-income residential areas in the south, as well as to the campus of the National University (UNAM) which represent another small but clear cluster in the south.

Another cluster locates in the west in the Santa Fe area. Santa Fe was a new corporate development area in the west of the city – planned in the 1980s by the local government with strong support from private capital – with a mixture of residential, commercial and services land use that became a pole of attraction for corporate offices of national and international companies (Aguilar & Hernandez, 2016).

If we compare visually the spatial pattern of the labour supply with that of labour demand, a very important difference emerges: while demand shows a greater tendency to locate and concentrate in the central city and the north and west surrounding areas, labour supply exhibits a pattern where high

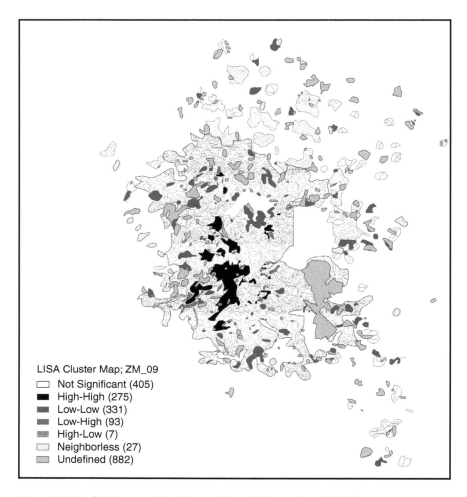

LISA Cluster Map; ZM_09
☐ Not Significant (405)
■ High-High (275)
■ Low-Low (331)
▓ Low-High (93)
▦ High-Low (7)
☐ Neighborless (27)
▨ Undefined (882)

Figure 7.6 Local indicators of spatial association of labour demand, 2008

Source: Based on INEGI (2009).

concentration is observed in parts of the northeast, east and southwest periph-eral areas. This suggests the presence of a significant spatial separation between jobs and workers.

The bivariate analysis – which relates the location between two variables – indicates a very low positive correlation between the concentration of popu-lation and the concentration of jobs; that is, people and jobs do not tend to concentrate in the same areas of the metropolis (Figure 7.7). LISAs show that a cluster of coincidence of population and employment takes place in the west (Santa Fe area), and smaller clusters locate in the central city and close to the

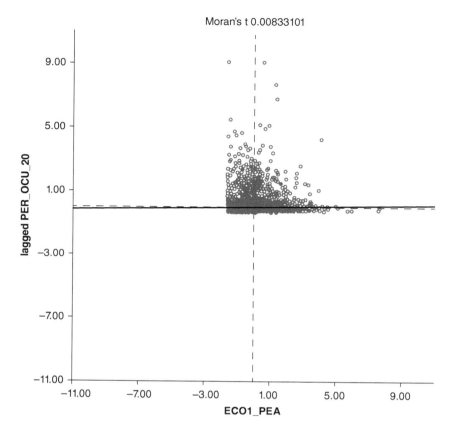

Figure 7.7 Bivariate global Moran's index labour demand and supply

Source: Based on INEGI (2009 and 2010).

centre towards the north. This confirms the existence of important spatial gap between jobs and places of residence. The places of coincidence probably cor-respond to high-income residential areas that locate close to high-income jobs such as those in Santa Fe (Figure 7.8).

The spatial separation between jobs and place of residence, in the presence of an inefficient transport system, implies not only high productivity costs but also significant losses in the living standards of the metropolitan population since commuting generates transport costs (in time and money) that reduce family income. In particular, low-income sectors located in the far peripheries suffer from low accessibility to jobs and services that concentrate predominantly in the central city. This is a common phenomenon across metropolitan areas in the world but the extent and significance of their consequences can be very locally defined. This is a very complex area of study as it involves the micro decisions

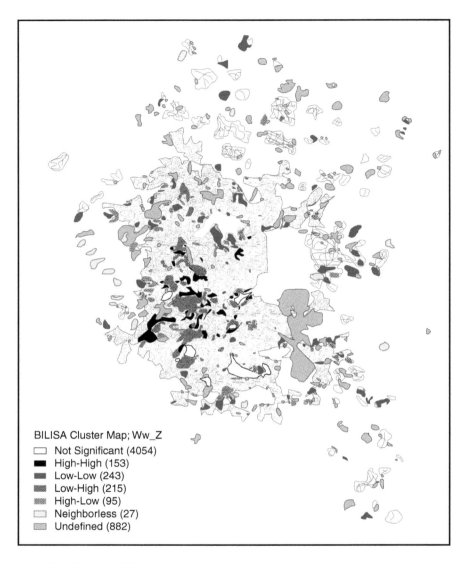

Figure 7.8 Bivariate LISAs labour demand and supply

Source: Based on INEGI (2009 and 2010).

of economic and residence location within the city. The spatial mismatch or imbalance opens the question of the role for local governments and companies alike to connect more residence places to job centres via public transit, to help lower-income residents stay in place as housing costs rise in the urban core and to make attractive jobs to commuters.

Political-administrative framework and metropolitan governance

As it has been argued, in Mexico there is an absence of clear and effective institutional arrangements for metropolitan development, urban services and infrastructure because of the complex, fragmented and often disorganised governance arrangements. MCMA has been identified nationally and internationally as an example of jurisdictional complexity because it is a very large conglomerate of local and state political-administrative divisions. MCMA faces two political-administrative systems: (1) Mexico City with its division into boroughs and (2) states and their municipalities. According to the current official delimitation, the territorial structure and the country's legal framework, this metropolitan area consists of 60 municipal governments located in two different states (State of Mexico and Hidalgo), and the government of Mexico City, together with the authority of its 16 boroughs that perform some functions and administrative powers; that is, 76 municipal-level governments, 3 state-level governments and the federal government. Mexico City proper is the seat of the federal government and the urban core of the metropolitan area. It is not a state in itself, though it is granted many state-level responsibilities and powers. As a consequence of a political reform in 2015 Mexico City was established as the official name of the former Federal District. Previously, the Federal District was a special political-administrative jurisdiction that contained Mexico City (the original urban centre). It was governed by a government statute and did not enjoy full autonomy. In fact, until the 1990s the population did not elect its government representative. With the reform, Mexico City proper maintained a special status but gained greater autonomy, and its first constitution was enacted in 2017. Currently, its boroughs are territorial and political-administrative divisions similar to municipalities, but with juridical, administrative and financial differences. The municipalities and boroughs are both led by publicly elected authorities, but in contrast to municipalities, boroughs cannot collect their own taxes and do not have autonomy.

Despite the economic, social and environmental problems shared between Mexico City and the metropolitan municipalities, the metropolitan area is highly unconnected in terms of its administrative and governmental organisation. Metropolitan governance depends on the interaction, coordination and cooperation of numerous actors, from local, state and national authorities to private companies and citizens. The overlapping powers of local, state and national governments often lead to contradictory policies and rules due to poor coordination and reduced willingness to cooperate. The infrequent cases of metropolitan coordination have taken place on specific sectors or specific events such as environmental contingencies.

Mexico has developed some avenues for intergovernmental horizontal and vertical coordination or association in recent decades. Article 115 states that municipalities can coordinate activities when there is a conurbation (i.e. urban municipalities that are adjacent). When such conurbation covers the territory of municipalities located in two or more states, then state governments also should coordinate. Coordination covenants are another mechanism for coordination. However, the national constitution has no provisions for a metropolitan level of government; it states that there is no intermediate authority between the municipality and the state government, and it does not mandate the creation of metropolitan agencies. The General Law of Human Settlements (GLHS) defines 'metropolitan' rather ambiguously. The constitution and the GLHS acknowledge the concept of 'conurbation' as the geographic continuity between two or more urban centres, but not the concept of 'metropolitan area' as the territorial space of influence of a dominant urban centre. Reaching covenants depends on political agreements (not on a legal mandate) and goodwill. Consequently, metropolitan governance arrangements remain weak given the ambiguous treatment of metropolitan areas within the national and local legislative framework, the weak legal framework for coordination and the low institutional capacities at the local level (OECD, 2015).

Metropolitan governance is not an emerging issue. In the 1970s some attempts emerged to implement metropolitan commissions and to design schemes of coordination agreements. However, in general, these efforts were ineffective due to the lack of financial, regulatory or decision-making authority (Cenizal, 2015). The Executive Committee of Metropolitan Coordination was established in 1998 and sought to involve the authorities of the State of Mexico, Hidalgo and Mexico City proper in specific projects focused on a topic or concrete problem. During the first years of the twenty-first century, six metropolitan commissions were established: (1) Metropolitan Environmental Commission, (2) Metropolitan Water and Drainage Commission, (3) Metropolitan Commission for Public Security and Law Enforcement, (4) Metropolitan Commission on Human Settlements, (5) Metropolitan Transportation and Roads Commission and (6) Metropolitan Civil Protection Commission. The Metropolitan Development Secretariat of the government of the State of Mexico and the General Secretariat of Mexico City's government, along with other dependencies, integrate these commissions. There is also a metropolitan fund which is a federal subsidy intended to finance studies, plans, evaluations, programs, projects, actions and public works of infrastructure and equipment, to promote the development of metropolitan areas (Sánchez, 2012). Yet, the existence of metropolitan funds and instances of coordination has not necessarily resulted in functional and operational advances or in metropolitan institutions (Cenizal, 2015).

Serious governance failures have inhibited adequate responses to critical urban development priorities. Legal and political complexities make urban management difficult, and fragmentation usually disperses responsibilities on problems to be addressed on a metropolitan basis. Such a metropolitan arrangement makes it difficult to implement planning schemes that seek to provide services and infrastructure efficiently (Perlman & Pineda, 2011). The fragmented urban landscape is reflected in the significant differentials in local government capacity to provide public services and to raise public revenue which affects the quality of life of the population between and within each jurisdiction (Graizbord, Rowland & Aguilar, 2003). For a small group of OECD countries, Ahrend, et al. (2014) find a tendency for more fragmented cities to have lower levels of economic productivity. Although the effect varies across countries, it is largest in Mexican cities; the discontinuity in personnel (municipal mayors and civil servants) may render it difficult to establish lasting cooperation across municipalities, potentially multiplying effects of fragmentation.

According to the OECD (2015), institutional deficiencies, combined with a limited focus on strategic urban planning and fragmentation, prevent the metropolitan area from achieving its full economic potential. The mechanisms that guide urban development are complex, fragmented and underdeveloped. MCMA requires integrated regional planning frameworks applied at the metropolitan level. Frameworks need to include greater coordination and collaboration across and among levels of government, strong financing mechanisms and participation from private actors. Stronger metropolitan governance is a precondition for comprehensive urban policy and for better economic performance.

Concluding comments: the challenges ahead for MCMA

MCMA has been growing constantly since the 1940s physically, demographically, and in complexity. The pace of urban expansion and metropolisation has been uneven over time. Demographic growth reached its peak in the 1960s, and up to the 1990s its physical expansion (urban sprawl) formed a more continuous and spatially increasing urbanised area. In the last three decades urban expansion has been characterised by a sort of leapfrog expansion, and urban spatial continuity is less clear; that is, land use bears limited contiguity to previously urbanised areas. Much of its urban expansion has depended on the governance, political and institutional processes surrounding the use and allocation of land, which, in turn, have had important impacts on the economic performance of this metropolitan area.

The central city has faced several decades of depopulation and deterioration, while many of the older social housing blocks built in the 1950s present problems of ageing infrastructure, poor maintenance and overcrowding. Newer social housing developments in the suburbs face rapid growth, but many of them also face accelerated deterioration. The most visible manifestation of a housing crisis is the large percentage of unoccupied, and in some cases abandoned, homes on the metropolitan periphery. In addition, population deals with costly public transport and deficient basic public services.

MCMA is a socially, economically and politically fragmented metropolis, with governance deficits and large and increasing differences in the coverage and quality of public services. While such a situation may not be uncharacteristic of other parts of the country, it imposes a particular penalty on a large metropolitan area. The political-administrative boundaries dividing the metropolitan area are ill-adapted to the functional city and the needs of citizens.

Governance structures create contradictions, conflicts and competition that prevent cooperation and collaboration. Most efforts to integrate metropolitan-wide mechanisms seem to be poorly linked to the political/decision-making channels. Historically, political economy factors involved in urban planning have played a determining role in sprawl, as well as in the prevailing metropolitan governance structures.

Fragmentation of urban management has had negative consequences for the development of the metropolitan area. There are multiple links, common dependencies and continuities within the metropolitan area in terms of availability of resources, urban markets, infrastructure, equipment, public services, economic and social conditions, processes and common relations. But fragmentation of legislation and regulations, the management of resources, planning and policies and concrete actions among multiple governments leads to oppositions, discontinuities, overlaps, lack of coordination, duplication and neglect of problems. However, along with the need for an integrated approach at the metropolitan level, Mexico has been struggling with the issue of decentralising its historically highly centralised national government.

The unequal metropolitan area represents an urban puzzle that is shaped by the complex alliance of public and economic power. Like numerous metropolitan areas, MCMA has high levels of income inequality. One aspect that reveals such disparities is the fragmented urban structure in terms of the location of jobs and place of residence. Nevertheless, problems are various and complex: water provision, environmental deterioration, poverty, segregation, housing and land, local and international transportation, crime, and so on and so forth. Challenges with the quality of governance and the lack of a metropolitan vision have detracted from agglomeration benefits and residents' wellbeing. All these problems question the position of one of the largest megacities in the world as a first-tier global player.

Notes

1 Although it expanded during the colonial period and again following independence in 1821, by the twentieth century the population in Mexico City was less than 600,000 (Alix-García & Sellars, 2018).
2 During the 1950s and 1960s the Mexican economy performed very consistently, averaging 6 per cent GDP growth annually and 3 per cent inflation rate, allowing the country to sustain a stable exchange rate with respect to the US dollar for more than 20 years.
3 Popular urbanisation referred to the process by which low-income urban population managed the occupation of land spaces to build their own homes and promote government intervention to regularise – when applicable – the possession of land, to improve housing conditions and to incorporate settlements into the urban area through the provision of basic services and equipment (González, 2013).
4 Two significant differences between the homebuilding industry in Mexico and that of developed countries must be noted: first, a very large segment of the residential construction was informal; second, the vast majority of loans in the country were from government lenders, INFONAVIT (Institute for the National Housing Fund for Workers) and FOVISSTE (Housing Fund of the Institute of Social Security and Services for State

Workers), which issued mortgages in a centrally planned manner. These credits were sub-sidised loans.

5   As defined in Chapter 3 of this book, *ejidos* are lands that the government expropriated from private owners after the Mexican Revolution and then were distributed among peasants. Initially, agrarian laws prohibited the rental or sale of ejidos. A reform of land tenure in 1992 gave ejidatarios formal title to their land, enabling them to lease or sell their plots if the majority of members of the ejido agreed.

6   In advanced capitalist countries, the term 'social housing' normally refers to social rented hous-ing, within the context of housing welfare regimes. In large parts of Latin America –because of minimal affordability and limited investment – 'social housing' is very much the low-cost housing segment which is facilitated by the state.

7   In this chapter, I use Mexico City proper to refer to the administrative jurisdiction that was formerly known as the Federal District.

8   http://gaceta.diputados.gob.mx/Black/Gaceta/Anteriores/62/2013/oct/20131002-IV/DictamenaD-6.html

9   AGEBS, or Basic Geostatistical Areas, are microscale statistics areas used by the Mexican statistical office.

References

Aguilar, A. G. & Hernandez, J. (2016). 'Metropolitan change and uneven distribution of urban sub-centres in Mexico City, 1989–2009'. *Bulletin of Latin American Research*, 35(2), 191–209. Available at: https://onlinelibrary.wiley.com/doi/full/10.1111/blar.12407.

Ahrend, R. et al. (2014). *What makes cities more productive? Evidence on the role of urban governance from five OECD countries*. OECD Regional Development Working Papers, No. 2014/05, Paris: OECD Publishing. Available at: https://doi.org/10.1787/5jz432cf2d8p-en.

Alix-García, J. & Sellars, E. (2018). Locational fundamentals, trade, and the changing urban landscape of Mexico. Selected Paper prepared for presentation at the 2018 Agricultural & Applied Economics Association Annual Meeting, Washington, DC. Available at: https://EconPapers.repec.org/RePEc:ags:aaea18:274238.

Carrillo, J. L. (2004). 'Ciudad de México: Una megalopolis emergente: El capital vs la capi-tal'. *Red de cuadernos de investigación urbanística*, No. 38. Available at: http://polired.upm.es/index.php/ciur/article/view/253/248.

Cenizal, C. (2015). *Governing the Metropolis: The evolution of cooperative metropolitan governance in Mexico City's public transportation*. Master dissertation. Massachusetts Institute of Technology. Available at: https://dspace.mit.edu/bitstream/handle/1721.1/98927/921883015-MIT.pdf.

Connolly, P. (2003). *The case of Mexico City*. UN Global Slums Report: Case Studies for the Global Report on Human Settlements, UN-Habitat [online]. Available at: www.ucl.ac.uk/dpu-projects/Global_Report/pdfs/Mexico.pdf.

González, J. R. (2013). 'La urbanización popular y los partidos políticos en México'. *Realidades*, 3(2), 79–89 [online]. Available at: https://dialnet.unirioja.es/servlet/articulo?codigo=4752296.

Graizbord, B., Rowland, A. & Aguilar, A. G. (2003). 'Mexico City as a peripheral global player: The two sides of the coin'. *The Annals of Regional Science*, (37), 501–518. Available at: https://link.springer.com/article/10.1007/s00168-003-0167-4.

INEGI (2009). *Censos Económicos 2009* [online]. Available at: http://www.inegi.org.mx/est/contenidos/espanol/proyectos/censos/ce2009/default.asp?s=est&c=14220.

INEGI. (2010). *Censo de Población y Vivienda 2010* [online]. Available at: www.beta.inegi.org.mx/proyectos/ccpv/2010/.

Ingram, G. K. (1998). 'Patterns of metropolitan development: What have we learned?' *Urban Studies*, 35(7), 1019–1035. Available at: https://doi.org/10.1080/0042098984466.

Isunza Vizuet, G. & Soriano Cruz, V. (2008). 'Mercado de trabajo y movilidad en la ciudad de México'. *Mundo Siglo XXI*, (11), 45–56. Available at: https://repositorio.flacsoandes.edu. ec/xmlui/handle/10469/7322.

Janoschka, M. (2011). 'Geografías urbanas en la era del neoliberalismo: Una conceptualización de la resistencia local a través de la participación y la ciudadanía urbana'. *Investigaciones Geográficas*, (76), 118–132. Available at: www.scielo.org.mx/scielo.php?script=sci_art text&pid=S0188-46112011000300009.

Janoschka, M. & Salinas, L. (2017). 'Peripheral urbanisation in Mexico City: A comparative analysis of uneven social and material geographies in low-income housing estates'. *Habitat International*, (70), 43–49. Available at: https://doi.org/10.1016/j.habitatint.2017.10.003.

Legorreta, J. (1991). 'Expansión urbana, mercado del suelo y estructura de poder en la ciudad de México'. *Revista mexicana de ciencias políticas y sociales*, 36(145), 45–76.

Martin, R. & Morrison, P. (2003). 'Thinking about the geographies of labour'. In Ron Martin, R. & Morrison, P. (eds.), *Geographies of labour market inequality*. London: Routledge, pp. 1–20.

OECD. (2015). *OECD territorial reviews: Valle de México, Mexico*. Paris: OECD Publishing. Available at: https://doi.org/10.1787/9789264245174-en.

Perlman, B. J. & Pineda, J. de D. (2011). 'Rethinking a megalopolis: A metropolitan government proposal for the Mexico City metro area'. *State and Local Government Review*, 43(2), 144–150. Available at: https://doi.org/10.1177/0160323X11414917.

Pradilla, E. (2005). 'Zona metropolitana del Valle de México: megaciudad sin proyecto'. *Ciudades*, (9), 83–104. Available at: https://dialnet.unirioja.es/servlet/articulo?codigo=2230701.

Sánchez, A. (2012). *La evolución de la Ciudad de México para el desarrollo social*. Informe del estado de desarrollo social en el Distrito Federal. México, D. F.: Evalua DF. Available at: https://evalua.cdmx.gob.mx/storage/app/media/uploaded-files/files/Atribuciones/inf-est/evo_cmexico.pdf.

SEDATU, CONAPO & INEGI. (2018). *Delimitación de las zonas metropolitanas de México 2015*. Secretaría de Desarrollo Agrario, Territorial y Urbano, Consejo Nacional de Población, Instituto Nacional de Estadística y Geografía. Mexico City. At: www.gob.mx/ conapo/documentos/delimitacion-de-las-zonas-metropolitanas-de-mexico-2015.

SEDESOL, CONAPO & INEGI. (2012). *Delimitación de las zonas metropolitanas de México 2010*. México, D. F.: Secretaría de Desarrollo Social, Consejo Nacional de Población, Instituto Nacional de Estadística y Geografía. Available at: www.conapo.gob.mx/es/ CONAPO/Delimitacion_zonas_metropolitanas_2010_Capitulos_I_a_IV.

Trejo, A. (2016). 'Nuevas Dinámicas Económicas Metropolitanas y Regionales en México y los Problemas de la Política Territorial'. In Negrete, M. E. (ed.). *Urbanización y Política Urbana en Iberoamérica: Experiencias, análisis y reflexiones*. México, D. F.: El Colegio de México, pp. 107–144.

Unikel, L. (2016). *El desarrollo urbano en México: diagnóstico e implicaciones futuras*. México, D. F.: El Colegio de México.

Valenzuela, A. (2017). 'Failed markets: The crisis in the private production of social housing in México'. *Latin America Perspectives*, 44(2), 38–51. Available at: https://doi.org/10.1177/00 94582X16682782.

8 Provision of urban services

How Mexico City performs
compared to other metropolitan
areas in Latin America

Introduction

Intense and accelerated urbanisation has been a remarkable trend in Latin American countries in the last half-century, leading to the incorporation into cities of vast areas around them. This has meant not only the expansion of urban areas but also the enlargement of social and economic spaces of activity, due to the location of population and businesses in conurbations and peripheral areas extending beyond the political-administrative limits of the central city. As a result, metropolitan areas now constitute the heart of urban systems in several countries in this region. Metropolitan expansion involves an increasing need to expand service provision to fulfil the population's social needs. But the questions of who implements policies and how, what service and infrastructure a government provides, who it pays for services and how frequently the service is provided find no clear answers in practice. Fragmentation, in particular, places significant pressure on metropolitan service delivery systems. It can result in numerous, uncoordinated and inefficient providers. Gaps between metropolitan service demand and its supply, and significant intra-metropolitan disparities can develop. Lack of coordination usually translates into inadequate provision of basic services and higher financial burdens. As a consequence, public services underperform in many metropolitan areas, and provision of public services becomes one of the most critical issues for their development.

A large body of research indicates that governance is highly significant in the effective delivery of urban services (Slack, 2007; Bird & Slack, 2007; Jones, Clench & Harris, 2014; Jones, Cummings & Nixon, 2014). Moreover, political economy factors are just as important for urban service delivery as funding and technical capacity (Jones, Cummings & Nixon, 2014). Overall, the body of knowledge about the key governance and political economy aspects specific to different metropolitan environments is not strong. There is also a lack of detailed international comparative analytical work. While the provision of public services in metropolitan areas is an issue of strategic significance in advanced countries, it has received relatively little attention in low- and middle-income countries, and there is a need for empirical and comparative evidence in this research area.

To gain insights into the delivery of public services in metropolitan areas a comparative approach is used in this chapter to assess how governance schemes for providing basic services accommodate different contexts in practice and what outcomes they produce. Mexico City Metropolitan Area (MCMA) is compared with Lima and Bogota. According to Trejo, Niño and Vasquez (2018), despite sharing some characteristics (e.g. they have cultural backgrounds and colonial roots in common, are national capital cities with a special political-administrative status and have all undergone significant decentralisation processes and intense metropolisation), these metropolitan areas offer the possibility of illustrating variability in metropolitan governance structures. They present different historical forms of metropolitan expansion and institutionalisation, and their countries operate under different political systems – with unitary governments in Colombia and Peru and a federal government in Mexico. When discussing metropolitan governance in MCMA two additional metropolises in Mexico are considered: Monterrey and Guadalajara are the second and third largest metropolitan economies in the country, just behind Mexico City. Despite their common national framework regarding legal, financial and political-administrative restrictions to metropolitan governance, their particular local context has brought contrasting experiences when compared to MCMA. The analysis involves three areas related to metropolitan governance and service delivery: coordination arrangements, financial sustainability and service coverage and quality.[1]

The analysis focuses on three key urban services: transport, urban waste collection and water. These services are almost entirely limited to urban areas and are services for which urban governments typically have responsibility (Jones, Cummings & Nixon, 2014). They are a priority in strategic metropolitan planning and pose unique challenges in metropolitan environments (Boex, Lane & Yao, 2013; Jones, Clench & Harris, 2014). Moreover, they are services that can have important direct impacts on urban productivity and competitiveness. Daily mobility is a major challenge, especially for low-income inhabitants living on the metropolitan peripheries. Governments not only struggle to provide adequate public transport, but they also have limited resources for the construction and maintenance of infrastructure. Waste management is another pressing issue, especially in low-income countries where a very large amount of waste is either dumped or sent to poorly managed landfills, because of the potential for various social and economic problems. Water provision is a problematic area because it is based on the availability of the resource, and rivalry over water increases in large urban areas because of greater demand.

In this chapter I start by synthetically reviewing the main theoretical approaches to metropolitan governance and delivery of urban services. This literature review underscores the differences between metropolitan government and metropolitan governance, and the important analytical distinction between the provision and the production of urban services. Next, the empirical cases of metropolitan delivery of services are discussed and contrasted. In addition to the role of metropolitan governance in determining public service provision, the chapter explicitly considers political economic factors such as political risk, political culture, political will and incentives in the practice of governance for services delivery. The chapter concludes with some final remarks.

Metropolitan government and governance

Metropolitan areas are highly problematic territories in urban planning and public policy implementation. Whereas spatial socioeconomic processes tend to transcend jurisdictional boundaries, the sphere of influence of city governments has no territorial continuity. In consequence, in metropolitan expansion there is usually little control over territorial development, weakening public management capacity (Sellers & Hoffmann-Martinot, 2008). When planning and government in metropolitan contexts are based in autonomous local authorities that are independent from each other, problems such as pollution, service and infrastructure provision, inequality, crime and violence, and many others, pose a serious challenge to the local governments concerned (Slack, 2007). Confronted with such political–administrative fragmentation, the absence of cooperation and coordination mechanisms can aggravate urban problems.

Academic debate on metropolitan governance is too often framed in the theoretical and normative discussion of government decentralisation and its consequences for efficiency and equity (Bird & Slack, 2007). As Lewis (2004) finds, the decades of debate on metropolitan political structure have included a tendency for excessive dichotomisation between government centralisation and decentralisation. In a given metropolitan area it is the role of the local governments to supply bundles of public goods and services that fulfil their constituents' preferences as nearly as possible, given the price of providing those services. The subsidiarity principle argues that greater welfare gains can be achieved by adjusting the provision of services to citizens' preferences and local costs (Oates, 1997). According to Tiebout (1956), decentralisation favours accountability and horizontal competition triggers a more efficient supply of public goods.

Consolidation enables the achievement of economies of scale, the management of externalities and redistributive policies (Treisman, 2000). Consolidation also contributes to minimising the dangers of elite capture and corruption, especially in developing countries (Prud'Homme, 1995). Thus, decentralised or polycentric government is seen as optimal because it provides a wider degree of choice for residents, who can vote with their feet, and more competition among service providers. In the opposite case, consolidation produces economies of scale, reduces duplicated effort, increases technical capacity in service provision and favours equity mechanisms (Lewis, 2004).

Echoing these principles, the school of public choice argues that decentralised metropolitan governments spur effective and efficient service delivery by promoting competition (Yaro & Ronderos, 2011), whereas regionalists and new consolidationists argue in favour of metropolitan governments (Lowery, 2000). In the public choice scholarship on metropolitan government structure and Tiebout's model of local public economies, the primary normative end goal is allocative efficiency. On the other hand, regionalism supports equity; thus, in practice, any particular government structure involves a natural trade-off between equality and efficiency (Lewis, 2004).

The type of metropolitan model implemented is generally conditioned by the different types of intergovernmental relations, sources of financing and the history and culture of the metropolitan area concerned (Slack, 2007). Attempts to implement metropolitan governments as such began in the 1960s with very varied practices and evolutions (Slack, 2007; Bird & Slack, 2007). Overall, four different models of metropolitan government can be pinpointed: the one-tier fragmented model, the single-tier consolidated model, the two-tier model, and the one-tier model with voluntary cooperation (Figure 8.1).

In contrast to traditional discourses on metropolitan government and decentralisation, much of the contemporary work on urban politics and public administration emphasises the distinction between government and governance (Feiock, 2004). It is now widely accepted that metropolitan governance can and does occur without metropolitan government, and that it can be effective even where a metropolitan area is highly fragmented across many small municipalities. Metropolitan areas can create governance structures not tied to a single dominant unit of government. Without a consolidated metropolitan-level government, metropolitan areas are able to generate a rich world of governance activity carried out on a metropolitan scale and tailored to their own specific contexts (Oakerson, 2004).

Whereas the metropolitan government is the formal administrative structure that exercises public powers of management, planning and administration in

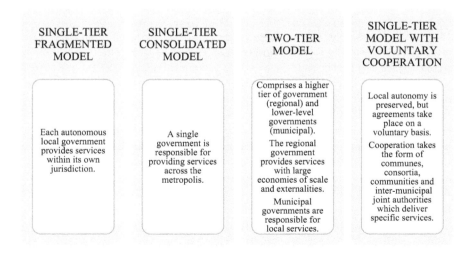

Figure 8.1 Models of metropolitan government

Source: Based on Slack (2007).

the metropolitan area (Pírez, 2014), the process of governance includes the entire set of related processes: prescribing, invoking, applying and enforcing the rules that regulate behaviour. The governance structures can be more or less elaborate, depending on the complexity of the relevant environment. These structures require access to governmental authority but need not be confined to governmental institutions, and therefore governments are a necessary but not a sufficient condition of governance (Oakerson, 2004).

Certainly the organisation and structure of city governments shape local governance by influencing public and private policy decisions and the ability of local units to act collectively to address regional problems (Feiock, 2004). However, specifying the institutional architecture of governmental authority in a metropolitan area does not describe its governance structure. Metropolitan areas that feature large numbers of small municipalities can generate very different governance structures, which can, in turn, be expected to yield different processes of governance (Oakerson, 2004).

A general but illustrative concept of governance refers to the process by which human beings regulate their interdependencies in the context of a shared environment such as a metropolitan area where streets and sidewalks, water resources and wildlife, markets and settlements are shared common resources. It can convey the idea that smaller communities are nested within larger communities (ibid.).

Metropolitan governance is the process by which a set of governmental and non-governmental actors interact in the formulation of policies and on the issue of collective goods on the metropolitan scale. It refers to multifaceted processes that pursue social goals in specific areas of development through the promotion of dialogues in the decision-making process and the participation of multiple actors (Tortajada, 2006). Metropolitan governance encompasses more than city and county governments, and includes voluntary, non-profit and private organisations, as well as intergovernmental linkages (Feiock, 2004). In metropolitan areas the governance processes are more complex, because various levels of government, private actors, non-governmental and social organisations and multiple local governments coexist in the same urban area. Regulating the interdependent relations among jurisdictions in the absence of a metropolitan-wide political authority is extremely complex due to institutional, territorial and administrative fragmentation (Storper, 2014). According to Parks and Oakerson (1989) rather than conventional governmental structures, metropolitan areas require governance arrangements that allow for diverse and flexible solutions in an environment of constant shifting conditions.

Approaches to metropolitan delivery of urban services

Jurisdictionally fragmented structures are an inevitable condition in metropolitan areas (Storper, 2014). But fragmented metropolitan structures do not necessarily imply institutional failure (Parks & Oakerson,1989; Parks & Oakerson, 1993). Acceptable and adequate governance structures can be achieved through a diversity of arrangements such as agreements and associations in which relevant actors agree to act together in a coordinated manner (Feiock, 2004). Thus, the structure of metropolitan governance will depend not only on the type of government or institutional and political framework in place, but also on the approach taken to handling coordination, on funding structures, and on the forms of private-sector and civil-society participation (Slack, 2007).

As prescribed by the new regionalist movement, a pattern of governance emerges from the centralisation and consolidation of governments and functions and the creation of regional organisations. An alternative decentralised regional approach emphasises self-governance through horizontally and vertically linked organisations. These linkages are primarily among governments but also include civil society, the private sector and service producers. This neo-progressive path to regional governance argues that the debate on centralised versus fragmented government should not be framed merely as a question of efficiency but also as a matter of both cooperation and competition mechanisms among decentralised governmental units in metropolitan areas (Feiock, 2004).

The institutional collective action (ICA) approach provides a theoretical framework for understanding a system of metropolitan governance without a metropolitan government. The widespread belief that competition makes cooperation on regional issues close to impossible leads to the conclusion that decentralised units of government are unable to deal with regional externalities or spillovers. However, local governments can act collectively to create a civil society that integrates a region across multiple jurisdictions through a web of citizens' voluntary agreements, associations and collective choices. The argument is that a decentralised system of local governments can simultaneously produce the benefits of competition and cooperation to address multijurisdictional and regional problems. Local governments' choices to cooperate or compete in response to external market forces reflect strategic interactions among local actors; thus, competition and cooperation can be complementary strategies (ibid.). ICA is a mechanism by which cooperation is achieved among local governments, between layers of government and between local government units and other actors in the community (Figure 8.2).

Collective action also deal with the problem of metropolitan coordination. Coordination problems arise when local governments attempt to organise interjurisdictional activities. Coordination is necessary when the tasks at hand are complex and the interconnectedness of activities and policies is critical for success. Local authorities may seek to coordinate their decisions around central actors through participation in mechanisms such as informal networks, regional organisations and formal, informal and contractual networks. Even though the ICA framework contains a multitude of potential issues, in practice one of the most common involves coordination over service delivery activities across jurisdictions to achieve economies of scale, minimise common-pool resource problems and internalise externalities imposed by other local authorities. Coordination gains and scale economies in service production are the

INSTITUTIONAL COLLECTIVE ACTION

Cooperation among local governments	Cooperation between levels of government	Cooperation between local governments and other actors in the community

Externalities or spillovers give communities in a metropolitan area a strong incentive to cooperate with each other to achieve joint or regional goals.	Cooperation arises when the potential benefits of cooperation outweigh the transaction costs of negotiating, monitoring and enforcing the political contracts.	Upper levels of government have an incentive to encourage local cooperation when it provides them with electoral advantages.	Where other political benefits to elected officials are high, they are willing to play the role of third-party enforcer of cooperation.	Private or non-profit organisations can participate in public–private regional partnerships for economic development.	Civil society partnerships with governments or with the private sector.

Figure 8.2 The institutional collective action approach to metropolitan governance

Source: Based on Feiock (2004).

primary motivations for inter-municipal collaboration in metropolitan areas (Feiock, 2013). However, political economy factors may deter coordination because local governments confront different sets of incentives (e.g. electoral votes, popularity, position in the political cycle, etc.) that influence the likelihood of cooperation.

Economic factors, local political culture and state-level rules can shape institutional supply in metropolitan areas and define the possibility of cooperation and coordination. Following Post (2004), three conditions influence ICA negatively: an increasing number of local governments attempting to cooperate, increasing heterogeneity in the population, and increasing regulation of local government by state laws. On the other hand, five conditions influence cooperation positively: the increasing geographic density of local governments, the increasing homogeneity of the populations served, common policy objectives among local governments, the presence of strong public and private leaders, and federal incentives to cooperate. Voluntary cooperative action usually occurs in small groups because the transaction costs, monitoring and identification of non-compliance with agreements are more difficult for large groups. Collective action among larger groups typically requires a third party to absorb the organisation costs, apply coercion and provide selective incentives (Feiock, 2004). Governance such as that arising from ICA can transcend municipal boundaries and allow problem-solving, rule-making and efficiency on a metropolitan scale. However, when close voluntary organisation and cooperation are not success-fully achieved, metropolitan governance weakens (Parks & Oakerson, 1993).

ICA in metropolitan areas has been difficult both to understand and to achieve because it involves strategic interaction among numerous organisations and juris-dictions, multiple potential scenarios and a high degree of uncertainty (Feiock, 2004, 2013). Although each jurisdiction chooses its own policies when making decisions with regards to economic development, land use management, ser-vice coordination and other areas, the outcomes are affected by the decisions of other local actors. Where benefit spillovers exist, each jurisdiction chooses its best response to the choices of other jurisdictions. Local governments have to anticipate how those with whom they interact will respond to the set of institu-tional incentives. There are select incentives for politicians because their careers are linked to the characteristics of their political constituencies (Feiock, 2004).

In the case of public services, efficient scales and preferences in metropolitan areas can be multiple and heterogeneous, and can evolve over space and time with diverse production functions and financial and cost structures (Parks & Oakerson, 1989; Slack, 2007). The distinction between the provision and the production of public services is necessary to understand the complexity of metropolitan governance (Parks & Oakerson, 1989). In decentralised intergov-ernmental relations, local authorities are provision units that use a variety of alternative production arrangements such as direct production, private con-tracting, coordinated and joint production, and franchising to deliver a set of services. Thus, metropolitan areas include multiple provision units that, in turn, are linked in numerous ways to a variety of production units. Governance structures for providing public services are then determined by the provision units, the production arrangements and the rules within which provision and production take place.

Traditional analysis of metropolitan governance mainly emphasises the gen-eral problems of fragmentation and overlapping jurisdictions. Metropolitan areas around the world, particularly in the Global South, are also daily confronted with the need to rethink and redesign the management of their urban services. As metropolitan governance is a determining factor in the definition of the quantity and quality of public services, the efficiency with which they are provided and the manner in which their costs are distributed, it is important to examine its type and structure (Slack, 2007). The variety of government and metropolitan govern-ance devices can also be recognised by their spatial coverage and their institutional consolidation (measurable by the level of financial autonomy and cooperation/coordination), as well as by their democratic intensity (Sellers & Hoffmann-Martinot, 2008). Relying less on the democratic and accountability dimensions of governance, next I discuss the governance of urban services addressing the issues of coordination, financial sustainability, and access, coverage and quality.

The following section offers an overview of the delivery of waste, water and transport services in MCMA and discusses the successful experiences of metropolitan consolidation in the second and third largest metropolitan areas in Mexico – Monterrey and Guadalajara.

Service delivery in Mexico City Metropolitan Area compared to successful experiences in Mexico

Waste collection, water and transport services in Mexico City Metropolitan Area

As explained in Chapter 7, MCMA is one of the largest metropolitan areas in the world with over 20 million inhabitants. This metropolitan area is highly fragmented in terms of its governmental organisation. There is currently neither a metropolitan government entity nor functional metropolitan structure. Officially called the Metropolitan Zone of the Valley of Mexico, it includes the administrative area of Mexico City, 59 municipalities in the State of Mexico and 1 municipality in the state of Hidalgo. Mexico City itself is divided into 16 boroughs, each with a local authority which, however, has less powers than municipalities. Political–administrative fragmentation in MCMA, measured as the number of administrative units with more than 100,000 inhabitants, indicates that 39 municipalities and boroughs have populations of over that benchmark.

Mexico has a federal structure that is divided into states and municipalities. In Chapter 5 I underscored that metropolitan areas in Mexico do not have a legal status as official jurisdictions, yet the constitution allows inter-municipal cooperation on a voluntary basis. Legal structures concerning planning and coordination and political factors have not been conducive to metropolitan-scale organisation, and efforts to produce effective metropolitan agreements and commissions have been largely ineffective. In brief, MCMA entails a complex set of governmental entities with overlapping federal, state and local powers and an intricate organisational structure which complicates metropolitan governance arrangements, particularly planning schemes seeking to efficiently deliver services (Perlman & Pineda, 2011).

As explained in Chapter 5, Article 115 of the Constitution of Mexico places the municipality at the core of the administrative and political organisation of the national state. Article 115 stipulates all the municipal functions which include the provision of local public services. These include waste management, pipe water and public transport. Given this delegation of local services to municipalities, metropolitan provision is shaped by the production schemes defined by municipal authorities.

As noted in the previous section, Parks and Oakerson (1989) indicate that in decentralised intergovernmental relations local authorities are provision units that use a variety of alternative production arrangements such as direct production, private contracting, coordinated and joint production, and franchising to deliver a set of services. Figure 8.3 summarises the provision and production

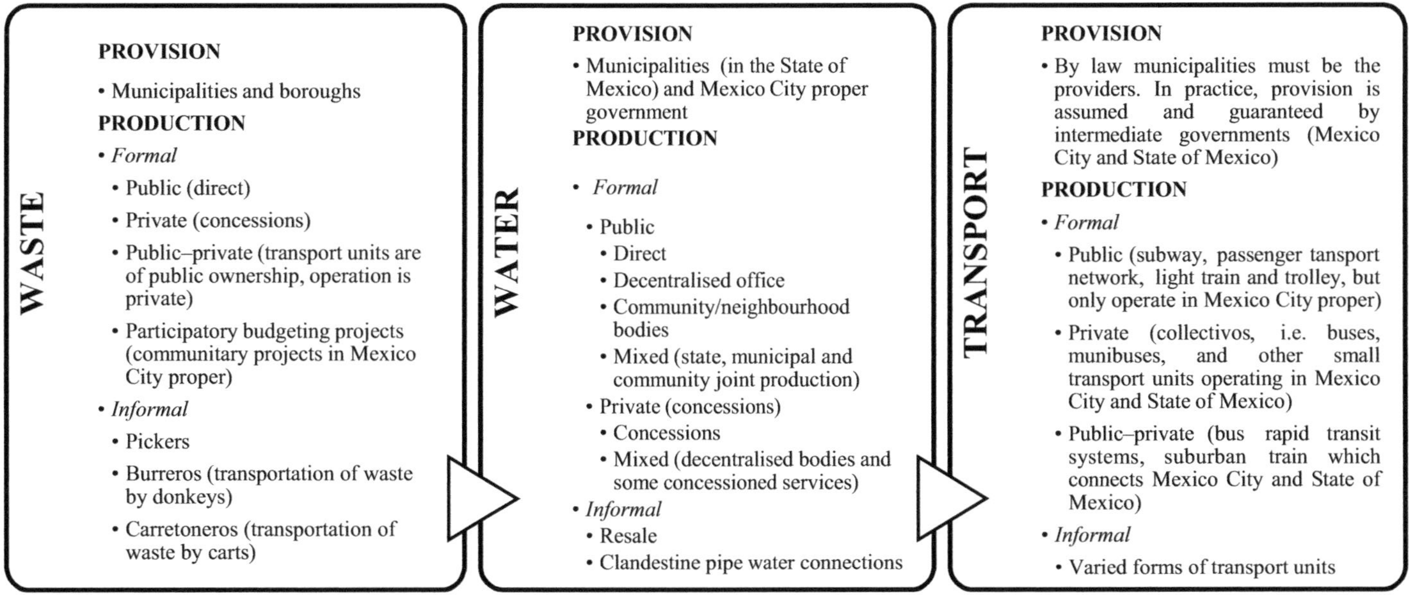

WASTE

PROVISION
- Municipalities and boroughs

PRODUCTION
- *Formal*
- Public (direct)
- Private (concessions)
- Public–private (transport units are of public ownership, operation is private)
- Participatory budgeting projects (communtiary projects in Mexico City proper)
- *Informal*
- Pickers
- Burreros (transportation of waste by donkeys)
- Carretoneros (transportation of waste by carts)

WATER

PROVISION
- Municipalities (in the State of Mexico) and Mexico City proper government

PRODUCTION
- *Formal*
- Public
- Direct
- Decentralised office
- Community/neighbourhood bodies
- Mixed (state, municipal and community joint production)
- Private (concessions)
- Concessions
- Mixed (decentralised bodies and some concessioned services)
- *Informal*
- Resale
- Clandestine pipe water connections

TRANSPORT

PROVISION
- By law municipalities must be the providers. In practice, provision is assumed and guaranteed by intermediate governments (Mexico City and State of Mexico)

PRODUCTION
- *Formal*
- Public (subway, passenger transport network, light train and trolley, but only operate in Mexico City proper)
- Private (collectivos, i.e. buses, munibuses, and other small transport units operating in Mexico City and State of Mexico)
- Public–private (bus rapid transit systems, suburban train which connects Mexico City and State of Mexico)
- *Informal*
- Varied forms of transport units

Figure 8.3 Production schemes of public services in MCMA

Source: Author's own elaboration.

schemes in the delivery of waste, water and transport services in MCMA. On the one hand, production is polarised between formal and informal segments in all services. The informal sector is a significant actor in the provision of urban services in MCMA, especially in the peripheries, in areas of the city that are difficult to access and in low-income neighbourhoods where irregular housing comes together with informal services. On the other hand, a variety of service schemes have developed depending on the specific service and on the jurisdictional location of demand (Mexico City or State of Mexico).

Metropolitan-wide provision of public services in MCMA is shaped not only by the political-administrative fragmentation and the particular dynamics of local, intermediate and national governments relations; different regulations determined at different governmental tiers also tend to congregate at the metropolitan level. Although local governments are responsible for providing collection services, the waste management process is regulated by norms and policies determined at higher levels of authority. The state government of State of Mexico formulates and conducts its own waste management policy through the Ministry of the Environment. In Mexico City, laws and regulatory considerations for solid waste management are the responsibility of the Ministry of the Interior, the Ministry of Works and Services, the General Directorate of Urban Services, the Ministry of the Environment and the Environmental Attorney of Land Management.

The National Water Commission – CONAGUA – is in charge of the use of national waters, bulk supply of water, construction and operation of infrastructure and monitoring the preservation of aquifers. The Watershed Organisation of the Valley of Mexico (Aguas del Valle de México), a subsidiary of CONAGUA, and the Water and Sewer Metropolitan Commission also participate in water regulation (Rosales, 2015).

In Mexico City the local Ministry of Mobility is responsible for planning and managing public transport. In the State of Mexico the Ministry of Mobility regulates public transport and authorises concessions, while the Ministry of Communications runs the rapid transit system, Mexibus. In the state of Hidalgo regulation and planning is based on the Transport Law and is carried out by a decentralised agency dependent on the Ministry of the Interior (OECD, 2015). The Metropolitan Commission for Metropolitan Transport (COMETRAVI), created in 1994, has had limited participation in public transport planning and operation.

Table 8.1 summarises the main aspects of service delivery in regards to coordination, financial sustainability and coverage, access and quality. In MCMA horizontal coordination is completely absent, with the exception of isolated cases of coordination among small municipalities in the provision of water services. Interjurisdictional coordination is equally absent between the state governments of Mexico City and State of Mexico. Financial sustainability is a critical issue altogether. However, the delivery of services in Mexico City proper perform relatively better than in the State of Mexico where municipalities struggle to finance direct production. Some services in Mexico City proper,

Table 8.1 Governance of urban services in MCMA

	Waste	Water	Transport
Coordination	Institutional coordination within Mexico City among local regulatory agencies and local authorities.	Fragmented model of provision.	High fragmentation between different transport systems and jurisdictions in Mexico City and municipalities in the State of Mexico.
	In municipalities of the State of Mexico some public–private coordination takes place with private companies granted concessions to provide the service.	A few cases of municipal association but weak inter-municipal coordination.	The exception is a coordinated payment system between the subway and the bus rapid transit (Metrobus) systems.
	The metropolitan commission focuses mainly on air pollution problems. Absence of horizontal coordination among jurisdictions.	Weak vertical coordination with federal and state institutions.	
Financial sustainability	Absence of official tariffs or fees.	Tariffs cover only 64 per cent of operating costs and governments subsidise the rest.	Transport systems operating in Mexico City are heavily subsidized.
	Payment is made via tips to drivers and waste pickers.	Subsidies in Mexico City are based on geographic criteria depending on neighbourhoods' socioeconomic classification.	Lack of technical analysis of costs and income structures to evaluate financial sustainability.
	Costs are shared between allocated budgets and other areas of municipal public services.	Significant heterogeneity in the financial situations among municipalities in the State of Mexico depending on the provision scheme.	High variability between systems and jurisdictions.
	Operates under a subsidy scheme.	Provision in Mexico City appears relatively financially stable.	Uncertain financial sustainability of Suburbano commuter train.
	Weak financial capacity and unsustainable provision.	Small municipalities in the State of Mexico that do not meet the criteria for establishing their own operator have worse financial conditions than municipalities with their own operator.	Concessioned services (small minibuses and buses) face important financial investment, maintenance and operation problems.
	High variability across jurisdictions. Larger differences between municipalities outside Mexico City and boroughs.		

(Continued)

Table 8.1 (Continued)

Coverage and quality	Covers between 88 and 98 per cent of households.	Approximately 79 per cent of population has piped water connection within the house unit.	High coverage in central areas, but problems with frequency. Poorer transport provision in the peripheries which in some cases lack formal transport services.
	Lower coverage in the northeast periphery.	72 per cent of population has daily access to water.	Concessioned services are highly inefficient with poor quality, poor safety and low environmental sustainability.
	Highly inefficient in quality and frequency with great variation across jurisdictions.	Highly uneven spatial distribution of access to the daily water service. Most peripheral municipalities and boroughs have lower availability than more central locations.	BRT system and subway operate beyond capacity, affecting quality. Suburban train best rated in terms of frequency, safety and quality, but it is the most expensive.

Source: Based on Trejo, Niño and Vásquez (2018).

such as water and public transport, are subsidised, especially transport systems (e.g. subway and some bus and train services).

Official data shows a relatively high coverage, but there are important territorial disparities between the peripheries and more central areas of the city. Furthermore, this data usually does not collect information in inaccessible parts of the city or in irregular settlements where services are not formally provided. More-differentiated coverage is observed in the provision of water – measured as the daily availability of the resource rather than the presence of pipe water connection within the house. Figure 8.4 shows that daily availability of water is consolidated in specific areas of the city. Figure 8.5 illustrates differences in coverage of public transport; Figure 8.6 shows the coverage of waste collection. Such disparities in the coverage of urban services usually embody the significant socio-spatial inequalities in the metropolitan area.

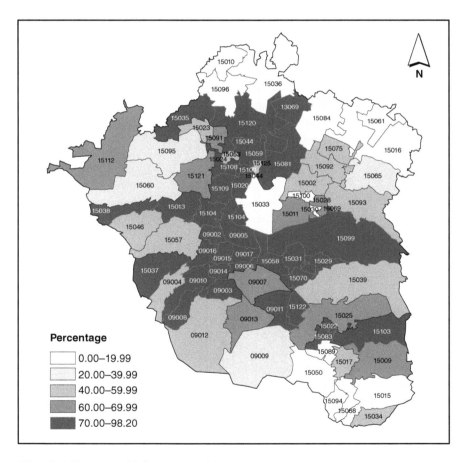

Figure 8.4 Coverage of daily water provision

Source: Author's own elaboration.

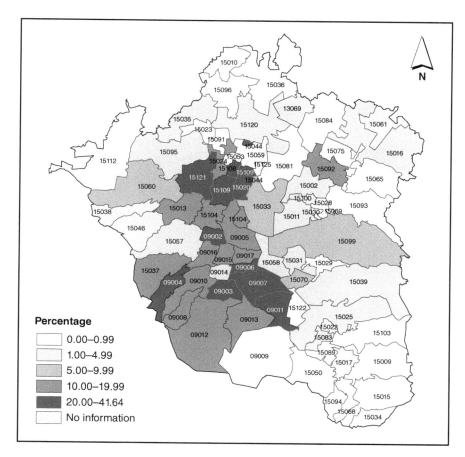

Figure 8.5 Coverage of transport services

Source: Author's own elaboration.

Overall, transport, waste and water services are considered of low quality. Most public transport systems operate with obsolete infrastructure and vehicles; issues of security and frequency are also of concern. In the case of water, there is a problem of frequency and bad quality of the water itself in several areas of the metropolis. However, quality of services is characterised by large spatial disparities, mostly affecting population in the peripheries and irregular neighbourhoods.

Metropolitan-wide provision of services in Monterrey and Guadalajara

Delivery of services in metropolitan areas in Mexico often suffers from the same flaws observed in MCMA: poor or absent coordination, financial burdens

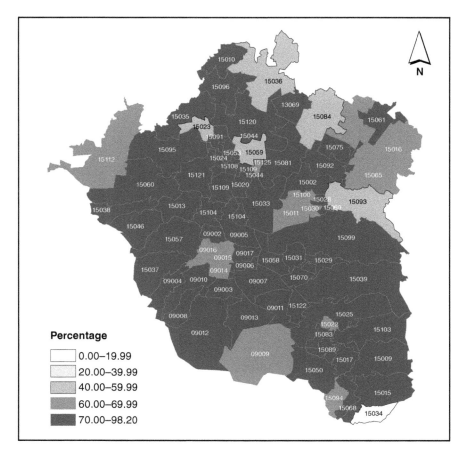

Figure 8.6 Coverage of waste collection services
Source: Author's own elaboration.

and deficient and inadequate coverage and quality of services. Spatial disparities are significant, mostly affecting low-income population in the peripheries or in irregular settlements. However, experiences vary according to different natural, economic, institutional and political conditions. For instance, some relatively successful experiences of metropolitan coordination have taken place in the Monterrey and Guadalajara metropolitan areas. Like Mexico City, these metropolitan areas have long experiences in the process of territorial metropolisation and institutionalisation of metropolitan structures. Alongside territorial expansion, efforts towards coordinated metropolitan governance have been put in place since the 1960s and 1970s (Table 8.2).

Table 8.2 Governance experiences in Monterrey and Guadalajara metropolitan areas

Metropolitan area	Number of municipalities	Metropolitan reform process	Successful experiences
Guadalajara	9	1977: State Congress enacts Human Settlements Law regulating intermunicipal coordination. 1978: Commission for the Urban-Regional Development of Guadalajara created. 1982: Plan for the Regulation of the Greater Zone of Guadalajara approved. 1989: Council of the Metropolitan Area of Guadalajara created. 1993: State Law of Urban Development recognises the Metropolitan Council. 2008 onwards: Metropolitan Fund provides resources for metropolitan projects. 2011: Jalisco State Metropolitan Coordination Law published. 2014: Metropolitan Coordination Agreement signed; Organic Statute of Metropolitan Coordination published; Metropolitan Planning Advisory Council established; Metropolitan Planning Institute created.	Inter-municipal Drinking Water and Sewage System Services (SIAPA) in charge of providing drinking water, sewerage and sanitation services to the metropolitan area. Metropolitan Transportation Commission plans and invests in infrastructure, and establishes prices and transport routes.

(Continued)

Table 8.2 (Continued)

Metropolitan area	Number of municipalities	Metropolitan reform process	Successful experiences
Monterrey		1967: Monterrey and Neighbouring Municipalities Regulatory Plan is enacted.	Monterrey Water and Drainage Services (SADM) provides public water and drainage services to the city of Monterrey, and through an agreement, to all the municipalities included in the metropolitan area.
		1984: Monterrey metropolitan area is officially recognised.	The Metropolitan Transportation Council plans and invests in infrastructure and establishes prices and transport routes.
	18	1987: Metropolitan Body for the Treatment and Management of Solid waste created.	Ecological Management and Waste Processing System (SIMEPRODESO) dedicated to the processing of non-hazardous solid waste generated in the metropolitan area.
		2003: Nuevo Leon Agency for Urban Development Planning created as a state agency, but its activities concentrate on the Monterrey metropolitan area.	

Source: Based on Garcia Ortega (1989), Ward (2011) and IMEPLAN (NA).

In Guadalajara, the Inter-municipal Drinking Water and Sewage System Services (SIAPA) in charge of providing drinking water, sewerage and sanitation services to the metropolitan area and the Metropolitan Transportation Commission which plans and invests in infrastructure and establishes prices and transport routes are two examples of successful metropolitan coordination. Similarly, in the Monterrey metropolitan area there are examples of coordinated mechanisms for providing services in waste, water and transport. The Monterrey Water and Drainage Services (SADM) provides water and drainage

services to the city of Monterrey, and through agreements, to all the municipalities within the metropolitan area. The Ecological Management and Waste
Processing System (SIMEPRODESO) is responsible for the management of
non-hazardous solid waste generated in the metropolitan area. The Metropolitan Transportation Council plans and invests in infrastructure and establishes
prices and transport routes.

Guadalajara and Monterrey metropolitan areas have the advantage of a less
fragmented and complex jurisdictional environment (9 and 18 municipalities
respectively). Moreover, coordination has been achieved through the regional
power of the state government. Nuevo Leon's government has been the major
power behind the existing metropolitan structures in Monterrey. Similarly, the
state-level powers have influenced metropolitan consolidation in Guadalajara. In Monterrey, consolidation of metropolitan services has been achieved
through the intense participation of the private sector.

Efforts are still limited, as municipal coordination has worked primarily in
favour of a more efficient provision of particular urban services, rather than
supporting a metropolitan-wide strategy for all areas of services, financing and
economic strategy. However, efforts towards the metropolitan consolidation in
the water, waste and transport sectors are remarkable advances towards the creation of special purpose districts as mono-sector and supra-municipal organisations that have brought improvements to service delivery.

Governance structures and service delivery in Lima and Bogota metropolitan areas

Lima metropolitan area

Peru is a unitary state with four levels of government: central, regional, provincial municipalities and local municipalities. The metropolitan area of Lima
includes the provinces of Lima and Callao. In the province of Lima, the Metropolitan Municipality has functions of a regional government and functions of
a provincial municipality. In the province of Callao, the Regional Government
of Callao and the Provincial Municipality of Callao exercise their respective
functions over the same jurisdiction. The province of Lima includes 49 districts
that are governed by 48 district municipalities, whereas the capital district is
governed by the Metropolitan Municipality of Lima. The Province of Callao has seven districts governed by six district municipalities, and the capital
district is governed by the Provincial Municipality of Callao (Trejo, Niño &
Vasquez, 2018).

Together, Lima and Callao had a population of approximately 645,000
inhabitants in 1940. The urban population began to grow rapidly in the mid-
twentieth century. In 1972, its population was over 3 million, and in 1993 it
was above 6 million. Around 1970, these two provinces became a conurbation
forming the metropolitan area of Lima. In 2013, the metropolitan population

was 9,752,000 inhabitants, of which 1 million were located in the province of Callao (INEI, 2014). Twenty-five out of 49 districts have a population larger than 100,000 people (51 per cent) of districts. Lima has special arrangements as a capital district, and has had a discriminatory treatment in the decentralisation process: whereas other regional governments have assumed functions such as health and education, in the Metropolitan Municipality of Lima the central government has remained as the provider of those services (Diálogos de Política Pública, 2015).

The Organic Law of Municipalities allows the use of municipal coordination mechanisms to ensure the efficient use of public resources, to provide services together and to implement infrastructure projects. Municipalities can create associations of municipalities that take the name of *mancomunidades*. In Lima, seven mancomunidades have made attempts to coordinate and provide services in public security and waste management in recent years (Trejo, Niño & Vasquez, 2018).

The multiactor governance structures in Lima are summarised in Table 8.3 which identifies those bodies, agencies or governments that participate in provision, production and regulation of service delivery.

Table 8.4 depicts the functioning of services delivery in Lima. A centralised water delivery makes vertical coordination necessary, but horizontal coordination is not an issue. There have been strong but slow efforts to consolidate waste and transport services through municipal associations (mancomunidades). Uncoordinated public transport delivery is more problematic than waste collection services. Centralisation of water provision improves financial sustainability, coverage and quality. Depending on the rate of payment, waste collection services rely on federal transfers to finance operation. The operation of bus rapid transit services is sustainable but they need subsidies to finance maintenance and investment.

Table 8.3 Stakeholders in the levels of governance in provision of services in Lima

	Waste	*Water*	*Transport*
Provision	District municipalities are responsible for the collection and transportation of solid waste and provincial municipalities for its disposal. In the capital districts of Lima and Callao the provincial municipalities are also responsible for collection and transport.	Provision of water services in Peru are not decentralised. According to Law 28696, Sedapal should provide water services to Lima and Callao provinces.	Services must be provided by municipal provinces.

(*Continued*)

Table 8.3 (Continued)

	Waste	Water	Transport
Production	Operates under a two-tier arrangement. Cleaning and waste collection are supplied directly by municipalities or private companies contracted to municipalities. Two large private companies, Petramas and Innova Ambiental, provide the service for other municipalities. Some municipalities run mixed production schemes.	Water is provided by the Lima Potable Water and Sewerage Service, Sedapal, a public company operating under a private legal regime which depends on the National Ministry of Housing and is controlled by the National Superintendence of Sanitation Services (Sunass).	Private companies have concessions to operate the metropolitan bus rapid transit system. Most metropolitan trips are taken on concessioned bus lines (buses and minibuses). This operates in a 'commission-affiliation' system in which companies are paid per vehicle operating and not per passenger.
Regulation	The Ministry of Health's General Directorate of Environmental Health controls landfills and authorises the work of companies to collect municipal waste. The Directorate of Environmental Quality formulates national policy on solid waste management but with limited normative prerogatives.	The National Water Authority administers and monitors natural sources of water and authorises the volumes of water that service providers can take. Sunass, a decentralised public organisation, regulates and supervises water and sanitation provision and pricing.	Provincial municipalities had been responsible for regulating public transport, but in the 1990s Peru adopted a largely unregulated public transport model that is dominated by private supply.

Source: Based on Trejo, Niño and Vasquez (2018).

Table 8.4 Governance of urban services in Lima

	Waste	Water	Transport
Coordination	The Metropolitan system for waste management does not include Callao. Despite strong normative incentives for cooperation, there are no adequate mechanisms to ensure imp lementation. Attempts at horizontal coordination through mancomunidades.	Inter-municipal coordination not necessary due to centralised provision by Sedapal. Weak vertical coordination between Sedapal and municipalities in Lima and Callao.	Fragmented but constant efforts to integrate metropolitan systems. Coordination with private operators.

(Continued)

Table 8.4 (Continued)

	Waste	Water	Transport
			Lima and Callao have each given permission to private companies to operate in both provinces.
			No integration or coordination between systems; e.g. in the city the Metro, the Metropolitano and secondary routes operate different fare systems.
Financial sustainability	Significant differences in payment rates across municipalities.	Operational costs covered by tariffs.	Bus rapid transit system operations are covered by customer fares
	Relies on intergovernmental transfers to provide the service where there is a low payment rate.	Infrastructure investments not covered by tariffs.	Other areas are subsidised by central government (maintenance and investment).
	17 districts have a 50 per cent deficit in expenditure coverage.	Large infrastructure projects financed by central government transfers.	
	Generally not self-sustainable, but there are significant differences across municipalities	Tariffs include subsidies based on consumption.	
		Transition to a subsidy system based on socioeconomic status.	
		Sedapal is a financially healthy company.	
Coverage and quality	Estimated 90 per cent coverage.	Around 89 per cent of households have water connection inside the house.	High coverage, low quality.
	Problems of low quality.	Service availability is a problem in the peripheries.	54 per cent of Limeños see transportation as one of the city's main problems.
	Variation across municipalities and neighbourhoods depending on socioeconomic conditions.	24-hour running water coverage on average in Lima Centro; 19 to 22 hours in the periphery.	

Source: Based on Trejo, Niño and Vasquez (2018).

Bogota metropolitan area

The Republic of Colombia is a unitary republic comprising 32 departments and a capital district. Departments, in turn, are divided into provinces, and provinces into municipalities. Bogota, officially Bogota Distrito Capital (D.C.), is the capital and largest city of Colombia. As a capital district, Bogota has a special status. The demographic growth and urban expansion of this city has created a functional structure that has surpassed municipal administrative borders. In the previous three decades, the population of Bogota multiplied by 1.9 times, while the urban areas grew 2.8 times. The metropolitan area of Bogota is formed by Bogota, Distrito Capital (the core municipality) and 17 municipalities (Guzman, Oviedo & Bocarejo, 2017). The metropolitan area is fragmented, but unlike Mexico City and Lima the dynamics of the metropolitan area concentrate strongly in Bogota Capital District (Trejo, Niño & Vasquez, 2018). The metropolitan population was 7,881,156 inhabitants in 2005 and around 9,348,583 inhabitants in 2015, which makes Bogota the largest metropolitan area in Colombia, one of the largest in South America, and one of the 33 most populated urban areas in the world (Smith, 2017).

Although metropolitan areas officially exist in Colombia, they are mostly administrative units, formed on a voluntary basis. Law 1625 of 2013 provides the formal framework for municipal associations which are formed as autonomous institutions with specific powers delegated voluntarily by the municipalities that belong to them. Therefore, in practice, these powers vary widely (Duranton, 2015).

Table 8.5 summarises the governance structure in the Bogota metropolitan area. In general, Bogota has a less complex multiactor structure, with the

Table 8.5 Stakeholders in the levels of governance in provision of services in Bogota

	Waste	Water	Transport
Provision	The service is provided by the Bogota District and the rest of the municipalities.	Centralised provision of water services.	Local provision.
Production	The city administration has implemented a new sanitary scheme which assigns five areas of service to five private enterprises. A number of recycling companies collect, transport and separate solid waste.	Bogota's Water Enterprise, Aguas de Bogota, supplies water services to Bogota and most nearby municipalities. It operates on a regional level as a private company. Aguas de Bogota is the subsidiary company of Acueducto, a public enterprise providing water and sewerage services in Colombia.	The bus rapid transit, Transmilenio, and local buses form the core of public transport.

(*Continued*)

Table 8.5 (Continued)

	Waste	Water	Transport
Regulation	The National Regulatory Committee for Drinking Water and Basic Sanitation is responsible for the normative control of waste collection services and regulating competition between service providers. The National Superintendence of Domestic Utility Services controls and inspects the service for efficiency. The Municipal Special Administrative Unit of Public Utilities directs, controls and supervises the provision of road-cleaning services. The District Department of Environment regulates environmental sustainability, and the Municipal Intercapital Consortium supervises the administrative, technical, operative, commercial, economic and financial aspects of solid waste collection.	Provision of water is regulated by the Potable Water and Basic Sanitation Regulation Commission which also sets the prices.	The Ministry of Transportation is responsible for formulating and adopting national policies, plans, programs and projects. A municipal Ministry of Mobility operates in Bogota and in Soacha.

Source: Based on Trejo, Niño and Vasquez (2018).

exception of the regulatory structure in the waste collection service. Like Peru, Colombia has a centralised provision of water services, where a single company provides the service. Although they are not included in the table, informality is another component in the delivery of these services, mainly in the periphery.

Table 8.6 shows the main aspects of the delivery of services in Bogota. Water service is centralised and a single company covers most of the metropolitan area. Transmilenio is the bus rapid transit system that service most of the metropolitan area by including a number of station in the municipality of Soacha. In the case of waste collections services, there is mostly an uncoordinated delivery. Waste and water services operate under a cross-subsidy scheme that seems to work adequately. A financially healthy operation is possible through this system. On the contrary, Transmilenio requires direct subsidies to operate. Official data shows adequate coverage but this information is collected only in legalised settlements. Low quality is perceived in the transport services.

Table 8.6 Governance of urban services in Bogota

	Waste	Water	Transport
Coordination	Uncoordinated delivery. Each municipality chooses a public or private operation	Centralised provision in most of the metropolitan area.	There is a consolidated model for infrastructure construction but without a metropolitan approach.
	Small municipalities allowed the Cundinamarca department company to provide the service.	Weak, coordinated provision to Soacha (largest municipality outside Bogota Capital District).	Inter-municipal transportation is the responsibility of departments.
	Some institutional coordination, mainly with the association of formal recyclers.		Transmilenio offers a service to only four stations outside Bogota's borders, in Soacha.
Financial sustainability	Fees subject to socioeconomic stratification (*estratos*, cross-subsidies).	Tariffs fixed according to the six socioeconomic levels (*estratos*).	Transmilenio funded directly by the Bogota district government.
	Fees include waste sweeping and cleaning, commercialisation, collection and transport.	6 m^2 of water provided to each household of *estrato*, 1 m^2 without charge.	The Integrated Public Transport System is not financially sustainable based only on fees paid.
	Financially sustainable.	Operational costs covered by tariffs.	Inter-municipal metropolitan buses are run privately; most of them have financial difficulties.
		Financially healthy delivery.	
Coverage and quality	Coverage of more than 90 per cent (official data collected only in formal settlements).	In Bogota 98.6 per cent of neighbourhoods are covered; in Soacha 82.8 per cent; in Sabana 96.3 per cent (these refer to legalised neighbourhoods).	High coverage.
	Reaches all socioeconomically vulnerable areas included in the stratification transfer system.		Problems of quality in municipalities outside the Bogota district.

Source: Based on Trejo, Niño and Vasquez (2018).

Provision of urban services, metropolitan governance and political economic factors

Ensuring an adequate provision of services in metropolitan areas is technically, financially and politically very complex. Metropolitan structures usually result in intricate arrangements for service provision and production involving varied organisations: public, private, formal, informal, community based or public–private partnerships. These arrangements are crucial in shaping service delivery in metropolitan environments, but as a result of their variation metropolitan service delivery can display some common and distinct characteristics across metropolises and across services provided.

Despite the common context of jurisdictional fragmentation, shifting inter-governmental relations and ongoing decentralisation processes, metropolitan governance structures in Mexico and Latin America differ not only across metropolises but also across sectors of the same metropolis. Service delivery practices often vary to accommodate specific needs, preferences, practices, institutions, legal structures and available resources (Trejo, Niño & Vasquez, 2018).

Compared to Lima, Bogota, Guadalajara and Monterrey, the metropolitan structures for service delivery in MCMA are the most fragmented. Provision of piped water, waste collection and public transport services are mainly provided by each of the multiple local governments and organisations, with almost a complete lack metropolitan cooperation and coordination. Consequently, the provision of services in this metropolitan area shows the worst performance in terms of coordination, efficiency and equity. Public transport is the service with the weakest governance and poorest performance. This is a particular sector affecting the overall socioeconomic performance of MCMA given the important spatial mismatches in the urban structure, as discussed in the previous chapter.

This may not be surprising as MCMA faces many of the same issues regarding effective governance as other large metropolitan areas, such as high fragmentation, multiple and overlapping administrative and governmental jurisdictions and a large and highly differentiated population. Furthermore, it has been identified nationally and internationally as an example of jurisdictional complexity because it is a very large conglomerate of local and state political-administrative divisions. MCMA faces multiple political-administrative systems: Mexico City with its division into boroughs, the states of Hidalgo and Estado de Mexico and their municipalities, and the national government.

It is important to underline that problems of collective action are preventing the coordination of relevant stakeholders to adopt a metropolitan-wide provision of urban services. Political short-termism, electoral cycles and political competition may preclude effective decisions on potentially unpopular or unattractive issues. In this case, the political economic context has to be understood as a deciding factor in the extent to which governance is implemented or achieves its aims. Integrating the political economy context into the metropolitan agenda can help to identify entry points for mobilising change and adjustment and determine alternative ways forward in the existing political and economic context, as prevailing relations of political power form an important part of the explanation of poor governance. Let us also recall that an increasing number of local governments attempting to cooperate, increasing heterogeneity in the population and the complex regulation of local governments, conditions that are found in MCMA, negatively influence collective action (Post, 2004).

In Mexico, Guadalajara and Monterrey provide examples of successful area-wide consolidation of the water, waste and transport sectors. Such consolidation has been triggered and facilitated to a large extent by the third party – the state government – that oftentimes is required to absorb organisation costs, apply coercion and provide selective incentives. In the metropolitan areas of Lima and Bogota services such as water are highly consolidated, whereas waste collection services seem to be in a process of consolidation, with inter-municipal agreements and associations seeking to coordinate the joint provision of the service. However, consolidation of the water provision responds to the centralisation of that sector in the national government or to the provision of a decentralised company that provides services as a private provider. Public transport in Bogota is also provided to almost the whole metropolitan area. Partial or complete consolidation of service delivery has positive effects on financial sustainability, coverage and quality, but do not fix problems (Trejo, Niño & Vasquez, 2018).

Concluding comments

The comparative evaluation of metropolitan governance and service delivery in MCMA has informed how service delivery adjusts to accommodate specific needs and sociopolitical contexts, even if such arrangements do not necessarily correspond to local rationalities. Service delivery in MCMA seems to be strongly affected by its extensive fragmentation. Implications of a fragmented supply of services has translated into social and financial inefficiencies, as well as into important spatial disparities. Certainly, fragmentation creates substantial difficulties in the provision of urban services. Yet, it is not possible to conclude that the lack of coordination and poor governance derive purely from the administrative fragmentation of the territory. Despite constitutional autonomy for voluntary inter-municipal cooperation, deep-rooted political interests and competition prevent such practice. Collective action problems derived from local politics and power imbalances have overpowered any approach to inter-jurisdictional coordination and cooperation for economic and social efficiency. In MCMA political economic factors appear to play a determining role in explaining the weak metropolitan governance structures, including party and political competition between states and between municipalities, the three-year term of municipal government, the culture of all-embracing political power and other factors.

In contrast, service delivery in Monterrey, Guadalajara, Lima and Bogota are supported by relatively stronger metropolitan structures, which bring an improvement in efficiency and sustainability. However, municipally guided projects and initiatives are still weak or absent. Consolidation processes have come from strong centralisation, initiatives from higher levels of government or the active participation of private companies. While the findings in this analysis are not generalisable, they illustrate the significant empirical variation found across metropolitan areas and sectors, demonstrating the need for a debate on metropolitan governance that goes beyond the traditional approach to jurisdictional fragmentation and metropolitan governments.

Therefore, the governance of service provision is place and sector specific depending on the extent of the territorial fragmentation, the local needs, the local political culture and the existing legal frameworks. In the absence of an overarching government for metropolitan areas, the relative significance of these factors will determine the lack of encompassing metropolitan arrangements that allow an improved provision of urban services.

Note

1   The data, results and discussion in this comparative analysis rely on the results of the BIARI collaborative seed research project on metropolitan governance in Latin America. The data was collected during fieldwork conducted in 2016 in Bogota, Lima and Mexico City. This included 9 workshops, 12 semi-structured interviews and 4 technical visits.

References

Bird, R. M. & Slack, E. (2007). 'An approach to metropolitan governance and finance'. *Environment and Planning C: Government and Policy*, 25(5), 729–755. Available at: https://doi.org/10.1068/c0623.

Boex, J., Lane, B. & Yao, G. (2013). *An assessment of urban public service delivery in South Asia: An analysis of institutional and fiscal constraints*. Washington, D.C.: The Urban Institute.

Diálogos de Políticas Pública. (2015). *Nota de política pública de descentralización: hacia la consolidación de un Estado unitario y descentralizado al servicio de los ciudadanos* [online]. Available at: www.dialogosperu.pe/files/downloads/cartilla_descentralizacion.pdf.

Duranton, G. (2015). 'A proposal to delineate Metropolitan areas in Colombia'. *Desarrollo y Sociedad*, (75), 223–264. Available at: https://dx.doi.org/10.13043/DYS.75.6.

Feiock, R. C. (2004). 'Introduction: Regionalism and institutional collective action'. In Feiock, R. C. (ed.). *Metropolitan governance: Conflict, competition, and cooperation*. Washington, D.C.: Georgetown University Press, pp. 3–16.

Feiock, R. C. (2013). 'The institutional collective action framework'. *The Policy Studies Journal*, 41(3), 397–425. Available at: https://doi.org/10.1111/psj.12023.

Garcia Ortega, R. (1989). 'El plan director de desarrollo urbano del area metropolitan de Monterrey: antecedentes, analisis y situacion actual'. In Garza, G. (ed.). *Una decada de planeacion urbano-regional en Mexico, 1978–1988*. El Colegio de Mexico, Mexico City. Available at: www.jstor.org/stable/j.ctv26d9b1.18.

Guzman, L. A., Oviedo, D. & Bocarejo, J. P. (2017). 'City profile: The Bogotá Metropolitan area that never was'. *Cities*, 60 (Part A), 202–215. Available at: https://doi.org/10.1016/j.cities.2016.09.004.

IMEPLAN. (NA). *Instituto de Planeacion Metropolitana*. Available at: http://imeplan.mx/en/acerca.

INEI. (2014). *Una mirada a Lima Metropolitana* [online]. Lima: Instituto Nacional de Estadística e Informática. Available at: www.inei.gob.pe/media/MenuRecursivo/publicaciones_digitales/Est/Lib1168/libro.pdf.

Jones, H., Clench, B. & Harris, D. (2014). *The governance of urban service delivery in developing countries* [online]. ODI Discussion Paper. London: Overseas Development Institute Report. Available at: www.odi.org/publications/8329-urban-services-poverty.

Jones, H., Cummings, C. & Nixon, H. (2014). *Services in the city: Governance and political economy in urban service delivery.* [online]. ODI Discussion Paper. London: Overseas Development Institute Report. Available at: www.odi.org/sites/odi.org.uk/files/odi-assets/publications-opinion-files/9382.pdf.

Lewis, P. G. (2004). 'An old debate confronts new realities: Large suburbs and economic development in the metropolis' In Feiock, R. C. (ed.). *Metropolitan governance: Conflict, competition, and cooperation.* Washington, D.C.: Georgetown University Press, pp. 95–123.

Lowery, D. (2000). 'A transactions costs model of metropolitan governance: Allocation versus redistribution in urban America'. *Journal of Public Administration Research and Theory*, 10(1), 49–78. Available at: www.jstor.org/stable/3525811?seq=1#page_scan_tab_contents.

Oakerson, R. J. (2004). 'The study of metropolitan governance'. In Feiock, R. C. (ed.). *Metropolitan governance: Conflict, competition, and cooperation.* Washington, D.C.: Georgetown University Press, pp. 17–45.

Oates, W. (1997). 'On the welfare gains from fiscal decentralization'. *Journal of Public Finance and Public Choice*, (2–3), 83–92.

OECD. (2015). *OECD territorial reviews: Valle de México.* Paris: OECD Publishing. https://doi.org/10.1787/9789264245174-en.

Parks, R. B. & Oakerson, R. J. (1989). 'Metropolitan organization and governance: A local public economy approach'. *Urban Affairs Quarterly*, 25(1), 18–29. Available at: https://doi.org/10.1177/004208168902500103.

Parks, R. B. & Oakerson, R. J. (1993). 'Comparative metropolitan organization: Service production and governance structures in St. Louis (MO) and Allegheny County (PA)'. *Publius: The Journal of Federalism*, 23(1), 19–40. Available at: www.jstor.org/stable/3330797.

Perlman, B. J. & Pineda, J. D. D. (2011). 'Rethinking a megalopolis: A metropolitan government proposal for the Mexico City Metro Area'. *State and Local Government Review*, 43(2), 144–150. Available at: https://doi.org/10.1177/0160323X11414917.

Pírez, P. (2014). 'El gobierno metropolitano como gobernabilidad: entre la autorregulación y la orientación política'. *Economía, Sociedad y Territorio*, 14(45), 523–548. Available at: www.scielo.org.mx/pdf/est/v14n45/v14n45a8.pdf.

Post, S. S. (2004). 'Metropolitan area governance and institutional collective action'. In Feiock, R. C. (ed.). *Metropolitan governance: Conflict, competition, and cooperation.* Washington, D.C.: Georgetown University Press, pp. 67–92.

Prud'Homme, R. (1995). 'The dangers of decentralization'. *World Bank Research Observer*, 10(2), 201–220. Available at: www.jstor.org/stable/3986582.

Rosales, A. (2015). *Economía política del servicio de agua y saneamiento en la Ciudad de México.* PhD Thesis. México, D. F.: CEDUA, El Colegio de México.

Sellers, J. & Hoffmann-Martinot, V. (2008). *Gobernanza metropolitana: United Cities and local.* Washington, D.C.: World Bank, 226–293. Available at: www.cities-localgovernments.org/gold/Upload/gold_report/09_metropolis_es.pdf.

Slack, E. (2007). *Managing the coordination of service delivery in Metropolitan Cities: The role of metropolitan governance.* Policy Research Working Paper, No. 4317. Washington, D.C.: World Bank. Available at: https://openknowledge.worldbank.org/handle/10986/7264.

Smith, D. A. (2017). 'World city populations 1950–2030: Proportional circle time series map'. *Environment and Planning A: Economy and Space*, 49(1), 3–5. Available at: https://doi.org/10.1177/0308518X16641414.

Storper, M. (2014). 'Governing the large metropolis'. *Territory, Politics, Governance*, 2(2), 115–134. Available at: https://doi.org/10.1080/21622671.2014.919874.

Tiebout, C. (1956). 'A pure theory of local expenditures'. *Journal of Political Economy*, 64(5), 416–424.

Tortajada, C. (2006). *Water governance with equity: Is decentralisation the answer? Decentralisation of the water sector in Mexico and intercomparison with practices from Turkey and Brazil.* Human Development Report Office No. HDOCPA-2006–15. United Nations Development Programme (UNDP). Available at: http://hdr.undp.org/en/content/water-governance-equity-decentralisation-answer.

Treisman, D. (2000). *Decentralization and the quality of government.* Los Angeles, CA: University of California.

Trejo Nieto, A., Niño Amezquita, J. & Vasquez, M. (2018). 'Governance of metropolitan areas for delivery of public services in Latin America: The cases of Bogota, Lima and Mexico City'. *Region*, 5(3), 49–73. Available at: https://doi.org/10.18335/region.v5i3.224.

Ward, P. M. (2011). 'Repensando el espacio geopolítico metropolitano en México: ¿Como lograr un verdadero gobierno y una gobernabilidad para todos?' In Capron, G., Icazuriaga Montes, C., Levi, S., Ribera Carbó, E. & Thiébaut, V. (eds.). *La geografía contemporánea y Elisée Reclus.* México, D. F.: Centro de estudios mexicanos y centroamericanos. Available at: https://books.openedition.org/cemca/2585?lang=es.

Yaro, R. D. & Ronderos, L. N. (2011). *International metropolitan governance: Typology, case studies and recommendations.* Washington, D.C.: The World Bank Group.

9 Urban policy agendas, governance and metropolitan economic development

Introduction

Metropolitan areas provide opportunities for economic growth and development, but the interplay of their challenges, on the one hand, and the economic and social opportunities, on the other, create significant responsibilities for policymakers. To varying degrees and in different ways numerous metropolitan areas around the world face the same problems of slow economic growth, inequality, segregation, unemployment, growing poverty and deficient provision of basic services to the population. These and other daunting development challenges, which have increased in scope and intensity in recent years, form part of the agendas of different levels of government. Local governments in particular do not only have to provide local services and maintaining infrastructure: changing political structures and decentralisation have placed increasing pressure and responsibility on territories and their authorities in the areas of job creation, poverty alleviation and economic growth. Local public policy and strategy are critical in metropolitan areas that are often required to reform the intergovernmental relations system for adequate governance and policymaking processes. Suitable and viable policy strategies are necessary to address metropolitan areas' pressing societal problems, which manifest through a myriad of phenomena.

In addition to their local and national specific frameworks, cities have to plan their economic destiny within a more or less common external developmental framework that includes globalisation, technological transformation and financialisation of housing. The framing of the New Urban Agenda, Habitat III, and the adoption of New International Development Agenda, Agenda 2030 for Sustainable Development strategically positioned urban economies to achieve broad development outcomes. For most nations, bigger cities mean greater production, higher per capita income and increased productivity; awareness of this is not new, but it has gained legacy and attention, with the urban economy a subject of interest and a crucial public policy issue from the highest to the lowest level.

Having discussed some of the theory and evidence on urbanisation and economic performance, in this last chapter I address two central issues in the political economy of metropolitan economic development: public policy and governance. International and national urban development agendas and the policies, strategies and activities that different tiers of government implement to promote economic development in metropolitan areas are reviewed. I include some references to Mexico's experience, particularly regarding urban and economic policy, and suggest some guidelines for the formulation of metropolitan economic strategies.

Differential public policy responses to the challenges of economic development may help to explain the spatial disparities and unequal economic positioning of metropolitan areas. However, there remains the question of whether there is significant room for public policy in shaping their economic development. Investigating whether economic advantage is policy dependent, whether policymakers, intentionally or not, shape cities' future and how much they grow, and whether policy can change even persistent and long-term economic patterns is a daunting prospect. Yet reviewing how political actors can reshape metropolitan economic development patterns is a decisive start. If the foundation and growth of cities are related to policy, this raises the question of how much agency political actors have to alter the path of development. If policy can change the attractiveness of a city, policy choices have important consequences for metropolitan development.

Metropolitan policies face great political, administrative and legislative difficulties given the inherent characteristics of metropolitan areas, and their governance, issues of coordination, cooperation, political will, political reform and decentralisation must be taken into account when formulating policies.

The international urban agenda

Most urban issues are articulated in the UN's International Development Agenda 2030 and the New Urban Agenda, which provide the overarching context within which the roles and responsibilities of different international, national and local stakeholders can be situated. In designing the global development agenda and the urban agenda, policymakers have understood and accounted for the political, social and economic importance of cities. Likewise, in the early 1990s the World Bank recognised the growing interdependence of urban economies and macroeconomic performance and the need to ensure cities' productivity and alleviate the growing incidence of urban poverty (World Bank, 1991). More recently, the World Bank has established a programmatic approach to identifying and designing effective policies and programs promoting inclusive city development, with the twin goals of ending extreme poverty and boosting shared economic prosperity (Shah et al., 2015).

The UN's thinking on international urbanisation has dominated the international agenda and was first integrated in the Habitat I Agenda at the First Conference on Human Settlements in Vancouver in 1976. The outcome of the Second Conference on Human Settlements in Istanbul in 1996 was the Declaration on Human Settlements, which was the official document of the Habitat

II Agenda (HIC, 2016). The Urban Agenda lays the groundwork for efforts to attend and resolve the most critical urban challenges in the world. It guides the efforts of a wide range of actors in urbanisation, from nation-states, city and regional leaders, international organisations to civil society, and provides a basis for a range of urban policies and approaches.

The legacy of the urban agendas validated their incorporation into the 2030 Development Agenda and the Sustainable Development Goals (SDGs) which highlighted the development challenges that are inherent in rapid urbanisation. The urban-focused SDG 11 was the result of explicit concerns about urbanisation and the need to 'make cities and human settlements inclusive, safe, resilient and sustainable' (UN, 2015). The Habitat Agenda also influenced the 2000 Millennium Development Goals, which include the target of achieving cities without slums, eradicating poverty and ensuring environmental sustainability.

The Habitat III Agenda, or New Urban Agenda, was adopted in Quito, Ecuador, in 2016 by the 197 UN member states. The New Urban Agenda seeks to create a closer relationship between urbanisation and economic development in order to strengthen the urban economy by offering guidelines and objectives for national urban policy, laws, institutions and systems of governance. The main enablers of economic development in the New Urban Agenda include local fiscal systems, urban planning, and basic services and infrastructure (UN, 2016a).

In the preparation of Habitat III a number of policy papers identified policy priorities, critical issues and action-oriented recommendations in relation to its implementation. Policy papers included 10 policy units, incorporating one for economic development and one for local finance and fiscal systems: (1) the right to the city and cities for all; (2) a sociocultural urban framework; (3) national urban policies; (4) urban governance, capacity and institutional development; (5) municipal finance and local fiscal systems; (6) urban spatial strategies; (7) urban economic development strategies; (8) urban ecology and resilience; (9) urban services and technology; and (10) housing policies.[1] Cohen (2015) points out that while subjects such as housing, infrastructure, community development, and environmental protection continue to deserve policy attention as in previous agendas, any progress in these areas depends on the income and public revenue available to cities. Both income and public revenue, in turn, depend on three foundational components of the urban economy: employment, productivity and urban finance.

The objective of inclusive and sustainable economic growth with full and productive employment and decent work for all summarises the Habitat III perspective on urban economic development. The Policy Paper on Urban Economic Development Strategies (UN, 2016b) recommends that cities proactively facilitate an inclusive economic development process with a strong rights framework. A supportive business environment in the formal and informal sectors, strong urban governance and institutions, a capacity for innovation, physical and social infrastructure and multilevel partnerships are identified as the enabling and supporting conditions necessary for inclusive urban economic development. According to this paper, no single prescriptive policy solution to economic development can solve the enormously diverse problems that cities face. Cities in both the developed and the developing world struggle with structural adjustment but they face different challenges. Urban economic challenges vary with income level, national context and city-specific peculiarities. In cities in the Global South, problems such as poverty, underinvestment in infrastructure, poor human development, financial weakness and others are most acutely felt (UN, 2016b). The urban economic development framework in the Habitat III Policy Paper is presented in Figure 9.1.

The New Urban Agenda recognises that several cities in the world have morphed into regions, corridors and metropolitan areas whose economic, social and political geographies defy the traditional concept of the 'city'. While metropolitan areas are seen as the major drivers of the global and national economies (UN, 2016a; UN, 2017), the Habitat III Agenda neither exhausts the debate on them nor provides sufficient guidance to address key urbanisation issues on the metropolitan scale (De Souza & Barcelo, 2016).

The Habitat III approach has received additional criticism. Satterthwaite (2016) argues that many of its commitments were already addressed by the SDGs and the Paris Agreement, and that international and national stakeholders often commit to undertakings that are actually the responsibility of local governments. Caprotti et al. (2017) raise questions about the Habitat III Agenda's potential for reductionism and argue for the need to be aware of types of urban space that may be dismissed by the new trends in global urban policy. They also

CHALLENGES	POLICY OPTIONS	ACTORS AND ENABLING INSTITUTIONS	DESIGN AND IMPLEMENTATION
• Productive and decent employment • Investment in housing, infrastructure, business and human capital • Governance, institutional structures, political economy, finance and resources	• Land use and land tenure regulation and planning • Business support initiatives (skills, industrial policy, technical support) • Infrastructure and service provision • Regulation and taxation schemes, extension of legal and social protection and support services for the informal economy • Strong urban finance, local autonomy, own resources • Urban governance and government capacity	• National and local governments • Private sector • Large multinational firms • Informal economy • Trade unions • Educational and training institutions • Non-governmental organisations • International organisations	• Involve all relevant actors • Research and analysis • Focus human, financial and physical resources on the development strategy • Support formal and informal economies • Build up human and social capital • Monitoring and evaluation through process, structure and outcome indicators

Figure 9.1 Urban economic development framework, Habitat III Policy Papers

Source: Based on UN (2016b).

call attention to the risky fetishisation of the role of experts in urban policy and development agendas. Rodríguez and Sugranyes (2017) express disappointment at the wishful thinking apparent in the agenda. Furthermore, the agenda does not assess the accomplishments of the Istanbul commitments or many new and emerging problems, and appears open to any possible position and purpose.

One improvement of the new international agendas is that national urban policies are recognised as instrumental in governments' coordination and articulation of their international and national goals of urban development. A national urban policy (NUP) is seen as a critical step in reasserting urban space and territoriality in the national development agenda.

National urban policy and its approach to economic development

A national urban policy is a tool by which governments can provide a guide to managing urbanisation with a coordinated approach and to offer a course of action that supports urban development. It should be used as the key reference for legislative institutional reform and as an instrument for public and political awareness of the gains to be obtained from urban development. It establishes the principles by which urban policy interventions are formulated and implementation is conceived. This should promote a common vision and include a clear strategy for effective coordination between policies and across spatial scales. Another key role of the NUP is supporting the alignment of different sectoral policies and ensuring that these policies are coherent for promoting urban development (UN-Habitat & OECD, 2018). NUPs can also enable subnational governments to shape their development policy in conformity with national and international policy goals (OECD & China Development Research Foundation, 2010). The OECD (2015a) argues that cities can only succeed when the NUP settings are sufficiently favourable. The framework set by a national government is of critical importance to its cities' initiatives and incentives.

This international commitment to urban development is a global inducement for countries to adopt NUPs and pursue a national urban strategy. UN-Habitat and OECD (2018) report that 150 of the UN's 193 member states have NUPs, but that of these only 76 are explicit policies. Some countries, such as the US, do not have a NUP because city planning and land use management is the responsibility of state and local governments. Even though the US does not have a single policy document regarding national urban planning and its national constitution limits federal government involvement in urban affairs (OECD & China Development Research Foundation, 2010), in practice the federal government promotes strong urban planning principles and supports state and local governments' urban planning (UN-Habitat & OECD, 2018). A US strategy for regional development is well framed in its national planning and has been 'consistent with the finest tradition of American politics and policy . . . since the earliest days of the Republic' (Yaro, 2009, p. 13).

There are also contemporary European precedents in national urban and regional policy that devote substantial resources to the development of under-performing urban regions, for instance, by means of EU Structural Funds (ibid.). While some OECD countries have a long-term national vision of urban development which is reflected in their national spatial planning frameworks, Japan and Korea appear to place special emphasis on the role of the central government in spatial planning. The NUPs of other countries such as France are exclusively conceptual, and the UK no longer has an NUP (OECD & China Development Research Foundation, 2010). There is a growing trend towards explicit NUPs elsewhere, especially in rapidly urbanising countries in regions such as the Arab States, Africa, Asia and the Pacific.

In Mexico the first postrevolutionary governments granted a special place to the reorganisation of territorial planning and policy on agrarian space when it was a predominantly rural country. With the advancement of its industrialisation policies, the Mexican state, consolidating itself as the leading planning body, recognised the wide territorial disparities across the country and the high concentration of population and economic activity in Mexico City. Attempts to address these inequalities were based on sectorial policies in specific regions of the country (Trejo, 2017).

Projects that can be considered part of its formal NUP started to appear in Mexico from the 1970s, with the enactment in 1975 of the Federal District Urban Development Law, the General Human Settlements Law in 1976, the National Commission for Urban Development in 1978 and the 1980 Federal District Urban Development Plan. According to Garza (1999), the greatest institutionalisation of urban planning occurred in the 1977–1982 presidential period when the federal government attempted to put into practice the guiding principles emanating from the General Law on Human Settlements related to rules on policy-setting and regulations on land use planning, to centralise urban and regional programmes under a state ministry, the Secretariat of Human Settlements and Public Works, and to draft state and municipal plans. However, the urban planning instruments failed to function due to two important shortcomings: they lacked specific and viable strategies for intervening in the structuring of national territory, and they did not have an adequate budget for the implementation of policies.

Despite the enactment of the 1984–1988 National Program for Urban Development and Housing, Mexico's urban policy weakened in the second half of the 1980s due to reduced state participation and financing cutbacks. With the implementation of neoliberal policy in the 1980s and 1990s, many instruments, programs and structures linked to planning were dismantled. In the absence of an explicit NUP, urban development was mainly driven by housing policy – more precisely, by housing finance – in a context of relatively weak public institutions and a strong private sector (OECD, 2015b). National policy primarily responded to the country's urbanisation through efforts to address the quantitative housing deficit. Attempts to improve urban development with specific programmes had little success. In 2012–2018 the government endorsed an explicit NUP to bring urban planning and policy into line with the NUPs of most other OECD countries. Table 9.1 summarises the recent state of Mexico's NUP and those of two other OECD federal countries that have experienced intense urban expansion: Belgium and the US.

Whereas there have been advances in the formulation of an explicit NUP in Mexico and Belgium, there has been much recent interest in the US, which has a long tradition of home rule for municipal authorities. Mexico's NUP explicitly refers to the problem of metropolitan sprawl; in the US there has long been debate about issues of coordination in metropolitan areas, while Belgium's NUP does not address metropolitan expansion explicitly. Lastly, Mexico's NUP includes economic development objectives and Belgium's shows interest in attracting high-value economic activity. The US's economic development strategy is largely formulated and implemented at the local and state levels.

Comparative analysis of NUPs across countries is difficult. Urban policy is a very broad concept, and policy objectives differ across countries because they are contingent on the specific challenges facing the cities and the urbanisation rates in each country. There are also varying degrees of political centralisation and forms of national government. Despite cross-country differences in urban policies within the OECD, a number of comparable trends can be identified: countries have recognised that national economic performance depends on the competitive capacity of their cities; development policies increasingly endorse a more pragmatic approach to balanced territorial development (while remaining concerned about territorial redistribution, national governments accept that a certain degree of concentration in the main cities is needed for national economic growth); and NUPs are becoming proactive and looking forward rather than acting remedially (OECD & China Development Research Foundation, 2010).

Spatial structure, economic development, human capital, climate resilience and environmental sustainability are five strategic policy sectors included in NUPs that represent long-standing issues with which governments have historically dealt, and reflect an array of urban challenges. NUPs appear to cover spatial structure and economic development extensively, in contrast to climate resilience and environmental sustainability (UN-Habitat & OECD, 2018). Table 9.2 includes the priorities and challenges of the NUPs in different regions in the world. All regions except Latin America identify economic competitiveness, productivity and the productive transformation of their cities as a thematic priority, despite the fact that cities in the region lag behind in terms of economic development, are not generating enough jobs to employ the expanding labour force and informal economic activity has risen considerably. However, a number of the regions' NUPs, Mexico's included, dedicate an extensive level of attention to economic development (Table 9.3).

Despite growing awareness of their key role in national policies, overall understanding of cities and the structural transformation represented by the dynamics of economic growth and productive organisation in metropolitan areas is still very limited. Urban planning has not included consistent links to

Table 9.1 NUPs in three federal OECD countries

Country	Name and year of last NUP	Form and stage of NUP	National urban agency	Characteristics of NUP
Belgium	Federal Big City Policy (FBCP), 1999	Partial NUP in the stage of implementation	Federal Public Service	No specific urban policy until the 1990s when the salience of urban issues rose, reflecting the rise of local right-wing political parties, urban rioting and the growth and segregation of minority ethnic urban communities. A strongly federalised governmental system and the differential economic experiences of Belgium's three regions have produced a divergence in policy approaches, with an initial focus on physical urban renewal in Wallonia, urban safety and poverty in Flanders and both in the Brussels region. The policy focus in the latter two regions has shifted recently towards an emphasis on social control and the attraction of high-income residents and high-value firms.
United States	NA	NA	NA	Strongly federalised system of government with a high degree of 'home rule' for municipal governments. Reliance on labour migration and low-welfare entitlements to overcome spatial economic shocks has created a highly fragmented and competitive system of government in which urban policies are unevenly developed and largely dependent on state–municipality relationships. Recent debates about 'new urbanism' and the potential benefits of 'regionalism' (i.e. metropolitan inter-municipal cooperation) for overall quality of life have encouraged a focus on the need for dedicated, bespoke urban policies, but seem unlikely to trigger fundamental change.
Mexico	National Urban Development Programme (NUDP), 2014	Explicit NUP in the process of implementation	Secretary of Agrarian, Land and Urban Development (SEDATU)	The NUDP aligns with Mexico's National Development Plan and contains six objectives: control urban sprawl; increase the wellbeing of city dwellers and guarantee social, economic and environmental sustainability; design and implement normative, fiscal, administrative and regulatory instruments for land use management; promote sustainable mobility; avoid risk zones and reduce the vulnerability of urban populations to natural disasters; consolidate the Regional Development Policy. Housing policy is regulated by the National Housing Programme (NHP). The NUDP and NHP work together to make resources and housing investment contingent on the application of an urban containment strategy by the relevant municipalities.

Source: Based on OECD and China Development Research Foundation (2010); OECD (2017); UN-Habitat and OECD (2018).

Table 9.2 Priorities and challenges in NUPs by region

Region	Thematic priorities of NUP	Thematic challenges in NUP
Africa	• **Economic development and poverty eradication** • Provision of adequate infrastructure and basic services • Curbing and upgrading informal settlements • Environmental protection • Urban–rural linkages and food security	• Rapid urbanisation outpacing policies and resulting in urban poverty and informal settlements • Urbanisation is caused by the push factor of rural poverty • Large urban youth cohorts lacking economic opportunities • Extreme vulnerability to climate change, particularly droughts causing food and water insecurity
Asia and the Pacific	• **Urbanisation as a means of economic transformation** • Improving the provision of housing and basic services • Improving land management • Balanced urban development and urban–rural linkages • Promoting resilience	• Low level of urbanisation but current and projected rates are extremely high • Urban poverty and large proportions of slum dwellers • Vulnerability to natural risks and hazards and to climate change, especially rising sea level and flooding
Arab States	• **Promoting cities as engines of economic growth and diversification** • **Job generation for urban youth** • Slum upgrading and provision of affordable and adequate housing • Heritage preservation and postconflict reconstruction • Balanced territorial development, steering urban pressure away from agricultural land and primary cities, sometimes through new towns • Energetic and economic transition	• Rapid urbanisation and growth of informal settlements • Large urban youth cohorts demanding equal social, political and economic opportunities • Extreme vulnerability to climate change, particularly droughts, causing food and water insecurity • Political conflict, turmoil and large population displacements • Economic reliance on fossil fuels
Europe and North America	• Balanced national and regional development, sometimes restraining the growth of major cities • Promoting sustainable urban growth • Urban renewal strategies • Cities as engines of economic competitiveness and productivity	• Ageing population • Stagnating demography • Deindustrialisation

(Continued)

Table 9.2 (Continued)

Region	Thematic priorities of NUP	Thematic challenges in NUP
Latin America and the Caribbean	• Curbing the housing and social housing deficit • Strong and comprehensive commitment to urban quality of life, ensuring the right to housing and the right to the city • Promoting a compact model of city planning and curbing sprawl • Developing a national system of cities • Metropolitan-level planning • Developing mass transport	• Rapid urbanisation has stabilised but caused unsustainable urban patterns • Extreme socioeconomic and spatial inequalities • Development of large metropolitan agglomerations • Environmental degradation caused by unplanned urban growth • Explosion of vehicle use has created traffic congestion and pollution • Vulnerability to natural risks and hazards and to climate change, especially rising sea level

Source: UN-Habitat and OECD (2018).

Table 9.3 Latin American NUPs with an extensive level of attention to economic development

Country	Economic development	Spatial structure	Human development	Environmental sustainability	Climate resilience
Chile	Extensive	Extensive	Extensive	Extensive	Low
Dominican Republic	Extensive	Extensive	Moderate	Low	Low
Mexico	Extensive	Moderate	Extensive	Moderate	Low
Nicaragua	Extensive	Extensive	Low	Low	Low
Paraguay	Extensive	Moderate	Moderate	Moderate	Low
Peru	Extensive	Extensive	Extensive	Moderate	Low
Uruguay	Extensive	Extensive	Moderate	Moderate	Low
Venezuela	Extensive	Extensive	Extensive	Extensive	Low

Source: UN-Habitat and OECD (2018).

local economic performance and policy, and the territorial approach of NUPs remains a pending paradigmatic change in how public intervention and action take place at the city level.

Policy approaches to territorial economic development

Economic development policies can be understood as activities to improve the economic wellbeing of a population. Territorial economic development policies usually imply different actions aimed at correcting spatial imbalances (equity objectives) and/or achieving economic efficiency and growth. Both types of policy tend to converge toward the need for instruments that allow adjusting and regulating the spatial expression of economic problems. These actions and activities can play a role in turning local capacities into advantages through the development of legal frameworks and the establishment of institutional and political arrangements that favour adequate implementation. Such public policies contribute to development to the extent that they promote and improve local wellbeing.

Peters and Fishers (2004) claim that defining economic development policy is problematic because it is often difficult to distinguish it from other state and local policy interventions such as housing provision, workforce improvement and community development. Nonetheless, economic development policy has been a part of state and local planning for many decades in countries such as the US, where local governments are increasingly active in implementing programmes and strategies to provide assistance and subsidies for individual businesses and sectors (Bartik, 1995).

While any discussion of metropolitan and local economic public policy can be improved by analysing the complete policy cycle, this section is only intended to identify and describe the most widespread goals, instruments and strategies that have been used for fostering urban prosperity. Because evidence on the effectiveness of economic development policies is inconclusive, there is also the question of which policies are most cost-effective in stimulating urban economies given the conflicting financial and fiscal pressures that policymakers face.

In territorial economic policy, local, regional and national levels of government each have a major influence on the objectives, instruments and scope of public policy. At the national level there are at least two main questions for policymakers: what are the best policy instruments for fostering urban performance? And how can strong cities be built while ensuring that others are not neglected? (Ronderos, 2009). Economic development strategies in local government, apart from the provision of public goods and services and the application of certain laws and regulations, have been an area of great and growing concern. Local officials attempt to provide the combination of factors that can make a city or metropolitan area economically attractive and active. Generally, local governments seek to retain and attract jobs and investment and to expand their tax base using a battery of strategies to reach these universal objectives of economic development. Some governments also aim to generate the multiplier effect, increase citizens' wages, salaries and social benefits; maintain low and stable unemployment rates; avoid poverty and emigration; and maintain sustainable productive systems (Bartik, 1995).

In a narrow sense, local economic development policy refers to programmes that intervene directly with businesses to encourage local industries and sectors to grow and develop. However, local economic development organisation may be diffused. It can be set up as an independent agency, as a regular local government department, as part of one or more local government departments, or as part of the mayor's office. Moreover, a wide variety of other organisations and actors are involved in economic development programmes and policy implementation: national or intermediate governments, coalitions of governments, chambers of commerce, public organisations, universities and private organisations. Programmes can be funded by a wide variety of sources: local finance, special funds, private contributions, federal and state grants, revenue from property redevelopment, etc. (Bartik, 1995). These factors mean that the organisational structure of local economic policy can be highly specific and complex.

Economic development policy poses difficult issues for local government officials and key policy questions emerge: What should the relative emphasis on different goals be? What instruments are adequate? Are the policies and their instruments cost-effective? (Bartik, 1995). A further consideration is that policymakers have additional goals besides economic development, including the equitable distribution of income (Ronderos, 2009). Bartik (1995) and Ronderos (2009) identify distinct approaches to the design and implementation of economic development strategies which represent general activities under the rubric of economic development. Table 9.4 contains a summary of the objectives, instruments and strategies most frequently used for local economic development policy.

The business-incentive approach, with the objective of attracting investment and creating jobs, has dominated public policy on economic development. A variety of tax instruments fall under the rubric of business incentives and

Table 9.4 Components of local economic development policy

Objectives	Strategies	Instruments
• Increase local employment	• Cluster policies	• Infrastructure improvement
• Increase the local tax base	• Regeneration policies for economic development	• Tax exemptions
• Retain and expand existing business	• Redevelopment of industrial areas to attract additional businesses and investment	• Subsidies and incentives (directly giving money to companies, a percentage of payroll)
• Increase competitiveness	• Sectoral and specialisation change	• Loans or grants to businesses
• Increase wages and social benefits to local citizens	• Place branding	• Assistance with entrepreneurship, exports, applied research projects, technology development programs, employee training, etc.
• Maintain low and stable unemployment rates • Reduce poverty • Sustainability	• Organisation of mega-events	• Advertising and marketing

Source: Based on Bartik (1995) and Ronderos (2009).

exemptions: property tax abatement, tax increment financing, sales tax exemptions and credits, corporate income tax exemptions and credits for investment or jobs, in addition to non-tax incentives such as business grants, loans and loan guarantees. In all of these cases the firm, not the worker or seeker of work, is the initial recipient (Peters & Fishers, 2004).

A widely used programme for economic development is competitiveness policy, which remains prominent on the national and local policy agendas in several countries. Certainly, since the 1980s urban policy has often focused on city competitiveness as a strategy for urban planning and the implementation of urban policies to boost private investment. This paradigm is based on the idea that competitiveness is a highly localised process that promotes specialisation and local efficiency. Competitiveness policies are largely directed at providing a good business climate to compete for investment and human resources. Local subsidies to businesses are commonly justified on the grounds of competitiveness, so this approach can involve a coalition between politicians and business managers. These subsidies reach consensus for most of the urban public policies, but it is the businesses who achieve the greater economic benefits. In this case local governance adopts an entrepreneurial approach. Yet when competitiveness is emphasised as the centre of an economic policy, other relevant internal areas such as quality of life, social inclusion and service provision may be neglected (Arroyo & Sandoval, 2016).

Upgrading the economy to more valuable and productive activities has also been persuasive and has become conventional wisdom in policy circles, influencing government spending priorities. However, this is not necessarily a distinctive approach, as many cities and regions seek to specialise in similar sectors.

In the face of growing economic pressures policymakers have been exploring new ways beyond low labour costs, lower property rents and government subsidies to increase the economic prosperity of their cities. Many devices have been deployed in the attempt to generate greater interest in investment, including city branding and the organisation of mega-events and urban regeneration projects, but there is little agreement on the most cost-effective approach. Differentiation may be seen as more constructive than head-to-head competition or upgrading (Turok, 2009). City branding has been used as a differentiation approach to economic development. This approach integrates economic strategy around a sharper market focus and reposition firms and institutions in new markets (ibid.), and regeneration and internationalisation policies have recently focused on development strategies.

A number of national governments such as those of Japan, Germany, Finland and Norway have also reoriented their economic spatial strategies, developing national policy on regional innovation systems in metropolitan areas, building universities and research centres and implementing major infrastructure projects. Successful urban regeneration policies (e.g. in Bilbao, Kitakyushu and Glasgow) have led to the development of tourism activity and creative industries (OECD & China Development Research Foundation, 2010). However, in other cases 'innovative' city-level strategies have been implemented without critical examination of their relevance to the local situation (Bartik, 1995). These and other policies tend to adopt a *tabula rasa* approach that lacks the necessary understanding to provide solutions for the needs of diverse cities (Ronderos, 2009).

With increasing national and international competition, economic development programmes have become more aggressive, diverse and sophisticated, but little information about them or evaluation of their effectiveness is available. Evaluations are rarely initiated by local officials, and usually claim credit for economic development (Bartik, 1995). According to the OECD & China Development Research Foundation (2010), there have been two, mostly unsuccessful, approaches to the problem of economic development policy: the most traditional relies heavily on attracting investment, and particularly foreign direct investment, through subsidies, tax exceptions and incentives of various kinds; the second approach sets unrealistic objectives for cities. While the former leaves cities vulnerable to investors who are mainly interested in lowering their costs and move on when the subsidy runs out or they find a cheaper location, the latter runs the risk of deciding that cities should develop prestigious high-value-added activities such as high-tech industries and advanced services where there is no prior experience or local production base in the sectors concerned, and it is unrealistic for a city to try to break into global competition based on such economic specialisation.

Bartik (1995) considers that a cost-effective local economic development policy requires careful targeting of the limited public funds and leveraging of private resources because economic development is a diffuse area of policy for which only small amounts of public funds are available. There is also strong polarisation: while funding for local economic development is generally low, some cities are able to spend a significant amount of their financial resources in implementing development policies. As Peters and Fishers (2004) point out, if the most economically depressed states and local governments are not more active in recruiting new investment, then it is because these poorer places have less money to spend on recruitment and incentives.

Offering business incentives has been regarded as the most expensive approach to economic development policy and receives the most intense criticism. Bartik (1995) considers that marketing, streamlining regulations and business problem-solving can be more cost-effective ways of making development happen. In the view of Peters and Fishers (2004), the very high expectations of many public authorities regarding their ability to micromanage economic growth through incentives and subsidies to a degree far beyond anything supported by even the most optimistic evidence has been a fundamental problem; moreover, subsidies seem to be a less technically complicated instrument to implement than other strategies.

In addition to cost-effectiveness and efficiency, other broad issues related to urban economic development policy include the still-limited integration of economic development strategy into wider planning functions (ibid.) and urban policymakers and spatial planners determining that particular economic activities such as information technology, biotechnology and financial services will thrive in a particular region without being guided by market signals (OECD & China Development Research Foundation, 2010). In metropolitan-wide economic policies the same problems emerge, but economic development goals – growth, development and inclusion – require distinct organisational approaches to the implementation of policies, as discussed in the following section.

Economic development policy in metropolitan areas: the role of governance and local political economy

Metropolitan economic development operates over broader geographies than the city and needs to rely on wider institutional collaboration than is usual for local government services and regulatory roles. Because it is not a conventional service delivery activity but involves strategic intervention, it requires different arrangements and often organisational innovation (Clark & Moonen, 2016). Suzuki (1998) underlines that nowhere is improved governance more critical than in metropolitan areas because urban policy and management have not been sufficient to address the pressing issue of economic prosperity.

Individual policies designed to stimulate economic development in metropolitan areas tend to fail because they lack both horizontal coordination between jurisdictions and sectoral coordination in the development strategy (Ronderos, 2009). Uncoordinated strategies waste resources and may fail to achieve the desired outcomes. Economic development efforts should be coordinated across the entire metropolitan area as far as possible. But the extent to which metropolitan economic development is coordinated can vary greatly, depending largely on local political interests (Bartik, 1995). Lewis (2004) argues that the political organisation of the suburban or peripheral portion of the metropolitan area is a potentially important policy determinant. He offers the example of Californian suburbs, which appear to have higher demand for economic development, are more enthusiastic about growth and are more willing to use complex policy tools to advance the development strategy. This situation implies greater competition for central city governments to maintain their preeminence. Formal rules, local political affiliations, partisanship, the form of local elections and the composition of local governments are other political explanations that shape the legal context in metropolitan decision-making (Johnson & Neiman, 2004).

According to Belligni and Ravazzi (2013), in complex and fragmented contexts, such as metropolitan areas:

> urban government cannot be practiced as hierarchical control (power over) by a group of elected decision-makers who impose unilateral decisions, but only as cooperation (power of) between political authorities and social actors. . . . In this perspective, urban decision-making systems ordinarily function as governance arenas where local authorities collaborate with private actors in order to formulate and implement public agendas.

With economic activity spreading beyond the city, the dynamics of metro-politan development require the cooperation from all actors in the metropo-lis. Because decisions made in one jurisdiction of a metropolitan area have consequences in others, some kind of institutional metropolitan arrangements must be established. To promote cooperation and coordination these should be win-win exercises, because without incentives and compensation for the rel-evant stakeholders, institutions will not work and policies will not deliver. This means that whereas government is a fundamental constituent of metropolitan arrangements, multilevel governance – the mobilisation of state and non-state actors – is crucial to meet metropolitan development challenges. Other factors in ensuring cooperation are the availability of reliable financial and human resources, and monitoring and evaluation (Suzuki, 1998).

Cities can adopt any particular arrangement to establish governance prac-tices. The urban regime approach, for instance, emphasises local political choices in understanding urban development, because they affect the social and economic system through the strategic action of local elites. Govern-ance takes place in a process of inducing cooperation between the public and private sectors through the formation of governing coalitions which define the orientation of economic development policy (Kantor, Savitch & Had-dock, 1997). This allows a distinction between pro-welfare and pro-economic growth regimes: pro-welfare regimes aim for equity, social cohesion, citizen empowerment and sometimes environmental sustainability as a strategy for supporting local demand, while in pro-growth urban regimes the main goal is economic growth and the strategic priority is to create a good business cli-mate to attract investment, high-value companies, managerial functions, skilled workers, the creative class and tourists by implementing supply-side policies (Belligni & Ravazzi, 2013).

Once more, discussions of how to manage metropolitan areas better revolves principally around a spectrum of governance schemes. In practice most existing metropolitan arrangements tend to respond to the lack of cooperation among local jurisdictions. These schemes usually bring solutions to problems affect-ing social and economic conditions, but do not explicitly provide a hands-on approach to an economic development strategy for the entire metropolitan area.

One practice for a collaborative framework aimed at facilitating a clear and coherent strategy for metropolitan economic development has been the crea-tion of a metropolitan development agency to integrate an area-wide economic development strategy into a wider governance system and facilitate the coor-dination of actors involved in economic development policies. In the OECD, Montreal and London offer two examples of a wider metropolitan governance reform process. The Metropolitan Community of Montreal is a metro-wide agency responsible for the planning and coordination of a number of met-ropolitan functions including economic development. The London Develop-ment Agency produces the Economic Development Strategy and implements economic development policies for the whole metropolitan region (Kamal &

Spiezia, 2004). However, policy responses to metropolitan development have not been adopted across all countries.

There is widespread agreement that metropolitan areas that have established cooperative arrangements designed to produce area-wide collective action are better equipped to improve their performance, and often unlock significant development potential (OECD, 2015a). While there is this consensus on the need for area-wide structures with legal capacity and authority, it is also clear that a uniform model cannot work for all cities, even within a single country (MacLennan, 2009).

In Mexico not only economic but also territorial, social and environmental challenges have drawn attention to the urgent need for effective metropolitan governance systems that facilitate coordination across levels of government and provide effective mechanisms for decision-making on the territorial and economic development of its cities and regions. But there is a gap between the growing expansion of cities on the one hand and metropolitan institutional development on the other. Metropolitan governance relies heavily on municipal authorities and real estate developers. Municipalities in metropolitan areas struggle with new responsibilities placed on them by higher levels of government, with weak public finances and with the increasingly complex planning challenges that arise from jurisdictional questions. Current legal frameworks reduce any possibility of metropolitan coordination to voluntary intermunicipal arrangement, where political will and the autonomy promoted by the decentralisation process remain essential constraints.

Although several government bodies have begun to address metropolitan planning, for instance, through the establishment of metropolitan coordination bodies in some metropolitan areas, the revision of the General Law of Human Settlements and the creation of a national Metropolitan Fund, metropolitan management and policy lack operative coordination bodies. The more challenging questions of how municipalities can best work together, particularly in the area of economic development, remain. Although there have been some relatively successful experiences of metropolitan coordination in the Monterrey and Guadalajara metropolitan areas (see Chapter 8), coordination has been achieved through the regional power of the state government and it has worked primarily to provide urban services more efficiently rather than to establish an explicit economic development strategy.

This absence of metropolitan public policy can be a significant factor contributing to productive inefficiency and low productivity in metropolitan areas and the country. Coordination and collective decision-making on metropolitan public policies require consensus-building, political cooperation, political settlement and will supported by corresponding policies, reforms and legal frameworks. State actors on various spatial scales, local businesses, global companies, real estate and construction companies, and local civil society can exert their influence on reform processes, but the lack of coordination demonstrates important imbalances of power.

Towards a public policy agenda for metropolitan economic development

There is unquestionably the need for change in the paradigms of metropolitan spatial policy. Since economic globalisation and the subsequent intensification of competition placed urban economic competitiveness at the top of the urban policy agenda, increasing attention has centred on policies and governance, particularly in the field of spatial development (OECD & China Development Research Foundation, 2010). Yet metropolitan areas are far from consolidation as a policy object because they are constantly being redefined and are frequently contested as a scale. Governments and institutions have had limited capacity and power within often ambiguous institutional frameworks. In this last section I call for research and policy agendas to work together to analyse the economic, political, social and legal dynamics of metropolitan areas in depth and to formulate well-informed public policies and strategies on the metropolitan scale.

Designing urban and metropolitan policy programmes that empower metropolitan areas as productive forces and spaces of economic restructuring is particularly relevant to overall development. Metropolitan economic development initiatives are difficult to execute in many countries because of weak governance conditions, uncompetitive local industries and other limited resources (Clark & Moonen, 2016). There are concerns that increasing decentralisation and fiscal constraints lead to the transfer of responsibilities across a wide range of policy sectors to cities and metropolitan areas, affecting their competitiveness and performance. These transfers are generally not accompanied by the necessary financial capacity or the ability to raise local taxes, thus putting pressure on municipal finances (OECD, 2001). Despite these financial and institutional constraints, all actors need to adapt, learn and reorganise for economic development to happen. Policy and research can guide such efforts.

Policy and the research agendas should work together, based on agreement about the relevant issues and taking into consideration some key general precepts about metropolitan policy:

- National, intermediate and local governments need to be empowered to deal with and manage metropolitan areas through the development of laws, institutional structures and agencies that guide their governance.
- Given the importance of NUPs, a combination of bottom-up and top-down approaches is needed.
- Political, power control and jurisdictional issues influence the policy and governance of metropolitan areas.
- Innovative fiscal and financial arrangements are needed to boost the public finances of metropolitan areas.
- Coordination, collaboration and cooperation mechanisms are required to address economic, social, environmental and institutional issues.
- Contextual differences should be considered, and governance, planning and public finance approaches should be implemented based on the precept that 'no one size fits all'.

- Policy design for metropolitan areas should include flexibility and complementarity with other policies.
- Most metropolitan areas have inadequate local data on which to base strategic decisions: statistical departments and agencies that collect data should accompany plans for metropolitan reform.
- Increased research on metropolitan issues is needed.

Some more general principles should also be considered when designing and implementing economic development agendas:

- Macroeconomic policy should be linked to metropolitan economic strategies.
- Metropolitan economic policy must be linked to other areas of urban development (social, environmental, urban planning, etc.).
- Performance indicators are needed.
- Metropolitan areas need to set realistic goals and to design effective incentives to encourage economic activity and job creation.
- Appropriate public services, infrastructure and urban conditions are needed to support economic development.
- Working on skills and distinctiveness is essential for efficient policy.

Lastly, Clark and Moonen (2016) argue that the agenda of inclusion is neither optional nor secondary to the pursuit of economic growth and efficiency, and in fact helps to create more innovative governance and economies in metropolitan areas. This brings up the recurring question of the definition and scope of economic development, which is usually confined to growth and efficiency. Matters such as sustainability and inclusiveness must also be included in the economic development agenda and analysis.

Despite these general guidelines, policy programmes and agendas are case-specific because each experience is shaped by unique historical, institutional, political, economic and social factors. In Mexico extensive urban and metropolitan reform is needed before any coherent effort can be made to deliver an economic strategy for its metropolitan areas. This reform must at least include legal recognition of metropolitan areas, a clear definition of governments' responsibilities, compulsory intermunicipal and interstate government coordination in metropolitan areas, alignment and coordination between sectors, and fiscal and financial reform to give each metropolitan area an adequate structure. In addition, an NUP that reflects the country's high urbanisation and increasing metropolisation is needed to support metropolitan reform and policy.

Given the current economic performance of metropolitan areas in Mexico, the specific strategies for each one should be highly differentiated. In the case of big metropolitan areas that are not growing fast but are very important in terms of population and output (e.g. Mexico City and Guadalajara), the problem of declining economic performance must be addressed. In particular, Mexico

City – which lost part of its manufacturing base due to macroeconomic policy changes in the 1980s – has positioned itself as the national centre for specialised services and commerce with the important role of linking the country with the rest of the world; it needs to strengthen this position and introduce ground-breaking economic development strategies to improve its business environment.

We know that improving the economic performance of metropolitan areas requires adequate governance and policies. These, in turn, depend on the country's institutional and financial framework, the design of intergovernmental relations and local circumstances and structures. In Mexico these endow public actors with limited and unequal powers and resources, hindering good urban management and improved performance: the forecast is one of protracted metropolitan reform.

Note

1 http://habitat3.org/documents-and-archive/preparatory-documents/policy-papers/.

References

Arroyo, J. J. & Sandoval, E. E. (2016). *Competitiveness of metropolitan zones in Mexico: A conceptual assessment.* Tokyo: Institute for Economic Studies, Seijo University. Available at: www. seijo.ac.jp/research/economics/publications/reserch-report/jtmo420000000mul-att/ keiken_green73_1.pdf.

Bartik, T. J. (1995). *Economic development strategies.* Upjohn Institute Working Paper No. 95–33. Kalamazoo, MI: Upjohn Institute for Employment Research. Available at: https://doi. org/10.17848/wp95-33.

Belligni, S. & Ravazzi, S. (2013). 'Policy change without metamorphosis: The 1993–2011 urban regime in Turin'. *Métropoles*, 12. Available at: http://journals.openedition.org/metro poles/4642.

Caprotti, F. et al. (2017). 'The new urban agenda: Key opportunities and challenges for policy and practice'. *Urban Research & Practice*, 10(3), 367–378. Available at: www.tandfonline. com/doi/full/10.1080/17535069.2016.1275618.

Clark, G. & Moonen, T. (2016). *The role of metropolitan areas in the global agenda of local and regional governments for the 21st century.* Working paper for the preparation of the 4th Global report on local democracy and decentralization (GOLD). Available at: www.gold.uclg. org/sites/default/files/BoC_Report.pdf.

Cohen, M. (2015). *Urban economic challenges and the new urban agenda.* United Nations Human Settlements Programme, Urban Economy and Finance Branch. Nairobi: UN-Habitat. Available at: https://unhabitat.org/wp-content/uploads/2016/03/Urban%20Economy%20 Paper.pdf.

De Souza, F. F. & Barcelo, J. (2016). 'Metropolitan issues and the new urban agenda'. *Policy in Focus*, 13(3), 34–36. Available at: www.ipc-undp.org/pub/eng/PIF37_A_new_urban_par adigm_pathways_to_sustainable_development.pdf.

Garza, G. (1999). 'Global economy, metropolitan dynamics and urban policies in Mexico'. *Cities*, 16(3), 149–170. Available at: https://doi.org/10.1016/S0264-2751(99)00013-X.

HIC. (2016). *Hábitat I, Hábitat II, Hábitat III: Habitat international coalition.* Mexico City. Available at: http://hic-gs.org/content/HIC_Habitat%201976%202016%20ES.pdf.

Kamal Chaoui, L. & Spiezia,V. (2004). 'Metropolitan governance and economic competitiveness'. *Urban Public Economics Review*, (2), 41–62. Available at: www.redalyc.org/articulo. oa?id=50400202.

Kantor, P., Savitch,V. H. & Haddock, S.V. (1997). 'The political economy of urban regimes: A comparative perspective'. *Urban Affairs Review*, 32(3), 348–377. Available at: https://doi. org/10.1177/107808749703200303.

Lewis, P. G. (2004). 'An old debate confronts new realities: Large suburbs and economic development in the metropolis'. In Feiock, R. C. (ed.). *Metropolitan governance: Conflict, competition, and cooperation.* Washington, D.C.: Georgetown University Press, pp. 95–123.

MacLennan, D. (2009). *Place policy, planning and new strategies for metropolitan management.* Report for Auckland Regional Council, Research and Evaluation Unit. Available at: http://knowledgeauckland.org.nz/assets/publications/Place_Policy_Planning_And_ New_Strategies_For_Metropolitan_Management.pdf.

Johnson, M. & Neiman, M. (2004). 'Courting business: Competition for economic development among cities'. In Feiock, R. C. (ed.). *Metropolitan governance: Conflict, competition, and cooperation.* Washington, D.C.: Georgetown University Press, pp. 124–146.

OECD. (2001). *Cities for citizens: Improving metropolitan governance.* Paris: OECD Publishing. Available at: https://doi.org/10.1787/9789264189843-en.

OECD. (2015a). *The metropolitan century: Understanding urbanisation and its consequences.* Paris: OECD Publishing. Available at: http://dx.doi.org/10.1787/9789264228733-en.

OECD. (2015b). 'Urban policy for more competitive, sustainable Mexican Cities'. In *OECD urban policy reviews: Mexico 2015: Transforming urban policy and housing finance.* Paris: OECD Publishing. Available at: http://dx.doi.org/10.1787/9789264227293-7-en.

OECD. (2017). *National urban policy in OECD countries.* Paris: OECD Publishing. Available at: http://dx.doi.org/10.1787/9789264271906-en.

OECD & China Development Research Foundation. (2010). *Trends in urbanisation and urban policies in OECD countries: What lessons for China?* Paris: OECD Publishing. Available at: https://doi.org/10.1787/9789264092259-en.

Peters, A. & Fisher, P. (2004). 'The failures of economic development incentives'. *Journal of the American Planning Association*, 70(1), 27–37. Available at: https://doi. org/10.1080/01944360408976336.

Rodríguez, A. & Sugranyes, A. (2017). 'La nueva agenda urbana: Pensamiento mágico'. *Hábitat y Sociedad*, 10, 165–180. Available at: https://doi.org/10.18537/est.v007.n014.a09.

Ronderos, L. N. (2009). 'Spatial strategies for U.S. economic development'. In Todorovich, P. & Hagler,Y. (eds.). *New strategies for regional economic development.* Cambridge, MA: Lincoln Institute of Land Policy, pp. 20–27. Available at: www.america2050.org/pdf/2050_ Report_Regional_Economic_Development_2009.pdf.

Satterthwaite, D. (2016). 'Successful, safe and sustainable cities: Towards a new urban commonwealth'. *Journal of Local Governance*, 19, 3–18. Available at: https://epress.lib.uts.edu. au/journals/index.php/cjlg/article/view/5446.

Shah, P., Hamilton, E., Armendaris, F. & Lee, H. (2015). *World-inclusive cities approach paper.* Report No. AUS8539. Washington, D.C.: World Bank Group. Available at: http://documents. worldbank.org/curated/en/402451468169453117/World-Inclusive-cities-approach-paper.

Suzuki, I. (1998). 'Metropolitan governance: Strategies for capacity building'. *Asian Review of Public Administration*, X(1–2), 285–297. Available at: http://unpan1.un.org/intradoc/ groups/public/documents/EROPA/UNPAN001434.pdf.

Trejo, A. (2017). *Localización manufacturera, apertura comercial y disparidades regionales en México.* México, D. F.: El Colegio de Mexico. Available at: www.jstor.org/stable/j.ctv1fxg2x.

Turok, I. (2009). 'The distinctive city: Pitfalls in the pursuit of differential advantage'. *Environment and Planning A: Economy and Space*, 41(1), 13–30. Available at: https://doi.org/10.1068/a37379.

UN. (2015). *Resolution adopted by the General Assembly on 25 September 2015*. Transforming our world: The 2030 Agenda for Sustainable Development. Seventieth session, United Nations, General Assembly. New York: United Nations. Available at: www.un.org/en/development/desa/population/migration/generalassembly/docs/globalcompact/A_RES_70_1_E.pdf.

UN. (2016a). *Draft outcome document of the United Nations Conference on Housing and Sustainable Urban Development (Habitat III)*. *United Nations Conference on Housing and Sustainable Urban Development (Habitat III)*. Quito: United Nations. Available at: http://nua.unhabitat.org/uploads/DraftOutcomeDocumentofHabitatIII_en.pdf.

UN. (2016b). *Habitat III Policy Paper 7: Urban economic development strategies*. United Nations Conference on Housing and Sustainable Urban Development (Habitat III), Quito: United Nations. Available at: https://webdosya.csb.gov.tr/csb/dokumanlar/mpgm0037.pdf.

UN. (2017). *The New Urban Agenda: Quito declaration on sustainable cities and human settlements for all*. United Nations Conference on Housing and Sustainable Urban Development (Habitat III). Quito: United Nations. Available at: http://habitat3.org/wp-content/uploads/NUA-English-With-Index-1.pdf.

UN-Habitat & OECD. (2018). *Global state of national urban policy*. Nairobi: United Nations Human Settlements Programme. Available at: http://dx.doi.org/10.1787/9789264290747-en.

World Bank. (1991). *Urban policy and economic development: An agenda for the 1990s*. Report No. 9576. Washington, D.C.: The World Bank. Available at: http://documents.worldbank.org/curated/en/914681468765339416/Urban-policy-and-economic-development-an-agenda-for-the-1990s.

Yaro, R. D. (2009). 'Toward a national reinvestment strategy for underperforming regions'. In Todorovich, P. & Hagler, Y. (eds.). *New strategies for regional economic development*. Cambridge, MA: Lincoln Institute of Land Policy, pp. 13–19. Available at: www.america2050.org/pdf/2050_Report_Regional_Economic_Development_2009.pdf.

Conclusions

Throughout history and across the world, urbanisation has proceeded in a non-linear fashion, advancing in some regions and stagnating or declining in others at different times. In the first decades of the twenty-first century this non-linearity is expressed in a variety of global trends and patterns, with today's urbanisation significantly different to that of the past. While urbanisation is a predominant fact in the world, there is limited information about *how* urbanisation, urban growth and urban expansion have evolved across different countries in the world, and in specific nations. Moreover, the intersection between urbanisation and development has not yet been studied extensively in particular contexts. In this book I have identified and discussed the most prominent issues facing Mexico's current urban trajectory, stressing the increasing predominance of its metropolitan areas, the relevance of the economic facet of urban development and the role of local political, demographic and economic dynamics in shaping its urban reality. Drawing on a documental review, empirical evidence and previous research, I have analysed metropolitan economic development of Mexico in the context of its economic, political and urban transition.

A multiscale outlook on urbanisation, urban development and economic performance has allowed me to make a comparative assessment of international urbanisation and metropolitan expansion; discuss urbanisation, the urban system, and the progression of the metropolitan phenomenon in Mexico; analyse the patterns, trends and drivers of economic development in its metropolitan areas, including their public finances; explain the metropolitan process and urban structure in Mexico City; compare the governance frameworks of specific city functions via case studies of different metropolitan areas in Mexico and Latin American; and survey diverse aspects of metropolitan economic policy and governance.

In these Conclusions, I review the main analytical assumptions in the light of a posteriori understanding of the topics discussed in the book, summarise the main findings, present the key implications and discuss the research and policy prospects.

From generalisations to diverse international evidence

For analytical purposes, this book began with a set of three generalisations that have often been in urban studies. The first sees the world as bifurcated into two sets of countries with different urbanisation paths. On the one hand, urbanisation occurred relatively rapidly in developed countries (i.e. in Western Europe and the US) during the Industrial Revolution of the mid-eighteenth century. The early urbanisation of this comparatively small set of countries was strongly associated with industrialisation and economic growth (Bairoch & Goertz, 1986). On the other hand, a big move to urbanisation has been spreading in numerous developing countries since the second half of the twentieth century. Three major features differentiate urbanisation in the developing nations from that in Europe and the US: in the former, compared to the developed countries, urbanisation is occurring more rapidly; more countries and larger numbers of people are involved; and it is less closely connected to income growth (UN, 2014; OECD, 2015; Fox & Goodfellow, 2016).

The second generalisation concerns the specific urbanisation path in the Latin American region which, as in other rapidly urbanising regions in the developing world, has not necessarily gone hand in hand with economic growth and development. Yet urbanisation in the region stands out in several ways: it is already 80 per cent urbanised, slightly higher than Europe (UN, 2018); the region became demographically urban within less than two generations due to the urban explosion in the 1940s (Lattes, 2000; Pinto da Cunha, 2002; Cerrutti & Bertoncello, 2003; UN-Habitat, 2012); compared to other regions in the world it has the highest urban primacy in the world (Chant & McIlwaine, 2009); and Latin America's cities exhibit several of the worst symptoms of underdevelopment (UN-Habitat, 2012; Klaufus & Jaffe, 2015; CEPAL, ONU-Habitat & MINURVI, 2016; Vargas et al., 2017; Jordan, Riffo & Prado, 2017).

The third generalisation refers to the rise of the metropolitan age. In both developed and developing countries, recent urbanisation has been connected to the geographical expansion of cities and urban sprawl. Metropolitan areas are emerging as functional economies that exceed both the administrative limits of the city and the jurisdictional scope of local authorities, with labour markets covering several municipalities and sometimes more than one state or province.

These generalisations were instrumental in introducing in this book the historical analysis of international urbanisation tendencies and patterns. However, as discussed in Chapters 1 and 2, generalisation conceals the wide diversity that we are witnessing today. These chapters discussed the considerable variation in the processes and levels of urbanisation across regions and countries, depending not only on location but also on income level and historic trajectories. In 2018 North America and Latin America and the Caribbean had the highest levels of urbanisation, at 82 and 81 per cent respectively, while Sub-Saharan Africa (40 per cent) and South Asia (36 per cent) remained mostly rural. Although Latin America's level of urbanisation is similar to that of North America's, it is high in the Southern Cone and Mexico, intermediate in the Andean region, and intermediate to low in Central America, with wide variation across the Caribbean countries (UN-Habitat, 2012). Similar variation can be found in Asia, for instance. In 2016, high-income countries were 81.5 per cent urbanised, followed by upper-middle-income (66.6 per cent) and middle-income countries (52.6 per cent); lower-middle-income (40.6 percent) and low-income countries (32.2 per cent) remained mostly rural.

The world's urban population is concentrated in just a few countries. China (758 million) and India (410 million) together accounted for 30 per cent of the urban population in 2018; and with the US (263 million), Brazil (173 million), Indonesia (134 million), Japan (118 million) and Russia (105 million) they comprised more than half of the world's urban population. Regionally, nearly 47 per cent of the world's urban residents are concentrated in East and South Asia, while Latin America and the Caribbean account for 14.3 per cent. Middle-income countries concentrate the greatest share of the world's urban population at 41.7 per cent. Although most urban dwellers live in urban centres of less than 300,000 inhabitants, over time the urban population has been absorbed mainly by megacities and cities with a population of 1 to 5 million. Outstandingly, 25 per cent of the world's population lives in supersized metropolitan areas that cut across jurisdictional boundaries.

Metropolitan expansion around the world has also been heterogeneous. Beyond some shared general characteristics, the size, shape and functioning of metropolitan areas vary considerably between the North and the South, and metropolisation has spread more intensely in the South, where metropolitan areas are becoming the territorial framework that prevails in processes of urbanisation and development. In fact, the size and growth of metropolitan areas in the South, where megacities of unprecedented size are multiplying, have now surpassed those of the developed world (Klaufus & Jaffe, 2015). In 2015 there were six megacities in China and four in India, with seven more in Asia, and Cairo, Kinshasa and Lagos in Africa. Latin America has four megacities, and the populations of Bogota and Lima are projected to grow beyond 10 million by 2030 to join Buenos Aires, Mexico City, Rio de Janeiro and Sao Paulo (UN, 2018).

In metropolitan areas in the Global South a significant proportion of their inhabitants live in irregular self-built settlements, and economic informality, poverty, segregation and spatial inequalities predominate (Sellers & Hoffmann-Martinot, 2008). While these metropolitan areas are commanding an increasingly dominant role in their national economies, their rapid urbanisation, expansion and urban growth seriously exceed their capacity to provide adequate services, jobs and infrastructure for their citizens (Cohen, 2006).[1]

Latin America is the clearest example of lost agglomeration advantages and metropolitan underdevelopment. Its patterns and trends are historically distinct from those of other developing regions. Urbanisation occurred earlier and more rapidly and is now at the level of advanced economies. Historic and contemporary urbanisation in Latin America is characterised by excessive urban primacy.

Compared to other regions of the world, distribution of the urban population by size is marked by the outstanding importance of megacities. Whereas cities with over 10 million inhabitants house around 15 per cent of Latin America's urban population, in Asia they house 13.4 per cent, in Africa 9.3 per cent and in North America 10.4 per cent. In addition, Latin America's large cities (1 to 5 million inhabitants) include more than a quarter of the region's urban population, a higher proportion than in any other region. Despite its substantial demographic concentration in megacities and large cities, countries in the region face significant economic and social pressure. Notwithstanding the relative importance of the largest cities as the engines of their national economies, it seems that economic growth and urbanisation do not reinforce one another at the national level. Moreover, Latin American cities are often regarded as the most unequal and most dangerous cities in the world, with social, economic and spatial divisions deeply rooted in urban society. Environmental deterioration and vulnerability to natural disasters are issues of rising importance.

In Chapter 2 I discussed the processes of historical-structural urban transformation in Latin America and how demographic, economic and political shifts have had major influences on the shaping of those urban challenges. Largely, unsuccessful industrial strategies at the macro level and lack of adequate urban planning and policies, mainly at the local level, have been blamed for the Latin America's urbanisation failure.

Within Latin America there is substantial heterogeneity, which may be accounted for by variations in different countries' implementation of economic models and demographic transitions. There appears to be some links between urbanisation and urban transitions, economic development and country size. I have argued that local social, legal, political and institutional arrangements explain the variability in urban development across countries and across cities in national urban systems.

The notion of the urban land nexus allowed me to pay attention to the specificities of local history, territory and politics in this study of urbanisation and development in Mexico. Using Mexico as a case study I provided an example of what happens to the urban and economic development of a country when the growth, complexity and expansion of its urban areas outpace the development of governance and institutional structures for managing them. This is typically found in metropolitan areas, which are multiplying in this already highly urbanised country. Chapters 3 to 8 presented the complex picture of Mexico's metropolitan reality and the economic development of its cities. In Chapter 9 a policy-oriented review was useful for the evaluation urban policies and governance. In the following sections I summarise the main findings.

Urban expansion and metropolisation

Observable trends in several Mexican cities illustrate that in the twenty-first century Mexico, like other developed and developing countries, is on its way to the 'metropolitan age', which began in cities such as Mexico City, Monterrey, Torreon, Tampico and Orizaba in the 1940s. Chapter 3 discussed the process of urban dispersal and its drivers. These include demographic factors (immigration and natural growth), economic factors (the suburbanisation of industrial economic activity and commerce), politics (clientelism, political leadership and vote capture) and policy (inadequate urban planning and weak enforcement), as well as land and housing market issues (limited availability of private land, irregular occupation and invasion, illegal sale of social land, cheaper land and house prices on the periphery, social housing construction, middle- and high-income gated housing complexes and self-build housing).

The land and housing sectors have contributed enormously to urban expansion. Due to the scarcity of private land, from the 1950s onwards, social land, and particularly ejidos, began to change hands to become, illegally or irregularly, private property which was incorporated into urban expansion in various modalities. In the second half of the twentieth century the low-income population drove substantial change in cities. Despite the land-ownership regime and regulations to control urban expansion, irregular ejido land transactions and invasions by poor urban dwellers were major factors in urban expansion. The commercialisation of land in a highly speculative environment and illegal and irregular occupation became the only way for broad sectors of the population to access housing in a situation with a growing need of housing and lack of accessible credit (Ziccardi, 2016).

The land tenure regime contributes to an explanation of the particular shapes and sizes of cities in this period. At the centre of the story is the composition of private, public and social land ownership, of which the latter comprises a large proportion and includes communal land, usually owned by indigenous communities or towns of indigenous origin, and ejidos, pieces of land expropriated after the Mexican Revolution for distribution among peasants. Before the 1990s ejido owners were not allowed to sell or rent their land. This feature of Mexico's land tenure regime is the distinguishing factor in its urbanisation that shaped the urban land nexus.

The functioning of both the legal and the irregular real estate markets was supported by political structures and corruption, with political parties seeking the votes of low-income settlers. In opposition to the idea of an anarchic and spontaneous process, urban expansion through the occupation of land followed the logic of the economic and political interests of agrarian leaders, local and national government officials, real estate agents and politicians. Clientelism and electoral politics were at the centre of the local politics of urban dispersal.

In the late twentieth century the National Housing Policy, based on deregulation and privatisation, led to important changes in the form and intensity of residential expansion in several cities. The ejido regime was modified so that under certain conditions ejidos could be traded. The construction of social housing in the form of large developments of identical, frequently small, tract houses for waged workers contributed substantially to urban sprawl. Social housing developments generally comprise low-quality houses with poor access to services and infrastructure. Local governments frequently grant construction permits without supervising the enforcement of legal regulations. To a smaller extent, expansion has also included real estate developments for the middle and upper classes. In these ways there has been a change from land-grabbing to developer-driven urbanisation.

This transition in the land and housing markets changed the political economy of urbanisation and urban expansion. National policy, market forces and local corruption reshaped the power balance in the urban expansion politics. Governments and other political structures have exploited discretionary powers to their own benefit. This simply brought a change from clientelism (offering protection against eviction or access to cheap and irregular land in return for political support) to more subtle forms of patronage practice, frequently compounded by rent-seeking behaviour, in the land and housing markets.

In 2015, 74 metropolitan areas were identified in Mexico, with a total of 75 million inhabitants, representing 63 per cent of the country's total population. Most metropolitan areas are in the centre and north of the country, with a high concentration of urban dwellers especially in Mexico City and the 'millionaire' metropolitan areas; that is, metropolitan areas with population of over 1 million inhabitants but lower than 5 million. Based on population data for 2015, the rank-size rule was confirmed, indicating a significant primacy in the urban system. Mexico City Metropolitan Area (MCMA) has remained as a primate city despite an important reorganisation of the urban system from the 1980s onwards, partly due to changing demographic dynamics and partly in response to various government measures to restructure the economy: population growth in the biggest metropolitan areas slowed while medium-sized metropolitan areas with seaports and those at the US border grew more rapidly, and urban growth was strongly related to new patterns of migration including increased inter-metropolitan flows.

Metropolitan economic development and finance

In Chapter 4 the assessment of indicators referring to the geographic distribution of production, productivity and efficiency, specialisation, informality and poverty across metropolitan areas provided a comprehensive panorama of their economic performance. Economic activity is very unevenly distributed across the Mexico's urban system, with a significant geographical concentration of jobs and production in the largest metropolitan areas, MCMA, Monterrey and Guadalajara. The import substitution industrialisation (ISI) model strongly fostered a centralised spatial pattern, making MCMA the heart of the national economy. The shift in the economic model and the industrial strategy of the 1980s, which included trade liberalisation, led to a change in the location patterns of the manufacturing industry, which now sought to take advantage of the improved access to the US market. Industrial relocation resulted in a group of winning metropolitan areas in the northeast of the country due to its links to the US economy, in the Mexican Gulf for its oil-related activity, and in the

Bajio region owing to its locational advantage and emerging specialised productive infrastructure.

Although shifts in its macroeconomic policies impacted on Mexico's economic geography, the spatial relocation of production did not modify the rankings of the largest metropolitan areas, that is, MCMA, Monterrey, Guadalajara, Puebla and Toluca, which together accounted for 55.2 per cent of the country's total gross metropolitan output in 2013. While the combined share of metropolitan output from the largest economies has fallen, due to decreases in MCMA and Guadalajara, two geographic concentration indexes reveal only a minor deconcentration of production between 1998 and 2008 before stabilising until 2013. A number of maquiladora and manufacturing centres in the north of the country which had initially benefited from trade openness, including Ciudad Juarez and Tijuana, have been losing their relative importance. Other metropolitan areas in the centre of the country and very close to MCMA – Puebla, Toluca and especially Queretaro – have experienced consistent progress. Tourist poles such as Cancun, Puerto Vallarta and Acapulco, which also saw a boom in the 1990s and at the beginning of this century, are decreasing in relevance. Metropolitan areas with oil-related industrial activity are a special group with high gross production but also high instability in their economic variables.

With regard to per capita output, MCMA is not well positioned. In contrast, in Queretaro and Monterrey output per capita is relatively high and increasing. MCMA has been the relatively efficient over time but as with most metropolitan areas it shows deteriorating productivity and efficiency, prompting questions about the beneficial effects of urban agglomeration. These productive efficiency deficits are not limited to the city level: the country as a whole has experienced significant deterioration in this area.

In contrast to some economic successes and improved average wellbeing, the poverty rates vary but are generally greater than 20 per cent, with the largest cities tending to a below-average incidence of poverty and most smaller cities being above the average of 40 per cent. This shows that inclusive development is still to be achieved in all of Mexico's metropolises. Cities in Mexico are becoming more service based, but relative specialisation is mostly oriented towards some traditional manufacturing industries, with the exception of MCMA which specialises in more advanced services. The clear division between the formal and the informal economy is another prominent feature of metropolitan areas in the country.

Cities attract businesses and residents by providing high-quality amenities, urban services and infrastructure, and other incentives. But providing these requires funding, for which various sources are used, including public, private and financial resources from the community itself. Balancing urban needs with the funding required is a problem characteristic of metropolitan areas. Chapter 5 highlighted public finances for urban and economic development as an increasingly relevant area of concern. I have argued that jurisdictional fragmentation in metropolitan areas creates a mismatch between the territorial scope of urban needs and the geographical scope of the public resources required to fulfil those needs. This is occurring in the overall context of constrained public budgets and local authorities being asked to do more with less. This is a daunting challenge for metropolitan areas because the availability, allocation and management of public financial resources define their ability to achieve their economic and social development objectives.

While developed countries have paid more attention to financing their metropolitan areas by granting special revenue-raising powers, instituting special intergovernmental transfer arrangements and conferring state-level status on metropolitan authorities, those in less-developed countries whose expenditure and revenue regimes are highly centralised depend less on local taxation and more on transfers. Chapter 5 has drawn attention to the critical need for a more metropolitan-sensitive approach to public finances and pinpointed guidelines for a normative model of metropolitan public finances. Fiscal and financial reforms are necessary to enhance metropolitan institutions' fiscal powers and financial autonomy and improve expenditure and revenue models for metropolitan-wide efficiency.

Like several other countries in the less-developed world, Mexico lacks the fiscal and transfer systems needed for metropolitan areas. Allocation of responsibilities, functions and financial resources is based on prevailing political-administrative structures. The current legal framework confers the provision of basic urban services and of financing that provision on municipal governments. Metropolitan finances are fragmented and usually uncoordinated, affecting their performance. Moreover, over the years financial and fiscal decentralisation has revealed a precarious federal design in terms of vertical balance, competition and autonomy, as well as a lack of coordination mechanisms. States and municipalities' own-revenue bases remain weak, and subnational governments are heavily dependent on federal transfers and less reliant on their own revenues. Municipalities in particular maintained a subordinate position and have developed very little their administrative, technical and human capabilities (Diaz, 2015). For the most part they face severe financial and fiscal constraints, as well as the increasing devolution of responsibilities, including economic development activities, to local government.

My assessment of public finances finds that despite the clear differences between metropolitan and non-metropolitan municipalities, mainly in the composition of revenue and spending and the dynamism of their different items, the wide-ranging trends reported in previous studies of Mexico's municipal finances are also largely confirmed at the metropolitan level. These patterns include increasing federal transfers and declining own revenues, in contrast to OECD countries; growing current and administrative expenditure in relation to investment spending; and a boom in public debt. There are, however, fiscal disparities across metropolitan areas. MCMA and other big metropolises stand out with their higher fiscal capacity due to collection of own resources via property taxes, and greater financial autonomy as they are less dependent on federal transfers.

Using indicators of financial dependence, capacity and leverage I have established a typology of metropolitan areas' financial performance. Less than half fall in the 'financial health' and 'stable' categories, demonstrating the problematic financial situation of the rest. Ten of Mexico's metropolises are in the worst position, 'high vulnerability', which describes a situation of low financial capacity, high dependency and high financial leverage. An important proportion of cities have 'financial weakness' and a 'propensity for financial instability'. In light of these findings, the questions of fiscal reform and a metropolitan-area-sensitive fiscal structure for Mexico remain critically important to support urban development strategies and wellbeing.

The low productivity and growth in Mexican cities have been attributed to several factors. Poor educational attainment, weak institutions, deficient infrastructure and connectivity all play a significant role in shaping their productive potential. Decision-making structures and coordination can also make a difference. In Chapter 6 a number of variables were tested in a model to assess their influence on productivity and per capita production. Capital accumulation, size, specialisation, human capital, institutions, public finances, urban spatial structure and territorial organisation were included as the factors driving the economic performance of cities in 2008 and 2013.

The results of the econometric estimations revealed the important role of traditional factors, such as physical capital accumulation, human capital and specialisation, formal employment and financial autonomy, in improving productivity. The presence of cultural and entertainment services does not appear to improve economic performance, but restricts urban productivity. It is particularly odd that city size, the presence of financial services, public debt leverage, connectivity, violence and fragmentation are not statistically significant. On the other hand, GDP per capita correlates only with capital accumulation, human capital and city size. Findings showing that city size is not significant in accounting for productivity clearly reveal the missing benefits of agglomeration economies in Mexican cities. Economic performance remains a fundamental problem that requires consideration of metropolitan areas in their own context, which is politically and administratively different to that of traditional cities.

Metropolitan structures, governance and policy

In Chapter 7 I assessed the urban transformation of Mexico City and the territorial changes that have occurred over the past century. Its economic function and productive structure were depicted, and the prevailing urban structure was identified. The chapter also reviewed the governance frame in which metropolitan development takes place. As described in Chapter 3, the transformation of Mexican cities began with the increasing commodification of urban land, the illegal and irregular occupation of land and informal housing developments predominating as a mechanism of urban expansion. This was replaced by the gradual proliferation of different forms of real estate production, mainly linked to the operations of the financial sector, in response to the reorientation of housing policies, which shifted the responsibility for providing social housing from the state to private actors, and the modification of the land-tenure regime. The functioning of these two models portrays the urban processes that took place in MCMA, where most of the irregular low-income housing has spread into the urban periphery, mainly in the neighbouring State of Mexico which lacks sufficient infrastructure to cater for the needs of the new residents.

Some local public policies targeting the densification of central areas of the city contributed to this peripheral expansion by activating the selective modernisation of certain neighbourhoods in the central city, resulting in a substantial increase in house prices there; this urban renovation and housing replacement chiefly favoured the middle and upper-middle classes, and triggered widespread gentrification. Territorial expansion of the metropolitan area continues integrating an increasing number of residential developments further from the city centre, which usually function as dormitory zones. Some expansion is also advancing on natural reserves and rural areas, and irregular settlements continue to contribute to some of the expansion of the municipalities of the State of Mexico with disorderly urbanisation. In the last three decades urban expansion has been characterised by leapfrog-like expansion, and urban spatial continuity is less clear.

The central city has faced several decades of depopulation and deterioration, and much of the older social housing built in the 1950s is presenting problems of ageing infrastructure, poor maintenance and overcrowding. Newer social housing developments in the suburbs are growing rapidly, but many of these are also fast deteriorating. The most visible manifestation of the housing crisis is the large percentage of unoccupied, and in some cases abandoned, homes on the metropolitan periphery, where the population has to cope with costly public transport and deficient basic public services.

While people are moving further from the city centres, jobs remain much more centralised, undermining the ability to match population with jobs. The spatial separation between the location of work and the place of residence, exacerbated by the inefficient transport system, brings not only high productivity costs but also significant losses to the living standards of the metropolitan population, as commuting is highly expensive. Low-income sectors in the far peripheries particularly suffer from poor access to jobs and services, which are predominantly concentrated in the central city.

MCMA is a socially, economically and politically fragmented metropolis. While this may not be uncharacteristic of other parts of the country, it imposes a particular penalty on a huge metropolitan area. The political-administrative boundaries dividing the metropolitan area into 16 boroughs and 60 municipalities in two different states, Mexico and Hidalgo, are ill-adapted to the functional city and the needs of its citizens. Fragmented and uncoordinated governance structures are the result of the politics of urban management, planning and policy. Local political forces, as well as some political determinants at other levels of government, have played a determining role in the urban sprawl and prevailing metropolitan governance structures. Fragmentation has led to opposition, discontinuity, overlaps, lack of coordination, the duplication of tasks and neglected problems.

Like numerous metropolitan areas, MCMA has important spatial inequalities. One factor that reveals this is the distance between the location of jobs and of places of residence. Other grave problems include inadequate provision of services, environmental deterioration, poverty, informality, spatial segregation, transportation, crime, and so on, all of which question the position of one of the largest megacities in the world as a global player. Institutional deficiencies combined with a limited focus on strategic urban planning and fragmentation prevent the metropolitan area from achieving its full economic potential. Challenges with the quality of governance and lack of a metropolitan vision have detracted from the benefits of agglomeration and residents' wellbeing, as evidenced by the relative decline in the concentration of its economic activity and decreasing per capita output.

Although the MCMA is among the most productive and efficient metropolitan areas in the country, it is also one of those with the greatest deterioration in its labour productivity (Trejo, 2016). OECD metropolitan areas with a comparable population share such as London and Paris produce around 30 per cent of national GDP, whereas MCMA produces less than 25 per cent. Likewise, MCMA is well below the economic potential of an urban agglomeration of its size in an emerging economy.

Recent research has highlighted increasing problems and disparities in the supply of public services in metropolitan areas. Public service provision is strongly linked to social urban development, but it also supports the economic performance of metropolitan areas. Chapter 8 provided some powerful insights on the relevance of metropolitan governance in the delivery of public services, depicting MCMA's fragmentation and collective action problems in comparison to Monterrey, Guadalajara, Lima and Bogota.

In the last decades there has been decentralisation, especially with regard to the autonomy of local governments in the organisation and management of public services in Latin America. The tendency is to transfer competencies, tasks and responsibilities, with central governments reluctant to decentralise public finances to deliver their responsibilities adequately. Municipalities are struggling to manage urban services and other tasks which require high operational capacity and finance on the part of the agents involved.

This situation, common across different countries and cities, intersects with particular local formal frameworks and informal practices. The comparative study of the provision of water, waste management and public transportation by metropolitan governance has demonstrated that in practice, governance is highly place specific and depends on the local political culture and overarching state legal frameworks. In the absence of formal metropolitan government, governance operating structures can reverse the negative impacts of fragmentation by accommodating the characteristics of the particular services provided with the overall institutional framework.

Service provision in MCMA is strongly affected by its extensive political-administrative fragmentation, which overpowers any approach to interjurisdictional coordination and cooperation for economic and social efficiency. Fragmented supply of services has translated into social and financial inefficiencies, as well as into important spatial disparities. Collective actions problems derived from local politics and power imbalances have overpowered any approach to interjurisdictional coordination and cooperation. Political economic factors appear to play a determining role in explaining the weak metropolitan governance structures, including party and political competition between states and between municipalities, the three-year term of municipal government, the culture of all-embracing political power and other factors.

Service delivery in Monterrey, Guadalajara, Lima and Bogota is supported by relatively stronger metropolitan structures, which bring an improvement in efficiency and sustainability. However, municipally guided projects and cooperation are still weak or absent. Metropolitan area-wide provision of services has derived from strong centralisation, initiatives from higher levels of government or the active participation of private companies. While the findings in the analysis of the waste collection, water and public transport are not generalisable, they illustrate that the metropolitan approach to service supply is not necessarily a process in which fragmented areas are governed by a single entity providing all services to the wider territory: it can be a slow process of consolidation led by various arrangements and actors across services and jurisdictions.

Metropolitan areas and their complex web of problems are one of the greatest challenges faced by government decision-makers and authorities, especially at the local level. This was addressed in Chapter 9. Policymaking and governance in metropolitan areas are particularly problematic, as they face incongruent territorial arrangements: economic and social urban realities do not match the political-administrative system. This is the major obstacle to the creation and implementation of metropolitan policy. Increasingly, local, national and international attention has centred on policies and governance, particularly in the field of spatial development. The most recent international development agenda, the 2030 Agenda for Sustainable Development, and the Habitat III New Urban Agenda, both recognise and underscore the fundamental relevance of public policy and good governance for addressing the most prominent urban issues facing the world today. Habitat III, a comprehensive international agenda for urban development, promotes the development of international goals, practices and compromises to deal with urban issues. It also fosters the elaboration of national urban policies to frame and ratify such goals and practices nationally. The development of explicit national agendas is generally on the increase, with Mexico one of the countries that has recently created explicit urban agendas, in contrast to other federalist countries such as the US, where strong local home rule prevails. The New Urban Agenda explicitly reacts to the growing relevance of metropolitan areas but without establishing particular guidelines. However, the growth of metropolitan areas leaves no room for doubt about the need for a change in the paradigms of spatial policies in general, and particularly urban policy.

Multilevel governance and policy programmes that empower metropolitan areas as productive forces and spaces of economic restructuring is particularly relevant to overall development. Metropolitan areas, whether growing or declining, face serious strategic issues in the arena of economic development. While this contributes to the argument favouring metropolitan institutional structures, actual metropolitan policies remain elusive. In practice most policies and governance structures are local and uncoordinated and follow old-style standards of economic strategy based on incentives to attract businesses and create employment. More politically and financially resourceful metropolitan areas across the world have implemented more sophisticated alternative approaches, but even here the metropolitan dimension is barely considered. Metropolitan economic development initiatives of any kind are particularly difficult to execute in many countries due to weak governance conditions, uncompetitive local industries, and limited resources. There are concerns that increasing decentralisation in many countries is leading to the transfer of responsibilities across a wide range of policy sectors to cities and metropolitan areas, which, together with fiscal constraints, is affecting their urban competitiveness and performance.

Key normative precepts about economic metropolitan policy would include empowering national, intermediate and local government to deal with and manage metropolitan areas; a combination of both bottom-up and top-down approaches; innovative fiscal and financial arrangements to boost public finances; coordination, collaboration and cooperation mechanisms among jurisdictions and tiers of government; macroeconomic policy linked to metropolitan economic strategies; metropolitan economic policy linked to other areas of urban development; and the provision of appropriate public services, infrastructure and urban conditions to support economic development.

These are general guidelines, but policy programmes and agendas are necessarily case specific. In Mexico extensive urban and metropolitan reform is needed, with clear definition of governments' responsibilities, compulsory inter-municipal and inter-state government coordination, alignment and coordination between sectors, and fiscal and financial reform. Incorporating pro-poor interventions within local economic development strategies will promote social and economic inclusion. The recognition and integration of the informal economy also will boost inclusion. Given the recent economic performance of metropolitan areas in Mexico, the specific strategies for each should be highly differentiated. The existing urban policy framework could also benefit from wider understanding of the role of cities in promoting economic growth and prosperity.

Lessons to be learnt, next steps in research and policy prospects

The experiences of highly urbanised or rapidly urbanising countries which have not yet become industrialised and/or achieved higher incomes and living standards demonstrate that the relationship between cities and economic development is complex. With the current urban landscape in several less-developed countries dominated by the emergence and consolidation of megacities and metropolitan areas, the relationship between development and metropolisation is of the utmost significance. Although some scholars, especially in the literature on the global city, tend to focus on the strategic role of certain metropolitan areas in the globalised economy, local and national dynamics must also play a significant role in analytical debate about cities and regions. While previous scholarly discussions have underscored the significance of socioeconomic forces beyond national borders, this book emphasises such forces at the local level, including their interplay with economic and political national and international powers, as a factor in understanding the condition of Mexico's metropolises in today's complex circumstances.

The book has shed light on how a specific emergent economy is coping with its intense urbanisation; the prominent demographic and economic role of metropolitan areas compared to non-metropolitan spaces, and how they struggle to maintain or advance their development path. Some of the issues, experiences, problems, challenges and solutions in Mexico are common to metropolitan development in other regions and countries, implying some cross-sectional commonalities.

At the same time there are processes, forces at work and results that are unique, showing that local and national conditions, structures and institutions are context specific and should also be made explicit. Even though the urbanisation of Mexico has been similar in several ways to that in other Latin American countries, its specific context determine how urban and metropolitan developments are experienced and what outcomes they bring. Macro tendencies tend to deliver common outcomes, but deep-rooted local practices, institutional cultures, legal frameworks and so on make a difference at the micro scale, as in the case of economic performance or the provision of urban services. The degree of the challenge can vary with city size and organisation. In metropolitan areas such as MCMA, traffic, accessibility, territorial and administrative fragmentation, and other problems are magnified due to its huge size, endangering its economic position in the national and international urban systems.

Thus, the political economy of urbanisation and development in Mexico can be understood as political and institutional capacity deficits and coordination failures that have resulted in development failure in most cities. The country illustrates how, in addition to its demographic shifts, its public policy action, legal structures and politics have resulted in a particular urbanisation model in which economic agglomeration is ineffective and inefficient.

While the decisions and actions of private individuals clearly shape urban landscapes in a market-driven society, governments, political powers and institutions play a pivotal role in shaping urban development trajectories. In many developed countries, local government, planning, property laws and the state have overseen the management of settlement patterns in metropolitan regions and limited social disparities. These tools are used neither as frequently nor as efficiently in countries such as Mexico.

At a time when the country is moving in a new political direction, the recognition of cities' positive contribution to development must serve to encourage a more active approach to managing urbanisation in a way that maximises both economic efficiency and public wellbeing. However, realising this opportunity requires a change in how the country approaches urbanisation and how metropolitan areas are placed as spheres for policy and territorial planning. The potential for long-term economic prosperity cannot be separate from social stability, inclusion, equity and environmental sustainability. Fiscal and financial reforms are needed, decentralisation must be efficient and legal recognition of metropolitan areas is essential. Coordination should be strongly enforced for more efficient governance. Public economic development policy should be formulated to reflect the new urban environment. Due to public financial constraints, authorities may experience difficulties even where legal mechanisms exist. The role of the private sector in urban management must be carefully considered. Importantly, at present few local and national statistical systems are engaged in the systematic collection of the spatially disaggregated data that are needed to investigate metropolitan issues, especially economic statistics such as GDP. For many reasons, then, there is a pressing need to develop local data sets that can illuminate local realities and inform local policy, planning and investment decisions.

Future international research should pay more attention to the local roots and routes of specific urban models and paradigms without losing the comparative angle. There is also a need to problematise urban buzzwords and theories when studying the political economy fields in which urban models are reproduced. I strongly recommend more critical attention to the mismatches that occur when trendy policy solutions are imported without accounting for the local political economy.

A number of significant issues are beyond the scope of this book or require further analysis. Analysis of the drivers of economic performance especially is flawed due to lack of data availability. In recent decades intermediate cities have grown somewhat faster than larger cities, and will soon experience the critical challenges faced by larger cities and metropolitan areas. Therefore, further study of intermediate urban centres is urgently needed. Inclusive development and environmental sustainability are critical areas of the development process that should be included in the economic agenda. Multiple dimensions of disparities and segmentation must be measured and understood. Large-scale national and international comparative studies and case studies are needed to reflect the general and particular lessons that can be learnt from urbanisation and development experiences around the world.

Note

1 At this point I should remind the reader that homogeneity in the developed world is a myth, at least regarding development levels. While some regions and cities have historically benefited from industrialisation and economic growth, others have lagged behind.

Outside the economic centres where production is concentrated, lagging urban areas suffer from persistent flaws in their living standards and economic opportunities (Calafati, 2011).

References

Bairoch, P. & Goertz, G. (1986). 'Factors of urbanisation in the nineteenth century developed countries: A descriptive and econometric analysis'. *Urban Studies*, 23(4), 285–305. Available at: https://doi.org/10.1080/00420988620080351.

Calafati, A. (2011). 'European cities' development trajectories: A methodological framework'. Issue paper commissioned by the European Commission (Directorate General for Regional Policy). Available at: http://ec.europa.eu/regional_policy/sources/docgener/studies/pdf/citiesoftomorrow/citiesoftomorrow_economic.pdf.

CEPAL, ONU-Habitat & MINURVI. (2016). *América Latina y el Caribe: desafíos, dilemas y compromisos de una agenda urbana común*. Documentos de Proyectos No. 716. Santiago, UN. Available at: https://repositorio.cepal.org/bitstream/handle/11362/40656/S1600986_es.pdf?sequence=1&isAllowed=y.

Cerrutti, M. & Bertoncello, R. (2003). 'Urbanization and internal migration patterns in Latin America'. Paper prepared for Conference on African migration in comparative perspective, Johannesburg, South Africa, 4–7 June, 2003.

Chant, S. & McIlwaine, C. (2009). *Geographies of development in the 21st century: An introduction to the Global South*. Cheltenham: Edward Elgar.

Cohen, B. (2006). 'Urbanization in developing countries: Current trends, future projections, and key challenges for sustainability'. *Technology in Society*, (28), 63–80.

Diaz, A. (2015). 'La oportuna fragilidad del municipio en México: Capacidades institucionales en el marco de un federalismo disfuncional'. *Revista Iberoamericana de Estudios Municipales*, (11), 145–172. Available at: www.revistariem.cl/index.php/riem/article/view/22.

Fox, S. & Goodfellow, T. (2016). *Cities and development*. 2nd edn. New York: Routledge.

Jordan, R., Riffo, L. & Prado, A. (eds.) (2017). *Desarrollo sostenible, urbanización y desigualdad en América Latina y el Caribe: Dinámicas y desafíos para el cambio structural*. Santiago: CEPAL. Available at: www.cepal.org/es/publicaciones/42141-desarrollo-sostenible-urbanizacion-desigualdad-america-latina-caribe-dinamicas.

Klaufus, C. & Jaffe, R. (2015). 'Latin American and Caribbean urban development'. *European Review of Latin American and Caribbean Studies*, (100), 63–72. Available at: https://doi.org/10.18352/erlacs.10127.

Lattes, A. E. (2000). 'Población urbana y urbanización en América Latina'. In Carrión, F. (ed.). *La ciudad construida: urbanismo en América Latina*. II Jornadas Iberoamericanas de Urbanismo sobre las Nuevas Tendencias de la Urbanización en América Latina. Quito: FLACSO-Ecuador, 49–76. Available at: https://biblio.flacsoandes.edu.ec/catalog/resGet.php?resId=19146.

OECD. (2015). *Governing the city*. Paris: OECD Publishing. Available at: https://doi.org/10.1787/9789264226500-en.

Pinto da Cunha, J. M. (2002). *Urbanización, redistribución espacial de la población y transformaciones socioeconómicas en América Latina*. Serie Población y Desarrollo. Santiago: UN, CEPAL, CELADE. Available at: www.cepal.org/es/publicaciones/7168-urbanizacion-redistribucion-espacial-la-poblacion-transformaciones.

Scott, A. J. & Storper, M. (2014). 'The nature of cities: The scope and limits of urban theory'. *International Journal of Urban and Regional Research*, 39(1), 1–15. Available at: https://doi.org/10.1111/1468-2427.12134.

Sellers, J. & Hoffmann-Martinot, V. (2008). *Metropolitan Governance*. United Cities and Local Governments. World Report on Decentralization and Local Democracy. Washington, D.C.: World Bank, pp. 255–279. Available at: www.cities-localgovernments.org/gold/Upload/gold_report/09_metropolis_es.pdf.

UN. (2014). *World urbanization prospects: The 2014 revision, highlights*. New York: United Nations, Department of Economic and Social Affairs and Population Division. Available at: http://esa.un.org/unpd/wup/highlights/wup2014-highlights.pdf.

UN. (2018). *World urbanization prospects: The 2018 revision*. New York: United Nations. Available at: https://population.un.org/wup/Publications/Files/WUP2018-KeyFacts.pdf.

UN-Habitat. (2012). *State of Latin American and Caribbean cities 2012: Towards a new urban transition*. Nairobi: UN-HABITAT.

Vargas, J., Brassiolo, P., Sanguinetti, P., Daude, C., Goytia, C., Álvarez, F., Estrada, R. & Fajardo, G. (2017). *Urban growth and access to opportunities: A challenge for Latin America*. Bogotá: Banco de Desarrollo de América Latina, CAF. Available at: http://scioteca.caf.com/handle/123456789/1091.

Ziccardi, A. (2016). 'Poverty and urban inequality: The case of Mexico City metropolitan region'. *International Social Science Journal*, 56(217–218), 205–2019.

Index

Note: Page numbers in *italic* indicate a figure and page numbers in **bold** indicate a table on the corresponding page.

Acapulco 47, 64, 86, 93, 95, 123, 127, 129, 131, 159
Africa 1, 36, 50, 53, 59, 74, 109, 123, 171, 248
agglomeration 24, 58, 65, 73, 78, 86, 88, 105, 121, 130, 131, 138, 199, 210; advantages 22, 23, 67, 68, 108, 198, 210, 267, 271, 273, 275; diseconomies of 112, 197; economies 20, 22, 27, 114, 131, 166, 170, 173, 174, 177, 180, 278; effects 107, 181, 182; evolution, 39; forces 22, 189; largest 5, 36, **38**, 187; positive 188
agriculture 21, 46, 61, 67
Aguascalientes 48, 64, 88, 90, 116, 121
Argentina 2, 31, 53, 54, 57, 109, 140, 154
Asia 1, 36, 50, 53, 59, 65, 75, 109, 123, 171, 248

Bogota 36, 44, 47, 59, 73, 214, 235–237, 240n1; governance 238–239
Bolivia 46, 67, 140
Brasilia 49, 59, 96, 110
Brazil 1, 31, 33, 45, 53, 54, 57, 67, 68, 96, 109, 140, 154
Buenos Aires 2, 36, 44, 47, 48, 58, 59, 73, 74, 76, 110, 112, 113

Cancun 61, 64, 79, 86, 88, 90, 91, 93, 114, 131
capital 21, 128, 167, 170; human 9, 135, 166, 170, 173, 174, 176, 177, 180, 181, 182, 183, 249, 273; investment 136, 138, 191; foreign 48; physical 121, 166, 180, 182; political 58; private 203; resources 53; social 175, 176, 177
Caribbean 31, 33, 53, 54, 59, 135, 145
centralisation 2, 8, 49, 58, 236, 239, 240, 248, 249; financial 141; of governments 215, 218; of power 190; water 232

Chile 2, 53, 54, 68, 109, 110
China 31, 33, 36, 66, 89, 109, 110, 154, 155, 171
cities: border 64, 90, 91; Caribbean 3; coastal tourist 64, 86, 88, 90, 91, 93, 129, 131, 271; colonial 46, 47, 49; industrial 48, 49, 64, 90, 112, 114, 116; Latin American 1, 2, 3, 36, 46, 49, 58, 59, **60**, 65, 66, 67, 73, 74, 80, 190, 195, 266, 268; Mexican **48**, 78, 80, *81*, 88, 89, 127, 180, 195, 209, 268, 273; pre-Columbian 45–46; primate 2, 58, 88, 190, 270
Ciudad Juárez 59, 61, 64, 86, 88, 90, 93, 114, 131
Coatzacoalcos 86, 94, 95, 116
Colombia 47, 53, 54, 57, 67, 68, 96, 109, 140, 214, 213, 231, 235, 236
commuting 20, 25, 26, 66, 83, 198, 199, 200, 205, 274; patterns 27
competitiveness 27, 28, 49, 77, 108, 135, 154, 168, 170, 171, 173, 174, 196, 200, 214, 249, **251**, 255, 277; economic 9, 70n3, 105, 137, **254**, 260; metropolitan 123, 127, 137
concentration 61, 96, 249; economic 22, 27, 86, 107, 109, 114, 173, 174, 181, 196, 199, 275; employment 114, 200, 201, 202, 204; metropolitan 62; of wealth 69, *69*; political 2, 49, 58; population 22, 27, 50, 52, 58, 67, 86, 88, 95, 105, 113, 114, 137, 154, 165, 173, 174, 181, 188, 196, 248, 268; production 114, 137; public finances 145; spatial 20, 23, 26, 131, 175; urban 4, 8, 33, 64, 270
conurbation 78, 82, 96, **193**, 198, 207, 208, 213, 231; commission 78–79; process 69, 74, 188, 190

coordination 23, 26, 41, 77, 144, **224**, 239, *see also* horizontal coordination and vertical coordination; agreements 141, 208, 214, 215; intergovernmental 137, 139, 175, 198, 207, 209, 210, 223, **224**, 231, 232, **233–234**, **237**, 247, 258; metropolitan 207, 213, 218–219, 220, 221, 223, 227, 228, 230, 249, 258, 259

corruption 77, 80, 215

costs 139, 181, 215, 239, 256; congestion 112, 174; construction 192; economic 76, 113; efficiency 137; environmental 76, 113; infrastructure 26; housing 206; labour 255; of land 197; political 160; productivity 205; provision of services 77, 154, 220, **224**; social 76, 113; transaction **169**, 176, *219*; transportation 19, 66, 176, 197, 200, 205, 274

creative class 9, 166, 173, 174, 177

crime 2, 22, 67, 90, 105, 154, 200, 210, 215

Cuernavaca 64, 78, 90, 93, 95, 123

decentralisation 5, 77, 140–144, 154, 168, 214, 215, 216, 218, 220, 221, 232, 238, 243, 244, 259, 260, 272, 277, 279; agency 223, 239; budgets 136; Caribbean 140; employment 25; federal government 210; municipal powers 78; population 25, 27, 64, 199; residential 200; revenue 150, 275; taxes 139, 145; urban systems 96

deindustrialisation 22, 67, 191, 197

delimitation 26, 82–86, 93, 198, 207

demographic: concentration 24, 88, 114, 137, 173, 181, 196, 268; forces 190; growth 49, 52, 90, **193**, 209, 235; transition 21, 52, 54, 57, 73; trends 27, 44, **48**, 278

deregulation 81, 113, 141, 192

developed world 36, 50, 67, 78, 80, 96, 130, 131, 136, 144, 177, 192, 246

developing world 7, 29, 36, 50, 65, 78, 96, 105, 130, 140, 246

development 2, 16, 22, 49, 135, 197, 213, 220, 266, 267; capitalist 107, 196; disparities in 155, 167, 176; *see also* economic development; governance 5; industrial 3; infrastructure 17, 41, 139, 199; local 141; metropolitan 5, 10, 29, 96, 207, 208, 210, 258, 259, 272, 278; political 86; social 3; sustainable 105; socioeconomic 65; spatial 166, 167, 260, 276; suburban 64; sustainable 3, 105; technology 19; territorial 28, 215, 249; transportation 52; urban 4, 5, 6–8, 24,

25, 45, 48, 58, 59, 61, 113, 127, 198, 209, 247, 265, 268, 275

developments 78, 79, 189, 199; commercial 191, 202, 203; residential 20, 82, 76, 79, 80, *81*, 82, 190, 193, 269, 270, 272, 274; tourist 93

disparities 170; economic 182; fiscal 136, 153–159, 160; income 41, 210; inter-metropolitan 9, 74, 106, 117, 213; inter-urban 7, 113; socio-territorial 67, 88, 113, 226; spatial 4, 167, 176, 227, 228, 239, 244; trends 50–61

displacement: industry 2, 73, 188, 190; population 2, 73; services 73; workers 199

Ecatapec 190, 198, 199, 201

economic development 1, 3, 7, 8, 16, 26, 28, 44, 54, 57, *63*, 65–67, 95, 105, 187, 190, 220, 268, 272, 279; driving forces 165–183, **178–179**; metropolitan 9, 106–109, 117, 132, 154, 160, 165–183, 187, 244–247, 265, 271, 277; Mexico 5, 9, 10, 127, 131; territorial 252–262, **254**; United States 249

economies of scale 22, 58, 107, 139, 170, 215, 218

education 20, 61, 123, **124**, 127, 142, 150, 232; poor access 77

ejidatarios 79, 191, 210n5

ejidos 79, 80, 100n1, 191, 195, 210n5

environmental: degradation 66, 105, 107, 112, 170, 210, 252; impacts 41; regulation 170; sustainability 50, 135, 245, 249, 258, 279

Europe 29, 31, 41, 47, 50, 74, 75, 109, 110, 171, 189, 248

federal transfers 136, *138*, 140, 142, 143, 144

federalism 161n1; fiscal 140–144, 214, 221, 247

fragmentation 5, 177, 180, 183, 213, 239, 273, 275; administration 187, 215, 223, 276, 278; cities 209; government 137, 207, 216, 221; jurisdictional 9, 135, 217, 220, 231, 238, 240; metropolitan areas 235, 257; social 26; spatial 2, 67, 113; territorial 240; urban functions 187; urban landscape 208; urban management 210; urban spaces 188; urban structure 210

GDP 22, 112, 123, 142, 177, 279; global 15; growth 109; national 39, 113, 130,

145, 196, 197, 275; per capita 106, 110, 113, 117, 172, 181, **181**, 183, 198, 273; regional 65

General Law of Human Settlements 78, 208, 259

gentrification 22, 66, 68, 193, 274

Germany 112, 146, 150, 172, 255

Global South 5, 6, 16, 24, 36, 50, 70, 105, 194, 220, 246

globalisation 3, 22, 61, 105, 107, 113, 183n1, 243, 260; consumption patterns 69; era 28

governance 5, 6, 24, 41, 68, 82, 171, 177, 182, 188, 213, 219, 239, 243–246, 257, 258, 260, 261, 262, 265, 268, 277, 279; Bogota 235, **235–236**, **237**; economic development 257–262; fragmented 176, 182; fiscal 138; Guadalajara **229–230**; integrated 77; Latin America 240n1; Lima 231 **232–234**; local 96, 255; metropolitan 8, 9, 105, 139, 140, 166, 207–209, 214, 215–217, 218, 228, 240, 259, 275, 276; Monterrey **229–230**; organisation 140; regional 218; structures 10, 19, 173, 175, 210, 214, 217, 220, 274; urban services **224–225**; weak 4

Guadalajara 47, 48, **48**, 49, 62, 64, 78, 82, 88, 89, 90, 91, 113, 114, 116, 121, 127, 131, 214, 221, 238, 239, 259, 261; conurbation 78–79

Guanajuato 47, 48, 64, 93, 95, 127

Habitat III Agenda 68, 243, 245, 246, *246*

Hermosillo 64, 91, 116, 121, 123

heterogeneity 5, 16, 45, 67, 90, 108, 180; economic 137; management 143; metropolitan areas 220; population 239; social 137; spatial 105, 123; structural 68; urban structure 188

Hidalgo 64, 127, 187, 208, 221, 223, 238

horizontal coordination 137, 175, 209, 218, 223, 232, 257

housing 5, 75, 127, 137, 142, 154, 190, 191, 192, 210, 245, 248, 253; access to 22; crisis 209; finance 243; high price 66; informal 80, 192, 273; irregular 80, 223; markets 68, 192, 269, 270; *see* also residential developments; self-constructed 191; shortage 66, 68; social 80, 269, 274

immigrants 52, 53, 90, 93, 95, 191

import substitution industrialisation (ISI) 49, 50, 52, 58, 59, 61, 62, 67, 74, 113, 114, 190, 196, 270

income 2, 7, 22, 31, 44, 58, 61, 105, 121, 123, 127, 160, 166, 172, 174, 181,

183, 191, 205, 245, 246; disparities 41; disposable 200; growth 20; per capita 65, 66, 167, 243; urban 21

India 31, 33, 36, 66, 89, 110, 154

Industrial Revolution 15, 19, 20, 24, 29, 266

industrial: activity 28, 78, 188, 190, 269; capitalism 61; cities 64, 90, 116; countries 25, 136, 140; development 3; local 260, 277; national policies 44, 59; parks 80; production 106, 108, 114; restructuring 112; sector 108, 168; strategies 268; structure 171, 197; zones 74, 169

industrialisation 4, 20, 22, 58, 61, 65, 66, 67, 78, 95, 113, 129, 188, 190, 196, 266; centralised 190; policies 61, 248; pre-45–50; programs 52

industry 2, 67, 73, 121, 116, 121, 174, 175, 191, 196, 197, 253; displacement 191; high tech 256; manufacturing 270; oil 271; real estate 161, 195

inequality 3, 4, 44, 49, 67, 77, 105, 106, 112, 210, 215, 243, 248; social 170

informal economy 66, 67, 123, 223, 245, 249, 271, 277

informality 2, 69, 77, 79, 113, 131, 135, 196, 236, 267, 270, 275

infrastructure 2, 5, 41, 77, 136, 144, 165, 166, 167, 170, 189, 192, 196, 207, 208, 210, 213, 214, 215, 223, 230, 232, 243, 245, 255, 261, 267, 277; costs 26; degradation of 154; demand 137; development of 139; financing of 160, 161; investment 61, 66, 231; lack of 76, 82, 274; local 142; quality of 107, 200, 209, 227; specialised 114; underinvestment 246; urban 22, 53, 135, 199

intermediate cities 59, 62

investment 3, 4, 5, 26, 70n3, 107, 136, 171, 232, 253, 254, 258; business 172; capital 138, 191; foreign 48, 256; infrastructure 61, 66, 196, 246; private 52, 192, 255; public 81, 145, 150, 151, 155, 160; social housing 211n6; spending 143, 144, 152, 160, 272

Japan 31, 33, 36, 110, 112, 248, 255

La Laguna 79, 88, 93, 95, 116

La Paz 123, 198, 201

labour 190, 197; costs 255; demand 19, 200, 202, 203, *203, 204, 205, 206*; division of 16, 19; informality 123, *125*, 127; migrant 61; skilled 173; supply 121–127, 201, *201, 202*, 203, *205, 206* labour force 10, 121, 249; spatial patterns 188

labour market 2, 3, 24, 15, 67, 78, 83, 113, 121, 131, 166, 181, 187; conditions 127; local 75; metropolitan 15, 25, 28, 108, 188; organisation of 46; regional 27; spatial 26, 182, 187; specialized 22; urban 53, 73, 82, 90, 106, 107, 198–207

land 210, 269; abuse 76; access 79; acquisition 191; allocation 79; commercialisation 80; consumption 26; cost 197; expropriated 79; grab 45, 76, 270; markets 187, 190, 270; ownership 79, 80, 195, 269; price 68, 174; regulation 82; occupation 188, 190, 194; rural 25; scarcity 41; speculation 80; urban 273; value 160, 161

land market 9, 82, 190, 192, 194; illegality 79, 80; irregularity 79, 80

land use 23, 24, 79, 187, 203, 209; irregular 81; management 220, 247, 248; planning 248

large cities 36, 58, 59, 62, 67

Latin America 3, 4, 5, 9, 41, 77, 79, 106, 131, 171, 194, 238, 249, 267; cities 1, 3, 36, 46, 49, 58, 59, **60**, 65, 66, 67, 73, 80, 187, 190, 195, 266, 268; decentralization 140; economy 110, 112, 131; governance 240n1, 265; land grab 76; metropolitan areas 2, 10, 74, *75*, 96, 109, 113, 135; national urban policies **252**; public services 8, 275; tax collection 142, 145, 146; *see also* urbanisation in Latin America; urban sprawl 76

Lima 44, 47, 58, 59, 73, 214, 231–234, 235, 240n1; governance 238–239

local government 2, 25, 26, 141, 146, 150, 203, 206, 215, 247, 254, 256, 270, 275, 277, 278; coordination 175, 219–220, 239, 260; centralisation 49; devolution 218, 272; fiscal health 153, 154; fragmentation 137; provision of services 135, 142, 208, 223, 238, 243, 257; revenue 160; structures 136, 147, 153, 194, 257; tax powers 136, 140, 145; United States 253

manufacturing 19, 61, 66, 121, 131, 171, 176, 188, 190; cities 64; hub 49

Matamoros 64, 86, 90, 93

Mazatlan 47, 91, 94, 121

medium cities 59, 64

megacities 2, 3, 36, 39, 50, 58, 59, 112, 210

Mérida 47, 49, 82, 88, 94

metropolisation 2, 9, 25, 27, 28, 73, 78, 82, 86, 92, 108, 121, 135, 187–190, **193**, 194, 198, 199, 267, 278; features 24, 96; Mexico 8, 95, 96, 209, 214, 228, 261; origins 8; rapid 86

metropolitan area 3, 8, 15, 22, 28, 39, 53, *75*, 77, 79, 86, *87*, 93, 183, 187, 189, 240, 273, 275, 276, 279; agglomerated 26; as regions 26–29; capital 110; challenges 105; definitions 16, 96; delimitation of 26, 74, 82–85, 198; economic activity 113–121; economic interpretation 106–108; emergence 73; financing 135, 136–140; fiscal decentralisation 140–144; fiscal disparities 153–159; governance 214–217, 257–259, 276, 277; growth 92, 170–176; growth rates 91, **91–92**; institutionalisation 96; international 109–113; labour supply 121–127; multiple jurisdictions 9, 25, 36, 41, 73, 74, 82, 135; peripheral zones 202; policy 261; problems 135; public finances 145; size distribution 114; service delivery 214, 217–221, 276; spatial structures 113

metropolitan areas in Mexico 83, *83*, 90, 96, 113, 176–181, 182, 187, 197, 270; economic activity in 113–121; Guadalajara 89; labour supply 121–127; *see also* Latin American metropolitan areas; *see also* Mexico City Metropolitan Area (MCMA); poverty 121–127; productivity 127–130, **128**

metropolitan coordination 23, 26, 41, 77, 139, 144, 207, 208, 209, 210, 213, 218, 219, 220, 227, 228, 230, 231, 232, 238

metropolitan development 5, 27, 29, 177, 183; economic 160, 165, 241–257, 260, 262, 277

metropolitan economies 74, 108, 112, **112**, 114, **115**, 128, 129, 135, 214; advantages *108*; development 9; growth *109*; output 109–113, **111**; performance 131; problems 123; production 106; significance 130; specialisation 108, 113–121

metropolitan expansion 2, 5, 6, 16, 69, 78, 80, *81*, 83, 95, 213, 214, 215, 249, 265, 267

Metropolitan Fund (MF) 144, 208, 259

Mexican Constitution 82, 96, 142; Article 115 78, 141, 142, 207, 221; Article 27 79

Mexican Revolution 49, 62, 79, 189, 269

Mexico 100n2, 113, 172, 196, 244; colonial 47; development 67, 165, 196, 265, 268; decentralisation 210; economy 131, 132, 182, 199, 271; federalism 141; finances 136, 144–152, 154, 160, 161, 272, 273;

governance 41, 214, 238, 238, 248, 259, 262, 277; history 46–50; labour 123; metropolisation 96, 265; metropolitan areas 109, 127, 166, 182, 221, 227, 261, 270, 277; metropolitan transition 78–82; migration 1; national urbanisation policy (NUP) 248, 249, 276; Northern 61; population 62, 64, 89, **92**, **97–99**; *see also* State of Mexico; states 83; tax revenue 142; urban concentration 53, 54, 57; urbanisation 2, 31, 44, 45, 61–65, 192, 267, 278; urban primacy 58

Mexico City 2, 5, 58, 64, 73, 74, 76, 235, 240n1, 269; average annual growth rate (AAGR) 90; connection to region 76; development 96; economy 110, 112, 113, 214; economic activity 114, 116, 121, 128, 131, 248, 261; finances 145, 161; governance 207–209; growth 90–95; history 10, 46–50, **48**, 189–190; informality 123; labour market 199, 202; megacity 36, 59, 267; metropolisation 82, 193; metropolitan transition 78–82; population 62, 88, 89, 210n1; primacy 62, 64, 90; poverty 127; urbanisation 44, 194, 273; urban economy 196–198; urban expansion 188; urban structure 265

Mexico City Metropolitan Area (MCMA) 5, 10, 44, 64, 88, 114, 270; challenges 209–210; economic output 271; evolution 188–193; fragmentation 274, 276, 278; governance 207–209, 215, 238; inequality 210, 275; finances 272; labour market 198–206, *199*; metropolisation 187; political economy 193–196; public financing 144–152, 155; service delivery 214, 221–231, *222*, 237–239; urban economy 196–198; urban expansion 189, 194, 274; urban structure 198–206, *199*

migration 20, 52, 53, 86, 93, 96, 173; international 4, 105; intra-metropolitan 93; rates 93; trends 93, 94

millionaire metropolitan areas 86, 88

Monterrey 49, 62, 64, 78, 82, 88, 89, 90, 91, 93, 113, 114, 116, 121, 127, 131, 214, 221, 238, 239, 259; conurbation 79

Moran's index 200, 201, 202, *201*, *203*

municipalities 53, 82, 85, *85*, 142, 150–151, 190, 191, 207, 208, 209, 217, 221, 235, 239; autonomy 141; budgets 145; conurbated 192; Mexican 83; migration attraction 93, 94, *94*

national urban policy (NUP) 247–252, **250**, **251–252**, 260, 261

New Urban Agenda 243, 244–247

North America 31, 33, 44, 50, 59, 75, 109, 110, 197

OECD 31, 39, 110, 112, 127, 144, 145, 146, 147, 149, 150, 151, 160, 172, 180, 197, 198, 199, 209, 247, 249, 256, 258

oil: activity 131, 270, 271; economy 116; production 64, 114, 128; revenue 142, 196

Peru 45, 46, 53, 54, 67, 68, 109, 214, 231, 236

political economy 10, 96, 140, 160, 161, 175, 177, 180, 188, 194–196, 210, 213, 215, 219, 239, 243; Bogota 238–239; economic development 257–262; Lima 238–239

pollution 44, 112, 174, 197, 215

population: concentration 95, 113; decentralisation 25; density 19, 47; distribution 88; overconcentration 88; size 26; spatial structure 28, 108; spatial concentration of 23

poverty 9, 44, 66, 67, 69, 77, 105, 112, 113, 121, 123, *126*, 127, 131, 135, 172, 197, 200, 210, 243, 244, 245, 246, 253; concentrated 22

primate cities 2, 58, 88, 190, 270

private: capital 203; financing 160; investment 52, 192; property 79, 269; sector 136, 144, 218, 231, 239, 248, 279

privatisation 81, 113, 141, 269; land 191

production: capacity 105; concentration 113; deconcentration 114; industrial 106, 114; metropolitan 114; per-capita 116, 117, *117*, **117**, 131; oil 64, 114, 128; spatial concentration 131

productivity 44, 66, 67, 109, 127–130, *130*, 131, 165, 166, 172, 173, 174, 175, 176, 177, 180, 181, 182, 198, 200, 209, 214, 243, 244, 245, 249, 259; deterioration 197; economic 19, 20; gains 22, 39; labour 197; loss 128; low 77; potential 110

public finances 5, 9, 6, 132, 135, 136, *138*, *143*, 154, 166, 259, 260, 265, 271, 272, 273, 275, 277; in Mexico 140–144, 160; management 142; metropolitan 136–140; trends 144–153

public services 5, 135, 136, 137, 143, 144, 150, 154, 208, 209, 210, 213, 214, 215, 232; delivery 215; in Guadalajara

227–231; in Monterrey 227–231; provision of 8; quality 44
public transport 25, 139, 199, 206, 209, 214, 238, 239, 274, 276; in Bogota 239; in Lima 232; in Mexico City 221–227, *227*
public: budget 135, 140, 142, 144, 145, 248; debt 77, 142, 150, 151, 152, 155, 160, 182, 196, 272, 273; investment 61, 66, 81, 138, 145, 150, 151, 152, 155, 160, 182, 196, 232; sector 28, 161n1, 192
Puebla 47, 48, **48**, 49, 62, 64, 78, 82, 121, 123, 127, 131
Puebla-Tlaxcala 79, 88, 114, 116
Puerto Vallarta 64, 86, 90, 91, 93, 114, 121, 129, 131

quality of life 3, 41, 44, 77, 79, 173, 209, 255
Queretaro 64, 88, 90, 91, 93, 113, 116, 131

rank-size rule *see* Zipf's law
revenue 137, 138, 139, 140, 152; authority 139; capacity 155; distribution 161n1; federal 141, 144; metropolitan 136, 137, 138, *138*, 145; municipal 141, 142, 144, 145, *146*, 148–149, *149*; oil 142, 196; public 245; tax *147*, 154, 172, 175
Reynosa-Rio Bravo 64, 86, 90, 93, 116
Rio de Janeiro 2, 36, 44, 47, 48, 59, 73, 76, 96, 110, 112
rural-urban migration 1, 50, 53, 59, 61, 93, 95

Saltillo 64, 116, 121, 123
San Luis Potosí 47, 49, 64, 82, 88, 116, 123
São Paulo 2, 36, 44, 47, 48, 59, 73, 74, 96, 110; connection to region 76
sectores populares 2, 80
segregation 2, 3, 66, 77, 113, 200, 210, 243
settlements 16, 26, 48, 190, 217, 236, 245, 278; indigenous 47; informal 25, 192; irregular 66, 74, 76, 127, 191, 193, 226, 228, 267; peripheral 80, 95; rural 29; urban 24, 46, 49, 59
small cities 48, 59, 64
social housing 199, 209, 210n6
social services 20, 77, 137
Spain 47, 48, 150, 172, 189
Spaniards 47, 69n1
specialisation 9, 19, 28, **118–120**, 121, 131, 139, 165, 166, 167, 170, 173, 174, 176, 177, 180, 182, 197, 255, 256, 262
State of Mexico 127, 195, 249; governance 194, 208, 223; municipalities in 198, 199, 200, 201, 207; service provision 223;

urban expansion in 187, 188, 190, 192, 193, 274
subsides 137, 150, 151, 155, 256; federal 144, 208; housing 192; services 143, 226; social 195; tariffs 77; to business 253, 255; transit 232, 236
suburbanisation 9, 190, 269
suburbs 20, 25, 209, 274; California 257; developments 64

Tampico 48, 49, 78, 79, 82, 86, 95, 116
tax 19, 136, 137, 138, 139, 140, 145, 141, 254, 260; -and transfer systems 136; burdens 154; base 138, 140, 145, 147, 253; capacity 144, 155; collection 66, 77, 143, 145, 207; incentives 255, 256; property 145, 146, 147, 148, 160; rates 138; reform 142, 147, 160; revenue 154; systems 155, 161n1
Tehuantepec 94, 95, 116, 127, 128
Tijuana 59, 61, 64, 86, 88, 90, 93, 131
Tlaxcala 48, 64, 123, 127
Toluca 48, 64, 79, 88, 90, 93, 114, 116, 127, 131
trade 46, 171, 189, 191; agreements 4; liberalisation 67, 114, 141, 183n1, 270, 271; unions 195
traffic 44, 112, 113, 189, 197
transfer 144, 151, 154; conditional 144, 145, 149; dependence 144, 149, 153, 154; disparities 154–155, *157*; federal 142, 143, 148, 149, 151, 154, 155, 160, 232; government 140, 155, 272; of resources 61, 77; of responsibilities 260, 277; systems 136, 141, 154; unconditional 145, 149, 150
transportation 52, 137, 142, 210, 214, 220, 230, 275; cost 66, 197, 200, 205; demand for 41; entry points 171; equipment 121; road-based 19, 25; sector 231, 239; supply 75; systems 19, 198, 205, 272; technology 20, 25; technological development 19; urban 19–20, 192

unemployment 67, 196; rate 112, 113, 243, 253
United Kingdom 110, 146, 172, 248
United States 3, 31, 36, 48, 61, 75, 89, 110, 112, 150, 154, 171, 172, 247, 249, 253; border 90, 93, 114; economy 114
urban amenities 20, 21, 22, 39, 82, 137, 271
urban bias 5, 44, 52, 61
urban core 82, 95, 206, 207
urban development 3, 4, 5, 6, 8, 10, 22, 24, 48, 113, 127, 160, 198, 208, 209, 243,

244, 247, 261; agenda 10; colonial 58; economic 6, 166–170, *167*, **168**, **169**; shaping forces 7;
urban dispersal 79, 269
urban economy 113, 117, 196–198, 244
urban expansion 8, 9, 18, 25, 26, 27, 45, 50, 69, 73, 74, 75, *76*, 78, 79, 80, 81, *81*, 83, 95, 107, 127, 128, 135, 165, 180, 187, 188, 190, 191, 194, 209, 235, 249; definition 17; delimitation 100n1; disordered 77; irregular 2; peripheral 199; regulation 80
urban growth 1, 16, 18, **30**, 41, 47, 48, 49, 50, **51**, 53, 61, 65, 78, 80, 95, 174; definition 17; explosive 189
urban land nexus 7, 9, 23, 24, 79, 268
urban management 68, 208, 210, 262, 274, 279
urban periphery 2, 73, 77, 79, 80, 82, 86, 96, 188, 189,190, 192, 198, 199, 201, 202, 203, 205, 209, 213, 214, 223, 226, 227, 228, 236, 257; expansion 95; settlements 95
urban planning 3, 9, 10, 44, 46, 47, 49, 68, 75, 77, 85, 96, 105, 209, 210, 215, 245, 247, 248, 249, 255, 256, 261, 268, 269, 275
urban population 1, 5, 17, 29, 57, 86, 88, 90, 210n3; global 15, 31, 33, *35*, 36, **37**, 267, 268; Latin America 45, **51**, 52, 53, 59, **60**, 268; Mexico 4, 49, 50, 62, 64, 78, 83; Peru 231
urban primacy 2, 4, 8, 44, 50, 58, 62, 64, 188
urban services 10, 22, 76, 81, 82, 127, 128, 136, 192, 195, 199, 207, 239, 240, 253, 259; Bogota 238–239; delivery 236, 243; Lima 238–239; metropolitan delivery of 217–221; piped water 10; waste collection 10; public transport 10
urban sprawl 2, 5, 9, 15, 16, 17, 20, 50, 73, 75, **75**, 76, 77, 78, 80, 86, 176, 182, 188, 209, 249, 266, 269, 274
urban structure 7, 9, 10, 76, 166, 175, 182, 188; Brazil 96; decentralisation 64; fragmented 210; impact on labour market 198–207; Mexico City 187, 265, 238, 265, 273
urban studies 3, 23; Latin America 3, 6
urban system 10, 27, 52, 73, 76, 86, 113; Brazil 96; colonial 47, 48; concentration

113; global 36, 106, 187, 188, 189, 278; Latin America 2, 58, 68, 113, 213, 268; Mexico 5, 8, 62, 64, 65, 88, 114, 121, 265, 270
urban transition 1, 4, 17, 52, 57; in developing countries 31; in Latin America 2, 3, 50; in Mexico 45, 265; preindustrial 45–50
urban-urban movement 53 59, 93
urbanisation 2, 28, 49, 77, 105, 110, 173, 174, 210n3, 246, 266; accelerated 1, 4, 21, 61, 213; benefits of 106; concepts 16–18; contemporary 15, 28, 135, 265; demographic 62; disorderly 193, 274; diversified 61; drivers of 18, 19–24, *21*, 54, 52, 92, 270; economic impact 6, 68, 106–108, 127, 243; explanations 19–24; first wave 29; global 1, 8, 29–41, **30**, 86, 244, 245, 249; high 3, 4, 68, 73, 261; informal 68; intensity 28, 61; levels *32*, 66; low 61; management 247, 279; metropolitan 61; origins of 9; peripheral 188, 192, 194–196; political economy of 270; rapid 5, 50, 61, 165, 248; rate 17, 114, 249; second wave 29, 36; theories of 6; trends 28, 29–41, 65
urbanisation in Latin America 1, 2, 3, 6, 8, 31, 33, 36, 44, 66, 67, 68, 69, 74, 213, 266, 267, 268; flaws 65–69 preindustrial 8, 45–50; trends 50–61, **51**, **55**, **56**, *57*
urbanisation in Mexico, 4, 5, 6, 8, 10, 44, 74, 88, 95, 194, 248, 261, 265, 267, 268, 269, 274, 278; contemporary 61–65, *63*; historical 45–50; metropolitan transition 78–82; trends 50–61
Uruguay 2, 53, 54, 58

Veracruz 47, 49, 82, 86, 93, 94, 95, 114
vertical coordination 137, 198, 209, 218, 232
violence 66, 90, 183, 215

waste collection 142, 214, 217, 220; in Mexico City 221–227, *228*; Lima 232
water 10, 19, 46, 139, 142, 214, 231; delivery 220; in Bogota 236; in Lima 232; in Mexico City 220, 221–227, *226*; in Monterrey 230; provision 210, 214, 232, 236, 238, 239, 275; resources 217; shortage 197; supply 48

For Product Safety Concerns and Information please contact our EU
representative GPSR@taylorandfrancis.com
Taylor & Francis Verlag GmbH, Kaufingerstraße 24, 80331 München, Germany